ANNUAL EDITIONS

Adolescent Psychology

Sixth Edition

D0521760

EDITOR

Fred E. Stickle

Western Kentucky University

Fred E. Stickle received his BS degree from Cedarville University where he majored in Social Science Secondary Education. He did his graduate study in counseling from Wright State University (MS) and Iowa State University (PhD). He is a professor at Western Kentucky University where he teaches adolescent counseling. Dr. Stickle maintains a private practice where by he provides counseling for adolescents and their families.

Boston   Burr Ridge, IL   Dubuque, IA   New York   San Francisco   St. Louis
Bangkok   Bogotá   Caracas   Kuala Lumpur   Lisbon   London   Madrid   Mexico City
Milan   Montreal   New Delhi   Santiago   Seoul   Singapore   Sydney   Taipei   Toronto

ANNUAL EDITIONS: ADOLESCENT PSYCHOLOGY, SIXTH EDITION

Some ancillaries, including electronic and print components, may not be available to customers outside the United States.

Annual Editions® is a registered trademark of The McGraw-Hill Companies, Inc.
Annual Editions is published by the **Contemporary Learning Series** group within the McGraw-Hill Higher Education division.

This book is printed on recycled, acid-free paper containing 10% postconsumer waste.

1 2 3 4 5 6 7 8 9 0 QPD/QPD 0 9 8 7

ISBN 978–0–07–339758–0
MHID 0–07–339758–X
ISSN 1094–2610

Managing Editor: *Larry Loeppke*
Production Manager: *Beth Kundert*
Developmental Editor: *Jade Benedict*
Editorial Assistant: *Nancy Meissner*
Production Service Assistant: *Rita Hingtgen*
Permissions Coordinator: *Shirley Lanners*
Senior Marketing Manager: *Julie Keck*
Marketing Communications Specialist: *Mary Klein*
Marketing Coordinator: *Alice Link*
Project Manager: *Sandy Wille*
Design Specialist: *Tara McDermott*
Senior Administrative Assistant: *DeAnna Dausener*
Senior Operations Manager: *Pat Koch Krieger*
Cover Graphics: *Maggie Lytle*

Compositor: Laserwords Private Limited
Cover Image: Stockbyte/PictureQuest and Royalty-Free/CORBIS

Library in Congress Cataloging-in-Publication Data
Main entry under title: Annual Editions: Adolescent Psychology. 2008/2009.
  1. Adolescent Psychology—Periodicals. I. Stickle, Fred E., Title: Adolescent Psychology.
658'.05

www.mhhe.com

Editors/Advisory Board

Members of the Advisory Board are instrumental in the final selection of articles for each edition of ANNUAL EDITIONS. Their review of articles for content, level, currentness, and appropriateness provides critical direction to the editor and staff. We think that you will find their careful consideration well reflected in this volume.

Preface

In publishing ANNUAL EDITIONS we recognize the enormous role played by the magazines, newspapers, and journals of the public press in providing current, first-rate educational information in a broad spectrum of interest areas. Many of these articles are appropriate for students, researchers, and professionals seeking accurate, current material to help bridge the gap between principles and theories and the real world. These articles, however, become more useful for study when those of lasting value are carefully collected, organized, indexed, and reproduced in a low-cost format, which provides easy and permanent access when the material is needed. That is the role played by ANNUAL EDITIONS.

The word adolescence is Latin in origin, derived from the verb *adolescere,* which means to grow into adulthood. Growing into maturity involves change. Most would argue that except for infancy, adolescence is the most change-filled period of life. The traditional definition was based largely on physical growth, as evident in the marked increase in height and weight.

Most researchers define the period of life between age 10 to 20 as adolescence. It is a period of transition in which a person moves from the immaturity of childhood into the maturity of adulthood. There is a growing realization that characteristics of adolescent behaviors do not result simply from the physical changes, but include a variety of psychological and social factors. Environmental settings such as family, peer, and school influence the development and the numerous and dynamic changes that take place.

It is commonplace to hear a discussion concerning adolescence as the years with new crazes and fads, or the problems of teenagers involving crime or sexuality. However, there are many strengths and even advantages to the teen-age years.

This anthology of readings will help you understand the bases of the developmental changes young people experience, and will present appropriate aspects of individuals, families communities and cultures that give richness to adolescent development. The selection of articles will include opinions of various authors. You may agree with some and disagree with others. Some may even spur classroom debate.

Fred E. Stickle

Fred E. Stickle
Editor

Contents

UNIT 1
Perspective on Adolescence

UNIT 2
Puberty, Physical Development, and Health

The concepts in bold italics are developed in the article. For further expansion, please refer to the Topic Guide.

UNIT 3
Cognitive Development and Education

The concepts in bold italics are developed in the article. For further expansion, please refer to the Topic Guide.

UNIT 4
Identify Social-Emotional Development

The concepts in bold italics are developed in the article. For further expansion, please refer to the Topic Guide.

UNIT 5
Family Relationships

The concepts in bold italics are developed in the article. For further expansion, please refer to the Topic Guide.

UNIT 6
Peers and Contemporary Culture

UNIT 7
Teenage Sexuality

The concepts in bold italics are developed in the article. For further expansion, please refer to the Topic Guide.

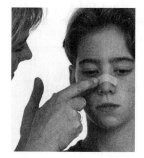

UNIT 8
Problem Behaviors and Intervention

The concepts in bold italics are developed in the article. For further expansion, please refer to the Topic Guide.

Topic Guide

This topic guide suggests how the selections in this book relate to the subjects covered in your course. You may want to use the topics listed on these pages to search the Web more easily.

On the following pages a number of Web sites have been gathered specifically for this book. They are arranged to reflect the units of this *Annual Edition*. You can link to these sites by going to the student online support site at *http://www.mhcls.com/online/*.

ALL THE ARTICLES THAT RELATE TO EACH TOPIC ARE LISTED BELOW THE BOLD-FACED TERM.

Academic performance
9. Help Us Make the 9th Grade Transition
10. Stories from Tween Classrooms
16. Leading Adolescents to Mastery
17. Healthier Students, Better Learners

Addiction, drugs, drinking, smoking
6. Prescription for Disaster
7. Youth Smoking Prevention: What Works
22. ADHD and the SUD in Adolescents
36. Alcohol Use among Adolescents

ADHD
22. ADHD and the SUD in Adolescents

Adjustment
23. Coping with Stress
29. Impact of Family Recovery on Pre-Teens and Adolescents
30. After Incarceration

Adolescent development
26. Parental Illness and Adolescent Development

Adulthood
3. The Future of Adolescence

Appearance/body image
20. Body Image: How Do You See Yourself?

Civic
4. Youth Engaged for Action

Computers
34. The Overdominance of Computers

Culture
1. A Peaceful Adolescence

Deviant behavior
28. Teenage Fatherhood and Involvement in Delinquent Behavior

Digital portfolios
8. Documenting Learning with Digital Portfolios

Dropout
12. The Dropout Problem: Losing Ground

Emotional
18. Fostering Social-Emotional Learning in the Classroom
19. The Consequences of Insufficient Sleep for Adolescents
25. Traumatic Stress in Adolescents Anticipating Parental Death

Emotional intelligence
18. Fostering Social-Emotional Learning in the Classroom

Exercise/fitness
5. Why Do Kids Eat Healthful Food?

Family
1. A Peaceful Adolescence
28. Teenage Fatherhood and Involvement in Delinquent Behavior
29. Impact of Family Recovery on Pre-Teens and Adolescents

Health
17. Healthier Students, Better Learners
19. The Consequences of Insufficient Sleep for Adolescents
28. Teenage Fatherhood and Involvement in Delinquent Behavior

High School
9. Help Us Make the 9th Grade Transition
10. Stories from Tween Classrooms
11. My Year as a High School Student
12. The Dropout Problem: Losing Ground
13. Let Seniors Lead
17. Healthier Students, Better Learners
18. Fostering Social-Emotional Learning in the Classroom

Homes
29. Impact of Family Recovery on Pre-Teens and Adolescents
32. Learning to Chill

Injuries
46. Adolescents Who Self-Injure

Interpersonal conflicts/social skills
18. Fostering Social-Emotional Learning in the Classroom
33. Risky Business: Exploring Adolescent Risk-Taking Behavior

Intervention/prevention programs
4. Youth Engaged for Action
33. Risky Business: Exploring Adolescent Risk-Taking Behavior
37. Terrorism, the Media, and Distress in Youth
43. School Bullying: Who, Why, and What to Do

Killing
35. Teaching Kids to Kill

Leadership
4. Youth Engaged for Action
13. Let Seniors Lead

Marriage/living together
41. The Perils of Playing House

Media
20. Body Image: How Do You See Yourself?
37. Terrorism, the Media, and Distress in Youth

Moral/ethical characters
1. A Peaceful Adolescence

Internet References

The following Internet sites have been carefully researched and selected to support the articles found in this reader. The easiest way to access these selected sites is to go to our student online support site at *http://www.mhcls.com/online/*.

AE: Adolescent Psychology 6th edition

The following sites were available at the time of publication. Visit our Web site—we update our student online support site regularly to reflect any changes.

General Sources

Search Institute
http://www.search-institute.org
ADOL: Adolescence Directory Online
http://www.education.indiana.edu/cas/adol/adol.html

UNIT 2: Puberty, Physical Development, and Health

Center for Change
http://www.centerforchange.com
Teens Health
http://www.teenshealth.org
Anorexia Nervosa and Related Eating Disorders (ANRED)
http://www.anred.com
Center for Adolescent Health: Confronting Teen Stress
http://www.jhsph.edu/adolecenthealth

UNIT 3: Cognitive Development and Education

School Stress
http://www.kqed.org/w/ymc/stress/index.html
Afterschool Alliance
http://www.afterschoolalliance.org
Educational Forum on Adolescent Health: Youth Bullying
http://www.ama-assn.org/ama1/pub/upload/mm/39/youthbullying.pdf

UNIT 4: Identity and Social-Emotional Development

Depression – Children and Adolescents
http://www.nimh.nih.gov/publicat/depchildmenu.cfnm

Teens in Distress Series: Adolescent Stress and Depression
http://www.extension.umn.edu/distribution/youthdevelopment/DA3083.html

UNIT 5: Family Relationships

National Council of Juvenile and Family Court Judges
http://www.ncifci.org

UNIT 6: Peers and Contemporary Culture

National Center on Addiction and Substance Abuse at Columbia University
http://www.casacolumbia.org

UNIT 7: Teenage Sexuality

Girls Inc.
http://www.girlsinc.org

UNIT 8: Problem Behaviors and Intervention

National Youth Violence Prevention Resource Center
http://www.safeyouth.org
Choices in Sport
http://www.drugfreesport.com/choices
Focus Adolescent Services: Alcohol and Teen Drinking
http://www.focusas.com/Alcohol.html

We highly recommend that you review our Web site for expanded information and our other product lines. We are continually updating and adding links to our Web site in order to offer you the most usable and useful information that will support and expand the value of your Annual Editions. You can reach us at: *http://www.mhcls.com/annualeditions/*.

UNIT 1

Perspective on Adolescence

Unit Selections

1. **A Peaceful Adolescence,** Barbara Kantrowitz and Karen Springen
2. **Youth Participation,** Jennifer L. O'Donoghue, Ben Kirshner, and Milbrey McLaughlin
3. **The Future of Adolescence,** Reed Larson
4. **Youth Engaged for Action,** Margaret Post and Priscilla Little

Key Points to Consider

• How can adolescents and families have a peaceful friendship?

• What does youth participation mean, what does it look like, and how does it happen?

• Are today's adolescents prepared to become adults?

• How does out-of-school programs promote youth involvement?

Student Web Site
www.mhcls.com/online

Exactly what characterizes adolescence is not clearly established. G. Stanley Hall, who is credited with founding the scientific study of adolescence in the early part of the 1900s, saw adolescence as corresponding roughly with the teen years. He believed individuals of this age had great potential but also experienced extreme mood swings. He labeled adolescence as a period of "storm and stress." Because of their labile emotions, Hall believed that adolescents were typically maladjusted. But what did he believe was the cause of this storm and stress? He essentially believed the cause was biological. Hall's views had a profound effect on the subsequent study of adolescence. Biological factors that underlie adolescence and direct the transition from childhood to adulthood have been repeatedly studied and refined.

Historically, other researchers hold very different views on the causes and characteristics of adolescence. For example, Erik Erikson (1902–1994), a psychologist interested in how people formed normal or abnormal personalities, believed that adolescence was a key period in development. He theorized that during adolescence, individuals develop their identity. Just as Hall did, Erikson believed that there was some biological basis underlying development. Unlike Hall, however, Erikson emphasized the role society plays in the formation of the individual. Erikson proposed that adolescents must confront a number of conflicts (for example, understanding gender roles and understanding oneself as male or female) in order to develop an identity. The form of these conflicts and the problems the adolescent faced coping with them were influenced by the individual's culture. If adolescents were successful in meeting the conflicts, they would develop a healthy identity; if unsuccessful, they would suffer role diffusion or a negative identity. Similar to Hall, Erikson saw adolescence as a period where the individual's sense of self is disrupted, so it was typical for adolescents to be disturbed. Today, Erikson's ideas on identity formation are still influential. The stereotype that all adolescents suffer because of psychological problems has been called into question.

Margaret Mead, an anthropologist who started studying adolescents in the 1920s, presented a perspective on adolescence that differs from both Hall's and Erikson's. She concluded that culture, rather than biology, was the underlying cause of the transitional stage between childhood and adulthood. In cultures that held the same expectations for children as for adults, the transition from childhood to adulthood was smooth; there was no need for a clearly demarcated period where one was neither child nor adult. In addition, adolescence did not have to be a period of storm and stress or of psychological problems. Although some of Mead's work has since been criticized, many of her ideas remain influential. Today's psychologists concur with Mead that adolescence need not be a time of psychological mal-

adjustment. Modern anthropologists agree that biology alone does not define adolescence. Rather, the socio-cultural environment in which an individual is raised affects how adolescence is manifested and characterized.

A cogent question is, what social and cultural factors lead to the development of adolescence in our society? Modern scholars believe that adolescence, as we know it today, did not even exist until the end of the 1800s. During the end of the nineteenth century and the beginning of the twentieth century, societal changes caused the stage of adolescence to be "invented." In this period, job opportunities for young people doing either farm labor or apprenticeships in factories were decreasing. For middle-class children, the value of staying in school in order to get a good job was stressed. Since there were fewer job opportunities, young people were less likely to be financially independent, and had to rely on their families. By the beginning of the twentieth century, legislation ensuring that adolescents could not assume adult status was passed, child labor laws restricted how much time young people could work, and compulsory education laws required adolescents to stay in school. In the 1930s, for the first time in this country's history, the majority of high school age individuals were enrolled in school. The teenagers were physically mature people who were dependent on their parents—they were neither children nor adults.

The articles in this unit provide a positive perspective on adolescents. The first manuscript provides evidence that teens and families can have a peaceful friendship. Youth participation is presented and myths in this area are debunked. Although there are increased risks and greater demands on youth than in past generations, Article 3 explains that many adolescents rise to the challenge. The last article in unit one examines how out-of-school programs promote youth involvement in civic action.

A Peaceful Adolescence

The teen years don't have to be a time of family storm and stress. Most kids do just fine and now psychologists are finding out why that is.

BARBARA KANTROWITZ AND KAREN SPRINGEN

At 17, Amanda Hund is a straight-A student who loves competing in horse shows. The high school junior from Willmar, Minn., belongs to her school's band, orchestra and choir. She regularly volunteers through her church and recently spent a week working in an orphanage in Jamaica. Usually, however, she's closer to home, where her family eats dinner together every night. She also has a weekly breakfast date with her father, a doctor, at a local coffee shop. Amanda credits her parents for her relatively easy ride through adolescence. "My parents didn't sweat the small stuff," she says. "They were always very open. You could ask any question."

Is the Hund family for real? Didn't they get the memo that says teens and their parents are supposed to be at odds until . . . well, until forever? Actually, they're very much for real, and according to scientists who study the transition to adulthood, they represent the average family's experience more accurately than all those scary TV movies about out-of-control teens. "Research shows that most young people go through adolescence having good relationships with their parents, adopting attitudes and values consistent with their parents' and end up getting out of the adolescent period and becoming good citizens," says Richard Lerner, Bergstrom chair of applied developmental science at Tufts University. This shouldn't be news—but it is, largely because of widespread misunderstanding of what happens during the teen years. It's a time of transition, just like the first year of parenthood or menopause. And although there are dramatic hormonal and physical changes during this period, catastrophe is certainly not preordained. A lot depends on youngsters' innate natures combined with the emotional and social support they get from the adults around them. In other words, parents do matter.

The roots of misconceptions about teenagers go back to the way psychologists framed the field of adolescent development a century ago. They were primarily looking for explanations of why things went wrong. Before long, the idea that this phase was a period of storm and stress made its way into the popular consciousness. But in the last 15 years, developmental scientists have begun to re-examine these assumptions. Instead of focusing on kids who battle their way through the teen years, they're studying the dynamics of success.

At the head of the pack are Lerner and his colleagues, who are in the midst of a major project that many other researchers are following closely. It's a six-year longitudinal study of exactly what it takes to turn out OK and what adults can do to nurture those behaviors. "Parents and sometimes kids themselves often talk about positive development as the absence of bad," says Lerner. "What we're trying to do is present a different vision and a different vocabulary for young people and parents."

The first conclusions from the 4-H Study of Positive Youth Development, published in the February issue of *The Journal of Early Adolescence*, show that there are quantifiable personality traits possessed by all adolescents who manage to get to adulthood without major problems. Psychologists have labeled these traits "the 5 Cs": competence, confidence, connection, character and caring. These characteristics theoretically lead to a sixth C, contribution (similar to civic engagement). The nomenclature grows out of observations in recent years by a number of clinicians, Lerner says, but his study is the first time researchers have measured how these characteristics influence successful growth.

The 5 Cs are interconnected, not isolated traits, Lerner says. For example, competence refers not just to academic ability but also to social and vocational skills. Confidence includes self-esteem as well as the belief that you can make a difference in the world. The value of the study, Lerner says, is that when it is completed next year, researchers will have a way to quantify these characteristics and eventually determine what specific social and educational programs foster them.

During these years, parents should stay involved as they help kids move on.

In the meantime, parents can learn a lot from this rethinking of the teen years. Don't automatically assume that your kids become alien beings when they leave middle school. They still care what their parents think and they still need love and guidance—although in a different form. Temple University psychology professor Laurence Steinberg, author of *The Ten Basic Principles of Good Parenting*, compares raising kids to building a boat that you eventually launch. Parents have to build a strong underpinning so their kids are equipped to face whatever's ahead. In the teen years, that means staying involved as you slowly let go. "One of the things that's natural in adolescence is that kids are going to pull away from their parents as they become increasingly interested in peers," says Steinberg. "It's important for parents to hang in there, for them not to pull back in response to that."

Communication is critical. "Stay in touch with your kids and make sure they feel valued and appreciated," advises Suniya Luthar, professor of clinical and developmental psychology at Columbia University. Even if they roll their eyes when you try to hug them, they still need direct displays of affection, she says. They also need help figuring out goals and limits. Parents should monitor their kids' activities and get to know their friends. Luthar says parents should still be disciplinarians and set standards such as curfews. Then teens need to know that infractions will be met with consistent consequences.

Adolescents are often critical of their parents but they're also watching them closely for clues on how to function in the outside world. Daniel Perkins, associate professor of family and youth resiliency at Penn State, says he and his wife take their twins to the local Ronald McDonald House and serve dinner to say thank you for time the family spent there when the children had health problems after birth. "What we've done already is set up the notion that we were blessed and need to give back, even if it's in a small way." That kind of example sets a standard youngsters remember, even if it seems like they're not paying attention.

Teens should build support webs of friends and adults.

Parents should provide opportunities for kids to explore the world and even find a calling. Teens who have a passion for something are more likely to thrive. "They have a sense of purpose beyond day-to-day teenage life," says David Marcus, author of *What It Takes to Pull Me Through*. Often, he says, kids who were enthusiastic about something in middle school lose enthusiasm in high school because the competition gets tougher and they're not as confident. Parents need to step in and help young people find other outlets. The best way to do that is to regularly spend uninterrupted time with teens (no cell phones). Kids also need to feel connected to other adults they trust and to their communities. Teens who get into trouble are "drifting," he says. "They don't have a web of people watching out for them."

At some point during these years, teen-agers should also be learning to build their own support networks—a skill that will be even more important when they're on their own. Connie Flanagan, a professor of youth civic development at Penn State, examines how kids look out for one another. "What we're interested in is how they help one another avoid harm," she says. In one of her focus groups, some teenage girls mentioned that they decided none would drink from an open can at a party because they wouldn't know for sure what they were drinking. "Even though you are experimenting, you're essentially doing it in a way that you protect one another," Flanagan says. Kids who don't make those kinds of connections are more likely to get in trouble because there's no one their own age or older to stop them from going too far. Like any other stage of life, adolescence can be tough. But teens and families can get through it—as long as they stick together.

With Julie Scelfo

Youth Participation
From Myths to Effective Practice

JENNIFER L. O'DONOGHUE, MPA, BEN KIRSHNER, PHD,
AND MILBREY MCLAUGHLIN, PHD

Five youth from the San Francisco Bay Area recently joined 25 other young people and over 100 adults at an international conference on the United Nations Convention on the Rights of the Child. "It was the most un-youth-friendly place," explained one young woman. "Every day we woke up early and spent hours listening to adults lecture about the experiences of youth. There was no time for us to talk to anyone, no time to move around, and when we tried to tell them about our feelings, they didn't really listen. Nothing really changed—until the last day when we finally got to do our presentation. One of the adults tried to come up and facilitate our question-and-answer period, and we just said, 'No, thank you. We're prepared to do this for ourselves. Sit down please.' I don't think the adults really got it until then."[1]

The concept of youth participation, whether under the name of youth voice, decision making, empowerment, engagement, or participation, has become a hot topic. The United Nations Convention on the Rights of the Child (CRC), the most widely ratified treaty in history, made participation a fundamental right of all young people. Advocates and researchers of youth development point to the developmental benefits of youth involvement in decision making and public engagement. (see for example Hart, 1992; Hart, Daitue, & Iltus,1997; Fittman, Ferber, & Irby, 2000). Youth participation has been linked to greater organizational sustainability and effectiveness (Zeldin, McDaniel, Topitzes, & Calvert, 2000; Rajani, 2000) and, on a macrolevel, national democratic, social, and economic development (Rajani, 2000). Not surprisingly, then, the idea of youth participation has garnered broad support across a range of disciplines and practices. However, the frustrations experienced by the young people cited at the start of this article point to a central issue within this growing field: even adults and youth with the best intentions struggle with just what youth participation means. What does it look like? How does it happen?

Participation is a broad term, encompassing several dimensions. The CRC defines youth participation as freedom of expression on issues affecting young people (Hart, 1992). Participation can also be organized around three general themes:

access to social, political, and economic spheres; decision making within organizations that influence one's life; and planning and involvement in public action (Tolman & Pittman, 2001). For the purposes of this article, we understand youth participation as a constellation of activities that empower adolescents to take part in and influence decision making that affects their lives and to take action on issues they care about.

This article provides a sketch of the state of the field of youth participation, reviewing what is known about what participation looks like, how it functions, and where it takes place (for a more complete review see Hart, 1992; Rajani, 2000; Irby, Ferber, & Pittman, 2001). As this is a developing field, a lack of empirical evidence and understanding can potentially fuel myths around youth participation. We address four of these myths here.

Youth Participation in Research and Practice

Youth development researchers have noted a shift in youth work in the past two decades from prevention (programs designed to treat and prevent the problems of "at-risk" youth) to preparation (building skills and supporting broader development for all youth) to participation and power sharing (actively engaging young people as partners in organizational and public decision making) (Pittman et al., 2000). These shifts represent a broadening of focus from looking solely at individual-level outcomes to also examining the impact of youth participation at organizational and community level.

The CRC defines youth participation as freedom of expression on issues affecting young people.

With this expanding focus, efforts to take youth participation seriously have extended beyond traditional youth development activities to embrace youth involvement in other areas. For example, researchers, policy-makers, and program evaluators are beginning to involve young people as research partners, working to understand better the lives of youth and the institutions that influence them (see also Kirshner, O'Donoghue, & McLaughlin, 2005). Internationally, young people have been central to grassroots social, environmental, and economic change movements (e.g. Brandao, 1998; Espinosa & Schwab, 1997; Hart & Schwab, 1997), a pattern that is beginning to show up in the United States as well. Moreover, many nonprofit and youth organizations have come to embrace the notion that youth voices should be part of organizational decision making (Zeldin et al., 2000), and young people have begun to be engaged in school reform efforts (Mitra, 2006; Fielding, 2001).

Most observers agree, however, that the corresponding research on youth participation—its prerequisites, organizational features, current scope, and impacts—remains in the early stages. In part, this reflects a lack of consensus on conceptual frameworks and definitions ("What Evidence," 2001), especially ones that take into account the influence of local contexts. Effective approaches to youth participation in Brazil, for example, have been shown to be less successful when implemented in the United States because of differing policy and organizational contexts (Brandao, 1998). Broad and meaningful participation seems to require a larger policy context in which the voices of youth are listened to and taken seriously, and we still have much to learn about the multiple ways in which context influences local efforts.

Similarly, little consensus exists on where youth participation most appropriately or effectively occurs. The majority of work around youth engagement has tended to focus on the experiences of young people in community-based or nongovernmental organizations (Hart, 1992; Hart et al., 1997; Ferber & Pittman, 1999; Pittman et al., 2000; Tolman & Pittman, 2001). These organizations often do not face the same sets of constraints as public institutions, and as a result, they may offer young people the type of alternative spaces that they need to reflect critically and build capacity for action. Youth organizing efforts are also typically based in community, whether in formal organizations or less-formal grassroots movements, and often work outside the system or act in opposition to public institutions. While acknowledging the strength and importance of such efforts, researchers and practitioners have begun to point to the need to bring youth participation to public institutions as well, working to create change from within. Many consider youth participation in schools, for example, critical to creating sustainable and significant change (Hart & Schwab, 1997; Rajani, 2000). Greater youth participation in public institutions can lead to substantive improvements in government effectiveness ("Youth Evaluating Programs," 2002).

Outcomes for Youth, Organizations, and Communities

Research on outcomes for youth and organizations has provided broad evidence of the benefits of youth participation. Some promising evidence about youth outcomes stems from research on student motivation in classrooms, in which participation in decision making has been correlated with greater effort, intrinsic interest, and more effective learning strategies (Ames, 1992; Eccles Wigfield, & Schiefele, 1998). Youth development practitioners also have found that participation

is an effective strategy for engaging youth, especially older high school students, who typically avoid youth organizations that do not give them a voice in decision making or planning (Ashley, Samaniego, & Chuen, 1997; McLaughlin, 2000). Such engagement has been found to have an impact on the host organizations, which report that youth participation in decision making leads to changes in the organizational climate and a deeper commitment by adults to youth development principles (Zeldin et al., 2000). Finally, meaningful participation is said to foster democratic habits in youth, such as tolerance, healthy disagreement, self-expression, and cooperation (Hart, 1992). Recent work studying community impact, although challenging to measure, has begun to document the ways in which youth participation has led to meaningful community change as well (Tolman & Pitman, 2001).

Myths of Youth Participation

Although youth participation is an international phenomenon, it is also closely linked to local context. As such, we focus our lens here on the current policy climate in the United States, which is often divided between defenders of more adult-controlled policies and practices for youth, on one hand, and adherents of youth participation, on the other. The first group tends to see youth as problems to be fixed or dependents to be taken care of. In the United States, these youth participation naysayers play a powerful role in shaping discussions of youth policy that often reinforce perceptions of young people as dangerous and disengaged. Studies showing the intractability of these negative constructions of youth in the minds of adults demonstrate the challenge of creating a broad movement of youth participation in the United States (Bales, 2000).

Participation in decision making has been correlated with greater effort, intrinsic interest, and more effective learning strategies.

In contrast, there are many who have wholeheartedly embraced the notion of youth participation, sometimes promoting an overly romantic notion of youth involvement. We refer to this often sentimental position as one held by the "true believer." Themes of voice and participation echo rich traditions in progressive education that value the autonomy of the child and the importance of appealing to his or her passions and interests. Yet in the struggle to convince others of the rights and abilities of young people to engage in organizational or public decision making and action, careful and critical understanding of youth participation is required.

As the idea of youth participation gains steam, the field is at a critical juncture. It is more important than ever before to identify and uncover the myths surrounding youth participation in order to build a convincing, evidence-rich case for its merits. We outline four such myths and discuss key issues facing supporters of youth participation.

Myth 1: Youth participation is accomplished by placing one youth on a board or committee

Many school boards, city councils, and boards of directors of nonprofit organizations have begun to create space for youth representatives. Although this marks a potentially important first step in opening the door to youth voice and participation, it also may limit the involvement of young people. Such a conception carries with it two related problems: tokenism and exclusivity.

Inserting one or a few youth into an adult-created and adult–driven process runs the risk of involving youth as tokens or "decorations," (Hart, 1992), precluding any opportunity for substantive influence. An authentic process is not one that is determined solely by adults. Rather, youth need multiple spaces for engagement. In this way, youth participation efforts can tap into the interests, passions, and skills of young people. Alternative points of entry can also open the space for youth to redesign and recreate the institutions that influence their lives.

In addition to the risk of tokenism, involving a few youth as representatives of larger groups may result in exclusivity, whereby only the most privileged or skilled youth are chosen to participate. Authentic youth involvement that creates space for broad and inclusive participation requires intentionality (Andersen, 1998; Baksh-Soodeen, 2001). This means building structures, practices, and cultures that support the participation of youth who may not come from privileged backgrounds or who may not yet have the skills to participate effectively. Creating inclusive participation also means overcoming the idea of representativeness. Although youth participation implies that youth share common interests, it is important to remember how multiple and diverse their backgrounds and experiences are. Young people engage with the public world as individuals, not as representatives of all youth, African American youth, or gay youth, for example.

Myth 2: Youth participation means that adults surrender their roles as guides and educators

Whereas Myth 1 is based on limited assumptions about the involvement of youth, the challenge with Myth 2 lies in limited assumptions about the involvement of adults. Too often, discussions of youth participation are silent about the roles that adults must play as supporters and educators, despite the fact that adults play critical roles providing guidance and connecting youth to needed information and resources.

In youth participation projects, adults socialize youth into practices and habits of the professional world. For example, Deborah Alvarez-Rodriguez points out her role as a "sympathetic critic" of the members of Youth IMPACT—a youth-led evaluation program in San Francisco. If youth made a presentation and the audience did not understand what they were saying or if young people did not take their professional obligations seriously, she gave them feedback to help them improve ("Youth Evaluating Programs," 2002). In other words, supporters of youth participation must be open to the unique voices and contributions of youth, but they also must help youth learn how to recognize the norms of the public arena or the specific practices of the field in which they hope to participate. This is not so that youth will merely adopt these norms, but so that they can be effective in shaping broader arenas.

Adults also often play roles as critical guides, especially in projects that are oriented toward civic participation or political activism. Youth wishing to make an impact on their community may need knowledge of political processes or an awareness of the multiple causes of deep-seated public problems. Without these, most would agree that such projects would be flawed efforts at youth participation.

Myth 3: Adults are ready for youth participation

An assumption of adult readiness brings some of the most intractable problems to youth participation efforts. As seen in the episode that opened this article, even the best-intentioned adults may not yet understand what youth participation means. Adults need to adapt to youth participation as much as (if not more than) youth do. This requires ongoing training and development of adults in how best to support youth and fulfill their roles as adult allies. Successful youth-adult partnerships recognize the importance of supporting adult learning and change to nurture effective youth participation.

> **Authentic youth engagement requires that young people be given the time and space to develop the skills they need to participate effectively.**

A greater challenge, however, may come from the need for adults to change their frames, that is, their understandings of youth and how to work with them. Even in institutions created to develop and serve youth, young people often face ambivalence from adults about their ability to participate in real-world decision making and action (see for example, Costello et al., 2000). True participation, then, means changing deeply held beliefs of adults—not just about age but also constructions around race, ethnicity, class, and "at-risk" status. At its most basic level, it requires a "willingness to be changed" (see "Youth Evaluating Programs," 2002).

Myth 4: Youth are ready to participate; they just need the opportunity

Just as adults need support and training, authentic youth engagement requires that young people be given the time and space to develop the skills they need to participate effectively. This does not mean that youth need to learn now and participate later, but rather that they have ongoing training and support during the participation process. This training includes domain-specific skills. Projects that involve youth in program evaluation, for example, need to train youth in research methods, such as interviewing or data analysis, which typically are not part of a regular school curriculum. Youth preparation also includes the development of broader skills. To engage meaningfully in decision making, youth (like adults) may need workshops and practice in facilitation, public speaking, and collaborative processes. Finally, youth too may need experiences that alter their frames about what is possible for young people. Involvement with real-world issues and projects where they can see the larger community or public impact may be the best way for youth to learn what they are capable of.

Moving Forward

The myths articulated here represent key barriers to meaningful youth participation. They highlight the need for honest discussion and analysis around issues of power. Are adults prepared to involve youth in meaningful ways? Are they prepared to look critically at patterns of privilege and exclusion that cut across age, race, ethnicity, class, gender, sexual orientation, and ability? How will they build structures and processes that work to overcome these? Are they ready to change, taking on roles as allies and partners rather than just directors or instructors? Equally important, are youth prepared to take on their roles as decision makers and public actors? Do they have access to the necessary knowledge and skills? Answering these questions will be crucial to understanding and strengthening youth participation efforts.

Note

1. Anecdote taken from researcher field notes, Aug. 22, 2002.

References

Ames, C. (1992). Classrooms: Goals, structures, and student motivation. *Journal of Educational Psychology, 84* (3), 261–271.

Anderson, G. L. (1998). Toward authentic participation: Deconstructing the discourses of participatory reforms in education. *American Educational Research Journal, 35*(4), 571–603.

Ashley, J., Samaniego, D., & Chuen, L. (1997). How Oakland turns its back on teens: A youth perspective. *Social Justice, 24,* 170–177.

Baksh-Soodeen, R. (2001). Lessons from the gender movement: Building a discipline to support practice. *CYD Journal, 2*(2), 61–64.

Bales, S. (2000). *Reframing Youth Issues for Public Consideration and Support.* Washington, DC: FrameWorks Institute.

Brandao, C. (1998). The landmark achievements of Brazil's social movement for children's rights. *New Designs for Youth Development, 14*(3). Available at: www.cydjournal.org/NewDesigns/ND_98Fall.

Costello, J., Toles, M., Spielberger, J., & Wynn, J. (2000). *History, Ideology and Structure Shape the Organizations that Shape Youth, Youth Development: Issues, Challenges and Directions.* Philadelphia: Public/Private Ventures.

Eccles, J. S., Wigfield, A., & Schiefele, U. (1998). Motivation to succeed. In W. Damon (Ed.), *Handbook of Child Psychology, Vol. 3: Social, Emotional and Personality Development* (pp. 1017–1094). John Wiley & Sons.

Espinosa, M. F., & Schwab, M. (1997). Working children in Ecuador mobilize for change. *Social Justice, 24*(3), 64–70.

Ferber, T., & Pittman, K. (1999). *Finding Common Agendas: How Young People Are Being Engaged in Community Change Efforts.* Takoma Park, MD: International Youth Foundation—U.S.

Fielding, M. (2001). Students as radical agents of change. *Journal of Educational Change, 2*(2), 123–141.

Hart, R. (1992). *Children's Participation: From Tokenism to Citizenship.* Florence, Italy: UNICEF, International Child Development Centre.

Hart, R., Daiute, C., & Iltus, S. (1997). Developmental theory and children's participation in community organizations. *Social Justice, 24*(3), 33–63.

Hart, R., & Schwab, M. (1997). Children's rights and the building of democracy: A dialogue on the international movement for children's participation. *Social Justice, 24*(3), 177–191.

Irby, M., Ferber, T., & Pittman, K. (2001). *Youth action: Youth Contributing to Communities, Communities Supporting Youth.* Takoma Park, MD: Forum for Youth Investment, International Youth Foundation.

Kirshner, B., O'Donoghue, J., & McLaughlin, M.(2005). Youth-led research collaborations: Bringing youth voice to the research process. In J. L. Mahoney, R. W. Larson, and J. S. Eccles (Eds.) *Organized Activities as Contexts of Development: Extracurricular Activities, After-School and Community Programs,* (pp. 131–156). Mahwah, NJ: Erlbaum.

McLaughlin, M. W. (2000). *Community Counts: How Youth Organizations Matter for Youth Development.* Washington, D.C.: Public Education Network.

Mitra, D. (2006). Increasing Student Voice and Moving Toward Youth Leadership. *The Prevention Researcher, 13*(1), 7–9.

Pittman, K., Ferber, T., & Irby, M. (2000). *Youth as Effective Citizens.* Takoma Park, MD: International Youth Foundation—US.

Rajani, R. (2000). *The Participation Rights of Adolescents: A Strategic Approach* (Working Paper). New York: United Nations Children's Fund.

Tolman, J., & Pittman, K. (2001). *Youth Acts, Community Impacts: Stories of Youth Engagement with Real Results.* Takoma Park, MD: Forum for Youth Investment, International Youth Foundation.

What evidence do we have that youth participation actually works? (2001, Spring). *International Insights on Youth and Communities, Volume II.* Forum for Youth Investment.

Youth evaluating programs for youth: Stories of Youth IMPACT. (2002). In B. Kirshner, J. O'Donoghue, and M. McLaughlin (Eds), *Youth Participation: Improving Institutions and Communities. New Directions for Youth Development Theory Practice Research.* (pp. 101–117). San Francisco, CA, U.S.: Jossey-Bass.

Zeldin, S., McDaniel, A. K., Topitzes, D., & Calvert, M. (2000). *Youth in Decision-Making: A Study of the Impacts of Youth on Adults and Organizations.* Chevy Chase, MD: National 4-H Council.

JENNIFER L. O'DONOGHUE, MPA, is a doctoral student in educational administration and policy analysis at the Stanford University School of Education. **BENJAMIN KIRSHNER**, PhD is an assistant professor at University of Colorado, Boulder. **MILBREY MCLAUGHLIN**, PhD is the David Jacks Professor of Education and Public Policy at Stanford University, executive director of the John W. Gardner for Youth and Their Communities, and co-director of the Center for Research on the Context of Teaching.

This article is condensed and adapted from O'Donoghue, J. L., Kirshner, B., & McLaughlin, M, (2002). Introdction: Moving youth participation forward, In B. Kirshner, J. O'Donoghue, and M. McLaughlin (Eds.), *Youth Participation: Improving Institutions and Communities. New Directions for Youth Development, 96,* 15–26. Copyright @ 2002, Wiley Periodicals, Inc. Reprinted with permission of John Wiley & Sons, Inc.

The Future of Adolescence

Lengthening Ladders to Adulthood

Navigating the social and economic complexities of adult life requires more savvy and education than ever.

REED LARSON

The life stage of adolescence is a crucial link in the future of society. It is a period when young people either become prepared for and enthusiastic about taking over adult roles, or they rebel against the expectations and responsibilities of adulthood. When things go right, adolescents enter adulthood with new energy and ideas that revitalize society and its institutions.

As we move into the twenty-first century, this life stage is changing rapidly across the world due to globalization, shifting job markets, and transformations in the family, among other things. It is crucial to learn how these changes affect young people's preparedness for the social and economic complexities of the adult world. The Study Group on Adolescence in the 21st Century, composed of a consortium of international scholars, examined the various contours of adolescents' preparation for the years ahead. The Group found that, although the demands on adolescents and the hazards they face in reaching adulthood are increasing, many young people are rising to the challenge.

A Raised Bar for Adulthood

What we expect of young people is extraordinary. First, we expect them to attend school for 12 to 18 years or longer without any guarantee that this education will match what they will need for career success. We ask them to make a leap of trust based on the assumption that the skills they are learning will be relevant when they eventually enter adulthood. Furthermore, we expect them to study without financial remuneration, accept a generic identity defined by their student role, and delay starting a family while in school. These circumstances put young people in a kind of limbo status for years.

As society evolves, this period of limbo continues to lengthen. Young people around the world are being expected to delay entry into adulthood ever longer. This is happening, in large part, because the platform one needs to reach for successful

adulthood is getting higher. An information society requires that young people learn more to become full members.

In postindustrial societies, we expect people to attend school until they're at least 22 years old—with no guarantee that their studies will lead to future employment, says author Reed Larson.

Education tops the list of new demands for adulthood, as more and more jobs, including manufacturing and service jobs, require literacy, numeracy, and computer skills. Brains are increasingly valued over brawn: In the United States, entry-level wages for people with only a high-school education have fallen by more than 20% since the 1970s. Job prospects are bleaker than ever for youths who do not continue their education after high school, and while there are exceptions—like the teenager who starts a basement computer business and becomes a multimillionaire—working a string of low-paying service jobs with no medical insurance is a much more common scenario for those with limited education.

The growing need for literacy skills in adult life extends beyond the workplace. Literacy is required to navigate complex insurance papers, retirement packages, legal regulations, and countless other complicated bureaucracies that are part of everyday life. Adults must be literate just to keep up with their own health care. Whereas 40 years ago patients were simply told what to do by their doctors, today patients are expected to be partners in their health management and to keep up with ever-changing research on diet, exercise, and disease prevention and treatment.

In addition to literacy, adolescents need to develop more versatile interpersonal skills to navigate the different worlds of home, work, and school—worlds of increasing complexity and diversity. Adult relationships are becoming less scripted and more transient, and teens need to develop skills for negotiating more *ad hoc* associations. Adults also must be able to operate in more-diverse social worlds. On the job, around the neighborhood, even within families, there is an increased likelihood that young people will need to know how to relate with people from different cultural and religious backgrounds. In developing the knowledge and vernaculars to move smoothly and communicate effectively across various social worlds, adolescents will need to acquire skills to change language, posture, tone, and negotiation strategies to adapt to multiple milieus. The adolescent who is able to function in only one world is increasingly ill-prepared for adult life.

Obstacles to Adulthood

As the platform of adulthood rises, the ladders required to get there lengthen. These boosted demands and longer ladders can increase the precariousness of adolescence, since a longer climb to adulthood creates new disadvantages for those who lack the financial means, emotional support, or mental capacity to keep climbing.

At work, at home, and at play, the human landscape increasingly features the co-mingling of individuals from different cultural, religious, and economic backgrounds. It is crucial for teens to develop social skills that will enable them to be comfortable and effective communicating with a variety of people in multiple milieus, suggests the author.

Acquiring advanced education and opportunities for learning diverse life skills often requires family wealth. In the United States, for example, annual college tuition generally ranges from $16,000 to $36,000—a full year's salary for many parents. Even

Education and Earnings in the United States

High School	$1.2 million
Bachelor's	$2.1 million
Master's	$2.5 million
PhD	$3.4 million
Professional	$4.4 million

Average lifetime work earnings by educational degree, based on 1999 earnings projected over a typical adult work life from age 25 to 64.

Source: U.S. Census Bureau

when tuition is covered by grants and scholarships, families must have sufficient wealth to be able to forgo the income their college-bound children would otherwise provide; many poor families, especially in developing countries, cannot afford this sacrifice. By contrast, middle- and upper-class youths throughout the world are gaining access to new resources, such as after-school programs, camps, tutors, travel opportunities, computers and new technologies, which will prepare them for both the literacy and life skills of modern adulthood.

Girls are at a particular disadvantage in many nations, facing sex discrimination as an obstacle to obtaining even basic education and social skills. In the Middle East and South Asia, girls are more likely to be pulled from school at an early age and are thus less likely to develop critical literacy skills. Across most of the world, girls face more demands for work in the home and restrictions on movement that constrain their opportunities to gain direct experience with diverse social worlds. As rates of divorce and abandonment rise worldwide, so do the risks for young women who fail to obtain skills to function independently. As they reach adulthood, uneducated women are increasingly vulnerable to poverty and exploitation.

Even academically skilled youths from middle-class families are subject to new perils on the climb to adulthood. The rapidly changing job market makes it difficult to predict what opportunities will be available when these adolescents finally seek employment. Entire sectors can disappear on short notice when industries move their operations abroad or close shop altogether.

High school and college curricula in the United States, many critics argue, provide a poor fit to the job market. Schools in many developing countries in South Asia and Africa are using curricula that have changed little since they were colonies of Western nations, focusing on memorization rather than critical thinking and on areas such as classics rather than marketable skills in computer technology or business. The result is growing numbers of youths who are educated but unemployed.

Backlash Against Limbo

It is also the case that a longer climb to adulthood, resulting in a longer period of limbo, can increase the stress experienced by adolescents. Even worse, it can lead to behaviors that arrest their process of preparation. In the United States, the experience of stress among young people has been steadily increasing. In 1999, 30% of college freshmen reported being "frequently overwhelmed," up from 16% in 1985.

The lengthening of ladders, then, increases the risk that more youths will "fall off." Adolescents who, for whatever reason, do not continue in education increasingly find themselves stuck in a low-paying and unstable labor pool.

Young people tend to live in the present moment and find immediate attractions much more appealing than long-term goals—especially when the achievement of those goals is abstract and being pushed further and further away. There is increasing possibility that adolescents will respond to the high-pressure, competitive worlds they are being asked to take on by turning off or turning away.

Web Resources on Youth Trends

- **Search Institute,** www.search-institute.org
  Social science organization focuses on youth development in multiple community and society settings.
- **2001 Monitoring the Future Study,** www.nida.nih.gov/Infofax/HSYouthtrends.html
  Study on the extent of drug abuse among eighth, tenth, and twelfth graders, conducted annually by the University of Michigan's Institute for Social Research and funded by the National Institute on Drug Abuse.
- **Ewing Marion Kauffman Foundation,** www.emkf.org
  Researches and identifies unfulfilled needs in society, then develops, implements, and/or funds solutions to help young people achieve success in school and life.
- **Youth Values 2000,** www.youthvalues.org
  International project, initiated by the International Sport and Culture Association, exploring young people's self-image, values, and beliefs about the world around them.
- **European Youth Forum,** www.youthforum.org
  Youth platform in Europe, composed of youth councils and nongovernmental youth organizations, that works to facilitate communication between young people and decision makers.

Societies must be concerned with a major unknown: whether young people, as a group, might rebel against the increasing demands placed upon them and the longer period of limbo they must endure. This result is increasingly probable as adolescents are spending more time with peers than they did in the past, which is creating distinct youth cultures in many societies. These youth cultures might become vehicles of mass resistance to adult society, like the hippie culture of the 1960s.

In New Zealand, Maori adolescents have drawn on American rap and hip-hop culture to resist assimilation into the mainstream. The attraction of radical Islam to many youths reflects a reaction against the competition and materialism of the new global world. In some cases these adolescents' resistance may lead to their joining militant groups, while in others it may simply mean that they enter adulthood unprepared to hold a job and raise a family.

However, we should not be too alarmist. Resistance is most likely when the ladders to adulthood are uninviting, poorly marked, and when the outcomes are uncertain—all things we can do something about. There is also a strong likelihood that the new youth cultures in the twenty-first century will lead society in positive directions. Often youth movements are inspired by pursuit of core human values: compassion, authenticity, and renewal of meaning. It is possible that generational "revolt" will pull societies away from the frantic lifestyles, shallow materialism, and divisive competitiveness that are accompanying globalization. It should be kept in mind that youths in most cases are a positive force.

Rising to the Challenge

The Study Group found that youths in most parts of the world report being optimistic about their lives and that, despite the greater demands and longer ladders, the majority of young people are rising to the challenge. Rates of illiteracy among 15-year-olds have fallen from 37% to 20% since 1970, UNESCO statistics show. Rates of high school and college graduation across most nations continue to climb. And there is little question that many young women have more versatile skills for taking care of themselves and navigating public environments today than 50 years ago. In the United States, teenage rates of pregnancy and violence have fallen substantially across the last decade, indicating that fewer teens are getting off track.

The most convincing scientific evidence of the increasing abilities of youth comes from IQ test scores. New Zealand political scientist James Flynn gathered intelligence test scores of young people over the last 70 years. Because new norms for the tests are established every few years, the publicly reported scores have shown little change. Once Flynn went back to the unadjusted scores, however, he found the IQs of young people rose dramatically over this period: The average IQ of a young adult today is 20 points higher than in 1940. There is no way to pinpoint what accounts for this increase, but it seems likely that youths' abilities have grown as they have responded to the increased complexity of modern life.

The general decrease in family size also contributes to youths' better preparedness for adulthood. Smaller families mean that parents can devote more attention and resources to each child. Parents in many parts of the world are adopting a more responsive and communicative parenting style, which research shows facilitates development of interpersonal skills and enhances mental health.

Other new supports and opportunities have also brightened the outlook for adolescents. Young people receive better health care than they did 50 years ago; consequently, youths around the world are much less likely to die from disease. The Internet provides an important new vehicle for some young people (though as yet a very small percentage of the world's youth) to access a wealth of information. Via the Net, adolescents can also run businesses, participate in social movements, and develop relationships; they are less handicapped by traditional barriers of age.

As a result of these opportunities and their own initiative, the current generation of youth is smarter, more mature, and more socially versatile than any generation in human history. They are better able to function in multiple worlds, collaborate in teams, and solve unstructured problems. We must not underestimate the ways in which adolescents in all parts of the world and of all social classes may draw on their youthful reservoirs of energy and optimism to forge fresh directions and develop new skills.

However, it would be a mistake to be too sanguine. Adolescence in the twenty-first century provides many opportunities for youths to make wrong turns or just become turned off, never to realize their true potential. In order to keep adolescents on the right track, society needs to provide more diverse kinds of ladders for people with different learning styles and socioeconomic backgrounds, regardless of sex or ethnicity.

Many jobs involve skills that do not correspond to those tested in school, and we need to provide avenues for them to receive non-academic opportunities to grow and shine—internships, job skills workshops, even art classes, to name a few.

There should also be way stations along the climb that allow young people to rest, gather themselves, and consider alternatives. The success of government, business, the arts, and private life in 2050 and beyond depends on how well we nurture and inspire the next generation to take over and give their best.

About the Author—**REED LARSON** leads the Study Group on Adolescence in the 21st Century, which was sponsored by the Society for Research on Adolescence and the International Society for Behavioral Development. He is a professor in the Department of Human and Community Development at the University of Illinois, 1105 West Nevada Street, Urbana, Illinois 61801. E-mail larsonR@uiuc.edu.

For more information on the Study Group, visit its Web site, www.s-r-a.org/studygroup.html.

Originally published in the November/December 2002 issue of *The Futurist*. Copyright © 2002 by World Future Society, 7910 Woodmont Avenue, Suite 450, Bethesda, MD 20814. Telephone: 301/656-8274; Fax: 301/951-0394; http://www.wfs.org. Used with permission from the World Future Society.

Youth Engaged for Action

MARGARET POST, MPP AND PRISCILLA LITTLE, MA

Youth participation in efforts to strengthen democracy has become a critical component of civic renewal in communities across the United States. Conversations about increasing civic participation have turned towards the ways in which young people can more actively engage in public life through their everyday environments. Youth development programs provide an important entry for youth to engage in action for social change, equipping young people with essential skills for healthy and successful lives (Gibson, 2001; Michelsen, Zaff, & Hair, 2002).

Within these programs young people develop skills, habits, and practices of democratic life, especially when done through tangible projects that make a contribution to the community. Commonly situated in the out-of-school time (OST) hours, these programs can be a bridge between youth and the community. As such, OST programs can provide opportunities for young people to become active citizens and participants in public life. Youth engaged for action in OST programs not only build skills but OSP programs also connect young people to larger civic purposes. This article sets a context for how OST programs can promote youth involvement in civic action by focusing on four interrelated programmatic strategies: establishing organizational readiness that fosters engagement, promoting youth–adult partnerships, engaging youth as leaders and decision makers, and involving youth in research and evaluation.

Why Engage Youth for Action?

"I think every teen should be involved in some sort of thing. Something outside of school that helps their community. 'Cause not only does it make you feel good about yourself, but it, it helps you a lot down the line, and it makes people give you a lot of respect."
—Youth Focus Group Participant

When youth experience themselves as active participants and have opportunities to take on leadership roles, they begin to see themselves as meaningful contributors to society. In OST programs geared towards youth engagement, skills are developed that promote positive youth development and enhance their capacity to act as citizens. Through their engagement, youth increase their civic efficacy and knowledge (Michelsen, Zaff, & Hair, 2002). They learn tools for problem solving and research, public speaking and negotiation, addressing issues of difference

and managing conflict, and working in collaboration with other youth and adults (Skelton, Boyte, & Leonard, 2002). Youth participation not only promotes social and emotional well-being, but also increases a young person's sense of self as a leader and citizen. It is important to note that efforts to build civic skills and enhance youth action need not exist solely as isolated programs; common principles that promote youth engagement can be embedded into all kinds of programs for young people in the non-school hours.

Four Programmatic Strategies
Organizational Readiness
In order to facilitate quality youth engagement, organizations should have in place specific structures and organizational processes that make it possible for young people to participate on a regular basis. At the center of these efforts is a participatory organizational structure, and culture, that values youth as active participants, not passive recipients, of programming. It is of central importance that organizations create structures and exhibit a culture that values the contributions of youth by making explicit the ways in which youth contribute to overall programs. Situating youth engagement at the center of programming is key to achieving organizational readiness.

To begin, organizations should assess the tangible and intangible characteristics of their organizations that reflect a commitment to youth participation. Some general characteristics of organizations with a participatory mindset include youth–adult teams to develop program ideas, youth involvement and leadership in decision making, and collective evaluation and reflection about what is working and what needs to be changed programmatically. Once these dimensions of programming have been evaluated by youth, program staff, and administrators, organizations can reflect on ways they can redefine their goals, articulating clear programmatic strategies for linking youth activities to their desired outcomes for youth involvement.

Youth–Adult Partnerships
Strong intergenerational relationships between youth and adults can serve important developmental functions such as promoting knowledge, competency, and initiative among youth (Zeldin, Larson, Camino, & O'Connor, 2005). Further, they often share three overlapping purposes: ensuring that youth have a right

to active participation in programs, facilitating positive youth development, and promoting community building and improvement. However, promoting youth–adult partnerships does not arise naturally for many programs; it requires a clear articulation of the roles of adults and youth in the program and a commitment to training and supporting staff to achieve the desired roles. This, too, is key to organizational readiness.

Three common pitfalls of establishing positive youth–adult partnerships illustrate the clarity that needs to be articulated for intergenerational relationships to be effective (Camino, 2005). First, adults may believe that youth should do everything of importance, thereby relinquishing their role as mentors and coaches. While a mindset that youth are capable is critical to the success of strong partnerships, equally important is the mindset that adults can facilitate youth learning and development. A second and related pitfall comes when adults think they need to "just get out of the way" of youth. While it is important that adult leaders give youth "space" to learn and grow, youth actually value the guidance and parameters that adult leaders can establish. Finally, a third and common pitfall in establishing effective youth–adult partnerships lies in the focus on the youth in the partnership, ignoring the role of adult development in creating effective partnerships. Partnerships are a two-way street and these pitfalls underscore that successful youth–adult partnerships are marked by a clarity of roles that recognizes the contributions that both parties can make toward a given endeavor.

Youth Leadership and Decision Making

Given the importance of articulating how to establish strong youth–adult partnerships, it is also necessary to clarify specific ways in which youth leadership and decision making can be promoted. The culture within youth-serving organizations should not only respect youth, but also be one where youth have an active and legitimate role in the program or organization's activities. Youth leadership and involvement in program decisions are critical aspects of effective youth civic engagement.

> *"I think a lot of what makes teens want to be involved is giving them an opportunity to do it themselves. At first it's a little weird when you realize, 'Hey, I'm making real major decisions!' But that gives them an opportunity to express themselves and they'll want to do more. And at first, our projects were little, and doing tiny stuff. And now they're getting, like, big, and we're going out and doing more 'cause we're realizing it. And that's more of an incentive, and a lot of my friends have come up to me, and said 'Oh, I want to do that kind of stuff, too. How do I get involved?'"*

— **Youth Focus Group Participant**

Both the physical and emotional spaces in youth programs can cultivate youth as leaders and decision makers. In turn, these spaces then reflect the organization's commitment to youth inclusion. Some examples of structured ways to develop these skills in youth include:

- Having youth and adults together set "ground rules" that are mutually agreed upon and reaffirmed periodically throughout the tenure of the program.
- Developing a clearly defined process for the roles youth can play in making decisions about the programs and the organization.
- Ensuring specific opportunities for dialogue and debate among youth and between youth and adults.
- Modeling conflict resolution that uses ground rules as a guide for norms of behavior and attitude, and pays attention to power dynamics that may emerge.
- Providing forums in which youth evaluate their actions and those of others, focusing on program content, individual growth and development as leaders, and the overall organizational process.

Youth as Evaluators

Youth participation in evaluation is a process of involving young people in assessing programs that affect their lives. It is not "token" involvement, but active engagement where youth have real influence in decisions. Increasingly, after-school programs, youth development initiatives, and community organizations are taking this participatory approach to research and evaluation. Programs are realizing that involving youth in evaluation and research about the programs in which they participate serves multiple purposes.

These purposes include:

- Enhancing the individual development of youth and encouraging their active involvement in the decisions that affect their lives.
- Contributing to organizational development and capacity building.
- Providing youth with the opportunity to create real community change (Checkoway, 2001).

Focus group data collected by Harvard Family Research Project (HFRP) suggest that after-school, youth development, and other community organizations involve youth at a variety of points in the research and evaluation process: developing research projects, designing research questions, creating data collection instruments, collecting information, analyzing data, presenting findings, and making recommendations for change (Horsch, Little, Smith, Goodyear, & Harris, 2002). Further, they involve youth in a range of activities—including community mapping, evaluation of programs and services directed at youth, community-based strategic planning processes, education, advocacy, and social change projects—usually taking place after the school day ends, on weekends, and during school holidays and vacations. Increasingly, programs are engaging youth as evaluators using technology and media as a "hook" for getting them engaged. For example, the Education Video Center in New York City engages and trains high school youth to research, shoot, and edit a documentary on a social issue of immediate importance to them. They then use the documentary to stimulate change in their communities (for more information about this and other youth, media, and evaluation efforts, see Harvard Family Research Project, 2004).

Youth Engaged for Action Requires Training

The four programmatic strategies described above underscore the importance of training for adults and youth alike. Caring adults are a key element to any program that wants to engage youth for action; however, it is important to recognize that many adults are not "wired" to think about youth as partners in leadership, decision making, and program implementation. Adults can be resistant to viewing youth in new ways, letting them play new roles, giving them the space to have a voice in decision making, and treating them as true partners. Meaningfully engaging youth for action challenges adults to take on new roles themselves, as partners rather than leaders, and to adapt the process to the needs and skills of the youth, and this often requires training.

Some programs have done a series of educational sessions with adults to improve their perceptions of youth credibility. However, training does not always come in the form of instruction and modeling. In some cases, adults' perceptions are changed through youths' actions. For example, youth members of a research project had difficulty getting adult participants to cooperate with a schoolwide survey. They faced both skepticism and unwarranted criticism. However, after a successful presentation of their findings, youth received greater adult acceptance and support from school staff. In addition, the adult response rate to a similar survey rose sharply the following year (Horsch et al., 2002).

While training for adults has become more commonplace, providing the right training and support to youth is equally essential to the success of engaging youth for action. It is important that youth understand the action project and have the skills necessary to do the work; this involves an orientation to this kind of work since having choice, leadership, and decision making responsibilities may be new for many young people. Adults also need to give them participatory roles that are appropriate to their level of development and expertise, and then provide them with training that matches their developmental level. For some, a gradual approach is successful; youth receive initial, well-defined tasks and gradually take on more, depending on their motivation, their time, and their ability to take on tasks by themselves. In other cases, youth involvement can take place in all of the tasks, but adults need to provide more intensive involvement early on, and then over time let youth take the lead. While age level can be an important consideration in determining how much direction youth need, their level of independence and maturity is also a factor. One way to support and train youth is to pair them with "expert" partners or coaches. This enables youth to learn how to take action and participate in social change.

Successful Strategies for Sustaining Youth Engagement for Action

Youth are typically not masters of their own lives or their own time—they may have to meet other school, extracurricular, or home commitments. Therefore, sustaining their engagement poses challenges to even the most adept adult facilitators. Table 1 lists a few strategies that may contribute to sustained engagement.

Conclusion

Any program that seeks to engage youth for action is by necessity multifaceted, drawing on the rich histories and lessons from youth development, community and grassroots activism, and participatory research and evaluation. While there are commonalities for successful youth action programs, as described herein, the projects themselves will differ from organization to organization. However, being intentional about your organization's

---

Table 1
Strategies That May Contribute to Sustained Youth Engagement

- *Develop lasting relationships.* Developing effective youth–adult partnerships is one of the most important factors that contribute to sustained involvement in youth programs (Lauver & Little, 2004). Youth themselves stress that there is a real and long-lasting value in developing close relationships with peers and adults (Horsch et al., 2002). These relationships can extend far beyond the bounds of the program endeavors to include attending sports games and recitals and getting to know parents.
- *Make results tangible.* A common motivator for engagement in social action is the ability to use information as a vehicle for change. Some youth are not satisfied with a report to a funder that sits on a shelf; they need to see the results of their work in tangible, immediate, and important ways. This can be through either program changes or the fact that others were willing to listen and consider what youth have to say. In either case, youth see tangible evidence that their efforts made a difference.
- *Compensate with visible rewards.* Providing youth with rewards and validation for their work helps to keep them involved. This validation can take the form of monetary compensation, a concrete product, utilization of results, presentation of findings to various audiences, travel to present or collect data and work with others, or making an impact in the community. The opportunity to gain skills, both practical and personal, is also a form of compensation.
- *Serve as mentors and role models.* Experienced youth who have worked on social action projects can be encouraged to be involved as mentors to newer members of these projects. Alumni of a project can play a strong role in recruitment, training, and maintaining connections and role models.
- *Provide logistical support.* Topping the list of requirements for a successful program for both adults and youth is food and transportation. Very simply, if youth are hungry, they will not be able to concentrate; if youth can't get there, they can't participate. Sharing meals also creates a congenial atmosphere conducive to work and relationship building.

desire to engage youth for action, fostering effective youth–adult partnerships, providing opportunities for leadership, and engaging youth as evaluators in participatory research projects are necessary ingredients to build youth skills and help them apply these skills to affect social change.

References

Camino, L. (2005). Pitfalls and promising practices of youth-adult partnerships: An evaluator's reflections. *Journal of Community Psychology, 33*(1), 75–85.

Checkoway, B. (2001). *Involving Youth in After School Evaluation.* Paper presented at the Harvard Family Research Project After School Evaluation Symposium, Washington, D.C.

Gibson, C. (2001). *From Inspiration to Participation: A Review of Perspectives on Youth Civic Engagement.* New York: Grantmaker Forum on Community and National Service.

Harvard Family Research Project. (2004). Harnessing the Technology for Evaluation. *The Evaluation Exchange,* Vol. 10, No. 3. http://www.gse.harvard.edu/hfrp/content/eval/issue27/fall2004.pdf

Horsch, K., Little, P., Smith, J., Goodyear, L., & Harris, E. (2002). *Youth Involvement in Research and Evaluation.* Cambridge, MA: Harvard Family Research Project.

Lauver, S., & Little, P. (2004). *Moving Beyond the Barriers: Attracting and Sustaining Youth Participation in Out-of-School Time Programs.* Cambridge, MA: Harvard Family Research Project.

Michelsen, E., Zaff, J. F., & Hair, E. C. (2002). *Civic Engagement Programs and Youth Development: A Synthesis.* Washington, D.C.: Child Trends.

Skelton, N., Boyte, H. C., & Leonard, L. S. (2002). *Youth Civic Engagement: Reflections on an Emerging Public Idea.* Minneapolis, MN: Center for Democracy and Citizenship.

Zeldin, S., Larson, R., Camino, L., & O'Connor, C. (2005). Intergenerational relationships and partnerships in community programs: Purpose, practice, and directions for research. *Journal of Community Psychology, 33*(1), 1–10.

MARGARET POST, MPP, is a consultant with Harvard Family Research Project (HFRP) at the Harvard Graduate School of Education, where her work has focused on youth development, civic engagement, and democratic participation. She has been a community organizer and educator for eight years, working primarily with young people, new immigrants, and parents in California, Minnesota, and Massachusetts. Post is currently a doctoral candidate in Social Policy at Brandeis University. **PRISCILLA LITTLE,** MA, is the Associate Director of Harvard Family Research Project (HFRP) at the Harvard Graduate School of Education (HGSE), where she also manages HFRP's out-of-school time learning and development initiative. HFRP strives to promote and support effective programs and practices to enhance children's learning and development in the nonschool hours; Little's primary focus is on the role that youth development and after-school programs play in complementing the school day. She is also an instructor of education at HGSE, where she teaches a course on after-school research, policy, and practice.

Acknowledgements—This article was prepared with support from the C. S. Mott Foundation and the W. K. Kellogg Foundation. The authors wish to thank Stacey Miller, HFRP, and Elaine Eschenbacher, Center for Democracy and Citizenship at the University of Minnesota, for their insightful review and comments.

Portions of this article were adapted from Horsch, K., Little, P., Smith, J., Goodyear, L., & Harris, E. (2002). *Youth Involvement in Research and Evaluation.* Cambridge, MA: Harvard Family Research Project. This brief draws on data from focus groups with 14 youth-involved research projects and provides strategies for engaging youth in evaluation.

UNIT 2

Puberty, Physical Development, and Health

Unit Selections

5. **Why Do Kids Eat Healthful Food?,** Jennifer A. O'Dea
6. **Prescription for Disaster,** Bob Smithouser
7. **Youth Smoking Prevention: What Works?,** Paula M. Lantz, Peter D. Jacobson, and Kenneth E. Warner

Key Points to Consider

- What are the barriers to a better lifestyle, and what can parents and schools do to intervene?

- What can be done about youth abusing prescription drugs?

- What makes prescribing drugs to teens different?

- What works to prevent youth from smoking?

Student Web Site
www.mhcls.com/online

Internet References
Further information regarding these Web sites may be found in this book's preface or online.

Center for Change
   http://www.centerforchange.com
Teens Health
   http://www.teenshealth.org
Anorexia Nervosa and Related Eating Disorders (ANRED)
   http://www.anred.com
Center for Adolescent Health: Confronting Teen Stress
   http://www.jhsph.edu/adolescenthealth

Emma Lee/Life File/Getty Images

The physical changes accompanying the onset of puberty are usually the first clear indicators that a child is entering the period of adolescence. The changes can be a source of both pride and humiliation for the developing adolescent. These physiological changes are regulated by a structure in the brain known as the hypothalamus. The hypothalamus is responsible for stimulating increased production of hormones that control development of the primary and secondary sex characteristics. Primary sex characteristics include physical changes in the reproductive system. Examples include growth of the ovaries and testicles. Secondary sex characteristics are physical changes not directly involved in reproduction. Examples include voice changes, height increases, growth of facial hair in males and breast development in females.

The hypothalamus signals the pituitary gland, which in turn stimulates the gonads to produce hormones (androgens and estrogens). The hypothalamus then detects the level of sex hormones present in the bloodstream and either calls for more or less hormone production. During childhood the hypothalamus is very sensitive to sex hormones, and keeps production at a low level. For some reason that is not yet completely known, the hypothalamus changes its sensitivity to the sex hormones in adolescence. As a result, significantly greater quantities of sex hormones are needed before the hypothalamus signals the pituitary gland to shut down production. The thyroid and adrenal glands also play a role in the development of secondary sex characteristics.

The physiological changes themselves occur over a five- to six-year span. Girls generally start to under go puberty 18 to 24 months before boys, with the typical onset at 10 or 11. The earliest pubertal changes in girls are breast budding, height spurt, and sparse pubic hair. Experiencing a first menstrual cycle is a mid-pubertal event, with the average age of menarche in the United States currently being 12 years old. For boys, initial signs of puberty are that the testicles begin to increase in size and the height spurt begins. Facial hair, deepening voice, and first ejaculation occur later.

The sequence of pubertal changes is fairly constant across individuals; however, the timing of puberty varies greatly from one person to the next. Some adolescents are out of step with their peers because they mature early, whereas others are late maturers. The advantages and disadvantages of early versus late maturation have been the subject of much research, so a few readings touch on this topic. One conclusion is that early maturation is correlated with earlier involvement in risk-taking behaviors like alcohol use and sexual activity. In extreme cases, biological disorders result in delayed or precocious puberty, but there are new medications for treating these conditions.

The onset of puberty is affected by diet, exercise, and genetic history. Largely due to improved nutrition and to better control of illnesses, puberty occurs three to four years earlier in the twenty-first century than it did 150 years ago. Adolescents today also grow several inches taller and weigh more. A visit to historical homes will show that the doorways and beds were much smaller in previous centuries. This trend toward earlier maturation is a worldwide phenomenon that has presumably reached a leveling-off point. Adolescents also experience psychological and social challenges related to puberty. For example, sexual arousal increases and the teenager must learn how to handle sexual situations. Likewise, gender-typical behavior is more expected by others observing the youth. The adolescent must also incorporate bodily changes into his or her self-image. Concerns about physical appearance become a major preoccupation and play a significant role in self-esteem at this time. These issues are addressed in this unit. In particular, the readings examine the body image concerns adolescents experience. This contributes to adolescents' anxiety about their bodies and how "normal" they are. On the other hand, other cultures employ rites of passage to mark entrance into manhood or womanhood. Many such rites of passage involve physical markings on the adolescent, such as circumcision or body tattooing.

Unit 2 starts with an examination of what teenagers perceive as the benefits of physical activity and good diet. The next article discusses the topic of addiction and prescribed drugs. Youth smoking is a serious concern. Article 7 presents what works to prevent youth smoking.

Why Do Kids Eat Healthful Food?

**Perceived benefits of and barriers to healthful eating
and physical activity among children and adolescents.**

The goal was to have children and adolescents identify and rank the major perceived benefits of and barriers to healthful eating and physical activity and to suggest strategies for overcoming barriers. Semistructured, in-depth focus groups were undertaken using standardized questions and prompts. Students in grades 2 through 11 (ages 7 through 17; N = 213) from 34 randomly selected schools participated in 38 focus groups. Major benefits of healthful eating included improvements to cognitive and physical performance, fitness, endurance, psychological benefits, physical sensation (feeling good physically), and production of energy. Barriers included convenience, taste, and social factors. Benefits of physical activity included social benefits, enhancement of psychological status, physical sensation, and sports performance. Barriers included a preference for indoor activities, lack of energy and motivation, time constraints, and social factors. Suggested strategies for overcoming barriers included support from parents and school staff, better planning, time management, self-motivation, education, restructuring the physical environment, and greater variety of physical activities. J Am Diet Assoc. 2003; 103: 497–501.

JENNIFER A. O'DEA

Health education theories (1–2) suggest that health behaviors are influenced in part by the perceived benefits of and barriers to a specified action. Social learning theory (3) emphasizes the importance of understanding personal beliefs and motivations underlying different behaviors, and the need to emphasize short-term and tangible benefits of behaviors. Obtaining a detailed understanding of the perceived benefits of and barriers to healthful eating and physical activity among children and adolescents forms the first step in designing appropriate dietary counseling and would be very valuable in the planning of health and nutrition education treatment and prevention programs, particularly obesity prevention programs.

There is a paucity of published studies about children's and adolescent's perceived benefits of healthful eating together with their perceived barriers to these practices. Several studies (4–8) have explored barriers to healthful eating, typically asking children and adolescents why they do not eat healthful foods and drinks, but few have investigated why they do eat healthful foods or what factors motivate this behavior.

Barriers to healthful eating, identified in previous studies, include a lack of sense of urgency about personal health; undesirable taste, appearance and smell of healthful food; lack of time; limited availability of choice; and convenience (5–8).

The major goal of this study was to answer the question, "Why do children and adolescents eat healthful foods and engage in physical activity?"

Methods

The focus groups included 213 school students (51% female) from school grades 2 through 11 in 34 schools representing all states and territories of Australia and including a representative mix of ethnicity and socioeconomic status. Forty school principals were invited to participate, and two declined because of time constraints. Participants were randomly selected from class lists and given parental consent forms to return (98.3% response rate). A total of 38 focus group discussions were conducted, each lasting 20 to 30 minutes. A total of 15.8 hours of tape-recorded interviews were obtained and transcribed verbatim to produce a manuscript. The data were then analyzed using content analysis (9–12), which involved the systematic examination of the transcripts to identify and group emergent clusters and themes, and then code, classify, and develop major categories of themes.

Results

Healthful foods were frequently defined by grade 3 through 11 students as fruits, vegetables, juice, pasta, rice, milk, and cheese, and less frequently as bread, cereals, meat, chicken, and water.

The most important benefits of healthful eating (Table 1) were enhancement of cognitive function, physical performance, psychological factors, and physical sensation, and production of

Table 1 Major Reported Perceived Benefits of and Barriers to Healthful Eating Identified by Children and Adolescents[a]

Major benefits (in descending order of importance)	Typical comments
Cognitive function/cognitive performance Enhanced concentration and mental function. Mental alertness/mental activity. Improved school performance.	"After eating healthy, it just cleans out the system and you focus better . . . I focus better on school work and everything." (11th-grade female)[b]
Physical sensation Feel good physically. Feel "fresh and clean" physically, not "clogged up."	"I feel good . . . I feel more refreshed . . . lighter . . . cleaner . . . I feel cleaner on the inside." (9th-grade female) "Eating healthy foods is like taking a shower." (8th-grade male)
Psychological benefits Self reward—have done something good for self. Cleans, refreshes, and clears mental function. Enhances self-esteem. Reduces guilt and anxiety.	"It's just a personal achievement . . . it's my personal feeling like I've done something for myself . . ." (8th-grade male) "I like feeling that I've done something good for myself, feeling good about myself . . . not feeling guilty." (11th-grade female)
Physical performance Enhanced fitness and sports performance. Enhanced strength, energy, endurance.	"It helps me run . . . it can make me do things like run . . . skip . . . jump . . . hop . . . walk a long way." (3rd-grade female) "It keeps you fit . . . like I've got heaps of energy and I eat healthy foods if I want energy . . ." (6th-grade male)
Increases production of energy "Creates" energy. Sustains energy and endurance. Regulates energy throughout the day.	". . . I eat a salad and I feel . . . fresh and I feel like going out and do-ing stuff . . . but if I sit there and pig out on junk food, I feel like a blob . . . I can't move . . ." (9th-grade female) "Every time I eat fruit, I feel revived . . . it's energizing." (7th-grade male)

Major barriers to healthful eating (in descending order of importance)	Typical comments
Convenience of less healthful alternatives Availability of "less healthful" alternatives. Easy and quick preparation of "less healthful" alternatives. Time costs involved in healthful foods.	. . . and when I get home from school, I think 'I should eat some fruits,' but then I see the chips . . . they're easier . . . it just feels like the easier thing to do." (6th-grade male)
Internal/physiologic preference Prefer taste of "less healthful" alternatives. Satiety of "less healthful" alternatives. Cravings for "less healthful" alterna-tives. Healthful food "looks and smells dull and boring."	"The sugar is . . . a tasty food and sometimes healthy food is kind of yucky and smelly. . ." (3rd-grade female) "Temptation for all those nutty chocolate things . . ." (5th-grade female)
Social reinforcement Peer pressure. Parental control over food. Lack of parental/school support and modeling.	"My parents buy the food . . . I think it's the availability of food that's around at the time . . ." (11th-grade male) "We have lots of junk food . . . my dad's into junk food . . ." (5th-grade female)
Reward driven/mood enhancement Treating oneself with unhealthful alternatives. Eating when bored/emotional eating. Relieve stress with less healthful alternatives. Less healthful alternatives improve mood and are more fun/exciting.	"Sometimes it all depends on your mood . . . if I'm feeling depressed, I just feel like eating chocolate . . ." (11th-grade female) "Sometimes I just have to have some junk food . . . it makes me feel better . . ." (9th-grade male)

[a] Results in Table 1 were obtained by using the following semistructured focus group questions and prompts: What does healthy eating do for you? How? What stops you from having healthy foods and drinks? How? Why? Can you vote on which benefit/barrier is most important or has the greatest effect on you?

[b] Approximate age ranges (in years) for school grade levels: 3rd grade = 8 to 9; 4th = 9 to 10; 5th = 10 to 11; 6th = 11 to 12; 7th = 12 to 13; 8th = 13 to 14; 9th = 14 to 15; 10th = 15 to 16; 11th = 16 to 17; 12th = 17 to 18.

energy. These five themes were consistently described by both sexes from all school grades and ethnic groups.

Older participants in grades 6 through 11 were able to clearly articulate the "refreshing" effect of healthful foods, particularly fruits and vegetables, as they related to the enhanced function of the body, mind, and psyche. Participants commonly used descriptive words such as "clean" "refresh," "feeling good," and "revived." Contrasting themes about the benefits of healthful eating included descriptions about the adverse effects of "junk foods" (defined as candy, chocolate, soda, fast foods, fried foods), which were described as slowing down the mind and body, draining the body of energy, making the body and mind feel "slow" and "heavy," and "clogging up the system." Eating "junk foods" was accompanied by guilt that contrasted with the psychological benefits of healthful eating, including personal pride, self-reward, and a sense of accomplishment and self-efficacy.

An overlapping theme was the clearly articulated link between healthful eating and physical performance. Participants clearly reported that the benefits of healthful eating enabled physical fitness, endurance, and physical well-being, whereas the impact of "junk food" reversed the beneficial physical effects and caused a "draining of energy" and subsequently resulted in more physical inactivity.

The benefits of healthful eating to appearance, weight control, immunity, longevity, and future health were articulated by males and females of all ages, but were ranked as moderately important, well below the importance of the other benefits.

The major barriers to healthful eating are given in Table 1. The theme of parental control over the food supply was notable, with the vast majority of participants of all ages indicating that they eat what is available and allowable at home, at school, and at friends' homes. Advertising for "junk foods" and price were identified as minor barriers.

Participants in grades 5 through 11 were able to suggest strategies for overcoming the barriers to healthful eating, but younger children could not. The major strategies included the following:

- Parental support, as described above;
- Planning to eat more healthful foods and drinks—carrying healthful foods to school; not taking money to school; reducing the availability of "junk food" at home, school, and community; increasing the availability of healthful foods at home and school to reduce boredom and to motivate interest;
- Cognitive strategies—using self-motivation strategies to remind oneself of the many benefits of healthful eating and the undesirable short-term impact of "junk foods"; and
- Educational strategies—-increasing information and education about food and nutrition; increasing advertising of healthful foods to make them more appealing; receiving personal advice from a doctor or dietitian about healthful eating habits.

The major benefits of and barriers to physical activity are given in Table 2. Minor benefits included health protection (e.g., heart health, bone strength, weight control).

The theme of feeling tired, sluggish, and lazy was clearly linked to the consumption of "junk food." Minor barriers included disinterest in current physical education activities, teasing, self-consciousness, lack of transport, and unsuitable outdoor environment.

Suggested strategies to increase physical activity were identified by participants in grades 5 through 11. These included the following:

- Planning/organization—making arrangements to play with friends, becoming involved in a team, prioritizing physical activity as important and fun;
- Increase variety and excitement of physical activity—participants, particularly teenagers, indicated boredom with existing physical education programs and expressed interest in new and unusual activities such as aerobics, martial arts, Tai Bo, yoga, archery, hiking, rock climbing, and water sports;
- Parental support and involvement—participants of all ages indicated that they would like to do outdoor games and activities with parents and they would like their parents to encourage them to become involved in various physical activities;
- Time management—participants of all ages indicated that they needed to rearrange the amount of time spent on homework, chores, part-time work, and family activities to make time for physical activities; and
- Restructure physical environment—female adolescents indicated that they would like female-oriented sports and activities taught by female teachers in private facilities. They suggested having doors on private showers and changing rooms, and self-selected physical education uniforms.

Children of all ages expressed the need for parents and teachers to help with these strategies.

Discussion

This study presents rich new data on a somewhat neglected area of research, namely, the specific benefits children and adolescents obtain from healthful eating and physical activity.

The study results suggest that the greatest motivator of healthful eating among children and adolescents in grades 5 through 11 is the desire to create a "cleansed," "refreshed," and "energized" mind, body, and emotional state. Participants of both sexes and all ages and ethnicities consistently reported having experienced short-term mental, physical, and psychological benefits from healthful eating as well as similar benefits from physical activity. In agreement with previous findings (5–7), motivating factors of less importance were health protection, benefits to appearance, and weight control, although these benefits were certainly not considered unimportant.

The strong social, psychological, and cognitive benefits of physical activity reported by participants add to the paucity of literature on this topic (13–16) and have the potential to help clinicians, educators, administrators, and parents better understand the strongest motivating factors behind children's health behaviors.

Table 2   Major Reported, Perceived Benefits of and Barriers to Physical Activity Among Children and Adolescents[a]

Major benefits (in descending order of importance)	Typical comments
Social benefits Fun/enjoyment. Socializing with friends. Enjoyment of teamwork, team identity. Fitness aids other areas of life (eg, coping). Development of life skills. Parental approval.	"It's fun . . . just playing with your friends." (4th-grade male)[b] "At physical culture . . . I just have all these friends that I've known for a long time and to have a social group outside of school . . . it just makes me feel better." (9th-grade female) "It's the social part of it that's most important . . . having friends in the team is really important so that you have fun and you learn to get on with people . . . and the life skills help with the social side." (11th-grade male)
Psychologic enhancement Sense of achievement, pride, self-esteem, confidence. Enhanced mood. Develop discipline. Sense of balance in life. Reduces guilt. Enjoyment of challenges and goals, excitement, adrenaline rush.	"You feel better physically and it increases your self-esteem . . . because you know you're doing something good for your body . . ." (11th-grade female) "Feelings about yourself . . . in the mind . . . the feeling that you've done something good for yourself . . . feeling good about yourself . . . not feeling guilty . . ." (9th-grade female)
Physical sensation (feeling good physically) Feel refreshed, "cleansed." Enjoy sensation of movement. Creation of energy, reduces fatigue. Sensation of well-being, strength, and fitness. Enhanced sleep.	"When you're dancing . . . you're sweaty but you don't care . . . you just keep on going and then when you go out you feel so good . . . you feel so healthy . . ." (11th-grade male) "It makes me feel good . . . afterwards my body just feels better. . ." (9th-grade female) "It uses my energy so I'm not restless in the night and I get good sleep." (6th-grade male)
Sports performance Improved sports performance. Skill development. Improved coordination, agility, flexibility, reflexes. Improved fitness, strength, endurance.	"It keeps you being able to play well for the whole game . . ." (8th-grade male) "Being able to turn and breathe after you run . . ." (10th-grade female)
Cognitive benefits Clears mind and thinking. Enhances concentration and brain function.	"It clears my mind for studying . . .if I go for a run I can come back and be sharper . . .better concentration . . ." (11th-grade male)
Coping strategy Stress relief, relaxation, distraction from worries, mental break. Outlet for aggression, frustration, and anger. Physical break.	"You get your mind off school, like all the pressures of school . . . you just forget about it . . . so that's a relief." (9th-grade male) "If I'm really, really angry, I can go outside and go for a big walk . . ." (11th-grade female) "Sometime I just need to go and punch the punching bag and kick it and it makes me feel heaps . . ." (8th-grade female)
Preference for indoor activities Prefer to watch television, videos, play on computer. Prefer to play with toys, games, books, music indoors.	"I'm stuck to the television sometimes . . . lots of movies . . ." (3rd-grade female)
Low energy level Feeling tired, lazy, and sluggish. "Junk food" snacks drain energy. Lack of energy.	"I just can't move . . . I just don't feel like moving . . . I feel tired or I feel lazy . . ." (6th-grade male) "Junk food makes you slow-down . . . really lazy . . . you don't feel like doing anything . . ." (3rd-grade female)
Time constraints Homework, jobs consume spare time. Other plans, commitments consume time.	"Sometimes I just don't have time because I've got school and I've got homework or I've got to go to work . . ." (11th-grade female)
Social factors Peer pressure—friends are involved in sedentary activities. Parental control/preferences. Lack of parental support. Lack of playmates or suitable playmates. Teasing/bullying from peers. Criticism from others (peers, teachers).	". . . it's like my social life as well . . . I just like to go and hang around with friends . . . sit and talk . . ." (9th-grade female) ". . .if I want to play with my best friend . . . my mom has to drive me there . . ." (5th-grade female) ". . . I hate physical education with boys . . . they hog the gear and they laugh at you and tease you . . ." (9th-grade female)
Motivation Low level of self-motivation. Low level of motivation from others. Low perceived rewards.	". . . I'd do more stuff it I had someone to do it with me . . . because you'd motivate each other . . ." (10th-grade male)

[a] Results in Table 2 were obtained by using the following semistructured focus group questions and prompts: What does physical activity do for you? How? What stops you from being physically active? Why? Can you vote on which benefit/barrier is most important or has the greatest effect on you?

[b] Approximate age ranges (in years) for school grade levels: 3rd grade = 8 to 9; 4th = 9 to 10; 5th = 10 to 11; 6th = 11 to 12; 7th = 12 to 13; 8th = 13 to 14; 9th = 14 to 15; 10th = 15 to 16; 11th = 16 to 17; 12th = 17 to 18.

Overlapping themes between the benefits of healthful eating and physical activity included beliefs that both food and exercise have a "cleansing" effect on the body, mind, and emotional state and that "junk food" has the reverse effect. Children and adolescents report that the combination of healthful eating and physical activity confers many benefits to schoolwork by enhancing clear thinking, concentration, sleep, stress control, and energy. Findings about barriers concur with those of previous studies (48, 13–16) with the expansion of themes and addition of a new barrier related to parental control, parental expectations, lack of parental and school support, and lack of role modeling.

Results clearly show that children and adolescents are looking to their parents and teachers to encourage, support, and enable them to be involved in more healthful behaviors.

Applications

The combination of these findings, applied within appropriate theoretical frameworks, could be a powerful way of motivating children to seek the health benefits that they identify as most important. In particular, the finding that children and adolescents believe that healthful eating and physical activity confer many interrelated cognitive, physical, and psychological benefits is a new and interesting result that has vast implications for motivating children and adolescents in clinical, community, and educational settings.

This research was supported by a Kellogg Australia Nutrition Research Grant.

Many thanks to the school staff and students who participated in this national research study.

References

Ajzen I, Fishbein M. Understanding Attitudes and Predicting Social Behaviour. Englewood Cliffs, NJ: Prentice-Hall; 1980.

Ajzen I. The Theory of Planned Behaviour. Organizational Behaviour and Human Decision Processes. 1991;50:179–211.

Bandura A. Social Foundations of Thought and Action: A Social Cognitive Theory. Englewood Cliffs, NJ: Prentice-Hall; 1966.

Ling A. Perceived benefits and barriers of increased fruit and vegetable consumption: Validation of a decisional balance scale. J Nutr Ed. 2001;33:257–265.

Gracey D, Stanley N, Burke V, Corti B, Beilin LJ. Nutritional knowledge, beliefs, and behaviours in teenage school students. Health Ed Res. 1996;11:187–204.

Neumark-Sztainer D, Story M, Perry C, Casey MA. Factors influencing food choices of adolescents: Findings from focus group discussions with adolescents. J Am Diet Assoc. 1999;99:929–934,937.

California Project Lean. Food on the Run Campaign. Key informant interviews with students, experts and LEAN regional coordinators about healthful eating and physical activity in multicultural youth. Sacramento, CA: Food on the Run Campaign; 1998.

Glanz K, Basil M, Maibach 2, Goldberg J, Snyder D. Why Americans eat what they do: Taste, nutrition, cost, convenience and weight control concerns as influences on food consumption. J Am Diet Assoc. 1998;98:1118–1126.

Miles MB, Huberman AM. Qualitative Data Analysis: An Expanded Sourcebook. Thousand Oaks, CA: Sage; 1994.

Pope C, Maya N. Reaching the parts other methods cannot reach: An introduction to qualitative methods in health and health service research. BMJ. 1995;311:42–45.

Britten N. Qualitative interviews in medical research. BMJ. 1995;311:251–253.

Mays N, Pope N. Rigour and qualitative research. BMJ. 1995;311:109–112.

Heath GW, Pratt M, Warren CW, Kann L. Physical activity patterns in American high school students: Results from the 1990 youth risk behavior survey. Arch Pediatr Adolesc Med. 1994;148:1131–1136.

Thompson JL, Davis SM, Gittlesohn J, Going S, Becenti A, Metcalfe L, Stone 2, Harnack L, Ring K. Patterns of physical activity among American Indian children: An assessment of barriers and support. J Community Health. 2001;26:423–445.

Wu TY, Pender N. Determinants of physical activity among Taiwanese adolescents: An application of the health promotion model. Res Nurs Health. 2002;25:25–36.

Leslie J, Yancy A, McCarthy W, Albert S, Wert C, Miles O, James J. Development and implementation of a school-based nutrition and fitness promotion program for ethnically diverse middle-school girls. J Am Diet Assoc. 1999;99:967–970.

J. A. O'DEA is a faculty member, Department of Education, University of Sydney, Australia, and a visiting scholar, Center for Weight and Health, Department of Nutritional Sciences, University of California, Berkeley, CA. Address correspondence to: Jennifer A. O'Dea, MPH, PhD, RD, University of Sydney, Faculty of Education, ASS, NSW 2006, Australia. E-mail: j.o'dea@edfac.usyd.edu.au

Prescription for Disaster

Bob Smithouser

The current enrollment at Fossil Ridge High School in Keller, Texas, stands at 2,147. It should be 2,148. That's because freshman Tyler Bailey, a promising athlete who dreamed of attending college on a football scholarship, died of a drug overdose and was buried in his black No. 86 jersey. The culprit wasn't cocaine or heroin. Tyler died from oxycodone intoxication after he and some friends raided a parent's stash of prescription drugs.

A growing number of families are discovering what that loss feels like.

"This is an entirely new category of substance abuse, and we're only seeing the tip of the iceberg," said Steve Pasierb, president and CEO of the Partnership for a Drug-Free America. "Ease of access is the number-one reason kids are abusing prescription drugs. They don't have to go to a scary street dealer, because the drugs are right there in Mom's or Grandma's medicine cabinet."

Illicit drug use among teens has dropped radically since 2001. There's also been a slight decline in alcohol and tobacco use. Yet several studies concur that the number of adolescents abusing prescription drugs has *tripled* since 1992. According to Columbia University's National Center on Addiction and Substance Abuse, 75 percent of them are "polysubstance abusers" who combine prescription meds with other drugs or alcohol. A Monitoring the Future study released in December found that 14 percent of high school seniors, 11 percent of 10th graders and 7 percent of 8th graders said they had used tranquilizers, barbiturates or sedatives for nonmedical purposes within the past year.

"This is an entirely new category of substance abuse, and we're only seeing the tip of the iceberg."

—Steve Pasierb, Partnership for a Drug-Free America

Donald Hauser serves as medical director with The Right Step, a drug and alcohol treatment clinic in Houston. He noted, "By far, the most common trend I think we're seeing are sedative hypnotics, particularly Xanax—'bars' is what they call 'em—and the opiates, the hydrocodone derivatives, the Vicodins, the Loracets. Almost every adolescent that comes in this program has used some of them."

Teenagers think that, because these products are FDA approved, popping pills from a pharmacy is safer than buying marijuana or Ecstasy from an unknown source. They don't realize the potential dangers and addictive qualities of depressants, antidepressants, stimulants, muscle relaxants, anti-anxiety medications, tranquilizers and opiate pain relievers—all modern drugs of choice. In fact, *USA Today* reported recently that only 48 percent of teens see "great risk" in experimenting with prescription medication.

Wendy is a 17-year-old who experimented mightily. One day she took Xanax and remembers nothing more than regaining consciousness in a garage, clearly a victim of sexual assault. "I don't even know who it was," said the young woman, now in a treatment program. "You have to hit your bottom. For me it was almost dying."

This problem is pervasive enough to have inspired *Rx,* a new teen novel by Tracy Lynn. Written from a teenager's point of view, it's the story of an overachieving 17-year-old who sneaks Ritalin to help her focus. Soon she finds herself trading and dealing a wide assortment of prescription drugs, both to fuel her own habit and to "help" peers facing similar challenges.

Pharm Country

How do teens score these drugs? They rummage through their parents' medicine cabinets or beat the system by phoning in prescriptions, forging signatures or duping the online questionnaires of Internet pharmacies. Ryan Haight got caught in that web. After faking his age and concocting an ailment to get drugs online, the 17-year-old died from an overdose of prescription pain meds.

Teens also purchase pills in school hallways (a single Vicodin tablet can fetch $4 or $5) and take advantage of relatives' existing prescriptions. "My mom was prescribed alprazolam, which is Xanax's generic name," a rehabbing teen told ABC's *Nightline.* "All I had to do was find the pill bottle and call CVS and type in the prescription number. And then maybe an hour later, you go pick it up and say, 'I'm picking up Blair's prescription.' That's how I got a lot of mine."

One of the trendiest, most social ways to get a pharmaceutical high is at "pharming parties," pot luck-style gatherings where teens contribute to a chemical "trail mix." Even those who would never do crack or cocaine think nothing of grabbing fistfuls of these diverse, colorful drugs and washing them down with alcohol. Ernest Patterson, a recovering addict, recalls,

Warning Signs

Parents should look for these common symptoms of prescription drug abuse in teenagers:

- missed prescription drugs
- slurred speech
- lack of concentration or coordination
- glassy eyes or frequent use of eye drops
- rapid weight loss
- secretiveness or dishonesty
- truancy or a drop in grades
- an unexplained change in eating or sleeping habits
- a constant need to borrow money
- less concern about hygiene or appearance
- waning interest in favorite sports or hobbies
- unusual emotional outbursts or a sudden change in friends

No Laughing Matter

Television sitcoms have a way of making light of heavy issues and ignoring consequences. Dr. David Crousman isn't amused. Specifically, he's upset about a running gag on *Will & Grace*, a recently retired, Emmy-winning series getting new life in syndication. Megan Mullally plays Karen Walker, a wealthy woman whose fondness for alcohol and prescription painkillers gets played for laughs.

"It's no joke at all," said Crousman, who runs an outpatient counseling facility in Beverly Hills. "It depicts a woman who's held hostage to her addiction. They're not showing her when she doesn't get her pain pill, when she doesn't have the alcohol. How she gets diarrhea, how she starts vomiting, how her skin will crawl, her legs will cramp. They don't show that because it's not cute."

It's the modern equivalent of the happy drunk. By downplaying the danger and cranking up the laugh track, the show's creators send a troubling message.

"They'll just reach their hands in there, take a handful and just take them. It could be anything."

Pharming parties also let users swap pills as if they were *Yu-Gi-Oh!* cards. "If I have something good, like OxyContin, it might be worth two or three Xanax," a girl told *Time*. "We rejoice when someone has a medical thing, like, gets their wisdom teeth out or has back pain, because we know we'll get pills. Last year I had surgery and I thought, Well, at least I'll get painkillers."

OxyContin seems to be the most popular . . . and deadly. Depending on the dose taken, OxyContin can slow or even halt breathing, especially when consumed with alcohol or other sedatives. Dubbed by one doctor "one of the strongest opiates and potentially addictive painkillers ever created," it was approved for round-the-clock pain, such as that experienced by patients with advanced stages of cancer. Its recreational use has increased 26 percent among 8th, 9th and 12th graders since 2002.

Dr. Nora Volkow, director of the National Institute on Drug Abuse, explained, "Some abusers bypass the time-release system by crushing or chewing the pills. That way, they get all of the drug their system at one time, and the body responds very differently. The risk of overdose then becomes huge. And an overdose of OxyContin can kill you."

That's precisely what happened to 17-year-old Julie Zdeblick. Julie's mother told *Family Circle*, "[Parents] are looking for alcohol and pot, not prescription drugs. It's like we got suited up for the game but were dressed for the wrong sport."

What Parents Can Do

With the medical community continuing to create stronger, more efficient drugs, the potential for this type of abuse will only get worse. Still, parents can take steps to keep teenagers from becoming statistics:

1. As part of an ongoing dialogue, give children a healthy respect for prescription medication. Express your strong disapproval of abuse. Silent or wishy-washy parents can be a teen's worst enemy.
2. Know which prescription drugs are in your home and keep them locked up. Even if your teens aren't tempted, guests could be. A New Jersey youth declared, "The best part about going to a new house was rifling through the medicine cabinet."
3. Be aware of how many pills remain in partially used prescriptions so you'll know if any are missing, and be sure to discard medications you're no longer taking.
4. Know which drugs are prone to be abused, including over-the-counter cough medicines containing dextromethorphan (or DXM), such as Robitussin DM and three of the four forms of Coricidin HPB.
5. Familiarize yourself with the warning signs of abuse *(see above)* so you can intervene before it's too late.
6. Explain the diminishing returns of drug abuse, which releases unnaturally large amounts of dopamine into the brain. Over time the brain gets used to it, and the addict ceases to enjoy life's normal pleasures without the dopamine flood that only the drugs can deliver.

Our overmedicated culture has a pill for just about everything. Ads for prescription drugs outnumber toothpaste commercials. So for many young people it's second nature to manage moods and stimulate performance with capsules that come in amber-colored plastic bottles. Members of Generation Rx need to know that, if not taken as intended, prescription drugs could land them in the emergency room . . . or the morgue.

Youth Smoking Prevention: What Works?

PAULA M. LANTZ, PhD, PETER D. JACOBSON, JD, MPH, AND KENNETH E. WARNER, PhD

A large body of research shows that very few people in the United States initiate smoking or become habitual smokers after their teen years. At the present time, nearly 9 out of 10 current adult smokers (89%) started their habit before age 19. Although many tobacco prevention activities have focused on youth, smoking among U.S. adolescents actually rose throughout most of the 1990s, until declining somewhat in the past few years.

Given the epidemiology of smoking initiation, a great deal of policy and programmatic attention has been directed at youth smoking in the United States. In this article, we synthesize the burgeoning literature regarding efforts to discourage youth from smoking. For those areas in which there is empirical evidence from evaluations and other research studies, we summarize the state of the science regarding the impact or effectiveness of these general strategies. In addition, we also comment on emerging initiatives and interventions that have not yet been evaluated or have not received much attention in the peer-reviewed literature in an attempt to identify emerging trends and promising innovations.

School-Based Educational Interventions

A large number of school-based programs have been implemented during the past three decades. Most of these efforts target elementary school and/or middle school students. As described in a 1994 Institute of Medicine report, the majority of these programs have tended to be based on one of three main approaches. The first approach is an *information deficit* or *rational model* in which the program provides information about the health risks and negative consequences of tobacco, most often in a manner intended to arouse concern or fear. The primary premise of this approach is that youth are generally misinformed about the risks of smoking and that educating them about the health and social detriments of smoking will provide a deterrent.

The second major educational approach to youth tobacco prevention is an *affective education model* in which the program attempts to influence beliefs, attitudes, intentions, and norms related to tobacco use with a focus on enhancing self-esteem and values clarification. This type of program emphasizes initiation influences within an individual, recognizing that knowledge deficits are not the only factors associated with smoking initiation.

> **Nearly 9 out of 10 current adult smokers (89%) started their habit before age 19.**

The third approach to tobacco prevention is based on a *social influence resistance model,* which emphasizes the social environment as a critical factor in tobacco use. In addition to individual factors, influences outside of an individual, such as peer behavior or attitudes, and certain aspects of the environmental, familial, and cultural contexts, are considered to be of great importance. As such, this type of intervention focuses on building skills needed to recognize and resist negative influences, including recognition of advertising tactics and peer influences, communication and decision-making skills, and assertiveness.

The results of several individual evaluations and meta-analyses strongly suggest that educational programs based on the social influence resistance model are the most effective of the three approaches. Several individual studies and meta-analyses suggest that programs that incorporate a social influences model and focus on skills in recognizing and resisting social pressures have a modest but significant impact on both smoking initiation and level of use. Even so, the long-term impact of school-based educational interventions is of concern. It appears that the effects tend to dissipate with time, with effects generally persisting in the range of one to four years. Program "boosters" or subsequent interventions appear to enhance the staying power of the intervention effects, although the most appropriate content of and timing for these booster sessions is not known.

Community Interventions

The increased understanding of the combined effects of environmental, social, and cultural conditions on tobacco use has resulted in an emphasis on interventions that include comprehensive, community-based approaches. Such an approach targets multiple systems, institutions, or channels simultaneously, and employs multiple strategies. In general, community interventions have multiple components, and involve the use of community resources to influence both individual behavior and community norms or practices related to adolescent tobacco use. This includes the involvement of families, schools, community organizations, churches, businesses, the media, social service and health agencies, government, and law enforcement, with intervention strategies generally focused on making changes in both the environment and individual behavior.

Although community interventions take a variety of shapes, common elements among them include a shared emphasis on altering the social environment or social context in which tobacco products are obtained and used, and a shared goal of creating a social environment that is supportive of non-smoking and cessation. Some of the components of community interventions, such as mass media campaigns and youth access restrictions, are also implemented as stand-alone interventions, as described below.

While an increasing number of communities are attempting to influence youth tobacco use with multiple-component interventions, there are few published reports of evaluations with rigorous designs. The available research results, however, are encouraging in many cases. For example, a community intervention involving mass media, school-based education, parent education, community organizing, and policy advocacy in 15 communities in the Kansas City area was found to be effective in reducing tobacco, alcohol, and illicit drug use. Regarding tobacco use two years past the start of the intervention, the rate of smoking in the last month among youth was reported to be 19% in the intervention communities versus 29% in the control communities.

School-based programs and community interventions involving parents, mass media, and community organizations appear to have a stronger impact over time when they work in tandem rather than as separate, stand-alone interventions. Mobilizing parents and community elements outside of the school (including the media) is seen as enhancing school-based interventions and increasing the potential for a lasting behavioral impact.

Although the results of a small number of controlled trials of community interventions attest to their ability to have an effect on youth smoking behavior, it is likely that broad-based community interventions alone are not sufficient to bring about a substantial and sustained decline in youth smoking. Community efforts, as symbolized by COMMIT, ASSIST, and other community interventions, likely need to be combined with stronger advocacy, taxation, media interventions, and policy formation and implementation, as discussed below.

Recently, several state health departments (including those in California, Massachusetts, and Florida) have implemented comprehensive tobacco prevention and control programs that attempt to tackle youth tobacco using multiple interventions aimed at a number of different levels. Each of these programs targets several populations concurrently, and uses multiple channels to disseminate the message. These programs are comprehensive both in using a variety of strategies to reach their audiences, in incorporating multiple types of intervention (i.e., education,

incentives, and regulation) at the state, regional and local levels, and attempting to have a strong policy component.

"Best practices" for this type of comprehensive tobacco control program were recently summarized by the Centers for Disease Control and Prevention. While these programs are in the early stages of development and implementation in many states, early results suggest that these comprehensive models have significant potential for youth tobacco control. Early lessons drawn from state experiences are that more comprehensive, aggressive, and better funded state programs will lead to greater reductions in tobacco use than less intense efforts. In short, a state's commitment to the program's intensity and comprehensiveness matters.

Mass Media/Public Education

Mass media strategies have been used for broad-based public education regarding a variety of public health issues, including tobacco use prevention and control. Mass media efforts are viewed as particularly appropriate for reaching youth, who are often heavily exposed to and greatly interested in media messages. Youth have been the primary target of some hard-hitting and sophisticated anti-tobacco media campaigns in several communities and states, including California, Florida, and Massachusetts as a major part of their comprehensive tobacco control programs. In addition, the American Legacy Foundation (the independent foundation established as part of the multi-state settlement with the tobacco industry) has launched a large and aggressive anti-tobacco media campaign aimed at youth. Despite some encouraging information from Florida regarding a sharp decline in youth smoking, the impact of anti-tobacco media campaigns on smoking behavior among youth in general or specific subgroups is unknown. The few existing studies of the impact of mass media campaigns on youth smoking have shown varying results.

The impact of anti-tobacco media campaigns on smoking behavior among youth in general or specific subgroups is unknown.

Media campaigns that involve essential elements of social marketing and are theoretically driven may well have an effect on the attitudes and behaviors of youth regarding tobacco use, although the impact of such campaigns is challenging to evaluate and has not yet been demonstrated. The literature suggests that mass media interventions increase their chance of having an impact if the following conditions are met:

1. the campaign strategies are based on sound social marketing principles;
2. the effort is large and intense enough;
3. target groups are carefully differentiated;
4. messages for specific target groups resonate with "core values" of the group (rather than simply preach

about the health risks of tobacco use), and are based on empirical findings regarding the needs and interests of the group; and

5. the campaign is of sufficient duration.

Tobacco Advertising Restrictions

Cigarettes are a heavily advertised and marketed consumer product. There is great concern that tobacco advertising and marketing—including the distribution of promotional products such as clothing, sporting equipment, and gear for outdoor activities—are positively associated with youth smoking. A growing amount of research evidence suggests that youth awareness of tobacco marketing campaigns, receipt of free tobacco samples, and receipt of direct mail promotional paraphernalia are associated with smoking susceptibility and initiation.

The technical limitations of econometric approaches to estimating the effects of advertising on cigarette consumption, combined with a lack of studies on adolescent smoking make this literature of little use in trying to assess whether advertising affects smoking by adolescents.

Similarly, the potential effect of cigarette advertising restrictions or bans on adolescent smoking behavior also is unclear. Some states and municipalities have implemented restrictions regarding tobacco advertising. These types of bans are too new to have been evaluated yet, and the implementation of similar bans nationwide has been delayed because of legal challenges. Researchers, however, have concluded that total bans on tobacco advertising would likely have a greater impact than partial bans, because partial bans afford tobacco companies the opportunity to switch advertising expenditures to other promotional media and methods.

Youth Access Restrictions

In the past decade, the issue of youth access to tobacco products has received an explosion of attention. Policy action has been seen in a number of areas, including regulation of sellers, regulation of buyers, restrictions on the distribution of free products or samples (including coupons), and regulation of the means of tobacco sale (where and how it can be sold). The latter includes state and local efforts to restrict or totally ban tobacco sales via vending machines.

Federal Public Law 102-321, commonly referred to as the Synar amendment and enacted in 1991, stipulates that states must enforce laws restricting the sale and distribution of tobacco products to minors and must demonstrate success in reducing youth tobacco access or risk not receiving the full complement of block grant funding for the treatment and prevention of substance abuse. Although the Synar amendment has led to a number of developments in youth tobacco control, it is believed that few jurisdictions seriously enforce laws regarding the sale of tobacco to minors. This is important, because while laws regarding sales to minors appear to be rather benign in

and of themselves, what seems to make a difference regarding illegal tobacco sales to minors is whether or not the laws are enforced.

Several controlled community intervention studies have demonstrated that increased enforcement of tobacco-sales laws can reduce illegal sales to minors. Unfortunately, however, the evidence that a reduction in sales actually translates into a reduction in tobacco consumption is limited. Several studies failed to look at the impact of enforcement interventions on smoking behavior. In studies that looked at both sales and behavior, the two did not always go hand in hand.

If the only or primary way in which youth gain access to cigarettes is through illegal sales, then we might expect the enforcement of youth access laws to have a powerful effect on smoking behavior. However, youth cite a number of "social sources" (such as family, friends, or even strangers) for their cigarettes as well as illegal purchase. Thus, what can be said with the evidence at hand is that youth access interventions can lead to a general reduction in illegal sales of cigarettes to minors. Whether this will translate into reduced and sustained reductions in youth tobacco use remains to be seen.

Tobacco Excise Taxes

Tobacco products are taxed by the federal government, states, and a few local governments. While generating revenue, tobacco taxation is also a policy that creates an economic disincentive to use tobacco. Theoretically, increasing the price of cigarettes through taxation could reduce adolescent cigarette consumption through three mechanisms:

1. some adolescents would quit smoking;
2. some would reduce the amount that they smoke; and
3. some would not start smoking in the first place.

The extent to which higher cigarette taxes will achieve these objectives depends upon how responsive smokers, and prospective smokers, are to price increases.

What seems to make a difference regarding illegal tobacco sales to minors is whether or not the laws are enforced.

Studies of the elasticity of demand for cigarettes have followed a long tradition, dating back more than half a century. Most of these studies have focused on the adult or overall demand for cigarettes, with comparatively few focused on teenage cigarette demand. In regard to youth, the evidence on the degree to which teenagers are responsive to changes in cigarette prices is mixed, but the general consensus is that higher prices are an effective deterrent to youth smoking. That is, increasing the price of cigarettes leads to lower consumption by both adults and teenagers. Because cigarette price increases have been relatively small (i.e., under a dollar and, in many cases, just a few cents), it is difficult to predict with confidence the impact that a large price increase—such as a dollar or more per pack—would have on teenage cigarette consumption. The effects might be expected to be proportionately greater than those of a small tax increase.

Recent Innovations

The purpose of this section is to identify emerging trends and promising innovations in policy and programmatic responses to youth smoking. The majority of strategies described below have received no or only cursory evaluations. Thus, while some of these approaches may be compelling or appear to have promise, there is little to no empirical evidence to support claims about their worth or effectiveness at this time.

Smoking Cessation Interventions

The results of a number of descriptive studies and focus group studies suggest that many teen smokers are motivated to quit smoking. The impact of smoking cessation interventions among adolescents, however, is not well understood. None of the nicotine replacement therapies currently on the market have been approved for subjects under the age of 18. In addition, until very recently, formal smoking cessation programs were aimed exclusively at adults. An important recent trend, however, is an increase in the number of such smoking cessation programs now available for youth. Given the cost-effectiveness of smoking cessation interventions for adults, and the large number of addicted teenagers, research on cessation programs tailored to youth is an important area and should be a high priority.

Computer-Based Systems

An important emerging trend is the use of computer-based systems to communicate messages about tobacco to teens. Some of these innovations have been evaluated, but because most are in various stages of development and implementation we consider them under the category of new innovations. The advantages of these efforts, if successful, are their low cost and adolescent receptivity to computer-based information.

Peer-Based Interventions

A major trend in school-based interventions is the use of peer-education programs, such as Teens Against Tobacco Use. These programs train older students to become positive role models for middle and elementary school students. Many of these programs include a media literacy component through which teens learn how the tobacco industry's advertising savvy has manipulated and distorted information about tobacco.

Penalties for Possession and Use

A controversial response to youth tobacco use that has emerged is the increasing willingness of state and municipal policymakers to fine underage youth for using tobacco products. Tobacco control advocates have vociferously protested this approach as an attempt to shift attention away from vendors who sell tobacco products to minors. Regardless, this shift appears

to be gaining momentum. Minors caught smoking or in possession of cigarettes can face a variety of penalties, ranging from a ticket or fine to suspension from school, denial of a driver's license, or any combination of these responses. Fines can also be combined with tobacco education or cessation classes. An additional important innovation to watch for in this area is the use of teen smoking courts.

School Policies

Schools may have their own smoking policies, which can apply even to those students over 18 years old. Penalties for violations include fines, smoking education and cessation classes, informing the student's parents, and suspension and/or expulsion. It appears that schools are increasingly willing to develop, implement, and enforce no-smoking policies. Recent school smoking policies seem to use a combination of punishments, rather than just fining or suspending students.

Restrictions on the Sale and Marketing of Tobacco Products

One way to restrict youth access to tobacco products is to physically remove the products from areas where youth can go. For example, recent restrictions on vending machines have been effective in removing them as a source of cigarettes for minors. In addition, the issue of billboard tobacco advertising was addressed in the 46-state settlement with the tobacco industry, which stipulated the removal of billboard advertisements by April 23, 1999. An emerging trend is to restrict self-service displays of cigarettes.

Direct Restrictions on Smoking

Policy efforts to restrict public smoking have proliferated since the 1980s. Such efforts include state and local restrictions on smoking in public facilities, outdoor spaces, worksites, hospitals, restaurants, bars, hotels, and on airline flights. Some econometric studies of teenage and young adult smoking behavior have found evidence that clean indoor air laws reduce teenage cigarette consumption. Although the reasons why such laws may be effective in reducing youth smoking are unknown, one could speculate that they simply reduce the opportunities available for smoking. Alternatively, or perhaps in conjunction with these reduced opportunities, clean indoor air laws may be a useful vehicle for creating a cultural norm that suggests smoking is socially unacceptable.

Interventions That Focus on Adolescent Risk Taking

Youth smoking occurs in a web of social relations that fosters many types of adolescent experimentation and that also may foster problem behaviors. Because of this social context, youth smoking arises from some of the same family, peer, and community influences that are also important to sexual risk-taking, crime and violence, and the initiation of harmful alcohol and illicit substance use. Existing prevention research regarding other adolescent problem behaviors therefore has potentially important implications for the design and evaluation of programs to curb youth smoking. Such interventions for older adolescents are often focused on improving academic skills. Many are also aimed at creating a sustained relationship with adult advisors or mentors who can provide social and emotional support while reinforcing appropriate social norms regarding substance abuse and other behaviors. An additional approach involves "family-focused" interventions.

There is no "magic bullet" in terms of youth tobacco control on the horizon . . . However, our review suggests a number of prevention strategies that are promising.

Discussion

The most obvious conclusion from this review is that adolescent smoking prevention efforts have had mixed results, and that there is no "magic bullet" in terms of youth tobacco control on the horizon. As a result, advocating for a focus on youth smoking prevention and control is somewhat controversial. Some policy analysts have suggested that the focus of public policy should be to reduce teenage smoking initiation rates. Others have suggested that the focus on children will undermine the broader and likely more fruitful initiatives and programs needed to attack smoking and to promote cessation among adult habitual smokers.

From a practical perspective, these different policy views are not mutually exclusive. Both can be implemented simultaneously, and should be considered as complementary rather than competing strategies. From a public health perspective, we are appropriately concerned that the prevalence of youth smoking remains high despite the amount of resources already devoted to this problem and the wide array of interventions that have been tried. Yet, it is possible that without these interventions rates of both experimental and habitual smoking among youth would be even higher.

Our review suggests a number of prevention strategies that are promising, especially if conducted in a coordinated way to take advantage of potential synergies across interventions. This includes such intervention strategies as media campaigns, teen cessation programs, community interventions that change the social context of smoking, and tobacco excise tax increases. Equally as important, there is great potential for these interventions to be cost-effective. Even modest gains from prevention and cessation efforts could lead to substantial reductions in the morbidity and mortality costs of smoking. We believe that previous calls for tobacco control efforts that are "youth centered" remain relevant and critically important as we move into the 21st century.

This review suggests that there are a number of interventions and strategies that deserve further consideration, dissemination, and evaluation. The resources available through the settlement with the tobacco industry provide an unprecedented opportunity to invest in youth tobacco control. Thus, we strongly advocate that this opportunity be seized and that significant state resources—along with other resources—be devoted to expanding, improving and evaluating tobacco prevention and control activities among youth.

PAULA M. LANTZ, PHD, PETER D. JACOBSON, JD, MPH, and KENNETH E. WARNER, PHD are with the Department of Health Management and Policy at the University of Michigan School of Public Health, Ann Arbor, Michigan.

This article was abstracted from P.M. Lantz, P.D. Jacobson, K.E. Warner, J. Wasserman, H.A. Pollack, J. Berson, and A. Ahlstrom (2000). Investing in Youth Tobacco Control: A Review of Smoking Prevention and Control Strategies. *Tobacco Control*, 9, 47–63. It appears here with permission from the publisher.

UNIT 3

Cognitive Development and Education

Unit Selections

Key Points to Consider

- How can youth use digital portfolios?

- What will ease 9th graders way into high school?

- What differences of maturity exist within and across grades?

- What does a high school teacher say after he experienced being a high school student again?

- Why is the dropout rate steadily rising and which programs convince students to stay in school?

- Should universities request depressed and suicidal students to drop out?

- How can high schools encourage leadership?

- How can schools teach students to not turn in substandard work?

- What is the link between student health and academic performance?

Student Web Site
www.mhcls.com/online

Internet References
Further information regarding these Web sites may be found in this book's preface or online.

School Stress
    http://www.kqed.org/w/ymc/stress/index.html
Afterschool Alliance
    http://www.afterschoolalliance.org
Educational Forum on Adolescent Health: Youth Bullying
    http://www.ama-assn.org/ama1/pub/upload/mm/39/youthbullying.pdf

Adolescence entails changes in cognitive capacities that are just as monumental as the biological changes. Whereas children tend to be more literal, more tied to reality and tied to the familiar, adolescents are more abstract, systematic, and logical. Adolescents can appreciate metaphors and sarcasm, they can easily think about things that do not exist, they can test abstract ideas against reality, and they can readily conceive of multiple possibilities. Many of these improvements in thinking ability contribute to conflicts with adults as adolescents become better able to argue a point or take a stand. They are better at planning out their case and anticipating counter-arguments. They are also more likely to question the way things are because they now conceive of alternate possibilities.

The study of cognitive changes that occur in adolescence has largely been based on the work of the Swiss psychologist, Jean Piaget, and his colleague, Barbel Inhelder. Piaget and Inhelder described the adolescent as reasoning at the formal operational stage. Children from the approximate ages of seven to 11 years old were described as being in the "concrete operational" stage. Not all researchers agree with Piaget and Inhelder that changes in adolescent cognitive abilities represent true stage-related changes. They do, however, agree that adolescent thought is characteristically more logical, abstract, and hypothetical than that of children. Recognize, though, that having certain mental capacities does not mean that adolescents, or even adults for that matter, will always reason at their rational best!

Piaget's views on cognitive development have been very influential, particularly in the field of education. Awareness of the cognitive abilities and shortcomings of adolescents can make their behaviors more comprehensible to parents, teachers, counselors, and other professionals who work with them. Similarly, as Piaget suggested, schools need to take the developmental abilities and needs of adolescents into account in planning programs and designing curricula. In addition, Piaget's general philosophy was that learning must be active. Others in the field of education, however, caution that there are other important issues left un-addressed by Piaget. For example, the U.S. has an elevated school dropout rate, so we need to find alternatives for keeping the nation's youth in school.

Building on the work of Piaget and Inhelder, David Elkind has argued that the newly-emerging formal operational cognitive abilities of adolescents lead to some troublesome consequences. For one thing, adolescents tend to over-intellectualize. They often make things too complex and fail to see the obvious, a phenomenon that Elkind calls pseudostupidity. Teachers often bear the brunt of this phenomenon as adolescents overanalyze every word of a multiple-choice question. Elkind also maintains that much of the extreme self-consciousness of adolescents occurs because of the construct of an imaginary audience. Formal operations make it possible for adolescents to think about other people's thoughts. Adolescents lose perspective and think that others are constantly watching them and thinking about them. A related mistake is that adolescents are likely to believe that everyone shares their concerns and knows their thoughts. This belief, that one is at the center of attention, further leads to the development of what Elkind calls the personal fable. Namely, if everyone is paying so much attention to me I must be special and invulnerable. Bad things won't happen to me. I won't get in a car crash. I won't get pregnant. The phenomena—pseudostupidity, the imaginary audience, and the personal fable—diminish as adolescents' cognitive abilities mature and as they develop friendships in which intimacies are shared.

While developmentalists in the Piagetian tradition focus on the ways in which the thought processes of children and adolescents differ, other researchers have taken a different track—a psychometric approach. In this approach, the emphasis is on quantifying cognitive abilities such as verbal ability, mathematical ability, and general intelligence (IQ). The measurement of intelligence, as well as the very definition of intelligence, has been controversial for decades. A classic question is whether intelligence is best conceptualized as a general capacity that underlies many diverse abilities, or as a set of specific abilities. Traditional IQ tests focus on abilities that relate to success in school and ignore abilities such as those that tap creativity, mechanical aptitude, or practical intelligence.

The role of genetic versus environmental contributions to intelligence has also been controversial. At the turn of the century the predominant view was that intelligence was essentially inherited and was little influenced by experience. Today, the consensus is that an individual's intelligence is very much a product of both nature and nurture.

Adolescents clearly have larger vocabularies, more mathematical knowledge, better spatial ability, etc., than children. Their memories are better because they process information more efficiently and use memory strategies more effectively. Adolescents possess a greater general knowledge base than children, which enables adolescents to link new concepts to existing ideas. Stated another way, psychometric intelligence may well increase with age. On the other hand, because of comparisons to age peers, the relative performance of adolescents on aptitude tests remains fairly stable. A nine-year-old child's outstanding performance on an IQ test, for example, is fairly predictive that the same individual's IQ score at age 15 will be better than the score of most peers.

Unit 3 starts with an article on digital portfolios. Several articles explain various aspects of high school discussing maturity within and across grades. Deborah Waldron reports on a high school physics teacher who enrolls in a 9th grade biology class. School dropout rate is steadily rising, and Paul Barton explains how some programs convince students to stay in school. One article explains how high school senior leadership programs nourish teachers-in-the-making. Bill Hemmer reveals both strengths and weaknesses in improving rates of high school and college completion for low income and minority students. The next article examines cheating in high school and how it can be cured. Kenkel and Hoelscher tell how one school taught middle school students to learn the benefit of not being able to turn in substandard work. The final article addresses the link between students' health and academic performance.

Documenting Learning with Digital Portfolios

Portfolios must be part of a purposeful assessment program with clear learning goals.

DAVID NIGUIDULA

Olivia, a sophomore at Ponaganset High School in North Scituate, Rhode Island, sat down last June with two of her teachers in front of her digital portfolio—a multimedia, Web-based collection of her best schoolwork. A menu listing the school's nine graduation expectations, including Effective Expression, Research Skills, and Critical and Creative Thinking, appeared on her portfolio's home page. The school's faculty had worked for a year developing these expectations and aligning them with the state's standards.

Clicking on the link to Effective Expression, Olivia and her teachers reviewed the list of learning outcomes associated with this expectation, including the ability to express ideas for various purposes and audiences and the ability to use communication skills in each subject area. The screen also contained links to about 20 entries, each showing a sample of Olivia's work that reflected this graduation expectation. During the last two years, Olivia had entered diverse work samples into her portfolio, including a sonnet, a solution to an open-ended algebra problem, and an audio file of her flute performance at the school's winter concert.

For each entry, Olivia had written a summary of how her work met one or more of the school's graduation expectations. Her teachers had assessed each entry using an online rubric and given her feedback, so that Olivia could review her work and the comments from her teachers at any time.

This end-of-year review was a chance to look at the portfolio as a whole. By this time, Olivia's portfolio contained two to four artifacts for every course. The review focused on a few artifacts that she had selected, each linked to one of three reflective prompts: Where have you done your best work? Where have you grown as a learner? What is your academic plan for next year?

Because Olivia's teachers had been able to look at and comment on her selected work online before meeting with her in person, they used this meeting to discuss with her what she had done well and what she needed to accomplish during her next two years to meet Ponaganset's graduation expectations.

Making Digital Portfolios Meaningful

Olivia's portfolio review is a snapshot of one moment in a well-coordinated digital portfolio assessment program. Digital portfolios are multimedia collections of student work stored and reviewed in digital format. Beginning in 1993, I led a team from the Annenberg Institute for School Reform and the Coalition of Essential Schools, which researched digital portfolios as an assessment tool and identified a set of essential questions that schools need to address:

As students look through the portfolio and read over their reflections, they recognize how their skills have grown over time.

- *Vision:* What skills and content should students master and demonstrate in their portfolios?
- *Purpose:* Why do we collect student work?
- *Audience:* Who are the audiences for portfolios?
- *Assessment:* How do the entries in portfolios reflect the school's assessment vision, and how can we assess the quality of those entries?
- *Technology:* What hardware, software, networking, and technical support will our school need to implement a digital portfolio assessment system?
- *Logistics:* How will students enter their work into digital portfolios?

- *Culture:* Is discussing student work already part of our school culture?

Although the technology of digital portfolios has changed significantly since the initial research, these questions still provide a guide for designing a digital portfolio program. As the leader of a team at Ideas Consulting, when I advise schools on using digital portfolios to enrich assessment of student work, I find that technology is the least important consideration. The essential element is integrating digital portfolios into a larger assessment system with clear learning goals. To do so, schools need to identify the purpose of their portfolios, the kinds of work students should enter into portfolios, and strategies for assessing portfolios.

What Is the Portfolio's Purpose?

The purpose of the portfolio drives the content. Digital portfolios can serve many purposes: showcasing students' best products; proving that students have mastered expectations required for graduation; and communicating with parents and other audiences about what students are learning. Ponaganset High School is at the forefront of implementing Rhode Island's "graduation by proficiency" initiative, under which students use their portfolios to show that they are meeting state standards. Starting with the class of 2008, all Ponaganset students will need to demonstrate their mastery of standards through a set of rigorous performance assessments—such as portfolios and senior projects—before they can graduate. The idea is for students to demonstrate that they can meet standards while also showing who they are as individual learners.

Teachers in the elementary schools of Barrington and Bristol-Warren, Rhode Island, use portfolios to communicate better with parents. At a parent conference, the teacher calls up the student's portfolio, which displays samples of the student's work in reading, writing, and math from kindergarten through 5th grade. Because the goal is to show growth over time, the portfolio contains only two or three samples in each subject area for each year.

For the reading component of the portfolios, for example, twice a year teachers videotape each student reading a brief passage and answering comprehension questions posed by another teacher. A 1st grade teacher can use the portfolio to show parents how their child has progressed from struggling with a level 5 text in October to confidently reading a level 11 text in April. Teachers report that the video component enables them to powerfully convey a students reading skills; just 60 seconds of video footage can provide the starting point for a rich discussion of the student's progress over time.

What Kinds of Work Should Portfolios Include?

Once a school determines the primary purpose of its portfolios, it can then decide what kinds of artifacts students should include. If the portfolio is meant to document how students are meeting graduation standards, then teachers need to provide opportunities for students to demonstrate their mastery of standards through work that can be digitally displayed. If the

school wants to show each student's growth over time, students must arrange portfolio samples in a sequence that shows such progress.

Schools need to identify the kinds of work students should enter into portfolios and strategies for assessing portfolios.

For example, Mr. Sangiuliano, a 4th grade mathematics teacher in Barrington, Rhode Island, wanted to show student progress in an area his students found difficult: solving open-ended word problems. He taught students a strategy for dealing with word problems: Students restated the problem in their own words and wrote an "I need to. . ." statement pinpointing the objective *(I need to figure out how many fish were caught),* followed by a strategy for approaching the problem *(I can make a table showing how many fish each person caught).*

To document students' progress at various points during the year, Mr. Sangiuliano recorded each student on video explaining how he or she applied the strategy to a word problem. Videos shot at the beginning of the year showed students needing prompting, with the teacher asking, "What was your 'I need to. . .' statement?" and helping students realize that there may be more than one workable strategy. Videos from later in the year showed that these 4th graders had internalized the method.

Assembling these video clips into student portfolios enhanced assessment in a few ways. As they watched their child successfully use the same approach to solve problems involving different mathematical operations, parents better understood the strategy used in class. Second, because Mr. Sangiuliano can easily pass these digital clips on to the 5th grade math teacher, work on a common problem-solving strategy can continue beyond his class. Finally, watching themselves on video helped students review and reflect on their own growth.

At the secondary level, portfolio-worthy assignments must be clearly linked to the portfolios purpose. If the portfolio is a vehicle for demonstrating student progress toward specific standards, then teachers must give plenty of assignments that tap into the skills and knowledge represented by each standard. Teachers should plan together how to align their assignments with the school's overall expectations.

For example, several middle schools and high schools in Rhode Island assign a geometry scavenger hunt. Teachers give students a list of geometric shapes and concepts—such as parallel lines with transversals, similar triangles, or complementary adjacent angles—and direct them to photograph buildings or objects around town that reflect these concepts. When introducing this assignment, teachers explain that the project meets the schools expectations of understanding geometric concepts and being able to communicate mathematically. The assignment could also demonstrate successful time management, skill in using technology to convey an idea, and aesthetic talent in photography.

How Should Schools Assess Portfolios?

Successful schools assess each student's digital portfolio by evaluating both individual entries and the portfolio as a whole. The entire faculty needs to develop common strategies so that students receive consistent feedback.

Develop schoolwide rubrics. As Ponaganset High School developed its learner outcomes, faculty members found that they needed to agree on how to communicate about those expectations. For example, teachers agreed that a graduate should be able to write a good lab report; but what made a lab report "good"? The school's science department created a rubric defining a good lab report as one that includes a clear statement of purpose and hypothesis; data in an easy-to-read format, appropriate to the kind of information collected; and a conclusion that is clear and concise and answers the intent of the purpose. Whether a student takes biology, physics, or chemistry, he or she has guidelines for creating a lab report that meets the school's standard. Ponaganset's teachers created similar rubrics for each of the learner outcomes. Outcomes such as demonstrating "initiative, responsibility, self-discipline, and perseverance" cut across all subject areas.

Include students' self-reflections. Students' reflections on their own work are a crucial part of assessment. Students should include such a reflection for each entry in their digital portfolios and for the portfolio as a whole. Reflections can be inspired by a prompt, such as "How does this entry fulfill the school's expectations?" or "What skills did you use in this project?"

The youngest students can reflect on their performances without writing. During a videotaped reading session, for example, the teacher might ask a student what words he or she found hard, or what strategies were helpful in figuring out new words.

When a student has to defend why an entry in his or her portfolio fulfills a particular learning expectation, the student will more thoroughly understand that expectation. When students make a conceptual link between their work and school standards, those standards become more than an abstract document to hang on the wall. As students look through the portfolio and read over their reflections, they recognize how their skills have grown over time and begin to see where they can go next.

Generate reports. Teachers and students should regularly create reports summarizing the contents and implications of students' portfolios. Digital portfolios offer teachers and students the advantage of creating reports in any number of ways. For example, a Ponaganset High School junior clicks on the link for each graduation expectation in his portfolio and instantly reviews how many entries he has for each expectation, and which expectations he still needs to provide evidence for. An advisor then helps this student plan how to fill in the gaps.

Reports of the class as a whole tell teachers a great deal. When a teacher can click on a button and see how all her students did on a particular rubric, she can determine how to adjust instruction. For example, an elementary teacher might use a report generated by compiling digital portfolio data to examine a class's performance on a writing rubric. She might see that certain students earn consistently low scores on word choice, a finding that would allow her to focus attention on these students.

In the end, the success of a digital portfolio relies on the clarity of a school's learning goals. Although the technology makes it convenient to organize student work and send that work to broader audiences, the effectiveness of the portfolio relies on a far more traditional practice: the ability of students, parents, and teachers to create a common vision.

DAVID NIGUIDULA is Founder of Ideas Consulting, 15 Houghton St., Barrington, RI 02806; 401–785–0401: david@ideasconsulting.com.

Author's note—For samples of digital portfolios, visit www.richerpicture.com and www.efoliominnesota.com (click on Gallery).

From *Educational Leadership*, November 2005, pp. 44–47. Copyright © 2005 by ASCD. Reprinted by permission. The Association for Supervision and Curriculum Development is a worldwide community of educators advocating sound policies and sharing best practices to achieve the success of each learner. To learn more, visit ASCD at www.ascd.org.

Help Us Make the 9th Grade Transition

No one knows better than students themselves what they need from teachers as they move into high school.

KATHLEEN CUSHMAN

By the time students hit 8th grade, the transition to 9th grade looms large. Middle school teachers are talking more urgently about the need to prepare for high school. Friends and siblings already in high school are warning that everything is about to change, big-time. The 8th graders worry about their social world turning upside down as they move from the top to the bottom of the grade-level pecking order.

In conducting research for a new book that brings middle school students' voices to the fore, I spoke with 16 students from Indianapolis, Indiana, just a few weeks after they started 9th grade at two large comprehensive high schools. They were just beginning to find their way in their respective schools and were still filled with the sense that they were exploring new territory.

These young teenagers made it clear that 9th grade marked the beginning of a new, high-stakes period of their lives. Out in the real world, people had been telling them, it would really matter how they behaved and whether they succeeded in high school:

> When you get to 9th grade, there's no more playing. You got to get about your work. You gotta find a study habit. You gotta do the right thing. Because after 9th grade, that determines where you're gonna be in life. How you gonna get paid, and how you gonna get treated—upper-class, lower-class. High school is going to follow you throughout your whole life. (Brian)

Kids had heard that in the social world of high school, the stakes were equally high. Even though they were eager to start, they also wondered whether they would be able to handle the new demands, fit in, and stay out of trouble.

As these students talked about what helped them most, they suggested how teachers might prepare middle school students for the high school transition and ease its difficulties in the crucial 9th grade year. The 9th graders pointed out that addressing the issues of transition early on—and continuing support through 9th grade—could bolster students' confidence and performance.

> **"I would tell middle school students the truth about what high school is like—that it's really nothing to worry about."**

What They Worry About

When they are imagining themselves in high school, kids draw on a vast storehouse of lore passed on from students who have gone before them. Fed by the rumor mill (and sometimes also by teachers' warnings), their worries fall into several categories.

High school will be huge and confusing. Unless they are headed for a small high school, kids imagine an overwhelming scene. In a crowded school short on human and financial resources, the prospect grows even scarier:

> All my buddies told me that high school was going to be a zoo, people running around, nobody going to class. Up on every corner, people just standing there like lightposts, with no worry about getting an education. It's so big here, there's like 2,000 kids. I'm thinking, "How they gonna manage it?" (Brian)

The work will be harder, and there will be more of it. With more classes and more at stake in each one, students know that high school will probably make new demands on them. They worry about losing their freedom to hang out with friends:

> They expect you to do, like, six hours of homework a night, 'cause each class will give you an hour's worth of homework. And I'm on the phone three hours after I get home, talking to my friends. (Rachell)

Older students will haze and bully the new ones. Exaggerated or not, stories circulate about how students in upper high school grades pick on and humiliate the new 9th graders. Shy, physically underdeveloped, or otherwise vulnerable kids worry especially:

> My brother said that they have a certain day that they throw the freshmen and some sophomores in trash cans

or in the creek, lock them out of their classrooms, hit them, pick on them. (Ashley)

When Reality Sets In

It doesn't take long, however, for new 9th graders to figure out which of their fears will actually come true. Only a few weeks after the start of high school, they describe their transition in more realistic terms.

High school gives you a fresh start. Not everyone knows your past when you arrive in 9th grade, so students sometimes take advantage of this to change their image, either academically or socially:

Once you get to 9th grade, you don't want everybody to think that you're a goofy or silly person. So you try to become more mature so everybody will give you more respect. They do give you a second chance. Last year, I wasn't that good in school, but right now, I'm doing pretty good. (Geoffery)

Guarding against social stigma also involves careful calculations about personal appearance. As in middle school, high school students sort themselves into cliques marked by clothing style and body decoration:

I see that a lot of people are cliqued off—maybe not purposely, but just by the way everybody's dressed. People who call themselves "alternative," they're all with the purple hair and the whatnot. Or "ghetto," where your shoes cost more than the rent. (Heather)

But 9th graders also notice that their high school peers cross those subgroups more than the middle school scene permitted:

Back in middle school, everybody wanted to be like everybody else. If you weren't like that, you got picked on. But now, you can do your own thing, and everybody's your friend. A lot of my friends in the beginning of this year were scary goth punk people. But now, I'm like a preppy person. (Rachell)

Classes build on work done in middle school. Students start 9th grade anxious that the academic work will be much harder than before. When their teachers build new material on their prior knowledge and skills, students regain confidence that they can do well:

I thought that with getting us ready for all the tests, we were going to have a hard time with math and language arts. But first [teachers] just review what you learned last year. Then they might add something that will help make it easier, like an easier method of doing fractions. (Geoffery)

High school teachers have less time for individual students. If they are responsible for the typical high school load of more than 120 students, teachers usually have little time to give 9th graders the individual attention they may have received in middle school. This can come as a shock, especially to students who struggle to keep up:

There's so many of us, it's hard for the teachers to get to know you. Kids expect that they're gonna get special help, like they did in middle school. But if you're really quiet, then teachers don't care. (Heather)

Teachers cut you less slack when you mess up. The workload escalates in 9th grade, so it's easy for students to fall behind:

Before, I could do one homework paper a night and still get an *A*. In 9th grade, there are more classes, and each class gives you double what you got in middle school. I can't get it all done. (Rachell)

Busy high school teachers often deal out matter-of-fact consequences for poor behavior, and students may have some difficulty adjusting to the harsher regime. Especially at a large high school organized in conventional ways, students may be on their way to detention or worse, with no questions asked:

[Students] are already realizing that school ain't a joke. You get a couple chances, then you're expelled. After that, that's when dropout comes. (Brian)

Your decisions have longer-lasting effects. As they mingle with older students in the larger universe of high school, 9th graders start to make more immediate connections between choices and consequences:

I thought I wouldn't survive high school, 'cause all you do is work and study. I thought maybe I wouldn't even go to class, I'd drop out. But now it don't seem that hard. When you start studying, you ain't got to worry about going out in the streets and getting into all types of stuff. (Nyesha)

As they try out new work and new ways, 9th graders gradually develop identities that may well continue through high school and beyond:

When I was in middle school, I felt like I was big. Kids felt like they gotta put on a front, try to do what the crowd do, be popular and cool. That's *all* middle school is about. But now that I'm in 9th grade, it's just, "Quit being childish, and be yourself." Everybody's starting to understand and get a better perspective. You have to strive to do your work, pass your class, graduate, go to college, marry a girl who's going to be something, have kids later on . . . live. (Brian)

Helping Students Make the Transition

Looking back after the first month of high school, these 9th graders offered four suggestions for how teachers can help middle school students make a successful transition.

Connect us up regularly with high school students. Teachers can talk about 9th grade all they want, but kids prefer to hear it straight from the source:

> I don't think that middle school students particularly listen to teachers' advice. But maybe they'd listen to high schoolers and feel better about what to expect at high school. Once I got into 6th grade, they had us write letters to 5th graders about what to expect. So maybe high school students could write letters to middle school students. (Heather)

Bringing 7th and 8th graders into contact with students who are already succeeding in high school gives them a useful perspective on why they should bother to work hard and master skills in the middle grades:

> We could pick a middle school class to go back and visit, like one of our favorite teachers. I would tell students the truth about what high school is like—that it's really nothing to worry about; you just need to work hard and be yourself. (Ashley)

Support us in developing skills and strategies for high school success. Teachers can start giving students new responsibilities, such as facilitating a class group, organizing an event, mentoring younger students, or mediating conflicts. At the same time, adults should provide the support that students need to succeed in their new tasks:

> We're starting to turn into adults, so we're not really sure what's expected. Maybe the schools can make middle school more mature, closer to high school, so it won't be that big of a change. (Geoffery)

Middle school students who participate in support programs start to develop attitudes that they will rely on later, when they face the challenges of high school:

> Our school established the Pink Ladies, for girls in 7th and 8th grade. Every Tuesday and Thursday, you meet with a speaker talking about the different things you can experience in your personal life. We also talk about what you can and cannot do to move forward in your life. (Nyesha)

Help us make strong and mutually respectful connections with adults. When teachers respond with empathy and respect to students' efforts, struggles, and worries, it can have a big effect on attitudes and behavior as students move on to high school:

> Eighth grade teachers try to scare students about high school, and then we come in really nervous. I don't think they should loosely say, "Oh, it's nothing." But they should tell us, "You're going to have a lot more work to do, and it's probably going to be a little harder." And not to be afraid, but not careless, either. (Heather)

Situations in which young people and adults work together doing things that matter create a context in which mutual respect grows. These include such activities as service projects, school publications or events, and discussion groups on important issues:

> When kids hang around kids, without adult supervision, they're going to act immature. But if you got the right adult there, showing the right way to be more mature, who's going to act childish? (Brian)

"All my buddies told me that high school was going to be a zoo, people running around, nobody going to class."

Provide bridge experiences in the summer after 8th grade. New 9th graders have a big advantage if they can start high school with some of their pressing worries put to rest. Being able to find their way around the campus, recognizing familiar faces in the crowd, and getting a jump start in the academic arena—all these can ease the newcomer's anxiety and make a successful transition more likely.

Training for an athletic team in the summer before high school offers many students this advantage. Even if team members have not yet been chosen, going to practices enables the younger students to get to know older students in an atmosphere of structure, discipline, and high expectations:

> In football practice, you get to know the upperclassmen better, before they put a label on you to say they don't like you. You get to talk to 'em, get to know their personality. (Christopher)

If adults present summer school as a chance to get a head start and make friends—and *not* as punishment for failure—kids are more receptive to the idea. It becomes even more of an advantage when the summer school takes place on the high school campus. Also, kids may find that summer school equips them with academic grounding for their schoolwork in the fall:

> They was teaching us stuff that was above us. But it was getting us ready before it comes. They was treating you like you was in high school. (Nyesha)

Helping 9th Graders Succeed

High schools can also take steps that help new 9th graders through the transition and build a solid foundation for their success. Even after only a month in their new high schools, students had plenty of advice for teachers about what worked best for them.

Create smaller learning communities for us. New high school students are more likely to find their academic and social bearings in a smaller learning community:

> In elementary and middle school, you interact more with the teachers, and they know you more. But at high school, you only see the teacher 40 minutes a day. By the time 9th grade came, [the 2,000-student high school] had already broken up into small schools. That kind of helped. Things been going all right for me. (Brian)

Group 9th graders together in one physical setting. It helps when 9th graders occupy the same physical spaces, especially when the building is large or the campus has more than a few hundred students. New 9th graders find it easier to get to classrooms, and proximity with classmates encourages social bonding and support:

> I was nervous, but I got over it after a week when I realized I had friends in all my classes. I only got lost my first day here, 'cause all my classes are really close together. (Amanda)

Start our year with a 9th grade orientation period. Coming into an unfamiliar high school, first-year students appreciate extra time to sort out their schedules, find their way around, get to know teachers and fellow students, and ask questions without fearing ridicule:

> We was in big groups, to help and support you. [Faculty advisors) gave each student a map of the school. They showed you your schedule, then they showed you the times that you go from class to class. (Nyesha)

Match us up with student mentors. Some high schools have a buddy system that pairs new 9th graders with a 10th or 11th grader. Mentors go through a training period, then check in with their 9th grade buddies regularly all year:

> I met my mentor the first day of school; he was one of the first people I talked to. First, we meet in a group; then we go one-on-one with them. They help you out, they take you different places, they introduce you to different things you've never seen. [My mentor] is like a big brother to me, a good friend. He's there for me when I need him. (Christopher)

Build advisory groups into our schedule. Belonging to a group of about 15 that meets regularly with a faculty advisor helps students better manage the high school transition. Whether the group consists of only 9th graders or includes students from upper classes, it can offer a haven in which to build relationships and get academic guidance and support:

> My advisor is one of my teachers, and we're real cool. I can go to her and tell her anything, and she won't say nothing. And sometimes at the end of the period, they ask if anybody needs homework help, or class help, or directions to any class. (Ashley)

Design classroom activities to connect with us personally. To new 9th graders, high school classes can seem intimidating at first. It helps when the teacher starts the year by showing interest in getting to know students and helping them get to know one another:

> Working in groups, and asking your group where they came from, where their name came from, what we like to do, what school we came from, stuff like that. We did that in my literature class, and in that class I actually talk to more people than in any other class, 'cause I know more people. (Brandon)

Lengthen class periods to give us more time to learn. In middle school, students may have grown used to longer blocks of time in which to work on academic material or projects. The typical fast-paced high school class period may not offer enough time for kids to understand a concept or practice a new skill, prompting some schools to revise and simplify their schedules:

> The classes are 40 minutes, and they go by fast. It doesn't seem like I'm getting enough of one thing—it's just jumping around, and it's too hard. And they give me a lot of homework—too much for that little class time, I think. (Kaitlyn)

Establish fair classroom norms and enforce them consistently. New 9th graders have the early adolescents need for order and structure in the classroom, but they also have the older teenager's passion for fairness and justice. They want to participate in setting classroom norms, and they resent it when unruly students take up all the teacher's attention:

> One or two people in a class just have to be the class clowns. If teachers have to mess with them for the first week, you don't get to know your teachers. If [these students] don't care about their learning, fine, but just don't interrupt everybody else's. (Rachell)

Give us extra help, both in and out of class. It is especially important to offer individual support with both classwork and homework so that 9th graders do not fall behind and get discouraged. One approach builds time into the school week for supported study groups or tutoring:

> On the football team, we have study table on Tuesday, Wednesday, and Thursday nights. The older kids can help you out with your homework if you need it. (Christopher)

Provide extra activities to help us succeed at things we care about. As new 9th graders work on meaningful activities with other students and adults, their identity as part of the school community grows stronger and more important to them:

> Two upperclassmen I know on the football team help in the cafeteria, selling candy and stuff. That's a good experience for us, to imprint on what they're doing so that when we get into the upper classes, we'll be able to help the school as well as they did. (Chandyn)

Looking Back, Looking Forward

Four weeks into their 9th grade year, students already have a good sense of being in a whole new world, with a new hierarchy of people and priorities. However, they will sometimes miss their younger selves. Said one student,

> The main message that I could give an 8th grade student is, "Be prepared, just not too prepared. And don't grow up too fast, 'cause once you start hitting your teen years, sometimes you wish you were just little again."

By listening to and acting on student concerns about high school transition, teachers can help students navigate their way through the ambivalence of the early teen years and step up to the plate every day with renewed interest and excitement.

KATHLEEN CUSHMAN (kathleencushman@mac.com) is author of *Fires in the Bathroom: Advice for Teachers from High School Students* (New Press, 2003). She is currently working on a sequel slated for 2007, which will feature the voices of middle-grades students. Both projects were funded by MetLife Foundation.

From *Educational Leadership,* April 2006, pp. 47–52. Copyright © 2006 by What Kids Can Do (www.whatkidscando.org). Reprinted with permission.

Stories from Tween Classrooms

**Two teachers describe the joys and perils of engaging
4th grade and 6th grade students in writing.**

BRUCE MORGAN AND DEB ODOM

Tweens are unpredictable. They go from being young adults to babbling infants in a second. One moment they are introspective and thoughtful; the next, they howl with laughter at an inappropriate remark. They look deeply into the meaning of text, and then grab their Pokémon cards and head to recess. They roll their eyes at you in disgust, then sit with you and cry at the ending to *Where the Red Fern Grows*. Academically, they swing from swagger and bravado to insecure blobs of protoplasm.

Teaching in a tween classroom is a daunting experience. And yet, we have both chosen to spend our teaching careers working with kids in this age group. Some call us crazy; we call ourselves courageous. The following stories from our two classes suggest the challenges and rewards of teaching tweens—specifically, of helping these students hone their writing skills.

Bruce Morgan's 4th Grade Classroom

For several years, I have taught students to use living books, or journals, to document their observations and thinking. But until recently, I had never asked them to record their thinking in the content areas. This year, I've been encouraging students to write more during math, science, and social studies. I have been intrigued by how deeply 4th graders think, but sometimes horrified by what actually gets onto the paper.

Last week, a group of students clustered around me for a math activity. I told them that one envelope contained 15 blue counters and 5 white counters; another envelope held 10 blues and 5 whites. Without telling the students which combination was in which envelope, I randomly pulled a counter from the first envelope and then returned it, shook the envelope, and pulled again. I wondered aloud how many times I would have to repeat this operation before it became safe to predict which envelope contained the most blue counters.

Aimee immediately announced, "It's envelope one."

Austin shot her a look and countered, "I say we pull a whole lot because we'll get closer. Since there are 15 blues in one of them, why not pull at least 20 different times just to see?"

Nathan added, "We have more chances to get a blue in the envelope that has 15 blues."

"It's envelope one," Aimee insisted again.

"It's too early, Aimee; hold on. You're rushing for nothing," Codi admonished.

"Aimee, we haven't even pulled from the second envelope yet—how could you know?" Collin asked.

Austin suddenly had an insight: "Hey, look at the numbers. It's a pattern—10 blues and 5 whites and 15 blues and 5 whites. Get it?"

"Ohhh, Austin. Give me the manipulatives!" Miranda demanded. She began to arrange piles of blue and white counters on the table. The kids watched as she matched blue and white counters together. "See, it is a pattern."

"There are 2 to 1 in one envelope and 3 to 1 in the other one. I'm sticking to pulling 20 times. Then we should know for sure," Nathan announced.

"Yeah, but think about what probability means," Carson added. "We won't ever know for sure. Even if we pull a million times, we'll get closer to being sure, but it might really suck and be wrong."

I summarized, "So it's a guideline, not a rule. We can use what we see to inform our decision, but we can't know for sure." Together we decided to pull 20 counters from each envelope and then predict which envelope contained 15 blue counters and which contained 10. After we pulled 20 from each envelope, most of the students predicted that envelope one had only 10 blue counters because we had pulled far fewer blues from that envelope. Their thinking was clear and made sense, but when we opened the envelopes and counted, the prediction was incorrect. As Carson had pointed out, with probability you can't ever be sure.

The kids were shocked, then excited. For the first time, they understood what *probable* meant.

I saw my chance to have the students document their thinking:

> You know, I want you to get your thinking into your living books. You don't realize how smart you are, and I really want you to have a record so you can look back on your

thinking when you're really old and marvel at how deeply you thought back in 4th grade.

They grumbled as they sat down to write. These brilliant, animated, reflective thinkers turned into zombies when they actually had to write about their ideas. They stumbled and faltered and produced works of staggering mediocrity.

Collin drew pictures of both envelopes and wrote, "Envelope 1, 15 w 5 B." That was it? No explanation, no thinking . . . nothing?

Christoph scrawled, "The first envelope is the fist chose. The senont chose is the sencont envalope more were pulled out of the seonct envope."

Aimee wrote, "1 can't really explane I got confused if envelop one was envelop 2. So I just prodiked."

Nathan sat there and sat there . . . and played with his pencil.

Their intelligence had blinded me to the fact that they were 9 years old and there was often a discrepancy between what they could think and what they could do. They needed guidance, structure, modeling, and a sense of security before taking an intellectual risk. I gathered them at the front of the room and apologized, and then busted them:

I blew it; I'm sorry, I set you up. And—your writing was pathetic. What is up with all these incomplete sentences? What about punctuation marks? Man, you sure used great spelling approximations, didn't you? Wrong! Look, let me do a quick demonstration of what I meant. Here's what I was thinking: When I began this experiment, I thought it would be obvious which envelope had the 15 blues because I was sure blue would be pulled more. . . .

I wrote as I talked, jotting down notes about what I was thinking before the experiment started, while we were conducting the experiment, and after we finished. Then I had several students synthesize their thinking out loud. I explicitly told them that the words they had just used should be in their written papers. I sent them back to their seats to give it another go.

This time, they were more confident and took more time. Christoph wrote,

There are two envalopes with a different numbers of chips in each one. One envalope has 10 blue chips and 5 white chips. The other one has 15 blues and 5 whites. I predicted that the first envalope has less bule than the second because more white chips were pulled out of first than the second envalope. I was wrong, but I should have been right.

Collin wrote,

I suspended belief until I had enogh information. It was very hard because the envlope that had the 10 blues and 5 whites really looked like it had the 15 blues. I waited, but not long enough. It's like the Broncos game we went to one time. We left early because they were so far ahead but then we found out they got beat. I never leave now until it's over. In my whole life I have learned from that, never leave early. It gets you every time.

And, true to the end, Aimee was confused. She steadfastly refused to believe that it made any difference: She still would make a prediction before pulling any of the counters at all. The range of thinking in a tween classroom is astronomical.

This lesson reinforced my beliefs about the necessity of discussing before writing, the role of demonstration lessons, and the importance of having high expectations for standard conventions of print. In addition, my reflections on the lesson gave me several other insights.

The boys talked more, and I allowed it. The girls had equally important observations to make, but were mowed down in the process. This can easily happen in intermediate classrooms. I forgot to pull the girls' thinking out and make it visible.

I was struck by the improvement in Christoph's writing. Not only did his thinking go deeper on paper, but his conventions of print also improved. The confidence he gained from the demonstration influenced his thinking and the quality of his writing because he had control and a sense of competence before he started.

I didn't give up on Aimee. I would continue to work with her to think more deeply and to communicate her thinking. I would help her jot down her ideas and make the thinking more explicit. This wasn't a one-shot deal. I had an entire year to continue working with all the students.

I was reminded that kids are kids. Smart, thoughtful Nathan had to stay in for three recesses to finish his writing. "I don't really want to do this," he told me honestly. Just as honestly, I responded in a voice filled with 26 years of empathy and compassion, "Too bad, Nathan—you're in until you finish." Ahh, this job!

Deb Odom's 6th Grade Classroom

Bruce's classroom and mine have many common threads. In tween classrooms, getting polished, finished written pieces can be torture. There are differences between 4th and 6th grade, though. Sixth graders are usually sick of personal narratives and the expectation that they will have a never-ending supply of fresh ideas flowing from draft books to publication. Engaging them in writing requires new, sometimes unconventional approaches.

One great way to get tweens' attention is to tap into their burgeoning—and usually quirky—sense of humor. Eleven- and 12-year-olds are just beginning to develop a sense of themselves as entities separate from their parents, and they often use humor to explore that independence.

I maintain a file of cartoons and comic strips that I use in various ways in my classroom. Sharing comics with kids is a quick, fun way to assess their ability to read between the lines and activate background knowledge. When I put a cartoon on the overhead projector, a quick glance around the room tells me who gets it and who is clueless. Talking about a visual joke, a play on words, or an implied outcome and then writing about what makes a particular comic strip funny—or not—provides an enjoyable alternative to prompt writing.

This year, I found a way to make comics and cartoons an integral part of vocabulary study. The book *Vocabulary Cartoons*, published by New Monic Books, presents words in an entertaining format. Each entry includes a soundalike word or phrase and a silly cartoon. For example, the word *vulture* sounds like *culture*. The cartoon shows two vultures in a tree, one painting at an easel while the other reads a stack of books. The caption below reads "VULTURES with CULTURE."

For the first quarter, I presented one new word a day. My students groaned at the silly cartoons, but they wrote great sentences with each new word. They also looked for the vocabulary words in their reading. Anyone who found a vocabulary word in context was allowed to write the sentence on chart paper with markers. As our bank of words grew, our walls got covered with rich examples of written language.

The maturity level in 6th grade classrooms varies greatly. I paired kids who understood the humor with kids who took a little longer to get it. Having a second voice explaining what we were doing provided enough support to enable all students to catch on.

When I started a mythology unit in the second quarter, I had one of those middle-of-the-night "Aha!" moments that soon become "Duhhhh . . . why didn't I think of this before?" Rather than give the class a list of 20 words with instructions to find the definitions and mythological origins—an exercise that had always seemed important but . . . well, deadly boring—I saw a way to make the words come alive.

I introduced my brainstorm with the tween attention grabber *aphroaisiac*. I wrote the word on chart paper and explained that we would be studying words that had their origins in the myths we were reading. I gave them the origin (from Aphrodite, goddess of love) and the definition (a love potion). I had their undivided attention.

"What is a love potion?" I asked. Hands flew up, but before I could call on anyone, Isaiah, my blurter, yelled, "Wine!"

Once I recovered, I continued with the instructions. Each day over the next few weeks, I would give them two new words and the origins of the words. Their assignment would be to find the current definitions and draw a cartoon for each.

Every morning for the next three weeks, I heard, "Are we doing vocab today?", "What are our words today?", and "Can we get more words?" We did vocabulary study right after specials, and by the time everyone was back in class, half of the students were already settled on the floor in front of the chart stand, vocab notebooks open, pencils poised, eagerly awaiting the days additions. I was astounded. The students' enthusiasm and motivation kept them engaged enough to allow me to work more with the kids who didn't understand the concept as easily.

As students worked on their cartoons each day, the room hummed with excited, insightful, and often hilarious conversation as they tried to tie the mythological origins to current usage.

To illustrate *fortune*, Alison drew a Magic 8 Ball showing the words "Better not tell you now."

Jack drew an *echo* powerful enough to knock a man off the rim of the Grand Canyon. As the man fell—portrayed by a series of tumbling stick figures—he repeatedly bounced off ledges and rocks, shouting "Ouch!" each time.

Meg's idea of a *labyrinth* was a hungry girl wandering through an endless maze, trying to reach the Pizza Palace.

In Alexa's cartoon, *hypnosis* was the only way a frustrated mom could get her daughter to clean her room.

As adults, most of these 6th graders will probably forget many of the mathematical formulas they learned, and none of them will ever write to a prompt. But I'd wager that most of them will never forget that wine is an aphrodisiac.

Helping Tweens Soar

In many ways, 4th graders and 6th graders operate on different levels. But all our students are capable of more than we sometimes believe. And all of them have the same basic needs: to be appreciated and accepted, to feel safe, to have fun, to feel that they're in control, and to feel competent enough to take risks and learn.

Like almost-grown eagles, what tweens need most is a safe place to fledge. They want to spread their wings and soar. Some days they are quite sure that they can. Then suddenly it looks like a really long way down to the rocky ground below, and all they want is a safe nest with a place to hide. Our job is to provide the high ledge, a gentle push, and the assurance that the nest is waiting for their return.

BRUCE MORGAN (bruce.morgan@dcsdk12.org) and **DEB ODOM** (deb.odom@dcsdk12.org) are teachers at Castle Rock Elementary School, 1103 Canyon Dr., Castle Rock, CO 80104. They are co-authors of *Writing Through the Tween Years: Supporting Writers, Grades 3–6* (Stenhouse Publishers, 2004).

My Year as a High School Student

A stint in students' shoes helped a science teacher examine her own practice.

DEBORAH WALDRON

Like countless other teachers, I decided to take a class last fall. Unlike most teachers, though, I chose to take a biology class at the school where I teach physics, Yorktown High School in Arlington, Virginia.

I had begun pursuing National Board Certification in Adolescence and Young Adulthood/Science, and I faced the hurdle of showing breadth of knowledge across the four major areas of biology, chemistry, earth and space science, and physics. My biology knowledge was woefully inadequate. Rather than enrolling in a class at the local community college, I decided to sit in on Allyson McKowen's 9th grade Intensified Biology class.

I attended class every day, took notes, did my homework, read the textbook, worked in a lab group, wrote up labs, and took the tests and quizzes. Except for my age and the fact that I came and went from class without a hall pass, I was a typical student. The amount of time I spent on after-school activities probably paralleled the time commitments of a typical high school student. I had family responsibilities as well as a fairly time-consuming "extracurricular activity"—I taught an evening physics class at the local community college. My stint in students' shoes gave me insight into the challenges that high school students face and led me to make changes in my own teaching. The following are my observations from the other side of the desk about practices that I believe help create the best conditions for learning.

What Looks Good from the Student Side

Give students more time for creative projects. Although I have fairly well-honed time management skills, I found myself starting a lot of creative assignments for class late at night. No matter how hard I tried, my daily responsibilities and workload kept me from getting a head start on a pending long-term assignment.

For example, one assignment involved creating an analogy for how a cell functions. I chose to compare a cell to a restaurant, reasoning that just as the various parts of a cell perform the functions necessary to maintain cell health, each staff member at a restaurant performs certain jobs to ensure the restaurant's continued success. Not only did I have to write a paper explaining the logic of my analogy, but I also had to create a physical model of the analogy. This was an incredible learning experience that truly taught me the structure of a cell and the functions of its parts—but it was one of several assignments I finished at 1:00 a.m.

I used to give my physics students a hard time when they complained about late-night study sessions. Now I realize that students' extracurricular and academic commitments often make it hard to work ahead. In teaching future classes, I plan to break long-term assignments into smaller chunks so that students have multiple deadlines along the way and to cut back on homework during weeks when longer assignments are due.

Occasionally use short, straightforward assessments. Although I believe all assessments should require students to demonstrate deep, authentic understanding, at times it is preferable to accomplish this with simple, straightforward assessments. These more traditional assessments can be structured in a way that gauges student learning and probes for true understanding. I remember one lab assignment in which Allyson told us that all we needed to do was analyze the data and complete six questions at the end of the lab. My lab partner and I looked at each other and almost simultaneously declared, "Thank goodness!" We had recently completed a formal lab write-up on a separate experiment, and neither of us had the energy or time to tackle another. The questions were enough for Allyson to make sure we understood the material and had completed the lab without drowning us in work.

Reinforce ethics and clarify plagiarism. In early October, our first formal paper was due. We had been studying water properties and had recently completed a lab on surface tension. This assessment required us to write the introductory section of a formal lab write-up as well as answer several in-depth questions about our data. My schedule that week was quite busy, and I didn't get a chance to sit down and start writing until 11:00 p.m. the night before the paper was due. Around 11:15 p.m., I thought to myself, "Hey, if I don't go to class tomorrow, I won't have to turn the paper in yet." The thought was extremely tempting, and

I went to bed. Somewhere around 3:00 a.m. I woke up, thought better about my choice, and finished my paper.

My year as a 9th grade student was enjoyable and stressful, and it provided a dose of reality that strengthened my teaching practice.

When I talked with Allyson about my dilemma, she mentioned that she always calls home to talk with the parents of a student who is absent the day a big assignment is due. I suspect that this kind of outside pressure helps students make wiser choices. Without such pressure, even as a teacher and a supposed role model, I made a poor choice for about four hours.

Later in the year, we had to create a brochure about a particular genetic disorder, explaining when the disorder was discovered, its symptoms, the genetic cause of the disorder, how common the condition is, and what treatments are available. I was assigned clubfoot and spent a significant amount of time researching it over the weekend. Although I had done the research and processed the information, I didn't get a chance to actually create the brochure until the following Thursday evening, after I had taught my night class.

That evening, as I drove home from the community college, I continued to plan my brochure in my head. I was tired and wanted to do it as quickly as possible while still doing a good job. At home, I started lining up Web sites from which I could cut and paste the information. After a few minutes, it dawned on me that I was about to plagiarize the entire assignment. When I thought about the situation later, I realized that as a teacher I simply expect my students to know what plagiarism is. Teachers need to be more specific with students and provide concrete examples throughout the year that will help them realize what is and is not academically acceptable.

Change student seats often. Simple as it sounds, shaking up student seating every six weeks or so makes a huge difference in the dynamics of the classroom. I initially knew none of the students in the class. At first, my lab partners were leery of me, but over time they warmed up to me and treated me as normally as possible, even teasing me about getting a low quiz

grade. However, had we stayed in the same seats for the entire year, I would have only gotten to know these 3 students in a class of 22.

My experience as the "new kid" made me realize the importance of creating an environment in which students can meet many other students. Because Allyson switched the student seats eight times over the course of the year, I got to know almost the entire class. The regular rearrangement of seats and reassignment of lab groups created a supportive classroom environment in which students felt comfortable asking any other student, not just a friend, for assistance. I now periodically rearrange student seats in my physics classes; I also assign lab groups rather than let students choose them.

How I Learned to Love the "Squishy Stuff"

The most enjoyable thing that I discovered in my year studying 9th grade biology was that it's the teacher, not the content, that makes the class. As a physics teacher, I had no expectation of enjoying biology. I called it the "squishy stuff." Allyson McKowen made me fall in love with biology. Her way of presenting the material and interacting with students made class enjoyable. Allyson's classroom was student-focused, and her leadership helped every student feel comfortable and courageous. Students asked and answered questions without fear. I looked forward to class and found myself doing outside reading in a college text so I could understand the material on a deeper level. I used to think that British physicist Ernest Rutherford was right when he said, "All science is either physics or stamp collecting." After a year of biology with Allyson, I know Rutherford was wrong.

My year as a 9th grade student was enjoyable and stressful, and it provided a dose of reality that strengthened my teaching practice. Although I learned an incredible amount of biology, I was more impressed with what I learned about teaching. A year from now, when I'm teaching physics to some of my former biology classmates, I'll draw on my experiences with them that have made me a better teacher.

DEBORAH WALDRON teaches physics at Yorktown High School, 5201 N. 28th St., Arlington, VA 22207; 703–228–5378; Deborah_Waldron@apsva.us.

From *Educational Leadership*, March 2006, pp. 63–65. Copyright © 2006 by ASCD. Reprinted by permission. The Association for Supervision and Curriculum Development is a worldwide community of educators advocating sound policies and sharing best practices to achieve the success of each learner. To learn more, visit ASCD at www.ascd.org.

The Dropout Problem: Losing Ground

As we strive to improve high school achievement, we must not forget the increasing number of students who fail to graduate.

PAUL E. BARTON

A recent upsurge of interest in the student dropout problem seems to have come as a surprise to U.S. school officials and policymakers. During the last two decades, complacency had set in as reports from the U.S. Census Bureau's household survey suggested that high school completion among young adults was approaching 90 percent, the goal set by the first National Education Summit in Charlottesville, Virginia, in 1989. The long-dormant concern about dropouts revived several years ago, however, when half a dozen independent researchers in universities and think tanks began publishing estimates of high school completion rates that contradicted the official rates. As a result, the issue of high school dropouts has returned to the front burner.

Many Estimates, Similar Results

The recent independent estimates of high school completion rates are almost always lower than the official estimates—including those that states have reported to the U.S. Department of Education under the requirements of No Child Left Behind and the state estimates from the National Center for Education Statistics. These independent estimates—derived through different methods and not always pertaining to the same year—vary somewhat, but they are all in the same ballpark. Jay Greene at the Manhattan Institute estimated a high school completion rate of 71 percent for 1998; Christopher Swanson and Duncan Chaplin at the Urban Institute estimated 66.6 percent for 2000; Thomas Mortenson of *Postsecondary Education Opportunity* estimated 66.1 percent for 2000; Andrew Sum and colleagues at Northeastern University estimated 68.7 percent for 1998; and Walter Haney and colleagues at Boston College estimated 74.4 percent for 2001. I describe these studies and their methodologies in detail in *Unfinished Business: More Measured Approaches in Standards-Based Reform* (Barton, 2005a).

The well-publicized contradictions of official estimates led to a minor political explosion, particularly after the Education Trust (2003) attacked the accuracy of the states' reports to the Department of Education. Then-Secretary of Education Rod Paige appointed a task force to look into the matter. Later, the National Governors Association convened a Task Force on State High School Graduation Data to propose a plan for how states could develop a high-quality, comparable high school graduation measure. All of this is being weighed in Washington and in state capitals.

A Closer Look at the Statistics

My own analysis (Barton, 2005a) confirmed the estimates of other researchers. I relied on two numbers I knew to be actual counts. One was the census count of the population cohort that would be of graduation age (17 or 18) in spring 2000; the other was the number of regular public and private high school diplomas awarded that year as reported by the National Center for Education Statistics. My final analysis estimated that 69.6 percent of youth who were of graduating age had received diplomas in 2000.

To measure change over time, I made estimates for 1990 using the same approach and found a completion rate of 72 percent for that year. For both 1990 and 2000, I also estimated individual state completion rates, which varied broadly. For 1990, the spread was from 90.6 percent in Iowa down to 61.7 percent in Florida (and 59.9 percent in Washington, D.C.). In 2000, the percentage ranged from 88.2 percent in Vermont down to 55 percent in Arizona (and 48 percent in Washington, D.C.). Only seven states showed an increase in high school completion rates during the decade; rates in the remaining states declined (Barton, 2005b).

Other researchers have found that minorities have lower completion rates than white students. For example, Elaine Allensworth (2005) carried out an excellent study of Chicago schools, which had individual student records available to track students. Among boys, only 39 percent of black students graduated by age 19, compared with 51 percent of Latino students and 58 percent of white students. Girls fared better: Comparable rates were 57 percent for black students, 65 percent for Latino students, and 71 percent for white students.

Research on the path that students travel through the grades may also shed light on the dropout problem. For example, one study identified an important trend that has developed over the last decade: the "9th grade bulge." Compared with past years, an increasing number of 9th graders are failing to be promoted to the 10th grade. Haney and colleagues (2004) found that in 2001, 440,000 more students were enrolled in grade 9 than in grade 8 the previous year. By 2001, seven states had at least 20 percent more students enrolled in the 9th grade than had been enrolled in that grade in the prior year, and one-half had at least 10 percent more. We know that there is an association between failing a grade and dropping out. And we know that more students are dropping out at younger ages.

The research conducted in the last couple of years raises many questions. One issue is why the U.S. Census Bureau household survey estimates differ from the lower completion rates found by independent researchers. We can explain this difference in part by the fact that the census lumped regular diplomas and GEDs together. The GED is a well-respected substitute, but it is not a regular diploma earned after completing four years of high school. Numerous research studies show that GED recipients tend to fare better than dropouts, but not as well as graduates with diplomas (Boesel, Alsalam, & Smith, 1998). Although the number of GEDs has become a growing proportion of total graduates, inclusion of GED recipients does not entirely account for the gaps among the estimates. Further analysis is needed to reconcile the remaining discrepancies.

Low achievement and grade retention are precursors to leaving school.

Another question raised by the research is why completion rates, in terms of regular diplomas, fell during the last decade in so many states. Some of the likely suspects include the decrease in two-parent families, the previously mentioned 9th grade bulge, and higher standards for graduation. However, my analysis did not produce evidence conclusively linking high school completion rates to any of these factors.

A Deteriorating Economic Position

At the same time that high school completion rates have fallen, labor market prospects for dropouts are becoming increasingly dire. In 2003, 1.1 million 16- to 19-year-olds did not have a high school diploma and were not enrolled in school. In the landscape of the economy, these dropouts are often lost travelers without a map. Only 4 in 10 of the 16- to 19-year-olds are employed, as are fewer than 6 in 10 of 20- to 24-year-old dropouts. Black and Latino youth are doing considerably less well than others (T. Morisi, U.S. Bureau of Labor Statistics, personal communication, July 14, 2004).

What about the earning power of those dropouts who do have jobs? Do they make enough money to support a household? For 25- to 34-year-old dropouts who manage to work full-time, the average annual salary of males dropped from $35,087 (in 2002

constant dollars) in 1971 to $22,903 in 2002, a decline of 35 percent. The comparable annual earnings for females without a diploma were $19,888 in 1971, declining to $17,114 in 2002. Even when they work full-time, the average earnings of this age group of dropouts are not far above the poverty line for a family with children—and most dropouts do not even reach this level of earnings. The earnings of high school graduates also have declined since 1971, but not as steeply as those of dropouts (National Center for Education Statistics [NCES], 2004, Tables 14–1, 14–2, and 14–3).

Factors That Affect the Dropout Rate

Which student conditions and life experiences are correlated with failure to complete high school? A 2002 report from the U.S. General Accounting Office (GAO)[1] summarized the research. Factors that correlated with low completion rates included coming from low-income or single-parent families, getting low grades in school, being absent frequently and changing schools. These factors vary considerably by state, as do high school completion rates.

These predictive factors do not determine completion rates, but they do show the conditions that schools need to overcome in their effort to maximize completions. Some schools rise above expectations, some schools meet them, and some schools do less well than expected.

To find out how the individual states performed in 2000 compared with what we might expect on the basis of conditions in each state, I computed the correlation of completion rates with expectations based on three factors: state average socioeconomic characteristics (family income, education, and occupation); the percentage of two-parent families; and the rate at which students change schools. I found that these factors accounted for almost 60 percent of the variation in state completion rates.

This comparison of the *expected* completion rates with the *actual* completion rates disclosed that the actual rate fell within 4 percentage points of the expected rate in 24 states. Except for Rhode Island and Hawaii, actual rates in the remaining states were within 10 points of the expected rates. The states doing the best in exceeding their expected completion rates were Hawaii, Maryland, Vermont, Connecticut, and West Virginia. The states doing the worst were Rhode Island, Indiana, South Carolina, and Arizona (Barton, 2005a). To learn more about increasing school completion rates, we should study both those states that greatly exceed the expected high school completion rate and those that fall far below it for clues about what these states are doing differently.

Increasing School Retention

The factors identified in the GAO report—that low-income students and high-mobility students are high-risk, that low achievement and grade retention are precursors to leaving school—provide a guide for what we need to do to improve high school completion rates. In my research, the factor *most* predictive was coming from a single-parent family (even after controlling for socioeconomic status). The extra effort that schools make to support students in all these circumstances will likely determine whether schools achieve higher or lower high school completion rates than expected.

In the landscape of the economy, dropouts are often lost travelers without a map.

Evaluations have established the effectiveness of a number of programs and models designed to increase school retention. The following models, described in more detail in *One-Third of a Nation: Rising Dropout Rates and Declining Opportunities* (Barton, 2005b), merit a close look by any state, district, or school wishing to embark on efforts to retain students in school.

- *The Talent Development High School* was developed by the Center for Research on the Education of Students Placed At Risk (CRESPAR), a collaboration between Johns Hopkins University and Howard University. This model emphasizes small learning communities, curriculum reforms, professional development, interdisciplinary teams of teachers, longer class periods, and employer advisory boards. There are now 33 such high schools in 12 states.
- *Communities in Schools* is designed specifically to keep students in school. Schools and community agencies form partnerships to deliver services and provide resources to students, such as individual case management, counseling, volunteers and mentors, remedial education, tutoring, classes teaching life skills and employment-related topics, and a variety of after-school programs.
- *Maryland Tomorrow* is a large-scale statewide dropout prevention effort operating in 75 high schools and is directed at students considered at risk of dropping out. Among other components, the program includes counseling, intensive academic instruction during the summer and the school year, career guidance and exploration, a variety of summer activities, and adult mentors.
- *The Quantum Opportunities Program* was launched in 1989 with funding from the Ford Foundation and the U.S. Department of Labor. Although the funding ended in 1999, the program's features offer a roadmap for providing supplemental services to students in schools that have large proportions of low-income and minority families. The program targeted randomly selected at-risk 9th graders entering inner-city high schools with high dropout rates. Using a comprehensive case management approach, the program provided year-round services to the participants throughout their four years of high

school. Components included tutoring and homework assistance, computer-assisted instruction, life and family skills training, supplemental after-school education, developmental activities, mentoring, community service activities, and financial planning.

The documented results of these programs, together with the growing research on public alternative schools (Kleiner, Porch, & Farris, 2002), provide a knowledge base about comprehensive approaches to increasing both academic achievement and high school completion rates—which generally go hand in hand.

Any reform initiatives that do not make inroads on the dropout situation can hardly be considered successful.

When it comes to working with individual students to avert a decision to drop out, however, there is a serious impediment. Guidance counselors, working with teachers, are the logical people to identify, track, and help students who show the well-known predropout behaviors: frequent absenteeism, course failure, and negative attitudes. But these professionals can hardly perform such work given the current ratio of 1 counselor to almost 300 high school students—a ratio that is even worse in high-minority schools (NCES, 2004, Table 27–1). In addition, almost all of a counselor's time goes to scheduling courses, helping students with college choice and admissions, performing hall and lunchroom duty, and, increasingly, dealing with test administration (NCES, 2001).

Somehow, schools must recruit individuals who have the time to interact with students one-on-one: more counselors, more volunteers, and more paid and unpaid mentors and tutors. How schools achieve this aim will vary, but any viable approach will require additional effort and resources at the school, school district, or state level (or all three).

Schools attempting to tackle the dropout problem face strikingly different circumstances. At one end of the spectrum are the schools in suburban neighborhoods where most students graduate and go on to college. Here, the relatively few students who appear dropout-prone can be identified, and resources are likely to be available to help them. At the other end are the schools in poor inner-city neighborhoods where families may have less time to supervise after-school activities or interact with the schools to address student absenteeism, misbehavior, or concerns about homework. Here, efforts to increase high school completion will require considerable additional resources, including the help of the larger community. All sorts of school situations lie in between, and no handy formula will apply across the board. But policymakers, administrators, and legislators have a base of knowledge to draw on, as well as information about good practices that work at the school and classroom levels.

A Battle on Two Fronts

The growing demands for high school reform have emphasized the need for higher achievement levels for students who graduate from high school so that they are prepared to either succeed in college or go directly into academically demanding jobs.

Although such efforts are important, any reform initiatives that do not also make inroads on the dropout situation can hardly be considered successful. We face a hard battle on two fronts—one to make high school more rigorous, and the other to keep more students in high school through graduation.

Note

1. Effective July 7, 2004, the GAO's legal name became the U.S. Government Accountability Office.

References

Allensworth, E. (2005). *Graduation and dropout trends in Chicago: A look at cohorts of students from 1991 through 2004*. Chicago: Consortium on Chicago School Research.

Barton, P. (2005a, January). *Unfinished business: More measured approaches in standards-based reform*. (Policy Information Report). Princeton, NJ: Educational Testing Service, Policy Information Center. Available: www.ets.org/Media/Education_Topics/pdf/unfinbusiness.pdf

Barton, P. (2005b). *One-third of a nation: Rising dropout rates and declining opportunities*. Princeton, NJ: Educational Testing Service, Policy Information Center. Available: www.ets.org/Media/Education_Topics/pdf/onethird.pdf

Boesel, D., Alsalam, N., & Smith, T. M. (1998). *Educational and labor market performance of GED recipients*. Washington, DC: U.S. Department of Education, National Education Library.

Education Trust. (2003, December). *Telling the whole truth (or not) about high school graduation*. Washington, DC: Author.

Haney, W., Madaus, G., Abrams, L., Wheelock, A., Miao, J., & Gruia, I. (2004). *The education pipeline in the United States, 1970–2004*. Chestnut Hill, MA: National Board on Educational Testing and Public Policy.

Kleiner, B., Porch, R., & Farris, E. (2002, September). *Public alternative schools and programs for students at risk of education failure, 2000–01*. Washington, DC: National Center for Education Statistics.

National Center for Education Statistics [NCES]. (2001). *Survey on high school guidance counseling*. Washington, DC: Author.

NCES. (2004). *The condition of education 2004*. Washington, DC: Author.

U.S. General Accounting Office. (2002). *School dropouts: Education could play a stronger role in identifying and disseminating promising prevention strategies*. (GAO–02–240). Washington, DC: Author.

PAUL E. BARTON is a Senior Associate at Educational Testing Service's Policy Information Center and an independent education writer and consultant; paulebarton@aol.com

Let Seniors Lead

JANICE DREIS AND LARRY REHAGE

Educators frequently bemoan the senior year of high school as a great wasteland—especially the second semester, when many students, with college acceptances in hand, lose all sense of engagement (Kirst, 2000). At New Trier High School in Winnetka, Illinois, we struggled with "senioritis" until we changed how we viewed senior year—and our seniors.

Seniors are the most knowledgeable and developed learners in the school. Instead of strategizing how we might prod them through a "status quo" senior year, we decided instead to view our seniors as a valuable source of leadership who could enhance how our teachers deliver instruction.

New Trier's Senior Instructional Leadership Corps (SILC), which puts any willing New Trier senior into a partnership assisting a classroom teacher, has infused vitality into our senior year. This leadership program, which involved 26 seniors in its first year, now enables more than 150 seniors to work with a teacher mentor each year. To date, 684 students have assumed a SILC role in their senior year, and 186 teachers have served as mentors.

Recasting Our View

The power of serving as a senior instructional leader is evident in Chris's reflection on his experience assisting a teacher in a sophomore acting class:

> Wow! That is how I feel when I look back at my semester as a SILC leader in Acting Workshop. . . . The connections that I made with students were incredible. . . . I truly got a sense of what it meant to be a teacher. It takes more than just a general knowledge of the material: It takes planning, flexibility, and understanding.

Such engagement through leadership is what we were after in creating SILC. The program evolved in the late 1990s out of concern over the lack of leadership opportunities available to New Trier seniors. New Trier is a large high school in an affluent suburban community north of Chicago, with a predominantly white student population. Among our 4,000-plus students, competition has always been fierce for a few coveted leadership roles in student government, clubs, service organizations, and athletics. Each year, when the rounds of applications

and interviews came to a close, we were concerned to see so many fine students turned away, dejected by an apparent belief that they did not measure up. Too often, we saw students' failure to acquire a leadership position lead to the beginnings of the disengagement on which senioritis feeds. In response to teachers, students, and parents who voiced concern about this problem, we established a schoolwide committee to create new leadership opportunities for seniors. As the guidance personnel for the senior class, we were in on the ground floor of creating and developing the program, and have been the SILC coordinators since its inception.

After only two meetings, a seemingly obvious idea surfaced: Given that our seniors admirably fulfilled leadership roles in athletics, government, and other extracurricular activities, they should have the opportunity to assume leadership roles in the classroom. Why not tap this resource and provide a whole new arena of learning for seniors themselves?

When New Trier High School invited its seniors to become instructional assistants, "senioritis" met its match.

This approach to senior year is rare. Many schools offer leadership programs in which senior students serve as teacher assistants to physical education teachers and coaches. But we are not aware of any student programs other than SILC that extend student leadership into the classroom and curriculum delivery.

Our goal was not only to provide meaningful leadership opportunities for seniors, but also to enhance the delivery of our curriculum through their talents. Participating teachers would mentor seniors, who would in turn serve as mentors to students in a given teacher's classroom.

Initial Explorations and Growth

After much discussion and planning, New Trier launched a semester-long pilot program in fall 1998. We introduced the program concept at a spring faculty meeting, and interested teachers immediately volunteered to approach potential SILC candidates. Twenty-six students and their mentor teachers enthusiastically initiated the first SILC session.

From the beginning, SILC leaders showed great potential for contributing in the classroom. Over the years, senior leaders have effectively offered individual tutoring, facilitated small-group work, prepared materials, designed enrichment activities, led discussions, and even taught minilessons. We initially articulated the following core expectations for SILC student leaders. The "SILCers," as they came to call themselves, must

- Work in a classroom with a mentor teacher two to five times a week, assisting in whatever curricular activities that the teacher deems appropriate.
- Meet with their mentor teacher once a week outside of class to plan these activities.
- Attend monthly seminars with the program coordinators for focused training and discussion of issues germane to their leadership role.
- Keep a journal of weekly activities and reflections.
- Write a self-evaluation at the end of their semester experience.
- Confer at semester's end with both the mentor teacher and a program coordinator.
- Adhere at all times to the SILC code of ethics.

Senior instructional leaders who fulfilled these expectations and received a positive teacher mentor evaluation would earn .25 credit in independent study from the department in which they worked.

These essential elements of the SILC program have changed little since the programs inception, but we have witnessed over and over students far exceeding these basic expectations. Many SILC leaders take their leadership beyond the classroom, offering individual and group tutoring sessions during the week. They have been incredible role models for freshmen from the very start. One of our first SILCers, Jessica, offered a special weekend review session at her house when she became aware of the confusion of freshman World History students who were preparing for their final exam. Nearly half the class showed up on her doorstep. For more than two hours, she helped them outline chapters, review terms, create timelines, and generally organize their materials for review.

Once a few teachers had had successful experiences with senior leaders, others were eager to give the program a try. Within two years after we launched the pilot, the use of instructional leaders in the classroom had become a powerful and pervasive instructional practice in our school. Students played a primary role in helping SILC flourish. They actively promoted the program to one another because they clearly perceived the role as an honored leadership position. Younger students who had seen SILC leaders at work in their classes emulated these role models when they became seniors.

Two years into the program, we faced a significant challenge when increased enrollment forced New Trier to open a separate freshman campus. Having witnessed the tremendous impact SILC leaders were having on freshmen, we felt it was worth making accommodations in scheduling and bus transportation to enable our senior leaders to continue to work with our youngest students.

How SILC Forms Leaders
Casting the Net Wide

A key way SILC departs from the conventional model of student leadership for seniors is that instead of just going for the "cream," we invite as many youth as possible to lead. Although many high school leadership programs have rigorous, often arbitrary standards for selection—such as specified grade point averages, test scores, teacher recommendations, or grueling interviews—we have deliberately avoided such gatekeeping. The only criterion for entry into the program is that an applicant must secure a teacher who wants his or her assistance in working with a specific class in the fall.

Students stepped up in remarkable ways to help deliver the curriculum.

The model of SILC that has evolved over the years is much more comprehensive than our early vision. We had imagined high-profile seniors working predominantly with freshman and sophomore classes. Within the first year, however, we saw seniors work effectively with classes at all grade and ability levels, even working with other seniors in advanced classes. Further, we discovered that it was not just the high-performing students and obvious leaders who made successful SILCers. Many students who are by nature quiet, studious, and conscientious stepped up in remarkable ways to help deliver the curriculum and serve as role models. A SILC leader named Tom, who had always been introverted, proved especially effective at explaining lab procedures and giving demonstrations in science class. He marveled,

I became able to interact with people better, not only in class but also in everyday life. SILC forced me to develop communication skills in situations that I would not have been able to handle normally.

In the final weeks of each school year, we discuss the program with all New Trier juniors during the teacher advisory period, and invite applications. Although most students now approach teachers to ask about serving as a SILC leader, many teachers initiate the connection as they did in the pilot year, and at times SILC coordinators simply make the match. Contrary to our expectations, we have found that a prior relationship between a student and teacher is not necessary for a successful partnership to evolve. What is most needed is a mutual desire between student and teacher to work together.

Orienting Leaders to Service

Each fall, SILC carries out an orientation for student leaders and teacher mentors. The orientation for seniors focuses on the seriousness of the commitment, adherence to a code of ethics, and an explanation of SILC's program goals. Each year's group creates the code of ethics to guide its work. Although codes vary slightly from year to year, they tend to consistently include a few key principles: maintaining student confidentiality, respecting the teachers authority, and, most important, striving continually to contribute to the educational effectiveness of the classroom.

We emphasize that being a SILC leader is, above all, about service, not about enhancing a student's résumé. In assuming a role as instructional assistant, seniors must understand that teachers and classrooms full of students are counting on them. In addition to assisting with all the basics of providing instruction, each SILC leader is explicitly asked to identify someone who is clearly disengaged and underachieving in that leader's assigned classroom and to try to make a real difference for that student. The senior leader is urged to do whatever she or he can, without becoming obvious or overbearing, to improve that student's performance, attitude, comfort level, and engagement in class. SILCers reflect on progress with the struggling student in their journals and apply what they learn about teaching in SILC's monthly seminars to their work with that student.

Status Quote
How wonderful it is that nobody need wait a single moment before starting to improve the world.

—Anne Frank

Caroline, an instructional leader in a sophomore French class, reflected on the rewards of reaching out to one learner:

> I am most proud of my work with one student who was very bright but did not have the same maturity level as others in the class. He frequently would act out to simply get attention. I showed him how to study effectively for tests, organize his homework, and participate actively without acting out. I believe that the student made a lot of progress throughout the first semester, and I have seen improvement in him. To know that I may have helped that student succeed is a wonderful feeling.

Working Together and Nurturing Leadership

The role a SILC student plays in a given classroom is entirely up to the mentor teacher. Clearly, teachers have different comfort levels with regard to how much responsibility they are willing to extend to SILC leaders, and seniors vary in their capabilities and confidence levels. We have found that it's essential for the mentor teacher and the senior to meet weekly outside the classroom to plan activities and set tasks appropriate for the week.

Teachers recognize the assets these seniors bring. One New Trier drama teacher commented, "My SILC leader was another pair of eyes and gave me a new lens through which to view my students." A math teacher noted, "The kids see how excited my

SILC leader is to be working with them, and they respond to that. Her enthusiasm for the subject is contagious."

On occasion, student leaders have unexpectedly assumed remarkable leadership roles, as Phil describes:

> One of my favorite memories of my first-semester SILC experience was a day in which my class had a substitute teacher. Our class was studying biomolecules on the Internet, and the sub really had no idea what was going on. I stepped forward and taught the class like it was my own. From that day on, I gained the confidence I needed to realize that I actually know what I am talking about in chemistry. The kids respected my leadership that day, and I could see a change in their attitudes toward me from then on.

We nurture these seniors' leadership and teaching skills at our monthly seminars, where we introduce topics and techniques associated with effective teaching practices, such as learning styles, group dynamics, personal relationship building, teacher expectations, and classroom management. The seminars offer SILCers the opportunity to share experiences and observations about their classwork. Seniors frequently discuss the difficulties they encounter in their classrooms; mutual support creates a strong bond as the leaders reflect on how to overcome challenges.

The seminars are instrumental in launching special SILC initiatives and reflective assignments, such as maintaining a journal of daily logs and weekly reflections, articulating the characteristics of an effective teacher, and formulating a vision of the ideal role students hope to assume in their SILC classrooms.

A Boon to School Culture

There is no question that New Trier's seniors have honed leadership skills, acquired insight into the art and science of teaching, and even sharpened their proficiency in the subjects in which they assist. Some seniors have indicated that they are seriously considering a career in education. The net result is students, in the capstone year of their high school experience, who are fully engaged, affirmed, and giving back to the community that nurtured them.

Beyond providing increased opportunities for senior leadership, the program has enhanced the culture and climate of our school. Most significantly, SILC leaders have become a vital force in helping to enhance and deliver our curriculum.

The program has also encouraged collegiality among teachers as they converse about how to bring SILC leaders into their classrooms and incorporate new teaching strategies. In addition, teachers now engage in a new kind of collegiality that brings students into the discussion of teaching and learning. These connections have deepened personal and professional relationships throughout our school community. Student relationships have benefited as well. As seniors go about their classroom leadership, interacting with students across grade levels, they engender a genuine spirit of good will. Younger students are now more likely to view seniors as approachable helpers rather than as agents of intimidation.

Insisting on a senior year that is essentially the same as the first three years of high school ignores seniors' developmental readiness to contribute to the world in significant ways. More than anything else, we have learned from our Senior Instructional Leadership Corps how capable seniors can be. Many seniors are ready to assume adult roles in their final year of high school, roles that provide the sense of purpose they so urgently need (National Commission on the High School Senior Year, 2001). The concluding paragraph of Molly's self-evaluation shows how helping in a freshman science class gave her a feeling of engagement of the highest order:

> I hope that I have helped these freshmen transition into high school as much as I know they have helped me transition into the real world. Next year I will be faced with many challenges and my newly learned leadership and personal relationship-building skills will be very useful. I look forward to each day with these students because they make me feel useful and appreciated. Some might say they helped me find joy. I would say they helped me find a purpose.

Seniors like Molly are incredible resources that can and should be called upon to serve the school. Recasting the senior year to allow our youth to lead creatively and invest in their community is the key to fostering meaningful engagement.

References

Kirst, M. W. (2000). *Overcoming the high school senior slump: New education policies.* Paper prepared for the National Commission on the High School Senior Year. Research supported by the Pew Charitable Trusts and the U.S. Department of Education (Office of Educational Research and Improvement).

National Commission on the High School Senior Year. (2001). *Raising our sights: No high school senior left behind.* Princeton, NJ: The Woodrow Wilson National Fellowship Foundation.

JANICE DREIS (dreisj@newtrier.k12.il.us) is a Senior Advisor Chairs at New Trier High School in Winnetka, Illinois. **LARRY REHAGE** (rehagel@newtrier.k12.il.us) is a Senior Advisor Chairs at New Trier High School in Winnetka, Illinois.

Studies Reveal Strengths, Weaknesses

Improving rates of high school graduation and college completion for low-income and minority students.

BILL HEMMER

An in-depth analysis of high school and college graduation data shows that only one in three eighth graders in 1988 earned an Associate's degree 12 years later.

At the same time, a new national study of public perceptions of our education system shows that most Americans recognize that a college degree is critical for economic success, yet most people also believe that our education system, particularly high schools, is failing to prepare young people for higher education.

The Boston-based Jobs for the Future (JFF) today released the two reports, conducted for JFF by the Parthenon Group and Lake Snell Perry & Associates (LSPA), at "Double the Numbers," a national conference focused on improving the rates of college success for youth who are underrepresented in postsecondary education. More than 400 education leaders, public officials, and policymakers are participating in this conference, which is exploring ways to "plug the leaks" in the so-called education pipeline and improve the high school-to-college transition rates, especially for lower-income and minority youth.

According to the national public opinion survey, Americans are aware of the barriers to success that students encounter in high school and college, yet many people also underestimate the challenges that young people—including lower-income and minority youth—face in attempting to earn a college degree. The results show near universal agreement that the high number of students who fail to graduate from high school and complete a college degree is a major problem for the national economy.

"The United States faces the daunting task of improving a major pipeline that is seriously limited," said Hilary Pennington, CEO of Jobs for the Future. "This pipeline is not in a foreign nation. It is our education system, which wastes human potential at an alarming rate."

At a news event in Washington, DC, Pennington and other experts called on states and the federal government to take a number of steps to improve high school graduation, college enrollment, and completion rates, especially for low-income, minority students.

Based on the reports, JFF issued recommendations for federal and state policies that would "double the numbers" of young people who complete college or earn another postsecondary credential:

- Align expectation, curricula, and assessments with those of postsecondary institutions.
- Provide all students with opportunities and support to take and succeed in advanced courses.
- Connect students to the world beyond the high school walls by internships, community service, and work experience.
- Set up data systems that track students over time and hold postsecondary and secondary institutions accountable for how well they help students complete a recognized postsecondary credential by age 26.
- Eliminate boundaries between high school and college. For example, early college high schools, middle college high schools, and dropout recovery programs at community colleges permit students to accelerate their route to higher education and earn college credit at the same time.
- Offer incentives that reward secondary and postsecondary institutions when students successfully progress to and through college.

"The nation can no longer focus on high school reform as a standalone endeavor and regularly ignore as many as half of the young people who drop out of the education system before earning high school and college degrees," says Pennington. "And we're spending millions of dollars and substantial political capital building high school exit exams that ignore the next part of the pipeline: how to ensure that students gain the credentials and the education required for career jobs and college-level studies."

The research by the Parthenon Group examined the return that states and the nation would gain on investments designed to increase the number of students attending college. Doubling the numbers offers potential economic, as well as social and civic benefits. Economic benefits include increased tax revenues; social and civic benefits include reduction in unemployment and increased voter participation rates.

The JFF/LSPA opinion survey shows that Americans are optimistic about many of the initiatives already in use nationwide to prepare all students for high school and college success: for example, smaller high schools, need-based aid, and scholarship programs. According to the poll, Americans believe cost is the most important impediment faced by students—especially from lower-income families—in the pursuit of a college degree.

The Gates Millennium Scholars (GMS)—supported by the Bill & Melinda Gates Foundation and administered by the United Negro College Fund—is an example of a scholarship program that helps qualified minority youth attend the higher education institution of their choice. Early analysis of the program shows that GMS scholarship recipients are more likely than non-recipients to attend and stay in a four-year or private college.

"Qualified students, regardless of the race, ethnicity, or financial background, should not have to trim their ambitions and be denied the opportunity to attend college," said Tom Vander Ark, executive director of education at the Bill & Melinda Gates Foundation. "Gates Millennium Scholars are showing that when financial and other barriers are removed, students from the most challenging backgrounds can achieve, attend college, and prepare to become leaders in a range of professions and our communities."

But cost is not the only obstacle, the poll says. A majority of Americans believes that high schools need to do more to prepare students for college. They want to see better high school teachers in the classroom. Moreover, they feel it is important for guidance counselors to do more to help students understand the value of college and to help them choose and apply to colleges that are right for them.

According to the JFF/Parthenon Group research, the barriers to college entrance and success are especially great for low-income families and other underrepresented youth, including minorities and immigrants who are learning English. For example, only 19 percent of lower-income families complete an Associate's degree or higher, compared to 76 percent of high-income families.

All states have room for improvement in overall degree attainment. However, the nature of the problem varies across states, driving the need for tailored solution sets to address state-specific challenges along the higher education pipeline. The emphasis in some states might be focused on high school graduation rates, while others might address post-secondary access and attainment issues.

According to the report, if the United States is to address anticipated shortages of 12 million highly skilled workers by 2020, we must radically change how we educate and support low-income students and minority students, who comprise the fastest-growing segments of the youth population. This requires transforming how we prepare young people for college, breaking down the barriers that separate schools and postsecondary education, and developing new incentives for individuals to attend college and for institutions to enroll and retain students.

The public opinion study found near universal agreement that the high number of students who fail to go from high school to complete a college degree is a major problem facing the nation. Moreover, most people appreciate that this problem threatens not only the economic well-being of students who leave school without a college (or even a high school) degree but also the potential of the U.S. economy as a whole.

References

National partners in the "Double the Numbers" conference include the Bill & Melinda Gates Foundation, Carnegie Corporation of New York, the Ford Foundation, and the W.K. Kellogg Foundation.

The national public opinion survey of 1,010 Americans age 18 and older was conducted by Lake Snell Perry & Associates in September through October 5, 2003. It included oversamples of African Americans and Hispanics. Altogether, 639 non-Hispanic whites, 161 non-Hispanic African Americans, and 171 Hispanics were surveyed. For results based on total sample, oversampled groups were weighted to reflect their true representative proportion.

The New Cheating Epidemic

More (and younger) kids are taking the easy way out to get good grades in school. Even worse, parents are actually helping students get away with it. *Redbook* reports on this troubling trend—and tells you how to keep your children honest.

ANNE MARIE CHAKER

While grading essays, Eileen Theim, a teacher in Bethesda, Maryland, came across some lines in a seventh grader's assignment that sounded suspiciously eloquent. After a quick search online, Theim found the phrase in question—a professional writer's Web site. When Theim confronted the student about the stolen lines, "the student said, 'Oh, OK,' as if she didn't know it was wrong," Theim recalls. Asked to redo the essay, the student chose to merely cut the lines she'd lifted and resubmit it.

If you think that this student was the exception and that most kids wouldn't dream of cheating on schoolwork, you're in for a surprise. Recent studies show that the majority of students cheat. In a survey by the Josephson Institute of Ethics, 74 percent of high schoolers say they've cheated on an exam at least once; this is up 13 percent from a decade ago. And 59 percent of middle schoolers admit to the same crime, according to a study conducted at Rutgers University in New Jersey. Even younger kids are cheating, according to one teacher's experiment in Rigby, Idaho: When the teacher, Sharon Jones, asked second and fifth graders to grade their own tests, all but three kids cheated to get the reward she'd promised high scores: a candy bar.

Making matters worse is that teachers and parents are allowing—even helping—kids to cheat, seeing it as the only way for them to survive and stay sane in these high-stakes, fast-paced times. Under more pressure to keep test scores up than ever, schools are sometimes abandoning their ethics to meet their goals. And parents, pained at the sight of their kids in tears or up late slaving over homework, are increasingly willing to finish those assignments themselves.

But what, exactly, is driving so many students, at such early ages, to cheat? And why are adults—their alleged role models—letting them get away with this deceit? *Redbook* reveals this disturbing trend and how you can encourage your kids to stay honest.

New High-Tech Hicks

We're all familiar with the usual ways kids cheat, from crib sheets written on sneakers to coughing codes between classmates. But these days, cheating has gone high tech. Pagers can transmit test answers without telltale whispers; Web sites such as school sucks. com hawk custom-written term papers on any topic. Ken Rodoff, a high school teacher in Springfield, Pennsylvania, was recently introduced to the powers of a laser printer when he uncovered a student's thumbnail-size crib sheet, printed in a font just large enough to read. "I have to admit it, it was impressive," he says. Though he failed that student, he doubts he's spotting every cheat sheet. "They're so small," he says.

These tech-savvy scams make it easier than ever for students to slide phony work by teachers, who are often unaware that cheating is going on—or just don't care. "Ninety-eight percent of cheaters don't get caught, and only half of those caught are punished," estimates Michael Josephson, president of the Josephson Institute, a Marina del Rey, California, research institute.

Sadly, it's the honest students who sometimes get the short end of the stick. "Once, an eleventh grader arrived at my after-school book club crying," says one school librarian. "She said that earlier that week, students in her history class had gotten a hold of their exam before they had to take it." But the girl had refused to look at it, and her grade ended up being lower than those of the cheaters. Even so, she refused to rat out her peers. The girl's teacher felt that little could be done, since she couldn't tell who'd cheated. "Here was a girl who was trying to do the right thing," says the librarian. But she was paddling against the current, which allowed others to thrive while she faltered.

Students in Crisis

Why are so many kids becoming cheaters? Largely because the pressure they're under to succeed is more intense than ever—and hits them as early as primary school. "These days getting on the honor roll or into elite secondary schools is increasingly difficult. I've seen third graders with private tutors," says John Dacey, PhD, an author of *Your Anxious Child*. Plus, the growing importance of extracurricular activities as a way to stand out to admissions boards is forcing students to spread themselves thin. Combine all this with the fact that young kids often lack the judgment or self-control to enable them to do the right thing, and some are bound to take the easy way out by copying their neighbors' test answers. "Kids are starving for some free time," says Dacey. "They'll do what it takes to get some hours to themselves."

One reason this pressure to excel starts early is standardized tests, now taken as often as once a year starting in kindergarten in some states, says Kevin Welner, a director of the Education and the Public Interest Center at the University of Colorado in Boulder. Kids who don't perform well may be held back, shuttled into less advanced curricula, or denied entrance into selective middle and high schools.

For Maria Vidal de Haymes, 40, this emphasis on standardized tests rather than on a school's curriculum convinced her to pull her seventh-grade son out of a Chicago public school at the end of the term and enroll him in a private school. "The better public high schools in this area pretty much only accept kids who score above the 95th percentile on the Iowa Test of Basic Skills [a standardized test]," she says. "These tests are demoralizing for kids, especially when their friends make it into good high schools and they don't. Parents with seventh and eighth graders are all panicking."

And as if high-stakes tests didn't produce enough anxiety, kids are doing nearly twice as much homework as they did 20 years ago, according to a study by the University of Michigan in Ann Arbor. Given these time constraints, Dianna Ewton, 40, empathized when her ninth-grade daughter confessed that she's copied friends' homework. "I gave her hell, but I can see why she did it," she says. "Her field hockey practice lasts until 5:30, and she also volunteers at the YMCA, babysits, and plays flute in the school band." Copying, she concludes, is her daughter's attempt to make ends meet.

School for Scandal

Perhaps most shocking, teachers themselves are cheating as well. Last October teachers and principals in 14 Chicago-area elementary schools were investigated for helping students answer questions on the Iowa tests, which are mandatory for students in the third, sixth, and eighth grades. So far, a substitute teacher and teacher's aide have been dismissed. What's more, some teachers claimed that their supervisors had told them to cheat on the tests to jack up the scores; one teacher claimed she'd lost her job after refusing to do it.

What drove these schools into such shady territory? A fear that low standardized test scores will have dire consequences for the school itself. "Last year alone, three Chicago schools were shut down as a result of their students' overall performance on the test," says the Chicago Teachers Union President Deborah Lynch. And President Bush's January 2001 signing of the No Child Left Behind Act ratchets up the pressure even more, requiring annual standardized testing of all students in third through eighth grade. High poverty schools that get federal funding and don't show an adequate yearly progress five years in a row face a state-government takeover. "This doesn't give schools much time at all to improve," says Melanie Mitchell, assistant director of the Keenan Institute for Ethics at Duke University. "I wouldn't be surprised if it tempts some schools to cheat."

Parents Who Help Too Much

With the stakes so high, even parents don't always play fair when it comes to their child's education. While most adults wouldn't approve of kids' copying each other's homework, more than one in

five parents say they've done part of a child's homework assignment themselves, according to a study by Public Agenda, a research firm in New York.

AnneLise Wilhelmsen, 41, of Los Alamitos, California, freely admits she's had a hand in doing her fourth-grade son's homework. In particular, she recalls watching her 9-year-old son struggle to complete a geography assignment. When she realized he couldn't get it done in time, she lent a hand. "Strictly speaking, this may have been cheating, but it was the right decision for this boy on this specific day," she says. "It [excessive homework] cuts into family time. It cuts into our children's opportunity to be children."

Etta Kralovec, an author of *The End of Homework: How Homework Disrupts Families, Overburdens Children and Limits Learning*, doesn't blame parents for helping so much. "Parents don't want to, but they also don't want their child to get bad grades or to have a meltdown trying to get everything done," she says. Another reason some parents do homework is so that they can spend more quality time with their kids. "We're increasingly protective of family time," Kralovec says. So much so, in fact, that at one school in Piscataway, New Jersey, parents staged protests decrying the amount of homework their kids received. The school now has "homework caps" limiting the amount of homework teachers can assign.

While schools often justify heavy homework loads by claiming that they boost standardized-test scores, this doesn't hold true for elementary school students, says Harris Cooper, professor of educational psychology at the University of Missouri in Columbia. "Younger kids don't have the cognitive skills or the attention span to benefit from long periods of study," Cooper explains. Some experts even say it's detrimental to young kids, who get frustrated and lose interest in subjects they once adored.

Why Cheating Goes Unpunished

Teachers say some forms of cheating are easier to spot than others. For instance, spotting homework that's benefited from a parent's "help" is a no-brainer. Some parents make it even more obvious by turning in assignments in their own handwriting. But calling parents on their rule-bending is often more trouble than it's worth. One New York middle school teacher says she argues with parents over grades on homework they've helped with "on a weekly basis." "They'll demand that I change the grade from a C to an A," she says. "I usually say, 'You get an A, but your kid gets a C.'" But more often than not, this teacher's principal recommends that she inflate the grade, and she does. "I'm an untenured teacher," she points out. "What else am I supposed to do?"

Christine Pelton, a former tenth-grade biology teacher at Piper High School in Kansas, knows all too well the consequences of standing up to irate parents. In December 2001, she found out that 28 of her students had cut and pasted essays off Web sites. She gave those students zeros, causing many to fail the course. A parental uproar ensued. "I got phone calls in the middle of the night from people cursing," she says. After the superintendent and the school board forced her to pass the students, she resigned in disgust. The superintendent and some board members have since left the district. "But I got a lot of respect from students," she says. "They said they were glad someone had finally stood up to the students who cheated."

How to Cheat-Proof Your Child

While containing such widespread cheating may seem daunting, parents can do so in various ways, starting in their own homes. Even before kids head off to kindergarten, you should have a talk with them, telling them that cheating is wrong and won't be tolerated (for tips on this topic, refer to "How to Talk to Your Child about Cheating").

But since even honest kids will be tempted to cheat if everyone else is getting away with it, parents also have to push for school-wide reform. The best place to do this is at a school board meeting. "Parents often make the mistake of approaching teachers," says Kralovec. But, surprisingly, teachers won't be able to do much; only principals and school boards have the power to put an end to rampant cheating, through changes in school policy (to find out when your local school board meets, inquire at the school principal's office).

What kinds of policies should parents request? For starters, ask that the board prohibit teachers from giving the same test to students in different periods of the same class, or from year to year. This measure will keep students from passing tests around to their peers who may be taking them later. You can also request that teachers keep a close eye on students during tests.

But teaching students to behave ethically on their own is a far more important and challenging goal for schools, says Don McCabe, founder of the Center for Academic Integrity. To this end, parents can ask the school board to write and enforce an honor code delineating what constitutes cheating and how students will be penalized if caught doing so. Having clear guidelines that are explained to students regularly goes a long way toward keeping students in line. Students and parents should receive a copy of this code at the beginning of every school year; after big tests, students should sign a waiver stating that they haven't cheated and are aware of the consequences if they do. These regular reminders will also discourage cheating.

Heavy homework loads may also be part of the problem. To keep your kids from feeling so pressed for time that they copy pals' assignments, ask the school board to make some homework non-graded (especially for younger kids) and to establish homework caps. Ron Bolandi, a school superintendent in Tewksbury, New Jersey, has implemented these policies, and while it's too early to tell how they will affect the incidence of cheating, Bolandi knows one thing for sure: "Students love it," he says. "They say now they can stop staying up until 3 a.m. doing homework and have a life."

How to Talk to Your Child about Cheating

Acknowledge the pressure he's under. Lecturing your child about cheating by simply saying "Don't do it" will create a you-versus-him dynamic that will likely cause him to stop listening to you. Instead say, "I know you're incredibly busy and stressed about school, and that it must be tempting to cheat. But it's still not right." This lets him know you're on his side without conveying that cheating's OK.

Don't say "You'll get caught." Too many kids get away with cheating for you to be able to convince your child that this is true. Instead appeal to his sense of morality by asking him, "How would you feel if someone cheated off you in your favorite class—and got the better grade?" It'll be much harder for him to cheat if he visualizes what it's like to be in the victim's shoes, says Caroline Watts, a psychologist at Children's Hospital in Boston.

Reassure him that grades don't matter that much. Kids often think that their getting high marks means more to you than their doing the right thing. Emphasize that this isn't the case by saying, "I'd be much, much more disappointed in you if you cheated than if you failed a test."

Is Your Child Cheating?
4 ways to find out if your kid earned his grades the honest way.

1. Even if you swear your child isn't cheating, it's good to check in with him regularly to establish that you're monitoring his work to see what he's learned. If you know that your child had a big exam, for example, ask him. "So what were some of the questions on that test you took today?" If he can't remember any, it may mean he copied off someone else, filling in the answers without really reading the questions.

2. Look in on your child frequently while he's doing homework, asking him if he needs any help. If he never has questions, is reluctant to . . . show you what he's working on, or refuses to work in the same room with you, it may suggest he's doing something you wouldn't approve of, such as exchanging answers with his friends.

3. Ask to see his resources—books, encyclopedias, etc.—for written assignments. If he can't provide them, it may mean he has pasted his essay off the Web or gotten it from someone else.

4. Read his written assignments. If a word he uses seems too sophisticated for someone his age, ask him to define it. If he can't explain it—or the overall point of his essay, for that matter—it may spell trouble.

Once You Know the Score

If your child fails three or more of these measures, there's a very good chance he's cheating. What then? While alerting his teacher and making your child face the consequences at school may seem the right things to do, Michael Josephson of the Josephson Institute usually recommends against this plan. "It may destroy any trust your child has in you," points out Josephson. "The important issue is that the child should be punished at home in a way that conveys that this is not acceptable." You should also address the underlying situation that led your child to cheat. If, for example, he's spread too thin by all his activities, suggest cutting a few of the less important ones so he'll have time to finish his schoolwork without cutting corners.

From *Redbook*, April 2003, vol. 200, issue 4, pp. 150–154. Copyright © 2003 by Anne Marie Chaker. Reprinted by permission of the author.

Leading Adolescents to Mastery

The ABCI approach leaves no assignment undone, no failure unchallenged, and no middle schooler unengaged.

SUE KENKEL, STEVE HOELSCHER, AND TERI WEST

On a crisp, sunny fall day at Bendle Middle School in Burton, Michigan, in 2003, with the wind shuffling red and gold leaves across the schoolyard, the students were talking about the new ABCI grading policy: "I've never gotten anything higher than a *D* in any class. How am I going to get at least a *C* on *every* assignment?" "I heard Ms. Kenkel talking about Saturday school! I'm not coming to school on the weekends!"

Bendle was less than two months into the ABCI program. Under this approach, students were required to achieve a *C* or higher on every assignment. If a student's work was judged to be less than *C* quality, that student received an *I* for Incomplete—and teachers gave the student as much time and support as needed to complete the work and get a higher grade.

Parent and student reaction to the policy was heating up. A typical parent response came from the mother of 7th grader Conner.

Conner had developed some poor study habits and had barely passed 6th grade. His mom, a single parent, worked the night shift at the local manufacturing plant. One afternoon, she blew into the principal's office at Bendle and, with fire in her eyes, shouted,

> Look, don't you understand that it takes everything I have just to get my kid up in the morning and get him here for school? He was doing just fine before this ABCI stuff. Isn't a *D* supposed to be passing? That's all he needs to get. Just give him the *D*s.

The season was about to change, and the culture of the school was changing drastically, too.

Cracking Down on Complacency

Bendle Middle School has a student body numbering 320; 97 percent of the students are white, and close to 60 percent qualify for free or reduced-price lunch. Many of the students live in rented two-bedroom bungalows; many are being reared by a single parent or another relative. Some parents have not earned a high school diploma themselves. Like all parents, they want the best for their children and do all they can to support them;

nonetheless, the home culture of many Bendle students is one of low academic expectations.

Bendle's teachers realized that the school needed to make changes when they reviewed final grades for the 2002–2003 school year. The data told the story: 29 percent of final grades for the 6th, 7th, and 8th grade classes were *D*s and *E*s. Staff members felt uncomfortable with these results and with students repeatedly not turning in homework. They believed that Bendle students were just as intelligent as more successful students, but that many of them came to the "game" with limited prior knowledge and support at home. Faculty members knew that they needed a new strategy to raise expectations and promote success among these at-risk adolescents.

In summer 2003, using a Comprehensive School Reform grant, Bendle staff members participated in a workshop facilitated by one of this articles authors, regional director of Michigan Middle Start Steve Hoelscher. Middle Start is a comprehensive school improvement program for middle schools and for schools with middle grades. ABCI is a two-year component of Middle Start that schools can also implement separately.

After much discussion of how to raise overall student achievement at Bendle, Steve and his team of Middle Start coaches recommended that the school consider implementing the ABCI approach, which they had seen spur tremendous results. The teachers had many objections, but no one could refute the point raised by the following question: "If an assignment is worth doing, then why isn't it worth doing well?"

Getting Teachers to "Aha!"

ABCI is borrowed and adapted from mastery learning theory, which was developed and promulgated by Benjamin Bloom (1968, 1971). More recently, the work of William Glasser and the Quality Schools movement (1990) has influenced the development of ABCI. ABCI embraces Bloom's concept that given enough time and quality instruction, all students can learn. With this approach, teachers insist that students complete every assignment to high standards.

Schools that adopt ABCI receive off-site training in implementing the program throughout the school year, including assistance with developing planning and communications strategies, coming to a consensus on what high-quality assignments look like, and networking with other ABCI schools. There is a financial cost to the program, and carrying it through takes enormous commitment and willingness to change.

The leadership team at Bendle made the commitment that all teachers would adopt ABCI; despite some doubts, all staff members agreed to move forward because of the irrefutable data showing that the school's current methods were not successful with many students. Bendle staff members participated in targeted training sessions that prepared them to manage and implement the ABCI program. Middle Start also provided an instructional coach who met weekly with the principal, the instructional teams, the building leadership team, and individual staff members.

But change can take time, and not all teachers valued ABCI right away. One veteran teacher came to the principal with tears in her eyes and a stack of papers a foot high. "I can't do this," she said. "I've been up until midnight almost every night this week. I've been spending my weekends grading these papers."

"What's different?" the principal asked.

"It used to be that only 40–50 percent of my students did the work, but now with this new policy, 90 percent of my classes are completing their assignments," she replied. As she spoke, this teacher had an "aha!" moment. She suddenly realized that she needed to reflect on what her students most needed to know and be able to do, to look at the assignments she was giving, and to ask herself which ones were truly worth assigning.

To bring more teachers to such "aha!" moments, throughout the 2003–2004 school year, the Middle Start coach facilitated staff reflections and dialogues that led teachers to analyze what they had been expecting from students and whether or not their expectations addressed the essential learning and skills that students needed to master. A goal of ABCI is to make teachers more thoughtful about the assignments they give and more consistent with how they grade those assignments both within the classroom and across classes.

These reflection sessions also guided teachers to look carefully at whether their instructional practices and assessments were appropriate for young adolescents—and to change practices to draw adolescents more fully into learning. Most teachers practiced the "stand and deliver" mode of instruction and used traditional forms of assessments, such as tests, worksheets, and individually graded assignments. These practices are not developmentally appropriate for young adolescents, who prefer active explorations, clear purposes, and opportunities to try out new concepts and skills in realistic settings. Students this age are also beginning to think about their position and potential in the world. Because middle school is the point at which many youth drop out, mentally if not physically, it's crucial that schools provide a curriculum that is socially significant and relevant to young adolescents.

Changing How Teachers Operate
From Examining Beliefs . . .

Bendles reflection discussions required teachers to examine their beliefs as well as their practices. Teachers looked at whether they believed that all middle school students *can* learn, regardless of home life, socioeconomic status, race, gender, ability, or any other characteristics. They questioned what was preventing many of Bendles students from achieving. In many cases, it came down to a question of time and support. One teacher reflected,

> Do we believe that at a certain point in time, the student should demonstrate mastery of what he knows, so that if he hasn't mastered it on that date, he either fails or gets a below-average grade?

The teachers realized that defending this practice was a way of sorting students and keeping those with a history of failure from succeeding. But if they began to expect *all* students to produce work that met high standards, then students who were just getting by or failing would be held accountable for measuring up.

. . . To Changing Practice

During their first year implementing ABCI, teachers at Bendle began to revisit and reteach lessons that many students clearly had not mastered. They became more comfortable modifying assignments to meet an individual student at his or her skill level. Three years into the approach, Bendle teachers now use instructional practices that engage young adolescents in the learning process. They modify lessons as necessary to meet the needs of all students, not just the special education students.

Students' expectations for what they can accomplish have increased dramatically.

For example, in an 8th grade language arts class studying capital punishment, students were required to read newspaper and magazine articles covering both sides of the argument and to present their own positions on the issue orally, in writing, or through a PowerPoint presentation. The teacher paired struggling readers with stronger readers to read articles together out loud and set up students to serve as peer reviewers for those who needed assistance in writing.

Teachers have made their practice public: Instructional teams are talking to one another about instructional practices and intervention ideas. ABCI has also spurred teachers to reflect together on how they deliver lessons and assign work. Because they know that students may have to redo an assignment several times, teachers think more deeply about how a given assignment aligns with standards and what the grading rubric should be for the assignment. Together, teachers look at student work to develop rubrics. As a result, teachers give more project-based assignments and fewer worksheets or busywork. The focus is on quality assignments rather than on rote learning.

Accommodations and Challenges

Bringing the ABCI approach to a middle school presents significant challenges and requires a leap of faith among school staff members and administrators. One challenge for Bendle has been the plethora of accommodations the school has made to provide the supports needed for all students to meet the newly raised expectations. These accommodations include an extended school day; an extended school year; a mandatory Saturday school; a homework club; tutoring; a "responsibility room" (a room within the school used as an alternative to suspension for disruptive students); and changes to extracurricular policies.

Drastic changes to a school culture demand sensitive, perceptive leadership. Some teachers will try to continue doing things the old way, so the principal needs to monitor whether these teachers are reaching the goal of having higher expectations and promoting engaged learning in their classrooms. Look at grade distributions and lesson plans. What kinds of work are teachers assigning? What kinds of grades are students receiving? How many students are getting Incompletes? Discuss with teachers how they are carrying out change. The reality is that not everyone in the school will buy into the new system. Teachers who have been giving students the same ditto sheets for years and believe that it's too bad if a student doesn't get it the first time are teachers who won't make the change.

It takes time for students and parents to realize that the school is doing business differently. Expect a huge learning curve and a transition period, but persist. ABCI coaches should guide and support teachers who need to develop new pedagogy. When a teacher shows reluctance to set high expectations or change instructional practice, that teacher and the principal should have a conference about why students need to be held accountable for high-quality work. Under the ABCI approach, teachers who seem unwilling to put effort into creating a climate consistent with ABCI's philosophy are required to develop a plan that shows how they can ensure all students' success. After each classroom assessment, the teacher reviews students' work and progress with the principal. The school administration may need to take disciplinary action with teachers who remain unwilling or unable to conform to the new policies. The ABCI philosophy, however, never recommends transferring a teacher who is not effectively holding students to high standards.

For many students, the ABCI program represents the first time in their education when teachers haven't let them squeak by.

The ABCI approach cannot succeed without the involvement of everyone at the school—teachers, support staff, guidance counselors, parents, students, and administrators. To make the change work at Bendle, we needed local businesses to provide tutors for the Saturday school, students to help one another after school or during lunch, teachers to give extra time, and parents to drive their students to school on Saturday and support them during homework time.

Seeing Positive Effects
Student Achievement and Behavior

Preliminary data indicate that adopting the ABCI approach at Bendle may have improved students' performance on state assessments. In academic year 2004–2005, for the first time in three years, Bendle made the adequate yearly progress required by NCLB. Student achievement scores on the Michigan Educational Assessment Program (MEAP) improved 11.7 percent in reading, 5 percent in English language arts, 2 percent in science, and 6 percent in social studies.

These days, it is common at Bendle to see students congratulating one another on "no Incompletes" with high fives. These adolescents are realizing a success they have never experienced before. Students frequently check their grades, stay after school for extra assistance, and celebrate when an assignment or project, completed to quality standards, is raised from an Incomplete to a letter grade. Their expectations for what they can accomplish have increased dramatically.

Teachers who have implemented ABCI in their classrooms have reported a drop in principal referrals and other discipline measures as well as increased student engagement in classroom activities. Students are more engaged not only because teachers hold them accountable, but also because their classrooms are more student-centered places where instruction is interactive, cooperative, and cross-disciplinary—in short, appropriate for young adolescents.

Student and Parent Reactions

Bendle students have given ABCI mixed reviews. Most students like the policy, particularly those who have traditionally fallen behind. For many students, this policy represents the first time in their education when teachers haven't let them squeak by. Finally, teachers not only expect these students to achieve at a higher level but also provide the support and guidance required to help students do so. As one student said, "It's so much better for me to stay after school to get help with my work. It's hectic at home, so I can't get much done." On the other hand, students who have traditionally received high grades, even when they didn't complete all the work, have been less likely to embrace the new policy.

Parent involvement at Bendle has increased. Parents now frequently call, e-mail, and come in to check on student grades, which are posted in the classroom weekly. Parents have higher expectations of what their children can accomplish. As one parent said, "My son has never achieved grades like this! His report card is hanging on the refrigerator!"

Doing Whatever It Takes

The National Forum to Accelerate Middle-Grades Reform has said middle schools should provide an academically excellent, developmentally appropriate, and equitable education for all young adolescents (1997). For middle schools that believe this is a charge worth accepting, the ABCI approach is an excellent start to matching beliefs with practice. The grading policy challenges middle school students to meet higher expectations; the training, structured reflections, and coaching provide teachers with essential supports and structures so that they can nurture achievement at high levels for all students.

At Bendle Middle School, all students are expected to achieve, whatever it takes.

After three years of implementation, ABCI has changed Bendle's school culture from one in which students, parents, and staff alike had become complacent and accepting of failing grades to one in which all students are expected to achieve, whatever it takes.

References

Bloom, B. (1968). Learning for mastery. *Evaluation Comment*, 1(2), 1–5.

Bloom, B. (1971). *Mastery learning.* New York: Holt, Rinehart & Winston.

Glasser, W. (1990). *The quality school.* New York: Perennial Library.

National Forum to Accelerate Middle-Grades Reform. (1997). *Vision statement.* Available: www.mgforum.org/about/vision,asp

SUE KENKEL is Principal of Davison Alternative Education Middle and High School Programs in Davison, Michigan, and former Principal of Bendle Middle School; skenkel@davison.k12.mi.us. **STEVE HOELSCHER** is Regional Director of Michigan Middle Start; 248–249–3265; stevehoel@sbcglobal.net. **TERI WEST** is Program Officer for middle school improvement programs at the Academy for Educational Development; 212–367–4595; twest@aed.org.

Healthier Students, Better Learners

The Health Education Assessment Project helps teachers provide the skills-based, standards-based health instruction that students need.

BETH PATEMAN

When we think back on health classes from our school days, many of us have only vague memories. We may recall some discussion of food groups, a film about puberty, or a lecture on dental hygiene conducted when the weather was too rainy to go outside for physical education. Few of us remember our K-12 health education experiences as being relevant to our lives outside the classroom.

Fortunately, that picture is changing. Asserting that "healthy students make better learners, and better learners make healthy communities," the Council of Chief State School Officers (CCSSO) and the Association of State and Territorial Health Officials (ASTHO) (2002) have summarized compelling research evidence that students' health significantly affects their school achievement. Even if their schools have the most outstanding academic curriculum and instruction, students who are ill or injured, hungry or depressed, abusing drugs or experiencing violence, are unlikely to learn as well as they should (Kolbe, 2002).

Effective health education programs have a vital role to play in enhancing students' health and thus in raising academic achievement. Kolbe's 2002 review of the research found that modern school health programs can improve students' health knowledge, attitudes, skills, and behaviors and enhance social and academic outcomes. How do these modern health programs differ from those that most of us remember from our school days? Thanks to growing knowledge about how to prevent unhealthy and unsafe behaviors among young people, today's exemplary health education combines *skills-based* and *standards-based* approaches.

Focus on Skills

The Centers for Disease Control and Prevention have identified six types of behavior that cause the most serious health problems in the United States among people over 5 years old: alcohol and other drug use, high-risk sexual behaviors, tobacco use, poor dietary choices, physical inactivity, and behaviors that result in intentional or unintentional injury. Stressing the importance of education efforts, the Centers state that

> these behaviors usually are established during youth; persist into adulthood; are interrelated; and are preventable. In

addition to causing serious health problems, these behaviors contribute to many of the educational and social problems that confront the nation, including failure to complete high school, unemployment, and crime. (n.d.)

Effective health education programs have a vital role to play in enhancing students' health and thus in raising academic achievement.

In response to the Centers' focus on these major health-risk behaviors, education researchers have worked to identify educational approaches that positively affect health-related behaviors among young people. Many research studies have established the effectiveness of skills-based school health education in promoting healthy behavior and academic achievement (ASTHO & Society of State Directors of Health, Physical Education, and Recreation, 2002; Collins et al., 2002; Kirby, 2001). Lohrmann and Wooley (1998) determined that effective programs

- Focus on helping young people develop and practice personal and social skills, such as communication and decision making, to deal effectively with health-risk situations;
- Provide healthy alternatives to specific high-risk behaviors;
- Use interactive approaches that engage students;
- Are research-based and theory-driven;
- Address social and media influences on student behaviors;
- Strengthen individual and group norms that support healthy behavior;
- Are of sufficient duration to enable students to gain the knowledge and skills that they need; and
- Include teacher preparation and support.

Health Education Standards

- *Standard 1: Students will comprehend concepts related to health promotion and disease prevention.* For example, students will be able to identify what good health is, recognize health problems, and be aware of ways in which lifestyle, the environment, and public policies can promote health.
- *Standard 2: Students will demonstrate the ability to access valid health information and health-promoting products and services.* For example, students will be able to evaluate advertisements, options for health insurance and treatment, and food labels.
- *Standard 3: Students will demonstrate the ability to practice health-enhancing behaviors and reduce health risks.* For example, students will know how to identify responsible and harmful behaviors, develop strategies for good health, and manage stress.
- *Standard 4: Students will analyze the influence of culture, media, technology, and other factors on health.* For example, students will be able to describe and analyze how cultural background and messages from the media, technology, and friends influence health choices.
- *Standard 5: Students will demonstrate the ability to use interpersonal communication skills to enhance health.* For example, students will learn refusal and negotiation skills and conflict resolution strategies.
- *Standard 6: Students will demonstrate the ability to use goal-setting and decision-making skills to enhance health.* For example, students will set reasonable and attainable goals—such as losing a given amount of weight or increasing physical activity—and develop positive decision-making skills.
- *Standard 7: Students will demonstrate the ability to advocate for personal, family, and community health.* For example, students will identify community resources, accurately communicate health information and ideas, and work cooperatively to promote health.

Source: Joint Committee on National Health Education Standards. (1995).

New Standards for a Skills-Based Approach

In 1995, the American Cancer Society sponsored the development of national health education standards that use a skills-based approach to learning (Joint committee on National Health Education Standards, 1995). The standards, summarized below, advocate health literacy that enhances individuals' capacities to obtain, interpret, and understand basic health information and services and their competence to use such information and services in health-enhancing ways (Summerfield, 1995).

Together with the Centers for Disease Control and Prevention's priority health-risk behaviors, the national health education standards provide an important new framework for moving from an information-based school health curriculum to a skills-based curriculum. Skills-based health education engages students and provides a safe environment for students to practice working through health-risk situations that they are likely to encounter as adolescents.

An information-based approach to tobacco use prevention might require students to memorize facts about the health consequences of tobacco use, such as lung cancer, heart disease, and emphysema. In contrast, a skills-based approach ensures that students demonstrate the ability to locate valid information on the effects of tobacco use. Students learn and practice a variety of skills: For example, they use analysis to identify the influences of family, peers, and media on decisions about tobacco use and they use interpersonal communication skills to refuse tobacco use.

The skills-based approach outlined in the national health education standards helps students answer questions and address issues that are important in their lives. For example, young children need to learn how to make friends and deal with bullies. Older children need to practice a variety of strategies to resist pressures to engage in risky health behaviors while maintaining friendships. Early adolescents need to learn how to obtain reliable, straightforward information about the physical, emotional, and social changes of puberty. High school students need to learn to weigh their health-related decisions in terms of their life plans and goals. All students need to learn how to respond to stress, deal with strong feelings in health-enhancing ways, and build a reliable support group of peers and adults.

The Health Education Assessment Project

Standards-based health education requires a new approach to planning, assessment, and instruction. Although many educators are excited about the prospect of standards-based teaching in health education, they may lack a clear picture of what standards-based performance would look like in their classrooms. To address this need, the Council of Chief State School Officers' State Collaborative on Assessment and Student Standards initiated the Health Education Assessment Project in 1993 (see www.ccsso.org/scass).

The Health Education Assessment Project develops standards-based health resources through a collaborative process. Funding for the project comes from the Centers for Disease Control and Prevention and the membership fees of 24 state and local education agencies. During its first decade, the project has built a foundation for a health education assessment system, created an assessment framework, developed and tested a pool of assessment items, and provided professional development and supporting materials to help teachers implement the assessment system and framework.

A skills-based approach to tobacco use prevention ensures that students demonstrate the ability to locate valid information on the effects of tobacco use.

Sample Performance Task: Advocacy for Mental Health

Student Challenge

Your challenge is to select and examine a mental health problem, such as anxiety, depression, eating disorders, suicide ideation, bipolar disorder, or schizophrenia. Your tasks are to

- Locate and analyze valid information sources to determine the causes and symptoms of the problem.
- Explore treatment options and health-enhancing ways of managing the problem.
- Recommend helpful tips for talking with friends or family members who might be experiencing the problem.
- Provide a list of helpful community resources.
- Design a computer-generated brochure or presentation targeted to high school students that includes a summary of your information on causes, symptoms, and management/treatment; tips for talking with others; and a list of community resources.

Assessment Criteria for a Great Presentation

Your work will be assessed using the following criteria. You will be required to

- Provide accurate and in-depth information and draw conclusions about relationships between behaviors and health.
- Cite your information sources accurately and explain why your sources are appropriate.
- Provide specific recommendations for health-enhancing ways of managing stress and ways of talking with others about the problem.
- Demonstrate awareness of your target audience (high school students) and persuade others to make healthy choices.

Additional criteria may be determined by class members.

The project helps educators translate theory into practice. It provides educators with a wide range of assessment items developed in a variety of formats, including selected response, constructed response, and performance tasks (see the sample below). The project provides teacher and student rubrics for assessing performance and examples of student papers for scoring practice. Perhaps the greatest benefit to educators has been the hands-on

professional development opportunities to practice aligning standards, assessment, and instruction for their own classrooms (CCSSO, 2003).

Classrooms in which students are evaluated by health education standards and criteria are substantially different from classrooms in which many teachers have taught and been taught. Teachers need hands-on preparation and experience with planning, implementing, and evaluating curriculum and instruction aligned with standards and assessment. The Health Education Assessment Project can improve the health of students by providing teachers with the tools they need to meet the important health needs of today's youth.

References

Association of State and Territorial Health Officials & Society of State Directors of Health, Physical Education, and Recreation. (2002).*Making the connection: Health and student achievement* (CDROM). Washington, DC: Authors.

Centers for Disease Control and Prevention, Division of Adolescent and School Health. (n.d.). *Health topics* [Online]. Available: www.cdc.gov/nccdphp/dash/risk.htm

Collins, J., Robin, L., Wooley, S., Fenley, D., Hunt, P., Taylor, J., Haber, D., & Kolbe, L. (2002). Programs that work: CDC's guide to effective programs that reduce health risk behavior of youth. *Journal of School Health, 72*(3), 93–99.

Council of Chief State School Officers. (2003). *Improving teaching and learning through the CCSSO-SCASS Health Education Assessment Project.* Washington, DC: Author.

Council of Chief State School Officers & Association of State and Territorial Health Officials. (2002). *Why support a coordinated approach to school health?* Washington, DC: Authors.

Joint Committee on National Health Education Standards. (1995). *National health education standards: Achieving health literacy.* Reston, VA: Association for the Advancement of Health Education.

Kirby, D. (2001). *Emerging answers: Research findings on programs to reduce teen pregnancy.* Washington, DC: The National Campaign to Prevent Teen Pregnancy.

Kolbe, L. J. (2002). Education reform and the goals of modern school health programs. *The State Education Standard, 3*(4), 4–11.

Lohrmann, D. K., & Wooley, S. F. (1998). Comprehensive school health education. In E. Marx & S. F. Wooley (Eds.), *Health is academic: A guide to coordinated school health programs* (pp. 43–66). New York: Teachers College Press.

Summerfield, L. M. (1995). *National standards for health education* (ERIC Digest No. ED 387 483). Washington, DC: ERIC Clearinghouse on Teaching and Teacher Education. Available: www.ericfacility.net/databases/ERIC_Digests/ed387483.html

Beth Pateman is an associate professor at the Institute for Teacher Education, University of Hawaii at Manoa, Honolulu, HI 96822; (808) 956-3885; mpateman@hawaii.edu.

UNIT 4

Identify Social-Emotional Development

Unit Selections

Key Points to Consider

- What is emotional intelligence and how can it be fostered?

- Is sleep deprivation of teens harmful to their health and emotional stability?

- Does stressful living contribute to psychological problems?

- How important is sufficient sleep on the emotional stability of teens?

- What is the overlap between teens who have ADHD and SUD?

- How does exposure to stress effect a teen's mental health and adjustment to problems?

Student Web Site

www.mhcls.com/online

Internet References

Further information regarding these Web sites may be found in this book's preface or online.

Depression–Children and Adolescents
  http://www.nimh.nih.gov/publicat/depchildmenu.cfnm
Teens in Distress Series: Adolescent Stress and Depression
  http://www.extension.umn.edu/distribution/youthdevelopment/DA3083.html

Each age period is associated with developmental tasks. A major aspect of psychosocial development for adolescents is the formation of a coherent personal identity. Erik Erikson referred to this as the adolescent identity crisis. Identity formation is a normative event, but it represents a turning point in human development that has consequences for later psychosocial skills.

Children's identities often represent an identification with parents and significant others. Adolescents reflect on their identity and come to some sense of who they are and who they are not. Identity formation involves an examination of personal likes and dislikes; political, religious, and moral values; occupational interests, as well as gender roles and sexual behaviors. Adolescents must also form an integrated sense of their own personality across the various roles they engage in (e.g., son or daughter, student, boyfriend or girlfriend, part-time worker, etc.).

To aid in the identity formation process, Erikson advocated that adolescents be given a license to explore alternative roles and values. He believed that such a moratorium period would allow adolescents to make commitments that reflect true personal choices. James Marcia elaborated on Erikson's ideas about identity formation. He described four identity statuses that depend on the degree of exploration an adolescent engages in and whether the adolescent makes choices or commitments to certain paths. Adolescents who are actively searching and evaluating options are said to be in a moratorium, as Erikson described. An identity-achieved status eventually is expected to follow this moratorium period. Other adolescents adopt values and life roles without experiencing a period of questioning. These adolescents are called identity-foreclosed, as they essentially conform to parental expectations for themselves. Conformity to parents is not automatically a sign of identity foreclosure, however. Identity-achieved individuals often make choices that fit parental values and expectations, but they do so only after some self-reflection. As a result, they are more invested in their choices and more self-confident. Finally, Marcia describes some adolescents as identity-diffused. These adolescents have not undergone a period of questioning and exploration, nor have they made clear ideological, occupational, or personal commitments. Identity-diffusion is expected in early adolescents, but it is seen as developmentally immature in college-age adolescents.

Erikson also proposed some differences in male and female identity development. Females were presumed to delay full identity development until the formation of an intimate relationship (that is, marriage). Interpersonal issues were seen more paramount in female identity development with the occupational domain being more relevant for male identity development. Recent research indicates that there are fewer gender differences in identity development than may have been true of earlier generations when Erikson did his work (1950s). Modern psychologist Carol Gilligan maintains that moral decision making

Think Stock/Jupiter Images

is another area of gender differences. She argues that females' moral values and moral judgments reflect more concern for interpersonal relationships and for caring about others. Males, she says, have a legalistic outlook which is less compassionate and more focused on the abstract application of rules. Unfortunately, Gilligan's ideas have not been fully tested to date.

An area that has received recent attention is how identity development may differ for minority individuals. In addition to ideological, occupational, sexual, and interpersonal commitments, ethnicity is a salient component that must be integrated into a person's identity. Adolescents may or may not identify with their respective ethnic group, but instead may reject their own ethnicity. Jean Phinney has articulated several phases characteristic of ethnic identity development. Similar to identity foreclosure, some minority adolescents adopt the values of the dominant culture and possess an unexamined ethnic identity. Others are in moratorium and are wrestling with conflicts between the dominant culture and their own culture. Finally, adolescents with an achieved ethnic identity feel an emotional attachment to their ethnic group, and come to some resolution integrating ethnic group values with the dominant culture's values.

Whether a person is male or female, minority or majority, identity issues have implications of emotional health, self-concept, and self-esteem. Adolescents' self-concepts become more and more abstract as they begin to think of themselves in terms of personality traits. They compare themselves to others in order to evaluate their own characteristics and abilities. They often construct an ideal self that is difficult to live up to. The abstract nature of their self-concept means that self-evaluation is more removed from concrete, observable behaviors and, thus, subject to distortion. Adolescents who are struggling with identity issues are also likely to undergo fluctuations in their self-concept as they explore alternative roles, values, and personalities.

Another important aspect of identity is self-esteem, which reflects how good one feels about oneself. The essential question is, "Am I okay?" Self-esteem is at a low point in early adolescence relative to other age periods. In adolescence, more dimensions contribute to self-esteem than is the case in childhood. Global self-esteem measures are often less informative, because adolescents' self-esteem varies in different domains (e.g., physical attractiveness, peer acceptance, academic competence, and athletic competence). Research by Susan Harter and her colleagues indicates that feeling good about one's physical appearance is the number one predictor of overall self-esteem in adolescents. Pubertal changes heighten concern about body image and appearance. Females compared to males are even more concerned about their looks and are much more likely to have a negative body image. Contrary to most expectations, recent studies show that self-esteem in African Americans is comparable to that of Caucasian Americans. Little work on self-esteem has been done in other minority populations.

Many students face social-emotional problems in schools. The first article in this unit explains how schools have become centers for teaching social skills. An important part of emotional stability is proper sleep. Ronald Dahl addresses this important topic. Body image and appearance is examined by Kathiann Kowalski. The next article discusses how stress and stressful life events account for psychological problems. The relationship between ADHD and substance use disorder are examined. The next article in this section addresses the central importance of coping with stress for prevention of adjustment problems. Social-emotional development is influenced by many factors. In the final article Paul Rudnick reports on a mother's story of her struggle with an unattractive daughter. A teen's emotional stability and development is greatly influenced by proper health habits.

Fostering Social-Emotional Learning in the Classroom

Teachers face enormous challenges meeting both the academic and social-emotional needs of learners in their classrooms. In this article we discuss ways in which teachers can promote social-emotional learning. First, we discuss the construct of emotional intelligence and how it can be improved through social-emotional learning. We then review strategies teachers can use to improve learners' emotional, social, and interpersonal problem solving skills.

LINDA K. ELKSNIN AND NICK ELKSNIN

It is estimated that between 15 and 22 percent of U.S. youth have social-emotional difficulties warranting intervention (Cohen, 2001; Mogno & Rosenblitt, 2001). Students at risk for school failure are particularly vulnerable for social-emotional problems. For example, 75 percent of students with learning disabilities (LD) exhibit social skills deficits (Kavale & Forness, 1996), and the U.S. Department of Education (1996) reported that 29 percent of adolescents with disabilities require social skills instruction beyond high school.

Regular education classrooms include ever-increasing numbers of at-risk students. For example, special education students receive most, if not all, of their education in regular education classrooms (U.S. Department of Education, 2001). It is clear that teachers face enormous challenges meeting learners' academic and social-emotional needs. In this article we discuss ways in which teachers can promote social-emotional learning in their classrooms. First we discuss the construct of emotional intelligence and how it can be improved through social-emotional learning. We then review strategies teachers can use to improve learners' emotional, social, and interpersonal problem solving skills.

Emotional Intelligence and Social-Emotional Learning

The term emotional intelligence was first used in 1990 by Salovey and Mayer, who offer this definition:

Emotional intelligence involves the ability to perceive accurately, appraise, and express emotion; the ability to access and/or generate feelings when they facilitate thought; the ability to understand emotion and emotional knowledge; and the ability to regulate emotions to promote emotional and intellectual growth (Mayer & Salovey, 1997).

Goleman (1995) popularized the construct of emotional intelligence in his book, *Emotional Intelligence: Why It Can Matter More Than IQ*. The term EQ, or emotional quotient, was coined by Bar-On (1997) to differentiate emotional intelligence from cognitive intelligence, which is measured by intelligence tests. EQ is thought to be comprised of five domains (Goleman, 1995; Mayer & Salovey, 1997):

- knowing ones' emotions
- managing one's emotions
- motivating oneself
- recognizing emotions of others
- effectively using social skills when interacting with others

Less genetically determined than IQ, emotional intelligence can be taught by teachers and parents. Even more encouraging is that EQ skills overlap, creating a "spillover" effect: Teaching one skill improves other EQ skills. Social-emotional learning (or social-emotional education) involves using procedures and methods to promote EQ.

Within two years after publication of Goleman's book, more than 700 school districts implemented social emotional learning (SEL) programs designed to teach students social-emotional skills (Ratnesar, 1997). SEL programs focus on emotional awareness, social skills, and interpersonal problem solving (Cohen, 2001). In the sections that follow, we discuss ways in which teachers can foster social-emotional learning in their classrooms.

Emotional Awareness

The ability to perceive and understand emotions develops with age. Children as young as three can identify sadness, happiness, and fear using nonverbal cues such as facial expression, gestures, and voice tone (Nabuzoka & Smith, 1995). At this age they begin to understand causes of feelings. However, children who are at risk for school failure may only acquire these skills through direct instruction (Gumpel & Wilson, 1996; Most & Greenbank, 2000). In addition, many children (and some adults) may require help in understanding subtle shifts in emotion represented by family groupings as identified by Bodine and Crawford (1999):

> *Anger: Fury, outrage, resentment,*
> *wrath, exasperation, indignation,*
> *vexation, acrimony, animosity,*
> *annoyance, irritability, hostility*
> *Sadness: Grief, sorrow, cheerlessness,*
> *gloom, melancholy, self-pity,*
> *loneliness, dejection, despair (p. 82)*

Understanding one's own emotions is prerequisite to self control and anger management (Bodine & Crawford, 1999). Understanding the emotions of others is essential if learners are to read social situations accurately and respond to them appropriately. Without emotional understanding, students will misread the behaviors of others. Teachers can help learners increase their emotional understanding by teaching nonverbal communication skills and by becoming emotion coaches.

Nonverbal Communication Skills

Most (i.e., 93%) of emotional meaning is conveyed without words: Fifty-five percent through facial expressions, body posture, and gestures, and thirty-eight percent through tone of voice (Mehrabian, 1968). In order to understand one's emotions and the emotions of others, learners must have adequate nonverbal communication skills. Nowicki and Duke (1992) and Duke, Nowicki, and Martin (1996) identified six areas of nonverbal communication: paralanguage, facial expressions, postures and gestures, interpersonal distance (space) and touch, rhythm and time, and objectics. Instructional goals are for learners to recognize nonverbal messages of others and to effectively express themselves nonverbally. Teachers can reach these goals by using activities described in Table 1.

Paralanguage. Paralanguage is comprised of nonword sounds that convey meaning. Examples include tone of voice, rate of speech, emphasis and variation in speech, and nonverbal sound patterns such as "mmmmmmmm." Learners need to understand how voice tone conveys emotion. In order to avoid cognitive conflict voice tone and words must match. Similarly, learners need to recognize that speech rate conveys emotion. They also should be aware of their own speech rate and be able to adjust it to meet listeners' needs. Emphasis and variation in speech conveys and changes meaning. The sentence "I didn't say you stole the car," takes on different meanings depending on which word is emphasized:

> **I** *didn't say you stole the car.*
> *I* **didn't** *say you stole the car.*
> *I didn't say* **you** *stole the car.*
> *I didn't say you* **stole** *the car.*
> *I didn't say you stole the* **car.**

Facial Expressions. People are expected to look at other's faces during conversation, and learners may need to be taught

Table 1   Activities for Teaching Nonverbal Communication Skills

Area of Nonverbal Communication Paralanguage	Activity
Tone of Voice	Identify emotions when teacher reads sentence using different voice tones.
	Read a script when given different situations surrounding different emotions.
Nonverbal Sound Patterns	Use different types of paralanguage to express feelings.
Rate of Speech	Match rate with emotions such as happy, angry, sad.
	Tape voice and count number of words spoken per minute; compare with others.
Facial Expressions	Demonstrate "resting face."
	Make facial expressions to convey different emotions.
	Identify emotions conveyed by people in public, on TV, and in magazines.
Postures and Gestures	Assemble a dictionary of gestures/postures conveying specific emotions.
	Demonstrate postures under formal/informal situations.
Interpersonal Distance and Touch	Identify types of conversations that should/should not occur in each spatial zone.
	Discuss feelings when personal space is invaded.
	Demonstrate a touch for an emotion when role playing.
Rhythm and Time	Estimate length of time to complete activities.
	Keep track of number of times late or on time.
	Describe examples of public and private time.
Objectics	Develop dress codes for specific situations and use magazine pictures to illustrate.
	Describe image conveyed by dress when observing people in public.
	Develop dictionary of "in" styles.

to engage in eye contact. Ability to read facial expressions is related to understanding that the face includes three zones: forehead and eyes, nose and cheeks, and mouth. Awareness of facial zones and the resting face (a person's unconscious facial expression) can be taught directly.

Postures and Gestures. Learners must learn to interpret postures and gestures and to use them appropriately. For example, the teacher may regard a student as bored and disinterested by how that student sits in class.

Interpersonal Distance (Space) and Touch. Hall (1966) identified four spatial zones among Americans: intimate zone (i.e., nearly touching to 18 inches away), personal zone (i.e., 18 inches to 4 feet away), social zone (i.e., 4 to 12 feet away), and public zone (i.e., 12 feet and more). Learners need to be taught about these zones as violating a zone may result in a serious faux pas. Learners who respect classmates' personal space are more accepted by peers and are less apt to get into difficulty when working with others. Learners also need to know about mental space that holds private topics. Learning to read people to determine if they feel that their mental space has been invaded is a useful skill. Finally, students also must learn what constitutes appropriate and inappropriate touching.

Rhythm and Time. Some principles of rhythm and time students need to understand and practice include being in sync with others, managing time, arriving on time, and knowing the difference between private and public time. Students need to be able to read messages conveyed through others' use of time (e.g., being made to wait in the doctor's office) and have their use of time match the intended message (e.g., spending time with friends means you care about them). Many learners need direct instruction in how to estimate and manage time.

Objectics. Objectics includes style of dress and hair, use of jewelry and cosmetics, and personal hygiene that allow learners to fit in with a group. Learners need to understand the difference between image (self perception) and impression (other's perception of an individual). Objectics are particularly important for young adolescents, whose desire to fit in is overpowering. Teachers and parents should not pretend to understand preadolescent and adolescent fashion rules, but should rely instead on observing children in school and magazines, at the mall, and on TV. Students may need to be taught how to dress to convey their desired image and how to dress for different situations.

Emotion Coaching

Once learners acquire adequate nonverbal communication skills, emotional understanding can be further improved through use of emotion coaching, a technique developed by John Gottman (1997). Teachers and parents acting as emotion coaches can use a five-step process to provide guidance about emotions. Parents and teachers first need to be aware of the learner's emotion. Gottman recommends that adults put the child's situation into an adult context. For example, how we feel when our boss dresses us down during a staff meeting is similar to how a child feels when a teacher reprimands the child in front of the class. Step Two involves recognizing uncomfortable emotions as teaching opportunities and discussing feelings rather than punishing or

criticizing. Emotions are validated rather than evaluated during Step Three. Step Four involves helping the learner label his emotion. The skills learned during nonverbal communication lessons will help learners use words to label how they feel. The final step involves helping the learner solve the problem that led to the feeling. Problem solving is discussed in detail elsewhere in this article.

Social Skills

Adequate interpersonal skills are an important component of emotional intelligence. Types of social skills include interpersonal behaviors needed to make and keep friends, such as joining in and giving compliments; peer-related social skills valued by classmates, such as sharing and working cooperatively; teacher-pleasing social skills related to academic success, such as listening and following directions; self-related behaviors, such as following through and dealing with stress; communication skills such as attending to the speaker and conversational turn taking; and assertiveness skills (Elksnin & Elksnin, 1998). Learners demonstrate two types of social skills problems: acquisition problems and performance problems.

Acquisition Problems

An acquisition problem occurs when a learner lacks specific social skills. Each social skill must be taught directly. Teachers can prepare to teach a social skill by providing the learner with a definition of the skill, the steps required to perform the skill, a rationale for learning the skill, situations in which to use the skill, role play situations in which to practice the skill, and social rules that govern skill use (see Elksnin & Elksnin, 1995).

Social skills are taught during role playing. The teacher first performs each skill step while talking out loud to model cognitive decisions. The teacher then guides the learner through the skill while providing specific, informative feedback to improve performance. Finally, the teacher provides opportunities for the learner to independently practice the skill. Many social skills curricula are available. A well-developed social skills program provides a taxonomy of social skills, along with analyses of skills steps.

Performance Problems

Performance problems occur when the learner knows how to perform the skill yet fails to do so. Causes of performance problems include failure to determine when to use a skill or failure to receive adequate reinforcement for skill use. In the first case, coincidental teaching can be used to encourage students to practice skills. In the second case, classmates can be recruited to praise the learner for using the skill.

Coincidental teaching. Coincidental teaching involves teaching social skills as situations occur in the natural environment (Schulze, Rule, & Innocenti, 1989). Teachers can use coincidental teaching in their classrooms and teach parents to use it at home. The first step is to identify social skills to target during the day and situations that call for skill use. For example, the teacher may identify "sharing" as the target skill and cooperative groups and free play as situations likely to require sharing. After situations are identified, the teacher determines times during the day that are supportive of coincidental teaching. For example, while the teacher is actively monitoring cooperative learning groups may not be the best time to coincidentally teach social skills. Once appropriate situations and times are identified, the teacher looks for opportunities for learners to use the skill, prompts learners to use the skill, and praises learners following skill use. Teaching parents to coincidentally teach provides students with even more practice opportunities (Elksnin & Elksnin, 2000).

Peer reinforcement. Often learners who perform social skills fail to receive reinforcement from classmates. These learners may even be punished for past mistakes (Scott & Nelson, 1998). In these situations, teachers must recruit peer support. Two examples of peer-mediated interventions illustrate the power of the peer group to enhance social skills performance. The first example is positive peer reporting, which involves reinforcing peers with tokens when they publicly praise appropriate social behavior. Jones, Young, and Friman (2000) taught peers to give positive feedback to socially rejected, delinquent adolescents by looking at the learner, smiling, stating a positive thing the learner did or said, and verbally praising the learner. Steps were posted on class bulletin boards as reminders. Peer acceptance of rejected learners improved and the number of positive statements made by their peers increased. In a second study, elementary-aged learners were taught how to recognize socially appropriate behavior (Skinner, Cashwell, & Skinner, 2000). They then were asked to "tootle," or tell the teacher when peers behaved in a socially appropriate manner, rather than "tattle," or tell the teacher when peers did or said something inappropriate. Socially appropriate behavior of students in this fourth-grade classroom increased substantially.

Problem Solving

In addition to possessing adequate social skills, emotionally intelligent learners are effective social problem solvers (Salvin & Madden, 2001). Problem solving can and should be taught, and it is important for teachers to model problem solving by "thinking out loud." Learners can be taught to problem solve using this sequence (D'Zurilla & Goldfried, 1971):

1. Define the problem.
2. Generate possible solutions.
3. Select a solution.
4. Predict outcomes if solution is implemented.
5. Select an alternative solution if predicted outcome is not positive.
6. Evaluate outcome after solution is implemented.
7. Decide what to do in a similar situation.

The FIG TESPN Routine and Social Skill Autopsies are two approaches that incorporate these steps that are especially useful in the classroom.

FIG TESPN Routine. Elias, Tobias, and Friedlander (1999) developed the FIG TESPN Routine as a process parents and children can use to solve social problems. Teachers also can use this routine. The eight steps of FIG TESPN include

1. Feelings cue me to thoughtful action.
2. I have a problem.
3. Goal gives me a guide.
4. Think of things I can do.
5. Envision outcomes.
6. Select my best solution.
7. Plan the procedure, anticipate pitfalls, practice, and pursue it.
8. Notice what happened, and now what?

During Step One, learners are taught that bad feelings signal a problem that needs to be solved. Learners are taught that problems cannot be solved effectively without labeling the emotion or the bad feeling. The teacher can use many of the strategies discussed earlier to increase emotional understanding. Step Two emphasizes that the learner "owns" the problem. He may not have caused the problem, but it is his responsibility to solve it. During this step, learners also learn that actions, not feelings, solve problems. Step Three focuses on goal setting to direct actions and reduce stress. Learners generate possible solutions during Step Four. Learners are taught that every action has consequences during Step Five. Based on predicted outcomes learners select a solution to the problem during Step Six. The original problem is revisited at this point. Step Seven emphasizes that problems are likely to occur when implementing any plan. By anticipating problems before implementing a plan, learners are less likely to become discouraged. During the final step of FIG TESPN, learners self-evaluate and are taught that not all plans will be successful. Several curricula that focus on interpersonal problem solving also are available.

Social Skill Autopsies. Lavoie (1994) recommends using social skill autopsies after the learner experiences a negative (or positive) social outcome. Autopsies involve analyzing the events surrounding a social outcome by asking the learner what she did, what happened when she did it, and what she will do in a similar situation based upon the positive or negative direction of the outcome. Autopsies should only be conducted privately and only after the learner has dealt with her emotions. For this reason, they can be used as part of the emotion coaching process. The obvious advantage of social skill autopsies is that they can be used any time and any place. If school personnel and parents "autopsy" social behavior, learners will become more skillful interpersonal problem solvers.

Conclusion

Emotional intelligence may be as important as, or even more important than, cognitive intelligence. Many learners, particularly those at risk for school failure, do not possess the social-emotional skills needed to be emotionally intelligent. However, these skills can and should be taught. In this article we reviewed ways in which teachers can improve learners' emotional understanding, social skills, and interpersonal problem-solving ability. Social-emotional learning enables learners to effectively "understand, process, manage, and express the social and emotional aspects of [their] lives" (Cohen, 2001).

References

Bar-On, R. (1997). BarOn Emotional Quotient Inventory, user's manual. Toronto, ON: MultiHealth Systems, Inc.

Bodine, R. J., & Crawford, D. K. (1999). Developing emotional intelligence. Champaign, IL: Research Press.

Camp, B. W., & Bash, M. A. S. (1985a). Think aloud, grades 1–2. Champaign, IL: Research Press.

Camp, B. W., & Bash, M. A. S. (1985b). Think aloud, grades 3–4. Champaign, IL: Research Press.

Camp, B. W., & Bash, M. A. S. (1985c). Think aloud, grades 5–6. Champaign, IL: Research Press.

Cartledge, G., & Kleefeld, J. (1991). Taking part. Circle Pines, MN: American Guidance Service.

Cartledge, G., & Kleefeld, J. (1994). Working together. Circle Pines, MN: American Guidance Service.

Cohen, J. (Ed.). (2001). Caring classrooms/intelligent schools: The social emotional education of young children. NY: Teachers College Press.

Coombs-Richardson, R., Evans, E. T., & Meisgeier, C. H. (1996a). Connecting with others, K-2. Champaign, IL: Research Press.

Coombs-Richardson, R., Evans, E. T., & Meisgeier, C. H. (1996b). Connecting with others, 3–5. Champaign, IL: Research Press.

Coombs-Richardson, R., Evans, E. T., & Meisgeier, C. H. (1996c). Connecting with others, 6–8. Champaign, IL: Research Press.

Duke, M. P., Nowicki, S., Jr., & Martin, E. A. (1996). Teaching your child the language of social success. Atlanta, GA: Peachtree.

Dygdon, J. (1993). CLASSIC. Brandon, VT: Clinical Psychology Publishing Company.

D'Zurilla, T. J., & Goldfried, M. R. (1971). Problem solving and behavior modification. Journal of Abnormal Psychology, 78(1), 107–126.

Elias, M. J., Tobias, S. E., & Friedlander, B. S. (1999). Emotionally intelligent parenting. New York: Harmony Books.

Elksnin, L. K., & Elksnin, N. (1995). Assessment and instruction of social skills. San Diego: Singular.

Elksnin, L. K., & Elksnin, N. (1998). Teaching social skills to students with learning and behavior problems. Intervention in School and Clinic, 33, 131–140.

Elksnin, L. K., & Elksnin, N. (2000). Teaching parents to teach their children to be prosocial. Intervention in School and Clinic, 36, 27–35.

Goldstein, A. P. (1997). The PREPARE curriculum. Champaign, IL: Research Press.

Goldstein, A. P., & McGinnis, E. (1997). Skill-streaming the adolescent. Champaign, IL: Research Press.

Goleman, D. L. (1995). Emotional intelligence: Why it can matter more than IQ. New York: Bantam Books.

Gottman, J. (1997). Raising an emotionally intelligent child. New York: Simon & Schuster.

Gumpel, T., & Wilson, M. (1996). Application of a Rasch analysis to the examination of the perception of facial affect among persons with mental retardation. Research in Developmental Disabilities, 17(2), 161–171.

Hall, E. (1966). The hidden dimension. New York: Doubleday.

Hazel, J. S., Schumaker, J. B., Sherman, J. A., & Sheldon, J. (1996). ASSET. Champaign, IL: Research Press.

Jones, K. M., Young, M. M., & Friman, P. C. (2000). Increasing peer praise of socially rejected delinquent youth: Effects on cooperation and acceptance. School Psychology Review, 15, 30–39.

Kavale, K. A., & Forness, S. R. (1996). Social skills deficits and learning disabilities: A meta-analysis. Journal of Learning Disabilities, 29, 226–237.

Lavoie, R. (Producer). (1994). Learning disabilities and social skills with Richard Lavoie: Last one picked . . . first one picked on. Washington, DC: WETA.

Mannix, D. (1993). Social skills activities for special children. West Nyack, NY: Center for Applied Research in Education.

Mayer, J. D., & Salovey, P. (1997). What is emotional intelligence? In P. Salovey & D. J. Sluyter (Eds.), Emotional development and emotional intelligence: Educational implications (pp. 3–31). New York: Basic Books.

McGinnis, E., & Goldstein, A. R. (1997). Skill-streaming the elementary school child. Champaign, IL: Research Press.

McGinnis, E., & Goldstein, A. P. (2003). Skill-streaming in early childhood. Champaign, IL: Research Press.

Mehrabian, A. (1968). Communication without words. Psychology Today, 24, 52–55.

Most, T., & Greenbank, A. (2000). Auditory, visual, and auditory-visual perception of emotions by adolescents with and without learning disabilities, and their relationship to social skills. Learning Disabilities Research & Practice, 15, 171–178.

Mugno, D., & Rosenblitt, D. (2001). Helping emotionally vulnerable children: Moving toward an empathic orientation in the classroom. In J. Cohen (Ed.), Caring classrooms/intelligent schools: The social emotional education of young children (pp. 59–76). NY: Teachers College Press.

Nabuzoka, D., & Smith, K. (1995). Identification of expressions of emotions by children with and without learning disabilities. Learning Disabilities Research & Practice, 10, 91–101.

Nowicki, S., Jr., & Duke, M. P. (1992). Helping the child who doesn't fit in. Atlanta, GA: Peachtree.

Ratnesar, R. (1997, September). Teaching feelings 101. Time, XXX, 62.

Salovey, P., & Mayer, J. D. (1990). Emotional intelligence. Imagination, Cognition, & Personality, 9, 185–211.

Salovey, P., & Sluyter, D. J. (Eds.). (1997). Emotional development and emotional intelligence: Educational implications. New York: Basic Books.

Schulze, K. A., Rule, S., & Innocenti, M. S. (1989). Coincidental teaching: Parents promoting social skills at home. Teaching Exceptional Children, 21, 24–27.

Scott, T. M., & Nelson, C. M. (1998). Confusion and failure in facilitating generalized social responding in the school setting: Sometimes 2 + 2 = 5. Behavioral Disorders, 23(4), 264–275.

Skinner, C. H., Cashwell, T. H., & Skinner, A. L. (2000). Increasing tottling: Effects of a peer-monitored group contingency program on students' reports of peers' prosocial behaviors. Psychology in the Schools, 37, 263–270.

Slavin, R. E., & Madden, N. A.(2001). One million children: Success for all. Thousand Oaks, CA: Corwin.

Shure, M. B. (2001a). I can problem solve, elementary. Champaign, IL: Research Press.

Shure, M. B. (2001b). I can problem solve, kindergarten. Champaign, IL: Research Press.

Shure, M. B. (2001c). I can problem solve, preschool. Champaign, IL: Research Press.

Stephens, T. M. (1992). Social skills in the classroom (2nd ed.). Odessa, FL: Psychological Assessment Resources.

U.S. Department of Education (1996). Eighteenth annual report to Congress on the implementation of The Individuals with Disabilities Education Act. Washington, DC: Author.

U.S. Department of Education (2001). Twenty-third annual report to Congress on the implementation of the Individuals with Disabilities Education Act. Washington, DC: Author.

Waksman, S., & Waksman, D. D. (1998). Waksman social skills curriculum. Austin, TX: PRO-ED.

The Consequences of Insufficient Sleep for Adolescents

Links Between Sleep and Emotional Regulation

Any review of adolescent lifestyles in our society will reveal more than a dozen forces converging to push the sleep/arousal balance away from sleep and toward ever-higher arousal. What harm could there be in trying to push back a little toward valuing sleep? The potential benefits, according to Dr. Dahl, seem enormous.

RONALD E. DAHL

A dolescents often "get by" with relatively little sleep, but it may be far less than they need. The observations of many parents, educators, and clinicians are in close agreement with a wealth of scientific data about the growing frequency of this worrisome pattern of behavior. As discussed in other articles in this special section, there has been recent progress in understanding many of the factors that contribute to adolescent sleep loss, including the role of early school starting times and the role of various biological and social influences on adolescents' self-selected bedtimes.

The increasing evidence that teenagers seem to be getting less sleep leads inevitably to the pragmatic question "How much sleep do adolescents really need?" Unfortunately, the medical/scientific answer to this question seems tautological. Sufficient sleep is defined as "the amount necessary to permit optimal daytime functioning."

As impractical as that answer may appear, there are two important reasons for such a definition. First, sleep requirements can be remarkably different across individuals. Second, at a physiological level, sleep and waking states are closely intertwined aspects of a larger system of arousal regulation. (Sleep researchers often use the Chinese symbol of yin/yang to designate the interrelationship of sleep/wake states.)

At the center of this discussion is a critical and pragmatic point: any evaluation of the sleep habits of adolescents must include a careful consideration of the *waking consequences* of sleep loss. The question becomes, in essence, "What are the daytime signs of diminished functioning that indicate insufficient sleep?" While there is a shortage of well-controlled research studies that seek to answer this question, this article focuses on the convergence

of evidence suggesting that *changes in mood and motivation are among the most important effects of sleep loss.* Thus an important place to begin looking for evidence of insufficient sleep among adolescents is in the area of emotional or behavioral difficulties.

There is no shortage of epidemiological and clinical studies documenting recent increases in the rates of many psychiatric disorders among adolescents. Certainly many complex factors are likely to have contributed to the emotional and behavioral problems of teenagers, but the possible link to adolescent sleep patterns bears some scrutiny. There is clear evidence that sleep loss *can* lead to the development or exacerbation of behavioral and emotional problems.[1] The key question is "How great is the contribution of sleep deprivation to these problems?" The magnitude of this link remains an open question that can only be answered through careful empirical research.

In the meantime, these issues have enormous ramifications for the fields of medicine and education with regard both to the physical and mental health of adolescents and to detriments to effective learning and social development. Many policy decisions will be influenced by our understanding and interpretation of the importance of sleep in these areas.

In this article I provide an overview of current scientific and clinical information regarding the consequences of insufficient sleep in adolescents. I pay particular attention to links between sleep and emotional regulation. The following is a brief outline of the main points to be presented:

1. *Sleepiness.* This is the most direct consequence of adolescent sleep loss, and it manifests itself most significantly in difficulty getting up on time for school

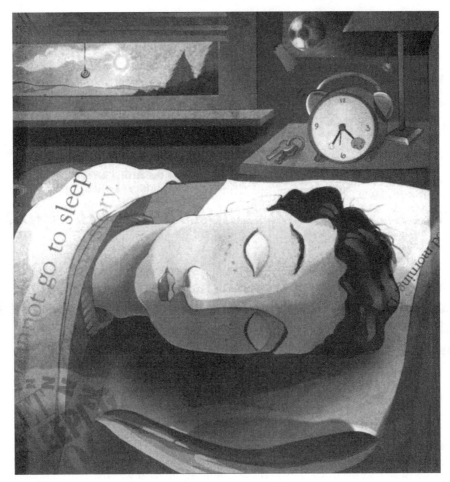

Illustration by Brenda Grannan

and in falling asleep in school. These problems can further contribute to conflicts with parents and teachers and to poor self-esteem. Sleepiness is also associated with a strong tendency toward brief mental lapses (or microsleeps) that greatly increase the risk of motor vehicle and other kinds of accidents.

2. *Tiredness.* This is a symptom of sleep loss and includes changes in motivation—particularly difficulty initiating behaviors related to long-term or abstract goals and decreased persistence in working toward goals.

3. *Mood, attention, and behavior.* Sleep loss can have negative effects on the control of mood, attention, and behavior. Irritability, moodiness, and low tolerance for frustration are the most frequently described symptoms in sleep-deprived adolescents. However, in some situations, sleepy teenagers are more likely to appear silly, impulsive, or sad.

4. *Impact of emotional and behavioral problems.* Emotional arousal and distress can cause both difficulty falling asleep and sleep disruptions. Behavioral problems and family chaos can contribute to even later bedtimes and to sleep schedules that are ever more incompatible with school schedules.

5. *Bi-directional effects.* There are bi-directional effects between sleep and behavioral/emotional problems. It

can be difficult at times to identify the causal links. For example, a depressed adolescent with severe sleep problems may be showing sleep disturbances that stem from depression or mood problems that stem from sleep disruption. Sleep loss can also contribute to a negative spiral or vicious cycle of deterioration. That is, sleep loss can have a negative effect on mood and behavior, which leads to subsequent emotional/behavioral difficulties that further interfere with sleep. This produces a sequence of negative effects in both domains. In some clinical cases, such negative spirals appear to be a pathway to withdrawal from school or serious psychiatric problems.

The Need for Sleep: An Overview

Before discussing the specific consequences of insufficient sleep in adolescents, it is necessary to begin with a general overview on what sleep is and why it is necessary at all.

Sleep is *not* simply rest. Mere rest does not create the restorative state of having slept. (Anyone who doubts this should try the following experiment tonight: spend eight hours resting in bed, with eyes closed, body relaxed, mind floating, in a deeply tranquil state, but without ever going to sleep; then keep track of your mood and performance tomorrow.) The fundamental difference between sleep and a deeply relaxed wakefulness is that sleep involves dropping into a state with a relative *loss of awareness of and responsiveness to the external world*. This state of unresponsiveness appears to be necessary for the restorative processes that occur during sleep to take place.

Furthermore, sleep itself is an *active* process. Sleep involves dynamically changing patterns and progressive stages, with some brain regions showing a great deal of activity in some sleep stages. Moreover, there are several aspects of sleep necessary for full restoration, including the continuity, timing, and patterning of different stages of sleep, as well as the timing of the sleep in relation to other biological rhythms.

For example, if subjects are permitted a full night's sleep but are awakened every 15 minutes for brief periods, on the following day they will report tiredness, fatigue, and emotional changes similar to having obtained insufficient amounts of sleep. Similarly, if subjects are permitted as much sleep as they need but are selectively deprived of one sleep stage—such as REM (rapid eye movement) sleep or delta sleep—they also report daytime consequences. And, as anyone who has experienced jet lag can attest, sleep that occurs at the wrong circadian phase is often fragmented and inefficient at restoration.

Sleep is not some biological luxury. Sleep is essential for basic survival, occurring in every species of living creature that has ever been studied. Animals deprived of sleep die. (Experiments with rats show that they can survive without sleep for about as long as they can survive without food.) Yet the specific function of sleep—*why* it is necessary for survival—remains a scientific mystery and the focus of a great deal of investigation.

Within this scientific mystery, however, are two important clues that are relevant to discussions of sleep and adolescent health. First, sleep seems to be particularly important during periods of brain maturation. (Across species, maturing individuals sleep more than fully mature individuals.) Second, sleep is naturally restricted to times and places that feel safe. Most species have evolved mechanisms to ensure that sleep is limited to such safe places as burrows and nests and to times of relative safety from predators. In humans, there is a similar tendency for safe feelings to promote sleep while feelings of threat or stress tend to inhibit sleep.

These links between sleep and stress are an important source of sleep disruption among adolescents. A key point can be best illustrated by a brief consideration of the evolutionary underpinnings of these biological links between sleep and emotion. For most of early human history, large nocturnal-hunting carnivores surrounded our ancestors, who had no access to physically safe sleep sites. (Humans cannot sleep in trees or on cliff edges, because we lose all muscle tone during REM sleep.) In the human ancestral environment, the main protection against predators was a close-knit social group. The human brain evolved under conditions that made this sense of social belonging and social connectedness the basis for feelings of relative safety. Natural tendencies in the human brain continue to reflect these links, so that fears of social rejection can evoke powerful feelings of threat and so lead to sleep disruption, while feelings of love, caring, and social connection create a feeling of safety and so promote sleep.

Finally, it is important to consider the ways in which the sleep and vigilance systems change during adolescent development. The maturation of humans during puberty includes physical and mental changes in preparation for taking on adult roles (with increased demands for threat appraisal and response). Changes in the vigilance system include a greater capacity for sleep disruptions from social stresses, including fears, anxieties, and emotional arousal.[2] Thus adolescent sleep systems appear to become more vulnerable to stress at a time when social turmoil and difficulties are often increasing.

Consequences of Insufficient Sleep in Adolescents

There is a surprising lack of controlled studies examining the effects of sleep deprivation or insufficient sleep among adolescents. However, there is extensive circumstantial evidence, clinical evidence, and research in adults that is relevant to these questions. While there is a general convergence of these findings, one important caveat is that we need a greater number of direct investigations. A second note of caution is that we lack information about *long-term* or *chronic* effects of insufficient sleep, since the limited data available have addressed only the immediate and short-term effects of sleep loss.

In brief, there are four main effects of acute sleep loss: 1) sleepiness, 2) motivational aspects of tiredness, 3) emotional changes, and 4) alterations in attention and performance. Before discussing each of these briefly, I wish to stress one general principle that applies across categories: the influence of *effort*. That is, the effects of sleep deprivation can be offset or even overridden for *short* periods of time by increased effort (or by increasing the external motivation to perform through rewards or punishments). The good news here is that most capabilities can be maintained over a short interval if necessary, while the bad news is that everything is harder to do. In some ways this is the cardinal feature of sleep deprivation: it takes increased effort to perform the same cognitive, emotional, or physical tasks.

1. *Sleepiness.* The most obvious and direct effect of inadequate sleep is a feeling of sleepiness. Sleepiness is most problematic during periods of low stimulation, such as in the classroom, when reading or driving, or when doing repetitive activities. Highly stimulating activities—particularly those involving physical activity or emotional arousal—can often mask moderate levels of sleepiness. Thus many sleep-deprived adolescents report that they can stay out very late at night and not feel tired, whereas if they were to lie quietly reading a book, they would fall asleep in minutes.

Another important aspect of sleepiness is the tendency toward brief mental lapses or micro-sleeps. Often, an individual is not even aware of these short gaps in awareness and responsiveness. However, such a lapse in the midst of driving, operating machinery, or doing anything else that requires vigilance can have dire consequences.

Several indirect consequences of sleepiness are also worth mentioning. These include adolescent conflicts with parents and teachers that arise from the difficulty of getting up in the morning or the ease of falling asleep in class; increased use of stimulants (particularly caffeine and nicotine); and synergistic effects with alcohol (the impairments from a combination of alcohol and sleepiness appear to be more than additive, resulting in a deadly combination of influences).

2. *Tiredness.* A separate symptom of sleep loss that can be defined as a feeling of fatigue or decreased motivation is tiredness. Tiredness makes it difficult to initiate (and persist at) certain types of behavior (especially tasks deemed boring or tedious). The effects of tiredness are less apparent when performing tasks that are naturally engaging, exciting, or threatening—perhaps because it is easier to recruit extra effort to offset tiredness. Conversely, the effects of tiredness are more pronounced for tasks that require motivation to be derived from abstract goals or consequences (e.g., reading or studying uninteresting material in order to increase the chances of attaining some future reward).

Tedious tasks without the imminent prospect of reward (or fear of immediate consequences) are much more difficult to initiate and complete when one has been deprived of sleep. Similarly, tasks that require planning, strategy, or a complex sequence of steps to complete are more difficult when one is tired. This general category of tasks (requiring motivation linked to abstract goals, delayed rewards/consequences, planning, strategy, and so on) involves abstract processing areas in the front of the brain (regions of the prefrontal cortex) that appear to be particularly sensitive to sleep deprivation.[3] The potential relevance of these types of motivational changes to educational goals and processes seems obvious.

3. *Emotional changes.* The emotional changes that are secondary effects of sleep loss are very important but very complex. There are at least three factors that make this a complicated area for investigators: 1) the emotional effects of sleep deprivation appear to be highly variable across individuals and across situations, 2) emotion and emotional regulation are very hard to measure accurately, and 3) there are bi-directional interactions between mood and sleep disturbances (this third aspect was noted above and will be addressed separately below).

One of the main sources of information in this area comes from clinical descriptions of children and adolescents with various sorts of sleep disorders or transient sleep disruptions. There are also a few studies (including ongoing research in our laboratory) that obtain measures of emotion before, during, and after a single night of sleep deprivation, and then again following a recovery sleep.

The major theme across these studies is evidence suggesting *mood lability.* Not only does there appear to be greater variability in emotional states following sleep loss, but there also appears to be less control over emotional responses in many adolescents. For example, if faced with a frustrating task, a sleep-deprived teenager is more likely to become angry or aggressive. Yet, in response to something humorous, the same subject might act more silly or inane. Several adolescents reported increased crying reactions during sad scenes in videotaped movies when they were sleep-deprived. Many subjects reported increased irritability, impatience, and low tolerance for frustration when asked to perform tedious computer tasks. In general, these findings often looked like a decrease in inhibition or conscious control over emotions following sleep loss. It is also important to point out that some subjects seemed to show no measurable changes in any emotion when sleep-deprived.

These results are quite preliminary, include a high degree of variability across individuals, and will require replication with larger samples to establish statistical significance. However, these findings fit very well within a general pattern of similar observations regarding *effortful control.* That is, the primary emotional changes following sleep loss suggest a decrease in the ability to control, inhibit, or modify emotional responses to bring them into line with long-term goals, social rules, or other learned principles. Effortful control over emotion involves regions of the prefrontal cortex of the brain that are similar to those discussed previously with regard to abstract goals.

Changes in emotional regulation that result in decreased control following sleep loss could have serious consequences in terms of many high-risk behaviors among adolescents. The inability to control emotional responses could influence aggression, sexual behavior, the use of alcohol and drugs, and risky driving. Clearly, additional research will be needed to better delineate these complex but important issues relevant to adolescent health.

4. *Changes in attention and performance.* Following sleep loss, changes in attention and performance also represent a complex area of investigation in children and adolescents. There are three main points. First, sleep loss is associated with brief mental lapses in attention during simple tasks that can be partially offset by increased effort or motivation. Second, sleep deprivation can sometimes mimic or exacerbate symptoms of ADHD (attention deficit/hyperactivity disorder), including distractibility, impulsivity, and difficulty with effortful control of attention. Third, there is also emerging evidence that sleep deprivation has marked influences on the ability to perform complex tasks or tasks that require attention in two or more areas at the same time.

While the first point about brief mental lapses has already been addressed, the latter two points warrant some discussion. A potential link between ADHD symptoms and sleep deprivation has received considerable discussion from several investigators.[4] Both ADHD and sleep deprivation are associated with difficulty with self-control of behavior, attention, and impulses. Both ADHD and the daytime symptoms of sleep deprivation will often respond to stimulant medication. Furthermore, ADHD symptoms are more frequent in children with sleep disorders, and there has been some reported improvement in ADHD symptoms in children following treatment of sleep problems. Finally, other studies have reported increased rates of sleep complaints and disorders in children diagnosed with ADHD. This is a very complex area, and disentangling the connections and relative contributions across these domains will require additional careful studies.

One pragmatic recommendation, however, is quite simple. For any child or adolescent who exhibits symptoms of ADHD, the importance of a good night's sleep and a regular sleep/wake schedule should be emphasized to avoid the consequences of sleep loss that could exacerbate symptoms.

One of the most interesting areas of study is evidence that some types of complex tasks may be particularly sensitive to the effects of sleep deprivation. James Horne has presented extensive evidence showing that dual tasks and tasks that require creative or flexible thinking are sensitive to sleep loss.[5] (These tasks all require abstract processing in areas of the prefrontal cortex.) Our own research group has generated similar findings in its examination of dual tasks following sleep deprivation in adolescents and young adults. For example, students with one night of sleep deprivation exhibited no significant changes in performance on a difficult computer task and showed no effect on postural balance. However, when the students performed both tasks simultaneously, sleep deprivation had a marked effect on balance.[6] In recent pilot studies we have also found the same pattern of results in adolescents performing cognitive and emotional tasks. Performance at either task could be maintained following sleep deprivation—but not both.

On one hand, detriments in performing a dual task (like controlling thoughts and feelings at the same time) might sound like an esoteric or subtle effect of sleep deprivation; on the other hand, it is important to point out that fluency in such dual tasks is the foundation of social competence. These are the daily challenges that must be balanced in the everyday life of adolescents: thinking and solving problems while navigating the emotional reactions of complex social situations, using self-control over impulses and emotions while pursuing goals, experiencing anger yet weighing the long-term consequences of actions. If further research substantiates the marked effects of insufficient sleep on these types of complex tasks in adolescents, then we should have significant concerns about the importance of sleep patterns in the normal development of social competence.

Sleep and Emotional Disorders in Adolescents

It is essential to underscore the complex intersection between sleep regulation and behavioral and emotional problems in adolescents. Clearly, there are two-way interactions between these systems. The regulation and timing of sleep can be altered by behavioral or emotional disorders, while cognitive, behavioral, and emotional control during daytime hours can be influenced by the way adolescents sleep. Furthermore, daytime activities, changes in the environment, and stressful events can have profound transient effects on sleeping patterns in the absence of any clear-cut psychopathology. In addition, medications used to treat psychiatric disorders often affect sleep, and sleep loss can exacerbate mood and behavioral symptoms.

Perhaps the best-studied example of such interactions is the relationship between sleep and depression. Subjective sleep complaints are very common in children and adolescents who have been diagnosed with Major Depressive Disorder (MDD). Symptoms include insomnia (75% of cases) and hypersomnia (25%). Hypersomnia difficulties are reported more frequently after puberty. Insomnia symptoms usually include difficulty falling asleep and a subjective sense of not having slept deeply all night.

Recently, clinicians and researchers have seen increasing numbers of adolescents with overlapping phase delay disorders or other sleep/wake schedule disorders associated with depression. Depressed adolescents frequently have difficulty falling asleep, are unable to get up or refuse to go to school, sleep until late in the day, complain of extreme daytime fatigue, and, over time, shift to increasingly more delayed sleep/wake schedules. Likewise, surveys reveal that adolescents who get less than 6¾ hours of sleep each school night or report more than a two-hour difference between school night and weekend bedtimes have a higher level of complaints of depressed mood than adolescents who get more sleep or who sleep on more regular sleep/wake schedules.

Clinicians who are experienced with these problems have pointed out that in many cases it is difficult to differentiate decreased motivation, school refusal/anxiety, delayed circadian phase, attention difficulties, and depressive symptomatology. Clearly, both sleep patterns and behavioral symptoms must be carefully assessed in an effort to prevent the problems, diagnose them accurately, and plan successful treatment.

There is also evidence of changes in the sleeping electroencephalograms (EEGs) of depressed adolescents, including increased time to fall asleep and altered patterns of REM sleep. Furthermore, changes in EEG measures of sleep predicted an increased recurrence of depressive episodes during longitudinal follow-ups in early adulthood.[7]

In some cases, treatment of sleep complaints and problems—including regularizing the sleep/wake schedule, cognitive behavioral therapy for insomnia, and short-term treatment with medication for severe insomnia—can have a positive impact on depressive symptoms.[8] On the other hand, effective treatment of depression can also be a critical aspect of improving sleep.

Negative Spirals?

As I described above, one area of concern with regard to the interconnections between sleep and emotional disturbances is the potential for a progressive sequence or spiral of negative effects. Insufficient sleep can amplify emotional difficulties, which can then produce further sources of distress and increased disruption of sleep. The reason for this concern arises more from clinical experience than from any controlled studies, and so the concern is perhaps best illustrated by describing a case.

Jay had a history of poor sleep habits (e.g., bedtimes past midnight, erratic sleep/wake schedule) beginning in about seventh grade. In ninth grade the problems became worse as he struggled to get to sleep at night (usually falling asleep at 1 a.m.) and to wake up in the morning and then had problems with distractibility and behavior at school. He also reported some symptoms of depression, including loss of interest in some activities, daytime fatigue, and worsening performance at school. His symptoms improved transiently in the summer, when he slept from 3 a.m. until noon.

In 10th grade Jay began attending a high school that started at 7:30 a.m., which required him to wake up at 6 a.m. to meet the school bus at 6:30 a.m. He had a very difficult time getting up for school at that hour because his average bedtime was 2 a.m. He made several attempts to go to bed earlier but found himself unable to fall asleep. He was never able to follow through in a way that would permit him to establish an earlier pattern of bedtime, and he quickly reverted to his 3 a.m.-to-noon sleep schedule on all weekends and holidays. Jay sometimes stayed up working at his computer or watching television—he says this was because he hated the feeling of lying in bed trying unsuccessfully to fall asleep. Before long, he was regularly missing school or arriving late and falling asleep in class.

Jay, who had at one time been identified as a gifted student, was failing most of his classes and appeared increasingly lethargic, subdued, and uninterested in school. His school counselor referred him to a mental health clinic. Over the course of several months, he was diagnosed as having depression with some ADHD symptoms (e.g., difficulty finishing tasks, distractibility). Trials of antidepressants and stimulant medication resulted in small transient improvements in some symptoms, but Jay was never able to reestablish good sleep patterns that were compatible with his school schedule. Eventually he withdrew from school, became increasingly depressed and withdrawn, and was hospitalized after a serious suicide attempt.

At the time of hospitalization, Jay had severe chronic insomnia and a major depressive disorder. Despite multiple interventions, these problems persisted. He showed very little motivation to return to school and appeared to have chronic depressive symptoms. At discharge his long-term prognosis was not promising.

In a case such as Jay's, it is impossible to disentangle the relative contributions of the sleep and mood dysregulations. While no general conclusions can be drawn from this single case, it does illustrate the complexity of these interactions and the importance of obtaining a better understanding in these areas.

Policy Decisions for Today and Direction for the Future

Frequently in this article I have cautioned readers about the need for additional research to improve our understanding of the complex issues arising from the consequences of insufficient sleep among adolescents. Our current knowledge is preliminary and based on a paucity of controlled data. Furthermore, we are probably at an equally early stage in our understanding of the behavioral and emotional problems of adolescents.

Nonetheless, behavioral and emotional difficulties are currently the largest source of morbidity and mortality among adolescents. While it is possible that sleep loss makes only a minuscule contribution to adolescents' problems with emotional regulation, it is extremely likely that it plays some role. It is also quite possible that insufficient sleep plays a significant role in leading up to some of these problems in a vulnerable set of individuals.

Identifying vulnerability to sleep loss may represent an important future direction for research, since there appear to be such large individual differences in the effects of acute sleep loss. Such vulnerability could be related to a tendency to need more sleep, to being a "night owl," or to a biological vulnerability toward emotional disorders.

Clearly, more research is needed to help inform policy makers, whose decisions will further affect adolescent sleep patterns. Cost-benefit analyses regarding the relative importance of sleep will require more precise quantification in these areas. In the meantime, one might make a reasonable case that the odds are heavily in favor of sleep as an increasingly important health concern among adolescents.

To reiterate the main point with which I began, adequate sleep is defined as the amount necessary for optimal daytime functioning. It appears that the potentially fragile underpinnings of adolescent social competence (controlling thoughts and feelings at the same time) may be most sensitive to the effects of inadequate sleep. Any review of adolescent lifestyles in our society will reveal more than a dozen forces converging to push the sleep/arousal balance away from sleep and toward ever-higher arousal. What harm could there be in trying to push back a little toward valuing sleep? The potential benefits seem enormous.

Notes

1. Ronald E. Dahl, "The Regulation of Sleep and Arousal: Development and Psychopathology," *Development and Psychopathology,* vol. 8, 1996, pp. 3–27.

2. Ronald E. Dahl et al., "Sleep Onset Abnormalities in Depressed Adolescents," *Biological Psychiatry,* vol. 39, 1996, pp. 400–410.

3. James A. Horne, "Human Sleep, Sleep Loss, and Behaviour Implications for the Prefrontal Cortex and Psychiatric Disorder," *British Journal of Psychiatry,* vol. 162, 1993, pp. 413–19.

4. Ronald D. Chervin et al., "Symptoms of Sleep Disorders, Inattention, and Hyperactivity in Children," *Sleep,* vol. 20, 1997, pp. 1185–92.

5. Horne, op. cit.

6. Abigail Schlesinger, Mark S. Redfern, Ronald E. Dahl, and J. Richard Jennings, "Postural Control, Attention and Sleep Deprivation," *Neuroreport,* vol. 9, 1998, pp. 49–52.

7. Uma Rao et al., "The Relationship Between Longitudinal Clinical Course and Sleep and Cortisol Changes in Adolescent Depression," *Biological Psychiatry,* vol. 40, 1996, pp. 474–84.

8. Ronald E. Dahl, "Child and Adolescent Sleep Disorders," in idem, ed., *Child and Adolescent Psychiatric Clinics of North America: Sleep Disorder* (Philadelphia: W. B. Saunders, 1996).

RONALD E. DAHL, M.D., is an associate professor of psychiatry and pediatrics at the University of Pittsburgh Medical Center, Pittsburgh, Pa.

From *Phi Delta Kappan* by Ronald E. Dahl, Vol. 80, No. 5, January 1999, pp. 354–359. Copyright © 1999 by Phi Delta Kappan. Reprinted by permission of the publisher and Ronald E. Dahl.

Body Image: How Do You See Yourself?

How you feel about your body has a big impact on your health. Learn to like the person you see in the mirror!

KATHIANN M. KOWALSKI

Brianna slipped quietly out of the house before dawn. She had lost 30 pounds by dieting, but now the weight was creeping back. She decided to try non-stop exercising for three days. Brianna wasn't thinking about missing school or even being alone by herself on the street. She would start walking and just keep going.

Fifteen hours later, Brianna walked into a police station. Her feet ached, and her sweat-pants were covered with burrs from wandering through a park. She was exhausted, scared, and hungry.

A poor body image had led to Brianna's eating disorder and depression. Her grand exercise plan failed, but it had one good outcome. Brianna finally got help dealing with her problem.

What You See and Feel

Body image is the way you see your body and how you feel about it. People with a healthy body image view themselves realistically and like their physical selves. People with a poor body image feel dissatisfied with their bodies, regardless of whether they are objectively healthy.

Different factors influence a teen's body image. "Certainly the media are setting standards for how girls and boys should look, defining what is beautiful in our culture," says Mimi Nichter. When the University of Arizona professor interviewed girls for her book, *Fat Talk: What Girls and Their Parents Say About Dieting,* most girls chose a "Barbie-doll" look: tall, thin, and large-breasted.

That same image pervades many ads on television and in magazines. When it comes to males, the media emphasize a tall, lean, muscular look. "People are paid to create an image or an illusion," says Sarah Stinson, head of the eating disorders program at Fairview Red Wing Health Services in Minnesota.

Only about 2 percent of women are as thin as most models, says the National Eating Disorders Association. Models work full-time with exercise trainers, makeup artists, and others to maintain their appearance. At photo shoots, clips and weights mold clothes to flatter a model's body. Once images are shot, computer artists take over. They airbrush pictures to remove any flaws. They can even change the shape of the bodies in the pictures. Thus, the standard media images of beauty often aren't true to life.

Faced with such unrealistic ideals, most teens feel worse about their bodies after reading teen fashion magazines. For those who felt unaccepted or unappreciated in their social environment—up to one-third of girls in one study—the effects lasted longer, according to Eric Stice at the University of Texas at Austin.

"From my perspective," says Stice, "this study is very damning for the mass media." In real life, he adds, most boys think a starved waif look is ugly for girls. And most girls don't like seeing mega-muscles on guys.

Peer pressure also influences a teen's body image. "Teasing can be very painful," says Nichter. "Kids seem to remember that for a very long time."

Frequently talking about weight can wear down someone's body image too. "I guess I started thinking I was fat at the start of high school," says Brianna. "Girls talk about it all the time at school—who's on diets. I would compare myself to other people, and I guess I thought I was fat."

"The majority of young women feel insecure," says Stinson. "What's happening is they're projecting those insecurities on each other, and you're getting this very competitive environment."

Families factor in too. When Brianna was little, her father sometimes commented on her eating a lot. Her brother sometimes called her a "fat pig." In other families, parents may tell a boy to eat so he grows up "big and strong." Or they may wistfully say that a daughter has "such a pretty face"—implying that the rest of her body is ugly.

Growing Pains

Young people internalize those messages. In a study by the Centers for Disease Control and Prevention (CDC), around 30 percent of students thought they were overweight. In reality, less than 14 percent of students were "at risk for becoming overweight." (The term refers to students whose body mass index was above the 85th percentile.)

Yet the 14 percent figure is also a problem. Nearly one-third of students get little or no physical activity, reports the CDC. Higher weight and a sedentary lifestyle increase the risks for diabetes, heart disease, and other health problems. Meanwhile, young people at the higher ranges of the weight scale often feel more frustrated by the gap between what they see in the mirror and what they see in the media.

Puberty complicates things. Girls get taller and gain an average of 25 pounds. They need the added fat for breast development and to enable them to conceive and carry babies as adults.

"Young women don't believe that they should gain fat," says Stinson. "They're terrified of it and don't understand the healthy role of natural body fat in development."

Boys get taller and more muscular as their bodies mature. That's generally consistent with our culture's ideal for males. But not all boys mature at the same rate. And not everyone gains muscle like the images featured in sports and fitness magazines.

When Problems Arise

When teens have a poor body image, self-esteem dips. Relationships suffer too. Conversations with friends may center on dieting and exercise, to the exclusion of other topics. Teens focus more on how they look than on what they want to accomplish in life. Instead of bonding with each other, teens often become competitive. That fuels feelings of isolation.

In the worst cases, eating disorders and other unhealthy behaviors develop. Eating disorders are more common among females than males. Yet the National Eating Disorders Association says about 10 percent of patients are male. (Besides a poor body image, other factors are often to blame. These include feelings of being out of control and, in some cases, a history of physical or sexual abuse.)

Brianna had anorexia nervosa. She did not eat enough to maintain a normal weight for her height. Besides looking very thin, she felt weak and had dizzy spells. Because girls need a certain level of body fat to menstruate, she stopped getting her period regularly. With her immune system weakened, Brianna came down with pneumonia during her sophomore year. Plus, Brianna recalls, "I lost hair. And I was cold all the time."

In addition to these problems, anorexia can cause loss of bone density, dehydration, and downy hair on the skin. When the heart muscle weakens and blood pressure drops too low, fatal heart failure can happen. By experimenting with diet pills, Brianna added to that risk. Even "natural" weight loss products can overstimulate the heart and cause heart attacks.

Binge eating disorder involves frequent episodes of uncontrolled eating, without regard to physical hunger or fullness. Patients suffer from guilt, shame, or disgust with their behavior. They often gain weight, which adds to any body image problems.

A person with bulimia experiences cycles of binging and purging. Even if a patient's weight stays normal, frequent vomiting causes decaying tooth enamel, swollen glands, a sore throat, and a puffy face. If patients take laxatives, they risk damage to their digestive systems and suffer from nutrient deficiencies.

Exercise bulimia compensates for eating with excessive physical activity. In her junior year of high school, actress Jamie Lynn Sigler exercised every day for hours. Her weight dropped to 90 pounds.

"As time went on, it began to take over my life and interfere with other things that were important to me," Jamie recalled, "like hanging out with my friends, my family, dance and theatre, and even my health." When she began thinking about suicide,

Jamie finally confided in her parents. The book *Wise Girl: What I've Learned About Life, Love, and Loss* tells the story of her recovery.

Body dysmorphia, a distorted body image, can also lead to excessive bodybuilding, especially among boys. Some also abuse steroids—drugs that unnaturally mimic the hormone testosterone to spur muscle growth. Risks of steroid abuse include possible outbreaks of violence during use and depression after cycling off the drugs, plus other physical and psychological consequences.

"When you have an eating disorder, you really don't want to talk about it," said Sigler. "You get very defensive. You isolate yourself a lot." If you're concerned about a friend, keep telling that person, "I'm here for you when you're ready to talk about it."

Building a Healthier Body Image

A doctor specializing in eating disorders gave Brianna a thorough check-up and prescribed medicine to help her clinical depression. Brianna also meets regularly with a psychologist, who has given her strategies to build a healthier body image.

"She had me write a list of things I like about myself," says Brianna. "When I start comparing myself to people, I think of one of those things rather than thinking, 'Oh, she looks so good and I look so bad.'" Among other things, Brianna is very intelligent. She is a hard worker. She is great at ballet. She plays the flute beautifully. And she likes her pretty blonde hair and blue eyes.

Dance class can still be a challenge, since the other advanced students are very thin. Brianna is learning to accept that people have different body shapes: ectomorphic, mesomorphic, and endomorphic. Ectomorphic people are very thin. Mesomorphic people are muscular. Endomorphic people tend to carry more fat. Many people's bodies mix these characteristics. Thus, one part of the body may be muscular, while another part may gain fat easily.

Brianna also met with a dietitian. When she was constantly dieting, she skipped meals. By nighttime she was so hungry that she might eat half a box of cereal. Now she's eating regular meals and including a reasonable amount of fat. She feels healthier and stronger. Now that she's eating regular meals again, she socializes more with other students at lunchtime too.

Another helpful strategy is to change the pattern of "fat talk" among friends. Sometimes teens join in the talk as a way to fit in. Other times, "I feel fat" can be code for other feelings that young people feel uncomfortable talking about: loneliness, disappointment, anger, insecurity, and so on. If teens encourage each other to talk about what's really bothering them, they can break the cycle of putting their bodies down. Clearer communication also frees teens to help each other deal with problems constructively.

Taking Charge

The media emphasize unrealistic standards of beauty. But, says Stinson, "You don't have to buy into these messages." She encourages young people to become activists: Write letters to companies praising ads that show normal teens with different body shapes and sizes. Conversely, send complaints and boycott companies that exploit young people by sexualizing them or glorifying thinness.

Don't Fall Prey to the Dieting Industry Either

Even "natural" weight-loss pills can contain stimulants that cause serious health problems. And despite "money-back guarantees," diet gizmos and gimmicks don't work. If any one did work, would Americans continue to spend $40 billion a year on books, diet programs, pills, gadgets, and everything else the dieting industry produces?

You can help educate other young people about having a healthy body image. In Minnesota, teen members of Red Wing GO GIRLS! make frequent presentations to help other young people develop a positive body image. By teaching others, the teens have become role models who are very proud of their own bodies.

Your Body, Your Health

"It's not your weight that determines your health," says Stinson. "It's your lifestyle." Here are some tips for a healthy lifestyle:

- Eat a variety of foods when you're physically hungry. Refer to the U.S. Department of Agriculture's Food Guide Pyramid (www.nal.usda.gov:8001/py/pmap.htm).
- Don't forget the calcium: The Food and Drug Administration (FDA) recommends four servings of calcium-rich foods a day for teens.
- Enjoy regular physical activities. Aim for at least 30 minutes a day most days of the week. Set realistic goals for yourself, and have a good time. The more your body can do, the better you'll feel about it.

Brianna is enjoying dance more now. She also has joined her school's swim team and enjoys the camaraderie with her teammates. When the team members feel tired after a practice, it's a good feeling. "As long as you're healthy and active, and your body is doing everything it's supposed to do, there's nothing wrong with your body shape," she says.

Based on her experience, Brianna adds this message to teens: "You're OK the way you are. Think of the many great things you are—you're like no one else. Just don't ever try to compare yourself with anyone because it's not worth it. You have to be yourself."

Reality Check: Show Your Appreciation

Real life heroes aren't people who stand around looking good. They're people who accomplish things and share their talents with others. In fact, you may be surprised about the things other people admire in you.

Try the following exercise:

1. Sit down with a group of classmates. Let each person take turns telling every other person something positive that they sincerely appreciate about the other person. The positive thing must be something other than physical appearance.
2. When group members hear something positive about themselves, they must look directly at the speaker and say thank you. No mumbling allowed!
3. Promise aloud to go for a week without commenting at all on anyone's weight or physical appearance. Enforce the agreement among yourselves.
4. For an added challenge, avoid looking at yourself in the mirror for two days. Talk with classmates about how hard or easy it was.

How Weight Changes Can Affect You

If you think losing 10 or even 20 pounds will make life wonderful, think again. The standard media images of beauty are not realistic. Even if you lost weight, you probably still would not match that ideal.

Initially, people who lose weight often feel proud of themselves. When many people hit a plateau, they feel frustrated. Weight levels off, despite continued dieting. The body naturally resists losing more than a small percentage of its weight too quickly. The metabolism slows down.

The National Eating Disorders Association says that 95 percent of people who diet gain back the weight within one to five years. That yo-yo effect places physical stress on the body. Gaining the weight back can further damage self-esteem.

More important, weight loss won't make all of life's problems go away. Dating and other social encounters can still be rocky. Family relationships can still be perplexing. School and work remain challenging.

Before you try to lose any weight, talk to your doctor or a dietitian. Body mass index (BMI) varies tremendously. Health professionals usually recommend weight loss only for people at the high end of the range. (BMI equals weight in pounds divided by height in inches, divided by height in inches again, multiplied by 703.)

Instead of going on a diet, many health professionals stress a healthy lifestyle. That includes a reasonable amount of enjoyable physical activity. It also includes healthy eating behaviors. Instead of wolfing down food on the run, for example, try slowing down and enjoying what you're eating. You can also learn to make smart nutrition choices by watching serving sizes and keeping the USDA's Food Guide Pyramid in mind.

From *Current Health 2*, March 2003, Vol. 29, Issue 7, pp. 6–12. Copyright © 2003 by Weekly Reader Corporation. Reprinted by permission.

Adolescent Stress

The Relationship between Stress and Mental Health Problems

KATHRYN E. GRANT, PhD ET AL.

Although exposure to some negative events is considered a normal part of development, stressful life experiences can threaten the well-being and healthy development of children and adolescents. Adolescents, in particular, are exposed to high rates of stressful life experiences (e.g., romantic break-ups, community violence, date rape), and there is some evidence that increases in stressors account, at least in part, for the increased rates of psychological problems adolescents experience (e.g., depression, conduct disorder, substance abuse) (Arnett, 1999).

This article will summarize recent research on the relation between stressful life experiences and mental health problems in adolescents. It will provide a definition of stress, present a conceptual model of the ways in which stressors affect adolescent mental health, and summarize research that has tested each of the basic tenets of the conceptual model. To clarify theory and research findings, illustrations based on the authors' own research with adolescents living in urban poverty will be provided.

Defining Stress

Few constructs in mental health have been as important, yet as difficult to define, as the concept of stress. The common theme across all prevailing definitions of stress is a focus on environmental events or conditions that threaten, challenge, exceed, or harm the psychological or biological capacities of the individual (Cohen, Kessler, & Gordon, 1995).

In recent decades, the most widely accepted definition of stress has been the transactional definition offered by Lazarus and Folkman (1984): "Psychological stress involves a particular relationship between the person and the environment that is *appraised* by the person as taxing or exceeding his or her resources and endangering his or her well being" (p. 19, emphasis added).

Recently, however, researchers have begun to question the appropriateness of a definition that relies on cognitive appraisals for children and adolescents. Results of research on stress during infancy indicate there are clear negative effects of maternal separation, abuse, and neglect on infants (Field, 1995). These negative effects occur, presumably, without the cognitive appraisal component that is central to the transactional definition. In addition, preliminary research indicates that cognitive appraisal processes that play a significant role later in development do not play the same role among younger children exposed to stressors (e.g., Turner & Cole, 1994). During adolescence, the brain continues to develop, and it is not clear when or to what extent cognitive appraisals influence the effects of stress.

Also, in recent years, theoretical models of the ways in which stressful experiences lead to mental health problems in adolescents have become more sophisticated, and there is greater emphasis on processes that influence or explain the relation between stressors and mental health problems (Cicchetti & Cohen, 1995). A model of stress that "lumps" potential intervening processes (i.e., processes that influence or explain the association between stressors and mental health problems), such as cognitive appraisal, in with stressors is conceptually unclear and poses problems for examining each of these factors individually (Reiss & Oliveri, 1991). To fully understand how stressful experiences and intervening processes relate to one another in the prediction of mental health problems, it is important to define and measure each of these variables, explicitly. This is particularly true in adolescent research, as the role of specific intervening processes is likely to shift across development.

Stressful life experiences can threaten the well-being and healthy development of children and adolescents.

For these reasons, we have proposed that stress be defined as *environmental events or chronic conditions that objectively threaten the physical and/or psychological health or well-being of individuals of a particular age in a particular society* (Grant,

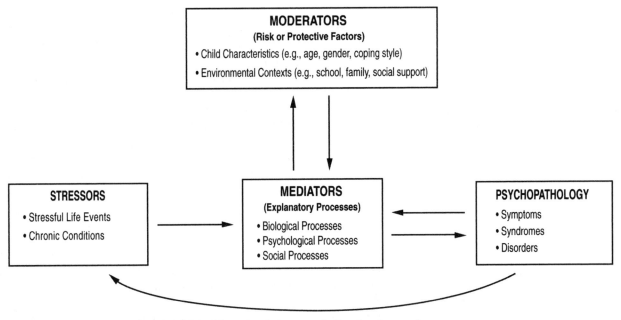

Figure 1 General conceptual model of the role of stressors in the development of mental health problems in adolescents.

Compas, Stuhlmacher, et al., 2003). Such a definition is consistent with traditional "stimulus-based" definitions of stress (Holmes & Rahe, 1967) and more recent definitions of "stressors" (Rice, 1999) and "objective stress" (Brown & Harris, 1989).

Relationship between Stress and Mental Health Problems

We (Grant et al., 2003) have proposed a general conceptual model of the role of stressors in the development of mental health problems for adolescents. This model builds on previously proposed specific models of psychopathology (e.g., Albano, Chorpita, & Barlow, 2001; Hammen & Rudolph, 2001) and includes five central hypotheses: 1) stressors lead to psychopathology; 2) moderators influence the relation between stressors and psychopathology; 3) mediators explain the relation between stressors and psychopathology; 4) there is specificity in the relations among particular stressors, moderators, mediators, and types of psychopathology; and 5) relations among stressors, moderators, mediators, and psychopathology are reciprocal and dynamic (See Figure 1). Each of these central hypotheses are described in detail below.

Stressors Lead to Psychopathology

The first hypothesis, that stressors lead to psychopathology, provides the conceptual basis for all studies of the relation between stressors and psychological problems in adolescents. Our recent review of longitudinal studies (Grant, Compas, et al., 2004) revealed consistent evidence that stressful life experiences predict psychological problems in adolescents over time. Likewise, there is growing evidence that youth who are exposed to high rates of stressful life experiences are at heightened risk for mental health problems.

For example, poverty sets the stage for an extraordinary number of stressful life experiences ranging from major life events (e.g., increased levels of child abuse), to chronic interpersonal stressors (e.g., marital conflict), to community violence, to the daily hassles associated with "trying to make ends meet" (Guerra et al., 1995). Extant research on psychological symptoms in low-income, urban youth has indicated that these youth are at heightened risk for a range of psychological problems including anxiety/depression, aggression, delinquency, social problems, withdrawal, and somatic complaints (Grant, Katz, et al., 2004). These findings provide further evidence of the most basic relation between stressors and psychopathology.

Influence of Moderators

The second tenet of the model is that moderators influence the relation between stressors and psychopathology. Moderators may be conceptualized as risk or protective factors, as they represent pre-existing characteristics (in existence prior to exposure to the stressor) that increase or decrease the likelihood that stressors will lead to psychopathology. Potential moderating variables include age, gender, social support, and coping styles. Moderating variables may be the result of genetic vulnerabilities (or protective factors), non-stressor environmental influences (e.g., parenting/peer influences), or, in some cases, stressful experiences. For example, exposure to severe and chronic stressors may lead to changes in the way adolescents view the world (e.g., they may develop a more pessimistic, less trusting perspective) and these changes in thinking may actually make adolescents more vulnerable to psychological symptoms when they are exposed to future stress (Grant et al., 2003).

Our recent review of the literature on moderators of the association between stressors and psychological problems in young people revealed few consistent findings (Grant, Compas, et al., 2005). One possible reason for the lack of consistency is that researchers have not focused on a particular risk or protective factor and examined it systematically across a number of studies. Unfortunately, this means that we know very little about factors that can break the connection between stressors and mental health problems in young people. Some individual studies have found evidence of particular protective effects and there is mounting evidence that having a cluster of protective factors is most beneficial (Beam, Gil-Rivas, Greenberger, & Chen, 2002; Meschke & Patterson, 2003). There is also some disconcerting evidence that youth exposed to the most pervasive and severe stressors (e.g., low-income urban youth of color) may be least likely to benefit from any particular protective factor (Gerard & Buehler, 2004; Luthar, 1991; Seidman, Lambert, Allen, & Aber, 2003). For example, in our own work with low-income urban youth, we have found preliminary evidence that youth who rely on particular individually-based coping strategies without broader supports may actually do more poorly over time than youth who report they don't have any protective factors at all (Grant, 2005).

Mediators

Although some factors may serve either a moderating or mediating function (e.g., cognitive attributions, coping), mediators are conceptually distinct from moderators in that they are "activated" or "caused by" the current stressful experience and serve to, conceptually and statistically, account for the relation between stressors and psychopathology (Baron & Kenny, 1986). Whereas moderators are characteristics of the child or his/her social network prior to the stressor, mediators become characteristics of the child or his/her social network in response to the stressor. Mediators may include variables such as coping styles, cognitive perceptions, and family processes (Grant et al., 2003).

Our recent review of the literature on mediators of the relation between stressors and psychological problems in young people (Grant et al., 2005) revealed that significant progress has been made in this area. The most frequently examined and empirically supported conceptual model has been one in which negative parenting mediates the relation between poverty (or economic stressors) and adolescent psychopathology (Grant et al., 2005). In particular, research suggests that, as parents experience economic pressures associated with poverty, they become less nurturant and more hostile toward their children, which leads to adolescent psychological problems (Conger, 2001). In our own work with low-income urban youth, we have seen evidence of similar patterns (Grant, McCormick, et al., in press).

Specificity

The fourth hypothesis is that there is specificity in relations among particular stressors, moderators, mediators, and psychological outcomes. According to this proposition, a particular type of stressor (e.g., urban poverty) is linked with a particular type of psychological problem (e.g., somatic complaints) through a particular mediator (e.g., a belief that expressions of anxiety or depression will make one look weak and leave one more vulnerable to victimization by others) in the context of a particular moderator (e.g., being a female adolescent). Analysis of full specificity models such as this one have yet to be reported in the literature.

There have been a large number of studies testing for specificity between particular stressors and particular psychological outcomes in young people, but these studies have yielded inconsistent results (McMahon et al., 2003). Nonetheless, some individual studies have found interesting evidence of specificity. For example, in our own work, we have found that particular types of psychological symptoms appear to be particularly common in the context of urban poverty. Somatic complaints is the internalizing symptom most frequently reported in our sample (Grant, Katz, et al., 2004). We have speculated that somatic complaints may be especially adaptive in a hostile urban environment. More stereotypically internalizing symptoms, such as anxiety or depression, may leave adolescents more vulnerable to victimization, but somatic complaints (like a stomach ache or headache) may allow them to avoid dangerous situations while still "saving face." Somatic complaints may also allow low-income urban youth to garner the most possible support from a network that may already be taxed with stressors of its own (Grant, Katz, et al., 2004).

Relations Are Reciprocal & Dynamic

The final hypothesis that relations among stressors, moderators, mediators, and psychopathology are reciprocal and dynamic broadly encompasses the following specific hypotheses: 1) each variable in the model influences the other (with some exceptions, for example, fixed moderators such as age will not be influenced by other variables); 2) the role of specific variables within the model may vary across specific stressors and shift over time (e.g., a mediator that developed in response to a particular stressor may become a fixed pattern of responding and, thus, interact as a moderator with subsequent stressors); 3) reciprocal and dynamic relations among stressors, moderators, and mediators will predict not only the onset of psychological problems, but also the exacerbation of symptoms and the movement along a continuum from low-level symptoms to the development of a clinically diagnosable disorder.

Of the basic tenets of our proposed conceptual model, this last hypothesis has received the least research attention. That is notable given that examination of this hypothesis, in particular, is essential for understanding the ways in which stressors influence adolescents, as it addresses the shifting nature of relations among variables across development. So far, the only consistent evidence for this proposition is that a number of studies have found that stressors not only predict psychological symptoms, but symptoms, in turn, predict exposure to additional stressful experiences (Grant, Compas, et al., 2004). In our own work with urban youth, we too have found evidence that psychological symptoms place youth at greater risk for exposure to additional stressors over time (Grant, Thomas, et al., 2005). This finding suggests that some youth are caught in a vicious cycle. Exposure to heightened rates of stressors places them at heightened risk for psychological symptoms, which, in turn, place them at risk for exposure to even more stressors, which place them at heightened risk for even more psychological distress (Grant, Thomas, et al., 2005).

Summary and Implications for Prevention

Recent research in the area of stressors and mental health problems in adolescents has led to the following conclusions:

1. Stress should be defined as *environmental events or chronic conditions that objectively threaten the physical and/or psychological health or well-being of individuals of a particular age in a particular society.*

2. There is strong evidence that stressful life experiences are predictive of mental health problems in adolescents. Adolescents exposed to high rates of stressful life experiences are at increased risk for a range of mental health problems.

3. The relation between stressors and mental health problems is thought to be affected by moderating variables. However, there is little consistent evidence of particular moderating effects. Additional research on protective factors is especially needed.

4. There is strong evidence that mediators explain the relation between stressors and mental health problems in adolescents. For example, the effects of poverty on adolescent mental health appear to be mediated by poverty's effects on family processes.

5. The relations among stressful life experiences, moderating and mediating processes, and psychopathology are thought to be specific, such that particular types of stressors are linked with particular types of mental health problems through particular intervening processes. There has been little systematic investigation of this hypothesis; consequently, little consistent evidence has been found for full specificity models.

6. The relations among stressful life experiences, moderating and mediating processes, and psychopathology are thought to be reciprocal and dynamic. This hypothesis has received little research attention, but there is growing evidence that stressors not only predict psychopathology, but psychopathology also predicts additional exposure to stress.

Implications

Given the risks associated with stressors, efforts to reduce adolescents' exposure to stressful life events are needed. These might include efforts at the individual family level to reduce marital conflict and domestic violence or to prevent child abuse. They might also include development of programs at the school or neighborhood level designed to reduce the effects of stressors associated with poverty, such as programs that provide affordable child care and job training. Most important are advocacy efforts at the sociopolitical level to address the inequities of our society that contribute to high poverty rates and childhood exposure

to community violence in economically disadvantaged urban settings.

In addition, more research is needed to understand what variables (if any) are actually capable of breaking the connection between stressful life events and mental health problems in young people. These protective factors could then be promoted through educational curricula, after-school programming, parent trainings, and other prevention efforts. Until stronger evidence is found for particular protective factors, it will be important to help young people develop protective contexts which facilitate development of a number of particular protective factors. For example, adolescents should be involved in at least one protective structure (e.g., family, school, church, after-school program), which facilitates the development of strong interpersonal relationships, which provide modeling, encouragement, and advice, which, in turn, facilitate the development of a positive value system or world view and healthy coping strategies (Grant, 2005). A constellation of protective factors, such as these, are likely to contribute to positive adolescent mental health.

References

Albano, A. M., Chorpita, B. F., & Barlow, D. H. (2001). Childhood anxiety disorders. In E. J. Mash & R. A. Barkley (Eds.), *Child Psychopathology. Second Edition.* New York, NY: Guilford Press.

Arnett, J. J. (1999). Adolescent storm and stress, reconsidered. *American Psychologist, 54,* 317–326.

Baron, R. M., & Kenny, D. A. (1986). The moderator-mediator variable distinction in social psychology research: Conceptual, strategic, and statistical considerations. *Journal of Personality and Social Psychology, 51,* 1,173–1,182.

Beam, M. R., Gil-Rivas, V., Greenberger, E., & Chen, C. (2002). Adolescent problem behavior and depressed mood: Risk and protection within and across social contexts. *Journal of Youth and Adolescence, 31,* 343–357.

Brown, G., & Harris, T. O. (1989). Depression. In G.W. Brown & T. O. Harris (Eds.), *Life Events and Illness* (pp. 49–93). New York: Guilford Press.

Cicchetti, D., & Cohen, D. (1995). Perspectives on developmental psychopathology. In D. Cicchetti, & D. Cohen, (Eds.), *Developmental Psychopathology Vol 1: Theory and Methods. Wiley Series on Personality Processes* (pp. 3–20). New York: John Wiley & Sons.

Cohen, S., Kessler, R. C., & Gordon, L. U. (1995). *Measuring Stress.* New York: Oxford University Press.

Conger, R. D. (2001). Understanding child and adolescent response to caregiver conflict: Some observations on context, process, and method. In A. Booth & A. C. Crouter (Eds.), *Couples in Conflict* (pp. 161–172). Mahwah, NJ: Lawrence Erlbaum Associates.

Field, T. (1995). Infants of depressed mothers. *Infant Behavior and Development, 18*(1), 1–13.

Gerard, J. M., & Buehler, C. (2004). Cumulative environmental risk and youth maladjustment: The role of youth attributes. *Child Development, 75,* 1,832–1,849.

Grant, K. E. (June, 2005). *Stressors and Adolescent Mental Health: Protective Factors in the Lives of Urban Youth.* Paper presented at the annual meeting of the William T. Grant Foundation Scholars' program, Jackson, WY.

Grant, K. E., Compas, B. E., Stuhlmacher, A., Thurm, A. E., McMahon, S., & Halpert, J. (2003). Stressors and child/adolescent psychopathology: Moving from markers to mechanisms of risk. *Psychological Bulletin, 129,* 447–466.

Grant, K. E., Compas, B. E., Thurm, A.E., McMahon, S. D., & Gipson, P. Y. (2004). Stressors and child and adolescent psychopathology: Measurement issues and prospective effects. *Journal of Clinical Child and Adolescent Psychology, 33*(2), 412–425.

Grant, K. E., Compas, B. E., Thurm, A. E., McMahon, S. D., Gipson, P., Campbell, A. J., & Krochock, K. (2005). *Moderating and Mediating Processes in the Relation Between Stressors and Child/Adolescent Psychopathology. Manuscript submitted for publication.*

Grant, K. E., Katz, B. N., Thomas, K. J., O'Koon, J. H., Meza, C. M., DiPasquale, A. M., Rodríguez, V. O., & Bergen, C. (2004). Psychological symptoms affecting low-income urban youth. *Journal of Adolescent Research, 19*(6), 613–634.

Grant, K. E., McCormick, A., Poindexter, L., Simpkins, T., Janda, C. M., Thomas, K. J., Campbell, A., Carleton, R., & Taylor, J. (in press). Family and neighborhood processes in the relation between poverty and psychological symptoms in urban African American adolescents. *Journal of Adolescence.*

Grant, K. E., Thomas, K. J., Apling, G. C., Gipson, P. Y., Mance, G. A., Carleton, R. A., Ford, R. E., Taylor, J. J., & Sajous-Brady, D. L. (2005). *Stressors and Psychological Symptoms in Urban Youth: A Test of a Conceptual Model.* Manuscript submitted for publication.

Guerra, N. G., Huesmann, L. R., Tolan, P. H., Van Acker, R., & Eron, L. D. (1995). Stressful events and individual beliefs as correlates of economic disadvantage and aggression among urban children. Special Section: Prediction and prevention of child and adolescent antisocial behavior. *Journal of Consulting & Clinical Psychology, 63*(4), 518–528.

Hammen, C., & Rudolph, K. D. (2001). Childhood depression. In E. J. Mash & R. A. Barkley (Eds.), *Child Psychopathology. Second Edition* New York, NY: Guilford Press.

Holmes, T. H., & Raye, R. H. (1967). The Social Readjustment Rating Scale, *Journal of Psychosomatic Research, 11,* 213–218.

Lazarus, R. S., & Folkman, S. (1984). *Stress, Appraisal, and Coping.* New York: Springer.

Luthar, S. S. (1991). Vulnerability and resilience: A study of high-risk adolescents. *Child Development, 62,* 600–616.

McMahon, S. D., Grant, K. E., Compas, B. E., Thurm, A. E., & Ey, S. (2003). Stress and psychopathology in children and adolescents: Is there evidence of specificity? *Journal of Child Psychology and Psychiatry and Allied Disciplines: Annual Research Review, 44,* 107–133.

Meschke, L. L., & Patterson, J. M. (2003). Resilience as a theoretical basis for substance abuse prevention, *The Journal of Primary Prevention, 23,* 483–514.

Reiss, D., & Oliveri, M. (1991). The family's conception of accountability and competence: A new approach to the conceptualization and assessment of family stress. *Family Process, 30,* 193–214.

Rice, P. L. (1999). *Stress and Health.* New York: Brooks/Cole Publishing Company.

Seidman, E., Lambert, L. E., Allen, L., & Aber, J. L. (2003). Urban adolescents' transition to junior high school and protective family transactions. *Journal of Early Adolescence, 23,* 166–193.

Turner, Jr., J. E., & Cole, D. A. (1994). Developmental differences in cognitive diatheses for child depression. *Journal of Abnormal Child Psychology, 22,* 15–32.

Kathryn E. Grant, PhD, is a licensed Clinical Psychologist, Associate Professor, and Director of Clinical Training at DePaul University. She and her research team are currently conducting a longitudinal study of stress and its effects on urban adolescents. Steven Behling, BS, is a doctoral student at DePaul University. His research interests include prevention of family violence and child maltreatment. Polly Y. Gipson, MA, is a doctoral student at DePaul University. She recently completed her thesis on stress and anxiety in urban adolescents. Rebecca E. Ford, MA, is a doctoral student at DePaul University. She recently defended her dissertation on the effects of acculturation on Latino adolescent mental health.

ADHD and the SUD in Adolescents

Timothy E. Wilens, MD

Overlap Between ADHD and SUD

The overlap between Attention Deficit Hyperactivity Disorder (ADHD) and alcohol or drug abuse (referred to here as substance use disorders [SUD]) in adolescents has been an area of increasing clinical, research, and public health interest. ADHD onsets in early childhood and affects from 6 to 9 percent of children and adolescents worldwide (Anderson, et al., 1987) and up to 5 percent of adults (Kessler, in press). Substance use disorders (SUD) usually onset in adolescence or early adulthood and affect between 10 to 30 percent of U.S. adults, and a less defined, but sizable number of juveniles (Kessler, 2004). The study of comorbidity between SUD and ADHD is relevant to both research and clinical practice in developmental pediatrics, psychology, and psychiatry with implications for diagnosis, prognosis, treatment, and healthcare delivery.

In adolescent studies incorporating structured psychiatric diagnostic interviews assessing ADHD and other disorders in substance abusing groups have indicated that from one third to one-half of adolescents with SUD have ADHD (DeMilio, 1989; Milin, et al., 1991). Data largely ascertained from adult groups with SUD also show an earlier onset and more severe course of SUD associated with ADHD (Carroll & Rounsaville, 1993; Levin & Evans, 2001).

ADHD as a Risk Factor for SUD

The association of ADHD and SUD is particularly compelling from a developmental perspective as ADHD manifests itself earlier than SUD; therefore, SUD as a risk factor for ADHD is unlikely. Thus, it is important to evaluate to what extent ADHD is a precursor of SUD. Prospective studies of ADHD children have provided evidence that the groups with conduct or bipolar disorders co-occurring with ADHD have the poorest outcome with respect to developing SUD and major morbidity (Biederman, et al., 1997; Mannuzza, et al., 1993). As part of an ongoing prospective study of ADHD, differences in the risk for SUD in ADHD adolescents (mean age 15 years) compared to non-ADHD controls were found. The controls were accounted for by comorbid conduct or bipolar disorders (Biederman, et al., 1997); however, we also show that the age of risk for SUD onset in non-comorbid ADHD is approximately 17 years in girls and 19 years old for boys (Biederman, et al., 2006a; Milberger, et al., 1997b).

SUD Pathways Associated with ADHD

An increasing body of literature shows an intriguing association between ADHD and cigarette smoking. It has been previously reported that ADHD was a significant predictor for early initiation of cigarette smoking (before age 15) and that conduct and mood disorders with ADHD put youth at particularly high risk for early onset smoking (Milberger, et al., 1997a) (*see Figure below*). Data also suggest that one-half of ADHD smokers go on to later SUD (Biederman, et al., 2006b); not surprising given that not only does smoking lead to peer group pressures and availability of illicit substances; but that nicotine exposure may make the brain more susceptible to later behavioral disorders and SUD (Trauth, et al., 2000). Furthermore, nicotinic modulating agents are increasingly being evaluated for the treatment of ADHD (Wilens, et al., 2006). Of interest, very recent NIDA-funded prospective data suggests that stimulant treatment of

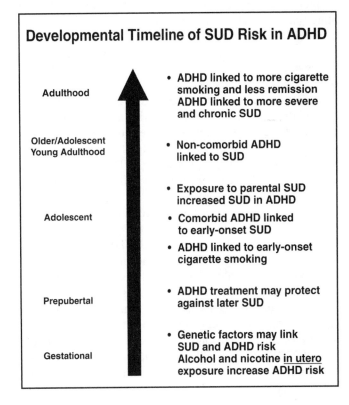

Developmental Timeline of SUD Risk in ADHD

Adulthood
- ADHD linked to more cigarette smoking and less remission ADHD linked to more severe and chronic SUD

Older/Adolescent Young Adulthood
- Non-comorbid ADHD linked to SUD

Adolescent
- Exposure to parental SUD increased SUD in ADHD
- Comorbid ADHD linked to early-onset SUD
- ADHD linked to early-onset cigarette smoking

Prepubertal
- ADHD treatment may protect against later SUD

Gestational
- Genetic factors may link SUD and ADHD risk Alcohol and nicotine in utero exposure increase ADHD risk

ADHD reduces not only the time to onset but also the incidence of cigarette smoking (Monuteaux, et al., 2004).

The precise mechanism(s) mediating the expression of SUD in ADHD remains to be seen. The self-medication hypothesis is compelling in ADHD considering that the disorder is chronic and often associated with demoralization and failure, factors frequently associated with SUD in adolescents. Moreover, we recently found that among substance abusing adolescents with and without ADHD, ADHD adolescents reported using substances more frequently to attenuate their mood and to help them sleep. No evidence of differences in types of substances has emerged between ADHD and nonADHD substance abusing teens (Biederman, et al., 1997). In addition, the potential importance of self-medication needs to be tempered against more systematic data showing the strongest relationship between ADHD and SUD being mediating by the presence of comorbidity in addition to familial contributions such as exposure to parental SUD during vulnerable developmental phases.

Diagnosis and Treatment Guidelines

Evaluation and treatment of comorbid ADHD and SUD should be part of a plan in which consideration is given to all aspects of the teen's life. Any intervention in this group should follow a careful evaluation of the adolescent including psychiatric, addiction, social, cognitive, educational, and family evaluations. A thorough history of substance use should be obtained including past and current usage and treatments. Although no specific guidelines exist for evaluating the patient with active SUD, experience has shown that at least one month of abstinence is useful in accurately and reliably assessing for ADHD symptoms. Semi-structured psychiatric interviews or validated rating scales of ADHD are invaluable aids for the systematic diagnostic assessments of this group.

The treatment needs of individuals with SUD and ADHD need to be considered simultaneously; however, the SUD needs to be addressed initially (Riggs, 1998). If the SUD is active, immediate attention needs to be paid to *stabilization of the addiction(s)*. Depending on the severity and duration of the SUD, adolescents may require inpatient treatment. Self help groups offer a helpful treatment modality for many with SUD. In tandem with addiction treatment, SUD adolescents with ADHD require intervention(s) for the ADHD (and if applicable, comorbid psychiatric disorders).

Medication serves an important role in reducing the symptoms of ADHD and other concurrent psychiatric disorders. Effective agents for adolescents with ADHD include the stimulants, noradrenergic agents, and catecholaminergic antidepressants (Wilens, et al., 2002). Recent findings from a metanalysis of 10 studies of open and controlled trials suggest that medications used in adolescents and adults with ADHD plus SUD have only a meager effect on the ADHD, but have little effect on substance use or cravings (Riggs, et al., 2004; Schubiner, et al., 2002; Wilens, et al., 2005). Of interest, no evidence exists that treating ADHD pharmacologically through an active SUD

exacerbates the SUD—consistent with work of Grabowski et al. (2004) who have used stimulants to block cocaine and amphetamine abuse. Not surprisingly, work by Volkow et al. (1998) have demonstrated important differences between binding at the dopamine transporter between methylphenidate and cocaine resulting in very different abuse liabilities.

Summary

There is a strong literature supporting a relationship between ADHD and SUD. Both family-genetic and self-medication influences may be operational in the development and continuation of SUD in ADHD. Adolescents with ADHD and SUD require multimodal intervention incorporating addiction and mental health treatment. Pharmacotherapy in ADHD and SUD individuals needs to take into consideration timing, misuse and diversion liability, potential drug interactions, and compliance concerns.

While the existing literature has provided important information on the relationship of ADHD and SUD, it also points to a number of areas in need of further study. The mechanism by which untreated ADHD leads to SUD, as well as the risk reduction of ADHD treatment on cigarette smoking and SUD needs to be better understood. Given the prevalence and major morbidity and impairment caused by SUD and ADHD, prevention and treatment strategies for these adolescents need be further developed and evaluated.

References

Anderson, J.C., Williams, S., McGee, R., & Silva, P.A. (1987). DSM III disorders in preadolescent children. Prevalence in a large sample from the general population. *Arch Gen Psychiatry* 44: 69–76.

Biederman J., Monuteaux M., Mick, E. et al. (2006a). Young Adult Outcome of Attention Deficit Hyperactivity Disorder: A Controlled 10 year Prospective Follow-Up Study. *Psychol Med* 36: 167–179.

Biederman, J., Monuteaux, M., Mick, E., et al. (2006b). Is Cigarette Smoking a Gateway Drug to Subsequent Alcohol and Illicit Drug Use Disorders? A Controlled Study of Youths with and without ADHD. *Biol Psychiatry* 59: 258–64.

Biederman, J., Wilens, T. & Mick, E. et al. (1997). Is ADHD a risk for psychoactive substance use disorder? Findings from a four year follow-up study. *J Am Acad Child Adolesc Psychiatry* 36: 21–29.

Carroll, K.M. & Rounsaville, B.J. (1993). History and significance of childhood attention deficit disorder in treatment-seeking cocaine abusers. *Comrpehensive Psychiatry* 34: 75–82.

DeMilio, L. (1989). Psychiatric syndromes in adolescent substance abusers. *Am J Psychiatry* 146: 1212–1214.

Grabowski, J., Shearer, J., Merrill, J. & Negus, S.S. (2004). Agonist-like, replacement pharmacotherapy for stimulant abuse and dependence. *Addict Behav* 29: 1439–1464.

Kessler, R.C. (in press). A recent replication of the National Comorbidity Study estimating the prevalence of adult ADHD among persons 18–44 in the US. *Psychol Med.*

Kessler, R.C. (2004). The epidemiology of dual diagnosis. *Biol Psychiatry* 56: 730–7.

Levin, F.R. & Evans, S.M. (2001). Diagnostic and treatment issues in comorbid substance abuse and adult attention-deficit hyperacity disorder. *Psychiatric Annals* 31: 303–312.

Mannuzza, S., Klein, R.G., Bessler, A., Malloy, P. & LaPadula, M. (1993). Adult outcome of hyperactive boys: Educational achievement, occupational rank, and psychiatric status. *Arch Gen Psychiatry* 50: 565–576.

Milberger, S., Biederman, J., Faraone, S., Chen, L. & Jones, J. (1997a). ADHD is associated with early initiation of cigarette smoking in children and adolescents. *J Am Acad Child Adolesc Psychiatry* 36: 37–44.

Milberger, S., Biederman, J., Faraone, S., Wilens, T. & Chu, M. (1997b). Associations between ADHD and psychoactive substance use disorders: Findings from a longitudinal study of high-risk siblings of ADHD children. *Am J Addict* 6: 318–329.

Milin, R., Halikas, J.A., Meller, J.E. & Morse, C. (1991). Psychopathology among substance abusing juvenile offenders. *J Am Acad Child Adolesc Psychiatry* 30: 569–574.

Riggs, P.D. (1998). Clinical approach to treatment of ADHD in adolescents with substance use disorders and conduct disorder. *J Am Acad Child Adolesc Psychiatry* 37: 331–332.

Riggs, P.D., Hall, S.K., Mikulich-Gilbertson, S.K., Lohman, M. & Kayser, A. (2004). A Randomized Controlled Trial of Pemoline for Attention-Deficit/Hyperactivity Disorder in Substance-Abusing Adolescents. *J Am Acad Child Adolesc Psychiatry* 43: 420–429.

Schubiner, H., Saules, K.K. & Arfken, C.L. et al. (2002). Double-blind placebo-controlled trial of methylphenidate in the treatment of adult ADHD patients with comorbid cocaine dependence. *Exp Clin Psychopharmacol* 10: 286–94.

Trauth, J.A., Seidler, F.J. & Slotkin, T.A. (2000). Persistent and delayed behavioral changes after nicotine treatment in adolescent rats. *Brain Res* 880: 167–72.

Volkow, N., Wang, G. & Fowler, J. et al. (1998). Dopamine transporter occupancies in the human brain induced by therapeutic doses of oral methylphenidate. *Am J Psychiatry* 155: 1325–1331.

Wilens T., Monuteaux M., Snyder L., Moore B.A. (2005). The clinical dilemma of using medications in substance abusing adolescents and adults with ADHD: What does the literature tell us? *J Child Adolesc Psychopharmacol* 15: 787–98.

Wilens T., Verlinden M.H., Adler L.A., Wozniak P.A. & West S.A. (2006). ABT-089, A Neuronal Nicotinic Receptor Partial Agonist, for the Treatment of Attention-Deficit/Hyperactivity Disorder in Adults: Results of a Pilot Study. *Biol Psychiatry* 59: 1065–70.

Wilens, T.E., Biederman, J. & Spencer, T.J. (2002). Attention Deficit/ Hyperactivity Disorder across the Lifespan. *Ann Rev Med* 53: 113–131.

Dr. Timothy E. Wilens is Associate Professor of Psychiatry at Harvard Medical School in Boston, Massachusetts. In addition, he is Director of the Substance Abuse Services in the Pediatric Psychopharmacology Clinic at Massachusetts General Hospital.

Dr. Wilens earned his BS in literature, science, and arts at the University of Michigan Honors College, and his MD at the University of Michigan Medical School in Ann Arbor. His peer reviewed articles concerning the relationship of Attention Deficit Hyperactivity Disorder (ADHD), bipolar disorder, and substance abuse and related topics number more than 170. Dr. Wilens has also published more than 65 book chapters, and 225 abstracts and presentations for national and international scientific meetings. He may be contacted at Twilens@ partners.org.

Acknowledgments—This research was supported by NIH BOI DA14419 and K24 DA016264 to TW.

Coping with Stress

Implications for Preventive Interventions with Adolescents

BRUCE E. COMPAS, PhD, JENNIFER E. CHAMPION, BA, AND KRISTEN REESLUND, BS

Considerable evidence suggests that exposure to stress and the ways that individuals cope with stress are of central importance for the prevention of psychopathology and other problems of adjustment during childhood and adolescence. Careful consideration of theory and research on stress and coping during adolescence is of potentially great importance for the development of preventive interventions for young people. In this article we first summarize the relationship between stress and psychopathology in children and adolescents, then discuss current research on coping. We conclude by discussing stress and coping approaches to preventive interventions, using an example from our current research with families of depressed parents.

Stress and Psychopathology

Traumatic events, stressful life events, and chronic stressful conditions affect the lives of millions of youth. Examples of these stressful experiences include natural and human disasters, neighborhood violence, economic hardship, personal or parental chronic illness, and minor events or hassles. Moreover, there is strong evidence that stress plays a clear role in the etiology and maintenance of psychopathology (Cicchetti & Toth, 1997; Haggerty et al., 1994). Research shows that stressors can be acute incidents (i.e., natural disaster, loss of a loved one) or more stable, chronic conditions (i.e., poverty, chronic illness) and that both types of stressors are associated with an increased risk for psychopathology in children and adolescents (Grant et al., 2003). Despite frequent exposure to acute or chronic stress, the vast majority of youth navigate adolescence without developing any form of psychopathology. For those who do develop psychological disorders, however, adolescence marks a period of significant increase in psychopathology across a wide range of disorders, including, for example, eating disorders, conduct disorder, and depression (Compas, 2004).

Research on child and adolescent stress has improved considerably over the past two decades (see Grant et al., 2003, 2004; McMahon et al., 2003). However, there is still considerable inconsistency in the field in the way stress is defined and measured. There is also much more to be learned about the impact that stress has on psychological outcomes in children and adolescents, and the implications that this has for prevention and intervention. There is strong evidence, though, that exposure to stressful events at one point in time predicts increases in internalizing and externalizing symptoms in adolescents above and beyond initial symptoms. However, the specific relationship between stress and outcome, as well as the mediators and moderators that affect this relationship are not yet well understood (Grant et al., 2004).

Current evidence shows that stressors are a general non-specific risk for psychopathology; however, the exact relationship between the two is yet to be defined. In their comprehensive review, McMahon and colleagues (2003) found that there is currently little evidence to support the specificity hypothesis in the relationship between stressors and outcome. An example of specificity would occur when a specific stressor (e.g., poverty) leads to a specific outcome (e.g., conduct disorder). Instead, there is more evidence to support the hypotheses of equifinality, where multiple stressors (e.g., poverty or loss of a loved one) lead to a specific outcome (e.g., conduct disorder), and multifinality, where a specific stressor (e.g., poverty) leads to multiple outcomes (e.g., conduct disorder or depression). Thus, exposure to stress appears to function as a non-specific risk factor for psychopathology. Recent research also shows that there is a reciprocal and dynamic relationship between stressors and psychological outcomes—stress leads to psychopathology but psychopathology also leads to the generation of stressful events in the lives of affected individuals (Grant et al., 2004).

Some children and adolescents exhibit a vulnerability to developing psychopathology. That is, these individuals when exposed to risk, in this case stress, are more likely to develop a negative outcome as compared to peers who do not have such vulnerability (Wolchik et al., 2000). Therefore, even when faced with similar levels of stress some youth may have risk factors, characteristics that are related to an increased probability of developing a negative outcome (Kraemer et al., 1997), whereas other youth may have protective factors, characteristics that are related to positive outcomes in the face of risk, and show resilience (Luthar & Cicchetti, 2000).

Coping with Stress

Conclusions regarding the association between stress and symptoms are insufficient without taking into account the ways that individuals cope with stress. Coping refers to self-regulatory processes enacted when faced with stress (Compas et al., 2001). The most widely cited definition of coping is given by Lazarus and Folkman (1984) as "constantly changing cognitive and behavioral efforts to manage specific external and/or internal demands that are appraised as taxing or exceeding the resources of the person" (p. 141). More specifically, coping involves conscious volitional efforts to regulate one's own behavior, emotions, thoughts, physiology, and the environment in response to a stressor (Compas et al., 2001).

Coping is one subset of a broader domain of self-regulation. It includes only regulatory efforts that are volitional and intentional responses to a stressful event or circumstance (Compas et al., 1999, 2001). These regulatory processes are influenced by the cognitive, behavioral, and emotional capacity of the individual as well as the social environment. Ways of reacting to stress that are involuntary or automatic are grouped into a more general classification of self-regulatory processes enacted in response to stress and are not considered coping (Compas et al., 2001). Furthermore, coping is situation specific—the ways in which an individual responds to a stressor is affected by the demands of the situation.

Stress responses can be broken down along two broad dimensions: voluntary (controlled) versus involuntary (automatic), and engagement versus disengagement. It is the distinction between voluntary and involuntary responses that distinguishes coping within the broader classification of stress responses; that is, coping refers to voluntary, controlled responses to stress. Both voluntary and automatic responses to stress can be further broken down into efforts to engage or disengage from the stressor

and one's responses. Engagement coping strategies are characterized by direct attempts to influence either the stressor itself or one's emotions in response to the stressor (primary control coping), or efforts to adapt to the stress by regulating one's cognitions (secondary control coping). See Table 1.

Primary control coping (also referred to as active coping in other theoretical models) includes strategies that are directed at actively changing the situation or one's emotional responses, such as problem solving (e.g., I try to think of different ways to change the problem or fix the situation), emotional expression (e.g., I let my feelings out by writing or talking with someone), and emotional regulation (e.g., I do things to calm myself down). Secondary control coping, on the other hand, involves adaptation to the stressor through acceptance (e.g., I realize I just have to live with things the way they are), distraction (e.g., I think about positive things to take my mind off the problem), cognitive restructuring (e.g., I try to see the good that will come from the situation or what I will learn from it), and positive thinking (e.g., I tell myself everything's going to be all right). Unlike engagement coping behaviors which are focused on dealing with the stressful situation or one's emotions, disengagement coping refers to efforts to distance oneself emotionally, cognitively, and physically from the stressor. Such coping includes behaviors such as avoidance (e.g., I try to stay away from things that remind me of the problem), denial (e.g., I tell myself that this isn't happening to me), and wishful thinking (e.g., I wish someone would come get me out of this problem).

Involuntary responses to stress can also be distinguished along the dimension of engagement and disengagement responses. Involuntary engagement refers to automatic responses oriented towards the stressor and is comprised of rumination, intrusive thoughts, and emotional and physiological arousal. Involuntary disengagement responses include uncontrolled behaviors

Table 1 Stress Responses

Voluntary/Controlled Responses (Coping)		Involuntary/Automatic Responses	
Voluntary Engagement Coping: Dealing with the stressful situation or one's emotions	**Voluntary Disengagement Coping:** Efforts to distance oneself emotionally, cognitively and physically from the stressor	**Involuntary Engagement:** Automatic responses oriented toward the stressor	**Involuntary Disengagement:** Uncontrolled behaviors focused away from the source of stress
Primary Control Coping: Direct attempts to influence the stressor or one's emotions in response to the stressor. Examples include: • Problem solving • Emotional expression • Emotional regulation	Examples include: • Avoidance • Denial • Wishful thinking	Examples include: • Rumination • Intrusive thoughts • Emotional & physiological arousal	Examples include: • Emotional numbing • Cognitive interference • Inaction
Secondary Control Coping: Adaptation to the stressor. Examples include: • Acceptance • Distraction • Positive thinking			

focused away from the source of stress, such as emotional numbing, cognitive interference, inaction, and escape (Connor-Smith et al., 2000).

Over 60 studies have established that coping is associated with symptoms of psychopathology in children and adolescents (Compas et al., 2001). More specifically, primary and secondary control coping efforts have both been found to be related to fewer internalizing and externalizing symptoms in various populations. Because coping is situation specific, the most effective coping behaviors are dependent on the characteristics surrounding the stressor. Primary control coping has been found to be most successful when dealing with stressors that are perceived as controllable, whereas secondary control coping efforts may be more adaptive with uncontrollable stressors (Compas et al., 2001). In contrast to the positive outcomes associated with engagement coping, disengagement coping is typically associated with increased levels of internalizing and externalizing symptoms.

The pattern of relations between coping and symptoms has been investigated across various populations. For example, in a sample of adolescents reporting on economic strain and family conflict, primary and secondary control coping were both related to fewer internalizing and externalizing symptoms (Wadsworth & Compas, 2002). Similarly, youth dealing with recurrent abdominal pain reported fewer somatic and anxiety-depression symptoms with higher levels of primary and secondary control coping (Thomsen et al., 2002).

One focus of our current research is the significant risk for adolescents associated with living with a depressed parent. When examining the relationship between coping and psychological functioning in children of depressed parents, adolescents' use of primary control coping to deal with their parent's depression was associated with fewer aggressive symptoms, while secondary control coping was found to be related to lower levels of both anxiety-depression and aggression (Langrock et al., 2002). Although primary control coping was associated with fewer symptoms, due to the context-dependent nature of coping and the uncontrollability of the stressor (as children of depressed parents can't relieve their parent's depression and thus aren't capable of changing their situations), secondary control coping behaviors appear to be most adaptive in this population. Involuntary engagement, conversely, showed significant increases in both internalizing and externalizing symptoms. These findings were further supported by a study conducted by Jaser et al. (2005), who compared adolescent reports of coping strategies in response to the stress of parental depression with parental reports of adolescent adjustment. In this research, secondary control coping was related to fewer symptoms of depression/anxiety, while involuntary engagement was associated with increased levels of these symptoms.

To fully understand the relation between coping and symptoms, however, it is important and necessary to consider the nature of the stressor and the role of coping as a mediator or moderator in the relation between a stressor and psychopathology. As a potential moderator or mediator in the link between stress and symptoms, coping may serve to influence or explain the relation between the two (e.g., Connor-Smith & Compas,

2002). A moderator may be conceptualized as a protective factor, meaning a pre-existing characteristic that increases or decreases the probability of developing symptoms of psychopathology in response to a stressor. Coping may perform in such a manner, with some individuals possessing a tendency to use more adaptive coping strategies when dealing with stress, while others cope in a less effective way that increases the likelihood of developing psychopathology regardless of the stressor. The role of coping as a moderator may also serve to explain the issue raised earlier regarding why a single stressor may lead to various symptoms or why various stressors may result in the same outcome.

Coping may also function as a mediator, which means that it is set off by the stressor and accounts for the resulting symptoms (e.g., Jaser et al., 2005). In this case, coping behaviors would serve as a direct cause of the preceding stressor and produce certain symptoms. When looking at the relationship between stress, coping, and outcome in children of depressed parents, adolescents' reports of secondary control engagement coping and involuntary engagement stress responses were found to mediate the relation between adolescents' reports of parental stress and parents' reports of adolescents' anxiety/depression symptoms (Jaser et al., 2005). This finding emphasizes the potential benefits for preventive interventions to increase adaptive coping skills by teaching secondary control coping strategies and reducing involuntary stress reaction in order to decrease symptoms and promote better adjustment.

Preventive Interventions

Given the significant role of stress as risk factor for child and adolescent psychopathology and the potential for coping to serve as a protective factor against the adverse effects of stress, it is logical that stress and coping processes are potential targets for preventive interventions. In simplest terms, prevention efforts could be designed to reduce stress and enhance adaptive coping in young people. However, this seemingly simple principle belies a much more complicated set of issues in prevention programs to reduce the adverse effects of stress.

Reducing stress. One target for preventive interventions could certainly be to reduce the burden on children by decreasing their exposure to stress. There are a number of significant sources of stress in the lives of young people that could be reduced, or exposure to these stressors could be reduced or altered. For example, stressors that arise within family environments are potentially reduced through interventions aimed at parents. These include interventions to reduce the incidence of physical and sexual abuse, family conflict, and parental psychiatric disorders. Stressors that arise in schools can also be reduced by restructuring school environments or school demands. For example, the timing of the transition from primary education to middle school can be adjusted to reduce the likelihood that this transition coincides with other developmental changes and challenges. Moreover, to the extent that dependent stressful events are associated with child characteristics, their incidence may be reduced by interventions that change relevant aspects of children's behavior or cognition.

However, the practical limits to reducing stress in young people's lives quickly become apparent because many sources of stress in children and adolescents' lives are uncontrollable. Parental divorce, parental death, neighborhood violence and other chronic stressors that emanate from poverty, and some forms of chronic illness are themselves not preventable. Thus, there will naturally be limits in the degree to which stress can be reduced.

Enhancing coping. Given the limited control that can be gained over young people's exposure to many forms of stress, a second important target for preventive interventions is to increase children's abilities to cope with stress. Improved skills in problem solving, emotion regulation, and access to adequate social support may increase children's resilience in the face of stress. The cognitive and behavioral skills that characterize effective coping with stress are malleable and there is promising evidence that these skills can reduce the adverse outcomes of stress in the lives of children. Several examples of preventive interventions that reflect a stress and coping framework can be found in the literature, including interventions for children of divorce and bereaved children (e.g., Wolchik et al., 2000). Our focus here is on a relatively new program that our research group has developed for children of depressed parents.

Preventive intervention for children exposed to parental depression: An example of stress and coping in prevention. The risk for psychopathology and other adjustment problems in children of parents who suffer from major depressive disorder is substantial. Estimates are that as many as 70% of children of depressed parents will develop a psychiatric disorder, including but certainly not limited to, depression. Several mechanisms are implicated in the transmission of risk from depressed parents to their offspring, including genes, innate disruption of biological regulatory processes, and stressful parent-child interactions. Clarke and colleagues (2001) have shown preventive effects for a group cognitive-behavioral intervention for adolescents of parents with a history of depression. Our current research builds on this research by intervening with parents and children to address both the sources of stress and ways of coping in families of depressed parents.

Sources of stress within families of depressed parents and the ways that youth cope with these stressors represent two possible targets for preventive interventions. Stressful interactions between depressed parents and their children that are the result of parental withdrawal and parental irritability/intrusiveness are associated with higher levels of both internalizing and externalizing problems in children (Jaser et al., 2005; Langrock et al., 2002). Further, the effects of these parental stressors on children's problems are mediated by the ways that children react to and cope with parent-child stress. Specifically, children who are more stress reactive (i.e., respond to stress with higher levels of emotional and physiological arousal, intrusive thoughts) are higher in internalizing and externalizing problems. In contrast, children who are able to enlist secondary control coping strategies in response to these parental stressors are lower in internalizing and externalizing difficulties.

Based on the identification of these risk and protective factors, we have developed a family-based preventive intervention to enhance the ability of depressed parents to more effectively parent their children (and as a result, reduce parental withdrawal and irritability/intrusiveness) and children's ability to use secondary control coping strategies in response to parental stressors (Compas et al., 2002). The intervention is comprised of eight weekly sessions and four monthly follow-up sessions delivered to four families at a time. Through didactic presentations and role plays during the sessions and extensive homework between sessions, the emphasis is on the development of skills that will lead to reductions in parent-child stress and the increased ability of children to cope with these stressors when they do occur.

Initial findings from an open trial with 30 families are promising. Risk factors were reduced from pre- to post-intervention, as reflected in significant reductions in parental depressive symptoms and parental withdrawal. Concomitantly, children's use of secondary control coping increased significantly from before to after the intervention. And most importantly, there were significant declines in both internalizing and externalizing problems from pre- to post-intervention. Effect sizes were generally moderate in magnitude. The intervention is now being tested in a clinical trial in which families are randomized to receive the group intervention or an information-only control condition. These preliminary data suggest that teaching parenting skills may contribute to reductions in parents' depressive symptoms, perhaps by helping parents interact with their children in ways that help them to feel competent. Enhanced parenting skills are also associated with decreased withdrawal by depressed parents, making them more physically and emotionally available to their children and thus reducing a significant source of stress for children.

Conclusion

Sources of stress in the lives of adolescents serve as a significant source of risk for psychopathology. However, the effects of stress are mediated and moderated by the ways that children and adolescents react to and cope with stress. As a consequence, interventions that aim to reduce sources of stress and enhance effective coping provide a promising avenue for preventive interventions aimed at improving the lives of children and adolescents who are at-risk for psychopathology. Interventions aimed at stress and coping processes within families may be a particularly fruitful direction for such work, as interventionists may be able to simultaneously reduce levels of stress within families and improve the coping abilities of children and adolescents.

References

Cicchetti, D., & Toth, S.L. (Eds.) (1997). *Developmental Perspectives on Trauma: Theory, Research and Intervention.* Rochester, NY: Rochester University Press.

Clarke, G.N., Hornbrook, M., Lynch, F., Polen, M., Gale, J., Beardslee, W., O'Connor, W., & Seeley, J. (2001). A randomized trial of a group cognitive intervention for preventing depression in adolescent offspring of depressed parents. *Archives of General Psychiatry, 58(12),* 1,127–1,134.

Compas, B.E. (2004). Processes of risk and resilience during adolescence: Linking contexts and individuals. In R.M. Lerner

& L. Steinberg (Eds.), *Handbook of Adolescent Psychology* (2nd ed., pp. 263–296). New Jersey: John Wiley & Sons, Inc.

Compas, BE., Connor, J.K., Saltzman, H., Thomsen, A.H., & Wadsworth, M. (1999). Getting specific about coping: Effortful and involuntary responses to stress in development. In M. Lewis & D. Ramsey (Eds.), *Soothing and Stress* (pp. 229–256). New York: Cambridge University Press.

Compas, B.E., Connor-Smith, J.K., Thomsen, A.H., Saltzman, H., & Wadsworth, M.E. (2001). Coping with stress during childhood and adolescence: Progress, problems, and potential in theory and research. *Psychological Bulletin, 127,* 87–127.

Compas, B.E., Langrock, A.M., Keller, G., Merchant, M.J., & Copeland, M.E. (2001). Children coping with parental depression: Processes of adaptation to family stress. In S. Goodman & I. Gotlib (Eds.), *Children of Depressed Parents: Alternative Pathways to Risk for Psychopathology.* Washington, DC: American Psychological Association.

Connor-Smith, J.K., & Compas, B.E. (2002). Vulnerability to social stress: Coping as a mediator or moderator of sociotropy and symptoms of anxiety and depression. *Cognitive Therapy and Research, 26,* 39–55.

Connor-Smith, J.K., Compas, B.E., Wadsworth, M.E., Thomsen, A.H., & Saltzman, H. (2000). Responses to stress in adolescence: Measurement of coping and involuntary responses to stress. *Journal of Consulting and Clinical Psychology, 68,* 976–992.

Grant, K.E., Compas, B.E., Thurm, A., McMahon, S., & Gipson, P. (2004). Stressors and child and adolescent psychopathology: Measurement issues and prospective effects. *Journal of Clinical Child and Adolescent Psychology, 33:2,* 412–425.

Grant, K.E., Compas, B.E., Stuhlmacher, A.F., Thurm, A.E., McMahon, S.D., & Halpert, J.A. (2003). Stressors and child and adolescent psychopathology: Moving from markers to mechanisms of risk. *Psychological Bulletin, 129(3),* 447–466.

Haggerty, R.J., Sherrod, L.R., Garmezy, N., & Rutter, M. (Eds.). (1994). *Stress, Risk and Resilience in Children and Adolescents: Processes, Mechanisms, and Interventions.* New York: Cambridge University Press.

Jaser, S.S., Langrock, A.M., Keller, G., Merchant, M.J., Benson, M.A., Reeslund, K., Champion, J.E., & Compas, B.E. (2005).

Coping With the Stress of Parental Depression II: Adolescent and Parent Reports of Coping and Adjustment. *Journal of Clinical Child and Adolescent Psychology, 34(1),* 193–205.

Kraemer, H.C., Kazdin, A.E., Offord, D.R., Kessler, R.C., Jensen, P.S., & Kupfer, D.J. (1997). Coming to terms with the terms of risk. *Archives of General Psychiatry, 54,* 337–343.

Langrock, A.M., Compas, B.E., Keller, G., Merchant, M.J., & Copeland, M.E. (2002). Coping with the stress of parental depression: Parents' reports of children's coping, emotional, and behavioral problems. *Journal of Clinical Child and Adolescent Psychology, 31,* 312–324.

Lazarus, R.S., & Folkman, S. (1984). *Stress, Appraisal, and Coping.* New York: Springer.

Luthar, S.S. & Cicchetti, D. (2000). The construct of resilience: Implications for interventions and social policy. *Development and Psychopathology, 12,* 857–885.

McMahon, S.D., Grant, K.E., Compas, B.E., Thurm, A.E., & Ey, S. (2003). Stress and psychopathology in children and adolescents: Is there evidence of specificity? *Journal of Child Psychology and Psychiatry, 44:1,* 107–133.

Thomsen, A.H., Compas, B.E., Colletti, R.B., Stanger, C., Boyer, M.C., & Konik, B.S. (2002). Parents' reports of coping and stress responses in children with recurrent abdominal pain. *Journal of Pediatric Psychology, 27,* 215–226.

Wadsworth, M.E., & Compas, B.E. (2002). Coping with economic strain and family conflict: The adolescent perspective. *Journal of Research on Adolescence, 12,* 243–274.

Wolchik, S.A., West, S.G., Sandler, I.N., Tein, J.Y., Coatsworth, D., et al. (2000). An experimental evaluation of theory-based mother and mother-child programs for children of divorce. *Journal of Consulting and Clinical Psychology, 68,* 843–856.

BRUCE E. COMPAS, PHD, is the Patricia and Rodes Hart Professor of Psychology & Human Development and Pediatrics at Vanderbilt University where he also serves as Director of Clinical Psychology Training and Director of Psychological Oncology at the Vanderbilt-Ingram Cancer Center. **JENNIFER CHAMPION,** BA, is a doctoral student in clinical psychology at Vanderbilt University. **KRISTEN REESLUND,** BS, is a doctoral student in clinical psychology at Vanderbilt University.

From *The Prevention Researcher,* September 2005, pp. 17–20. Copyright © 2005 by Integrated Research Services, Inc. Reprinted by permission. www.tpronline.org

A Mother's Story

PAUL RUDNICK

. . . Parents would certainly deny it, but Canadian researchers have made a startling assertion: parents take better care of pretty children than they do ugly ones.

—*The Times.*

Until I saw the article in *The Times,* I'd felt so utterly alone. Was I the only one? The sole parent on earth who knew the anguish, the heart-shattering despair of—All right, I'll just say it, right out loud. I am the mother of an ugly child. She's not deformed or handicapped or odd; she's unattractive.

Even during my pregnancy, I'd had my suspicions. I remember peering at the ultrasound screen as my obstetrician told me, "Look, it's a brand-new life," and all I could say was "Fine, but why are we watching the Discovery Channel?" And then, after I gave birth, a nurse placed something on my chest and cooed, "Here's your little miracle," and I glanced down, bewildered, and asked, "Who ordered the veal scaloppine?"

For the next few years, when guests would drop by, I'd pretend that Lisa, as we'd named her, was a Duraflame log. As she grew older, I referred to her as our new cocker spaniel, although no one really believed this, because, of course, cocker spaniels are adorable. I did, however, begin to read to Lisa, and the titles included "The Four Little Pigs" and "The Little Engine That Settled."

When Lisa turned five, I was faced with an agonizing decision: where could we send her to school? Shockingly, there are no facilities in this country specifically designed for the education of ugly children, except for a few fringe programs dedicated to computers. So we were eventually forced to send her to school in England, where she was extremely popular. But I remained torn—she was an American child, and sooner or later, at least on vacations, she'd have to return home. The solution became obvious: a large box. I'd have the headmistress simply FedEx Lisa to our address, although whenever the package arrived there'd always be that terrible moment when my heart leaped, because I'd think, Someone's sent me a gift! Perhaps it's a fully outfitted wicker picnic basket, or a case of champagne! But then I'd hear that sound—the breathing.

I tried to be a generous, loving parent; whenever Lisa clawed at her paper bag I'd murmur, "Oh, but sweetheart, it's from Hermès." Still, there were those mornings when she'd want to leave the house in just jeans and a T-shirt, so I'd improvise. I'd say, "When we're in the park, let's play a wonderful game. Let's pretend that I'm a beautiful princess and you're a bench." And if strangers stared at us and asked, "Why are you sitting on that poor child and enjoying your lunch?," I'd defend Lisa, proudly declaring, "She's not poor!"

Our favorite holiday was, naturally, Halloween. I'd get all gussied up as a lovely ballerina, and Lisa would be my pancreas. We also liked to take long autumn drives through the countryside, to see the leaves change; whenever I'd spot a particularly vibrant red maple or a blaze of yellow, I'd cry, "Look!," and pause to listen for her delighted knock from the trunk. Malls and other public spaces could still be a challenge, but this was handily solved when I learned to play the concertina and bought Lisa a little felt hat and lederhosen. Still, perhaps it was Lisa's older sister, Renee, who suffered the most. Renee was stunningly gorgeous, and she always felt the most profound tenderness for the sibling she called her little brother. As a lesson in compassion, I'd say, "Who does Mummy love the most?," and Renee and Lisa would giddily shriek, "Me! Me!" And then I'd ask, "And who does Mummy pity?"

Despite all of this joy, this infinite maternal concern, I always knew that a dreaded era loomed: puberty. How could I make Lisa understand that, although she was a brilliant, vivacious young lady and the balm of my soul, dating would be impossible, even underwater? But then I hit upon a remedy. For Lisa's first formal dance, I arranged for her to be escorted by Bobo, an adolescent male grizzly bear. "It's just like Noah's ark!" I trilled, as I snapped their photo; Lisa was a bit apprehensive at first, until I pointed out that the arrangement was for only one night, and that they would both be muzzled. I'm pleased to report that the evening was a huge success, thanks to a few open garbage cans, a dab of lard behind Lisa's ear, and the fact that no one will ever know that I slipped Bobo five hundred dollars and got him drunk.

Blessedly, today Lisa is well over thirty and happily married to Jorge, our houseboy, who now has his green card, a Chelsea duplex, and one of Lisa's kidneys. And just the other day Lisa said to me, "Mom, it's really inner beauty that counts, isn't it? Isn't that what life's all about?" I took her face in my hands and I replied, "Yes, of course it is, my darling." And I smiled, because, thankfully, it's true—ugly kids will believe anything.

From *The New Yorker,* May 23, 2005, pp. 46. Copyright © 2005 by Paul Rudnick. Reprinted by permission of International Creative Management.

UNIT 5
Family Relationships

Unit Selections

Key Points to Consider

- What effect is experienced by a teen who is exposed to a deteriorating, dying parent?

- What is the impact of parental illness on adolescent development?

- What effect may over-protective parents have on their teens?

- How does family exercise help adolescents?

- Is there a relationship between teenage fathers and delinquent behavior?

- What are the stages and types of family recovery?

- What is the impact of parental incarceration on teens?

- How do teens react when they see their own parent start to date?

- Why are today's youth so busy and distressed? What can families do about it?

Student Web Site
www.mhcls.com/online

Internet References
Further information regarding this Web site may be found in this book's preface or online.

National Council of Juvenile and Family Court Judges
  http://www.ncifci.org

In order to understand the influence of a family on its members, the family needs to be viewed as a system. This means that parents do not simply shape their child; rather, each part of the family influences the other parts. For example, just as parents influence their children's behavior, children not only influence their parents' behavior, but their parents' relationship with each other. A child who complies with parental rules may put less stress on the parents than a child who is consistently in trouble. The compliant child's parents may argue less with each other over issues like discipline. Similarly, the parents' marital relationship influences how each parent interacts with the children. Parents whose marriage is stressed may have less patience with the children, or may be less available to their children. This means that factors affecting one part of the system have implications for the rest of the system.

We can describe adolescents as changing in three major areas: biology, cognition, and social skills. Adolescents enter puberty, and parents see their children become sexually mature individuals. How parents react to this may be influenced by a variety of factors, including the parents' view of their own development. Parents who see their own attractiveness, health or sexuality decline may react to their child's development very differently than do parents who have a more positive view of themselves.

Adolescents' cognitive development may also distress their relationship with their parents. As adolescents become more cognitively sophisticated, they frequently become more questioning of parental rules. Although the adolescent's demand for

reasons underlying parental judgments may reflect newly developed cognitive skills—a positive development from an intellectual perspective—it may increase conflicts with parents. Parents who expect their rules to be obeyed without question may be more upset by their child's arguments than parents who expect to discuss rules and rule violation.

Concurrent with these physical and cognitive changes, adolescents also undergo social changes. These include increased demands for autonomy and independence. Parents whose children were docile and compliant prior to adolescence may feel their authority threatened by these changes. Parents may find it more difficult to discipline children than before. This may be especially problematic for families who had difficulty controlling their children earlier in childhood.

Although families maybe viewed as a system, there is no one form that this system takes. In the 1950s the ideal form of the family system was a breadwinner father, a homemaker mother, and "Leave it to Beaver" type children. Today families take many different forms. About 50 percent of American adolescents will live in single-parent families for some period. This rate is higher for African Americans. About 75 percent of women with school-age children are employed outside the home. About 21 percent of American children live in blended families, with stepsiblings and a stepparent. It is clear that there is no "typical" family. Does this mean that the family plays a less significant role in the life of the adolescent? There search indicates no. The family is still among the most important influences on an adolescent. How well adolescents resist peer pressure, how successful they are developing an identity, and what they strive for in the future all seem predominantly influenced by the family.

The first three articles address the topics of how dying parents, parental illness and overly protective parenting may have an adverse effect on adolescents. The next article deals with a teenage fatherhood and various indicators of deviant behavior. The impact of family recovery on pre-teens and adolescents is examined. The reunification of parent adolescent after incarceration is explored by Gretchen Newby. Many teens today experience their parents dating; this topic is explored by Josh Bailey. The last article discusses parents' reactions to an important topic, youth's busy schedules.

Traumatic Stress in Adolescents Anticipating Parental Death

Amy Saldinger, PhD, Albert C. Cain, PhD, and Katherine Porterfield, PhD

A 16-year-old recalls her father's gruesome decline from lymphoma:

"I get these terrible flashbacks of the last . . . months of his life. . . . This memory, is fighting a war within the walls of my body, desperately straining to burst forth in a violent explosion to free my soul of this intensity." (Waisanen, 2004, Project participant.)

A father reflects on his children's exposure to their mother's mental deterioration when cancer metastasized to her brain: [This exposure] "concerned me more than anything, even the death itself."

Trauma has traditionally been viewed as the special province of unexpected or atypical deaths: homicides, accidents, combat fatalities. Professionals helping families grieve *anticipated* deaths rarely consider their potentially traumatic impact. Anticipated deaths are considered to be the "good" deaths, with forewarning providing loved ones the chance to come to terms with death ahead of time, emotionally, cognitively and practically. Even leaving aside the empirical question of whether people actually take advantage of the opportunities for accommodation to impending death, this romantic view ignores the many logistical, financial, and emotional strains of terminal illness, chief among them the traumatically intrusive images of graphic parent decline. Moreover, the very anticipation of death has adverse psychological consequences including the undermining of the sense of the world as a stable, predictable place; panicky questioning about one's ability to cope; death anxiety ("will she actually die?," "could I die too?"); and an overwhelming sense of helplessness because of one's inability to change the dreaded outcome (Rando, 2000; Saldinger & Cain, 2004).

Experts maintain children can cope with any exposure to terminal illness providing parents frame and support it appropriately. Such assumptions ignore the realistic capacities of well parents (who may be overburdened caring for a dying spouse) to play their customary, pivotal role in helping children weather emotional crises. Nor do traditional assumptions account for individual differences in terms of what exposure children can tolerate, however appropriately framed.

To better understand the impact on children of exposure to traumatic stimuli during terminal illness, as well as the parent's role in modulating the impact, we interviewed spouses and children in families who had experienced parental death.

Methods

Data come from a qualitative community study of 65 families with children (ages 6 to 16) coping with parental death. Here we examine the 35 anticipated deaths, of which 86% were due to cancer. (Of the remaining 30 deaths, 7 were from suicide; 23 were sudden.) Participants were predominately Caucasian (91%) and largely middle-income. Sex of surviving parent was 71% female and 29% male; children were 52% female and 48% male. All families were intact at the time of parental death. Exclusionary criteria ruled out preexisting major life stressors such as mental illness or other deaths within the nuclear family.

Family members were interviewed 8 to 36 months after the death. Length of interviews ranged from 6 to 10 hours with surviving parents and 2 to 4 hours with children. Participants were asked about changes in daily life and family relationships during the illness and about their reactions to parental decline and impending death.

Findings
Range of Exposure

Illness length ranged from 2 months to 10 years. Some illnesses included lengthy remissions; others featured persistent decline. Children witnessed graphic physical decline including limb loss, unusual body odor or color, expectorating blood, prominent tumors, seizures and paralysis. Visible treatment side effects included weight loss, fatigue, bloating, vomiting, and hair loss. Medicalization of the home was common since diapers, catheters, feeding tubes, and oxygen tanks were required for such symptoms as incontinence, eating or breathing difficulties. Many children were also exposed to a dying parent's emotional volatility throughout the illness with end stages involving hallucinations, dementia, emotional withdrawal, and comas.

One mother captured the range of exposure facing families when she compared her husband's 5-year battle with lymphoma to her mother's breast cancer:

[Lymphoma] "is a terrible way to die. [After his transplant] Leo had graft versus host disease. For one year I fed him by machine. . . . We had a machine for his lungs. We never, ever, had one day that we didn't have to do something medically with him . . . [Whereas] my mom's breast cancer—she had it for 18 months and we had maybe one month [total] . . . that she was really ill."[1]

Children's Reactions to Exposure

Maturity affected youngsters' comfort with exposure. As a group, adolescents reacted more negatively to graphic exposure than did younger children, perhaps because their cognitive capacities made it easier to comprehend the significance of the changes they witnessed. Aaron, age 16, recalls strong revulsion:

I didn't want to spend . . . time with [mom]. . . . I was scared of the fact she was dying. . . . It's different than you're used to. You're kind of speechless and you don't know what to say."

To Aaron's brother, Barry, age 10, however, mom still seemed like herself, "almost all the time," and Barry wanted to be with mom to give "her hugs and kisses and [talk] to her."

Some very young children displayed not only tolerance, but even unabashed interest in graphic change. As one mother explained:

Stresses for Adolescents with a Dying Parent

1. Physical, mental and emotional deterioration of dying parent.
2. Forced exposure to dying parent. Teens less protected from exposure than younger children.
3. Fear of the unknowable; traumatic helplessness in the face of death.
4. Secondary traumatic stress: Inability to help traumatized, dying parent or to attenuate reactive distress of other family members.
5. Loss of sense of world as a safe, predicable place.
6. Teen's fear of intensity *own* emotional reactions.
7. Guilt over inability to tolerate exposure. Guilt compounded by unrealistic expectations of parents and teens about teenager's capacities to manage exposure.
8. Surviving parent physically unavailable.
9. Surviving parent emotionally depleted.
   a. Surviving parent unable to recognize and appropriately respond to child's reactions to impending death and dying parent.
   b. Parentified Child. Surviving parent seeking support from child.

"They asked to see everything. All the yucky smelly tubes . . . [He had a draining tube in his stomach.] For 6 days before he died he drank cranberry juice. . . . As soon as the juice went in, it went right out this tube. The girls and I sat and watched and laughed."

Most children, of whatever age, however, reacted negatively to the dying process, their reactivity stemming both from sensitivity to graphic stimuli and to fears of the uncontainable. Recalls one boy: "I was kind of scared [of being with mom.] Pretty much anything could happen . . . . She could pass out or do something I didn't know about."

Terrifying, as well, for youngsters was the intensity of their own emotions: "It felt like these feelings weren't normal . . . because I never felt this stressed out . . . about something like that before." Teens, in particular, struggled with guilt about an inability to tolerate exposure, a guilt to which they attest when recollecting their dread of hospital visits:

[Adolescent boy] "I never went to see her, because I was afraid of hospitals. . . . I felt guilty and disappointed, 'cause I knew if I wanted to, I could get up the courage to see her, but I still didn't."

[Adolescent girl] "I felt ashamed when I thought of all the times I made an excuse not to go see him just because I didn't like to see him that way. I was so selfish."

Teenagers with high tolerance for graphic stimuli are afforded some protection from traumatic stress. But for those with low thresholds, or for whom horrific stimuli exceed even a high threshold, guilty tension develops around desires to avoid the dying parent. This tension, is, itself, a traumatic stressor of anticipated death.

Parents' Role in Mediating Traumatic Exposure for Children

Some parents were extraordinarily thoughtful in helping children cope. One mother describes handling her son's response to the news that dad would die:

"He reacted . . . by being afraid of Allen. He was afraid death was going to happen. [I told him] 'Dad's not just going to die, we will know before he dies' . . . But he was afraid and he didn't want to stay with Allen. . . . If *I* was there, he was fine . . . but he didn't want me to leave. So for a few nights I didn't, but then I did go for a short walk, and eventually he got over that." [The last week, I suggested he sleep in the den so he] wouldn't . . . hear [dad's heavy breathing]. . . . [The last day] I gave [him] the choice of going to grandma's. It was hard for me not to have him there, but . . . I had the sense [he] was going to climb out of his skin."

This mother recognized that the very concept of death frightened her son. When verbal reassurance proved insufficient, she used her physical presence to help him master his fears. She discriminated among exposure worth mastering (staying connected to dad in the remaining 6 months); needless exposure (dad's heavy breathing); and exposure that merited a choice (exposure to the death). She asked only what was reasonable and supported her son throughout.

Many parents, however, preoccupied with their dying spouse, could barely handle ordinary parenting duties let alone help children grapple with impending death.

> [Surviving mother] "I don't remember much about my role with my boys. . . . I don't think they had *any* parent during those last few months."

Such parents, psychologically primed to assume "no news is good news," left children on their own to cope with stimuli which parents themselves found distressing:

> [Surviving dad] "She went from a healthy-looking person, to a person with the physical likeness of an 80-year-old . . . with osteoporosis. I don't remember [the kids] having any big reaction to her appearance. . . . They didn't go up to her and say . . . 'what's wrong?' They never asked me questions."

> [Surviving mom] "He looked horrible . . . that was the worst part, that he had to see himself. . . . I didn't want to cover the mirrors . . . I probably should've. . . . [But] because the changes were so gradual . . . [the kids] accepted everything."

The tendency to take children's reactions of nonchalance at face value testifies to overwhelmed parents' need to believe their children could cope, and cope, moreover, without adult intervention. Intuiting parental needs, children responded protectively, avoiding overt expression of distress. Clarifying why he did not share his feelings when his mother was dying, one youngster explains:

> "I didn't know . . . if [dad] would have any knowledge about how I felt or how to help me get rid of . . . unwanted feelings. I didn't think he had ever experienced this, so I didn't want to take a chance that he couldn't help me."

Some adults, alert to their child's discomfort did not insist on contact:

> "When . . . Eric was in a wheelchair . . . they got scared: 'this is my strong father, now basically he can't do anything.' They didn't know how to deal with it. . . . [A]s far as going to see him—it was up to them. I didn't say, 'you have to.'"

Unfortunately, allowing children—even mature teenagers—to determine *unaided* the amount of contact with a dying parent may burden them with guilt for eschewing connection. A laissez-faire stance, however, is preferable to that of the least protective parents—those who forced contact on terrified youngsters:

> "I always brought the kids to see their dad. . . . Ellen would throw up and get migraines when it was time to go. . . . But it's an important part of growing up . . . to see that sometimes people get sick, and we have to deal with them."

Subtler forms of coercion were imposed on children who were urged to make hospital visits for the sake of the dying parent:

> [Surviving father] "My [son] didn't like to go. I'm sure it scared him. . . . But I made him come. . . . It gave [his mom] a reason not to think about herself."

However altruistically motivated, when parents insist that children exhibit a level of self-sacrifice that exceeds their level of maturity or individual tolerance, the anticipatory experience of parental death can become painful, if not toxic.

Parenting Decisions around Mental and Emotional Change

Personality and emotional changes accompanying anticipated parental death are heartbreaking for children: children view these states as personally directed against them, rather than as manifestations of, or responses to, terminal illness.

> [Surviving dad] "My wife was pushing everyone away . . . Mona felt that. . . . Mona said things like, 'she doesn't think I'm important to her anymore.'"

As adults we appreciate mother's retreat from the intolerable impending loss of her parental role or from life itself. But from a child's perspective it would be natural to conclude, as Mona did, that she was no longer important to her mother. A son describes similar incomprehension at father's rejecting outbursts:

> [Brandon] "He never seemed like my dad any more. He yelled at me if I did anything. If I came too close . . . he made me go farther away. . . . I have no idea [why]. . . . I was sad I couldn't go near him."

> Reflects Brandon's mom: "[Brandon] got scared of him. . . . He was snotty, ignored him and refused to visit him in the hospital . . . because he didn't want to have to see [his father] like that. I worry some day that's going to really bother him: 'I was really mean to my father, and he was dying.'"

As outsiders, we see that Brandon already struggles with remorse, for while mom explained to one interviewer that Brandon *refused* to visit dad, Brandon defensively explained to a different interviewer that he was *unable* to visit: "I had chicken pox, and then I got a sore throat. . . . I wanted to go really bad . . . but I couldn't." Devastated by dad's rejection, Brandon responded in-kind. Mom understood Brandon's distress, but did nothing to assuage it.

Even the most thoughtful parents struggled to help children adjust to a parent's altered state.

> [Surviving mother] "When Ron was [in a coma] . . . I didn't think the kids should see him. . . . I didn't want them to remember Ron like that. But after four weeks, they wanted to see their Dad. . . . I couldn't talk them out of it. I took them, and it was horrible. . . . He wasn't really what they had thought."

Moms predicament highlights competing risks in anticipated deaths: denied access to a dying parent, children may feel abandoned and develop frightening fantasies unchecked by reality; but granted access, reality may be grimmer yet.

Secondary Traumatic Stress

A nearly intolerable emotion for bystanders is watching a dying loved one succumb to incapacitating fear of impending death (Rando, 2000). This is secondary traumatic stress, a stress that compounds the primary stress of witnessing deterioration and death itself. A boy recalls sheer helplessness observing mother's response to dialysis.

"I saw how upset she was. . . . I couldn't really help her. I had to sit there and watch. . . . She'd end up at the hospital because she was making herself sick, because she was getting too excited for [dialysis] to end. [That] scared me."

The concept of secondary traumatic stress can be fruitfully expanded to encompass exposure to the reactive distress of *non-ailing* family members. Children are especially vulnerable to the reactive distress of the well parent given their dependence on that parent for a sense of security, a security already shaken by impending death. Some parents reported consciously attempting to contain expression of their own emotions for their children's sake; other parents were less contained.

[Surviving father] "When I had a lot of anxiety, I would seek out my children. Just to distract me. One time . . . I asked my boy to sleep with me in bed. Just to be close to somebody. Other times I found myself withdrawing."

Some parents struggled to control their anger.

"Our relationship got more conflictual. . . . [The girls weren't] doing anything worse than normal, but I wasn't able to cope with my own emotions enough to deal with it."

One dad recalls his overreaction to his sons altercation with his bedridden wife:

"He sassed her . . . turned his back and walked out. . . . I went up there, and she was crying. . . . I whipped him with a belt. . . . I told him if he ever talked back to his mom again, I'd break his neck. I'm not very proud of that. . . . That's one of the low points."

Helpless to forestall death, Dad lashed out at what he could control: his son's sass.

Thus, traumatic stimuli in anticipated death extend beyond the direct stressors of patient deterioration. Behavioral reactions of well members reverberate throughout the family. Just as children may lack the capacity to understand or tolerate an anxious, angry or depressed dying parent, the reactive behavior of the well parent may leave them similarly perturbed.

Conclusions

Box 1 briefly outlines a number of stressors adolescents with a dying parent may experience. Additionally, following parental death, whether sudden or anticipated, children deal with graphic memories of real or imagined scenes of the moment of death. Traumatic too, after the death, is separation anxiety as youngsters contemplate surviving in a world without the protective presence of the deceased. Secondary stress is common, too, as children witness survivors' despair over the loss, and anxiety about the future. In *anticipated* death, however, traumatic stimuli begin long before the death itself: disease processes ensure repeated exposure to graphic stimuli; anticipation itself leads to ruminative anxiety; and the depleted emotional resources of both dying and well parents subject children to secondary traumatic stress. Guidance suggestions for parents, to help their children during these stressful times are listed in Box 2.

The applicability of these findings to other populations is limited by the relative homogeneity of our sample composition in terms of race, marital status and socioeconomic background. However, the use of a community sample, the decision to limit participation to families that had been intact prior to the death, and the use of selection criteria to rule out preexisting major life stressors has allowed us to examine traumatic stress under the "best possible" conditions, and provides some assurance that what we see is related to traumatic stress unconfounded by other stressful life events.

Note

1. Identifying information has been changed to protect the confidentiality of Project participants.

References

Rando, T. (2000). *Clinical Dimensions of Anticipatory Mourning.* Champaign, Illinois: Research Press

Saldinger, A., & Cain, A.C. (2005) Deromanticizing anticipated death: Denial, disbelief and disconnection in bereaved spouses. *Journal of Psychosocial Oncology, 22*(3), 69–92.

Saldinger, A., Cain, A.C., Porterfield, K., & Lohnes, K., (2004). Facilitating attachment between school-aged children and a dying parent, *Death Studies, 28*(1), 915–940.

Parent Guidance Suggestions

1. Expect adolescents to be strongly affected by exposure to impending death, however adequately prepared and whatever their maturity level.
2. Proactively suggest to teens that parental decline is distressing, inviting them to share concerns.
3. Offer teens choices around exposure, but remain involved in the decision.
4. Ease the guilt of adolescents who forge direct contact by encouraging alternate ways to stay connected to dying parents such as letter-writing, phone calls and emails. (For a detailed look at staying connected to dying parents see Saldinger, Cain, Porterfield & Lohnes, 2004)
5. Since trauma cannot be resolved until danger and unpredictability pass, expect working through of traumatic stress to continue post-mortem.
6. Help teens to identify important and trusted people who can be counted on to support them.

Waisanen, E. (2004). Daddy. *Journal of Loss and Trauma, 9,* 291–298.

Additional suggested reading related to this article is available at www.TPRonline.org.

AMY SALDINGER, PhD, is Assistant Research Scientist, University of Michigan, Ann Arbor, and Associate Director of the Family Styles Childhood Bereavement Project. **ALBERT C. CAIN,** PhD, is Professor, Department of Psychology, University of Michigan, Ann Arbor, and Director of the Family Styles Childhood Bereavement Project. **KATHERINE PORTERFIELD,** PhD, is Clinical Director, Bellevue/NYU Program for Survivors of Torture, Bellevue Hospital, New York.

This article is condensed and adapted from A. Saldinger, A. Cain, and K., Porterfield. (2003). Managing traumatic stress in children anticipating parental death. *Psychiatry,* 66(2), 168–181. Copyright © 2003 The Guilford Press.

Parental Illness and Adolescent Development

Nancy L. Worsham, PhD, and Emily K. Crawford, BA

Even though 16 years have passed, I (NLW) still recall vividly an interview with a 15-year-old male whose mother had been diagnosed with breast cancer six months previously. My interview with John[1] marked our third given the initial one when his mother was diagnosed and follow-up interviews every three months. Interviews targeted John's stressors and coping efforts associated with parental cancer. Once again I asked John about his experience and much to my surprise he said, "Nancy, the thing that helps the most is knowing that every three months you will come and talk to me and I can talk about everything including how scared I am." Although obviously we cannot generalize from John's response, it lends insight into the experience of parental illness for an adolescent, and in this instance a sense of loneliness this child experienced in facing his mother's illness. This story suggests that access to supportive adults may be especially helpful to youth facing traumas such as a parent's illness.

Although it is difficult to establish the specific numbers of adolescents who are impacted by parental illness, incidence and prevalence rates of acute and chronic illnesses for adults of child-rearing age would seem high. For example, Worsham, Compas, and Ey (1997) cited the U. S. National Center for Health Statistics (1993) epidemiological data in suggesting that "as many as 5–15% of children and adolescents may have parents who suffer from a significant disease" (p. 196). As an example, a disease such as multiple sclerosis (MS) typically presents between the ages of 20 and 40, a time of child-bearing and child-rearing (DeJudicibus & McCabe, 2004). Additionally, 2% and 4% respectively of the population between the ages of 18 and 44 suffer from cancer or heart disease (Centers for Disease Control and Prevention [CDC], 2004). Furthermore, an estimated 6,000 to 7,000 HIV-infected women give birth annually in the U.S. (CDC, 2005), and 850,000 to 900,000 North Americans are living with HIV/AIDS (CDC, 2003). A recent national study (Naiditch, Levine, & Hunt, 2005) looked at the prevalence of child caregivers (those youth who provide care to a parent, grandparent, sibling, or other relative) and found an estimated 1.3 to 1.4 million children (ages 8 to 18) provide some type of caregiving to family members. Given these large numbers, concerns about the impact of parental illness on adolescent development arise. Specifically, busy practitioners might be unaware that their adolescent patients or clients have ill parents. Furthermore even if aware, practitioners might be uncertain of how parental illness impacts their adolescent patients or clients and how best to assist these adolescents. In this article we provide a brief overview of both what we know and how we can best help.

The Adolescent Experience: Development and Parental Illness

Adolescence is characterized by multiple and significant developmental changes: striving for independence, the importance of friendships and peer relations, an overall sense of both uniqueness and belonging, and occasional acts of rebellion or at least questioning of authority figures (such as parents or teachers). Thus coping with parental illness can be especially difficult for adolescents, who are in the midst of substantial physical, hormonal, and cognitive changes with puberty's onset. Adolescents encounter increased pressure to engage in risky behaviors (e.g., unprotected sex) and are also at increased risk of developing various mental health problems (e.g., depression) (Compas, 2004). During the adolescent years, youth desire independence that is attained via experimentation and testing boundaries (Santrock, 2003). However, due to various responsibilities at home, youth with ill parents may be prevented from engaging in extracurricular activities to the extent that their peers are able, thus limiting social interaction with non-family members and potentially leading to decreased support systems. Also, the additional roles and responsibilities that may emerge at home may put adolescents at risk for unhealthy role reversals (Faulkner & Davey, 2002).

> **Coping with parental illness can be especially difficult for adolescents, who are in the midst of substantial physical, hormonal, and cognitive changes with puberty's onset.**

Furthermore, parenting includes several important aspects such as aiding the youth with emotion management and monitoring social relationships. If parents are ill and unable to perform these tasks, adolescents may be left to manage their social lives independently and thus may become involved in unhealthy relationships and/or behaviors. Faulkner and Davey (2002) further suggest that parental cancer can lead to depressive mood in both parents. This depressed mood may lead to impaired parenting characterized by less psychological availability, less communication, decreased supervision, lack of consistency in discipline and initiative, as well as more hostility, irritability, and coerciveness. These impairments compromise adolescents' adaptations in the form of behavioral, social, and self-esteem problems. Additionally Faulkner and Davey cite adolescents' reports of complications due to their mothers' illness, such as feelings of conflict between the desire to break away from the family of origin and the knowledge that they were needed both emotionally and physically at home, and frequent feelings of burden associated with additional roles and responsibilities.

Impact of Parental Illness

On a positive note, a great deal of research (specifically in the areas of cancer and AIDS) targeting the impact of parental illness on children and adolescents has been published in the past two decades. Although the total number of publications is still small in relation to other areas of research (for example, impact of illness on adults themselves), our empirical knowledge base has expanded.

Cancer

In the last 20 years, progress has been made in exploring the effects of parental cancer on adolescents. However, existing research is still hampered by methodological limitations such as nonrepresentative samples (primarily Caucasian, upper-middle class, two parent family), reliance on subjective measures (e.g., parent and self-report questionnaires), and cross-sectional vs. longitudinal research. Despite these methodological limitations, research indicates that parental depression in either parent, as well as a higher number of illness-related demands experienced by the parent with cancer often correlates positively with adolescents' higher total behavioral problems scores, externalizing problems, and internalizing problems (Birenbaum et al., 1999; Lewis & Darby, 2003; Welch, Wadsworth, & Compas, 1996). In a review of core results from four study samples, Lewis (1996) reported that adolescents coping with parental cancer had abnormally low self-esteem scores (28%), abnormally high behavioral problem scores (11%), abnormally low scores on quality of parent relationships (18%), and abnormally low scores on quality of peer relations (32%). Furthermore, female adolescents tend to have higher levels of anxiety/depression symptoms and more aggressive behavior (Welch et al., 1996).

HIV/AIDS

In comparison to research targeting cancer, less has been completed with regards to parental HIV/AIDS. Parental HIV/AIDS may present a different experience for youth than parental cancer given its greater associated stigma. Although the prognosis for AIDS has improved markedly, the likelihood of parental death cannot be overlooked. Rotheram-Borus and colleagues (2003, 2005) completed a majority of the existing research investigating the impact of parental HIV/AIDS on adolescents living in New York City where one-third of parents living with HIV/AIDS reside. In contrast to samples studied with cancer, these youth were primarily poor, Latino or African American, and lived in single-parent households. Employing both parental and adolescent reports, cross-sectional and longitudinal research, and including quantitative and qualitative methods, Rotheram-Borus and colleagues provide both descriptive research and a randomized controlled intervention trial investigating the impact of cognitive behavioral therapy in small groups on both parents and adolescents in comparison to control condition. In terms of descriptive findings, adolescents of

parents with HIV/AIDS are more likely to hold increased household responsibilities, experience anticipatory loss and anxiety, and experience compromised psychological adjustment (Rotheram-Borus et al., 2003). In terms of intervention, they found treatment benefits both in the short-term (3–21 months: emotional distress, self-esteem, and negative family life events) and long-term (4 years: teen pregnancy rate, conduct problems) (Rotheram-Borus et al., 2003). Additionally, Rotheram-Borus and colleagues (2005) investigated the impact of parental death and found youth to be especially distressed (i.e., elevated self-reports of depression) more than one year *prior* to death and had more contact with the criminal justice system prior to their parents' deaths than non-bereaved peers.

Other Illnesses

Although greatly limited in both number and date of publication relative to coverage targeting cancer and HIV/AIDS, other disease entities affecting parents and adolescents have been explored, including multiple sclerosis (DeJudicibus & McCabe, 2004; Steck et al., 2005), hemophilia (Kotchick et al., 1996), and pain and migraine (Fagan, 2003; Kopp et al., 1995).

Although adolescents cope fairly well overall it does appear that their parents' illnesses place them at risk for problems with psychological adjustment and might negatively affect both peer and family relations. Furthermore, additional responsibilities associated with parental illness might negatively impact normative developmental trajectories. How parents cope with their illnesses may have a very negative effect on their children; specifically adolescents experience more difficulty if their parents engage in avoidant coping (Kotchick et al., 1996), minimize communication and family openness (Kopp et al., 1995), and/or experience negative affect such as depression (DeJudicibus & McCabe, 2004; Fagan, 2003). Additionally, Steck and colleagues (2005) found that 54% of children of MS patients would benefit from psychotherapy, a need largely tied to the children's compromised ability to cope. Of additional concern, DeJudicibus and McCabe found that although a majority (85%) of parents saw little or no impact of their illness on their children, their children were in fact at risk for psychological problems (especially for internalizing disorders which tend to be underreported when relying solely on parent reports).

How We Can Help

In investigating the impact of parental illness on adolescents, a key concern is how these unique stressors might compromise normative adolescent development. Given those concerns and our review of the empirical literature we make the following recommendations (please also see Table 1).

Cancer

In their research with breast cancer patients and their children, Kristjanson, Chalmers, and Woodgate (2004) reported that adolescents desire content information such as whether their mothers are going to survive, information regarding the seriousness of the illness, potential treatment side effects, alternative therapies, other 'facts' associated with breast cancer, and how best to help their mothers. Adolescents valued information regarding normal feelings of other adolescents in similar situations and about the feelings and mood changes occurring in their mothers. The authors also reported that adolescents viewed their needs as "unique and dependent on their

Table 1   Recommendations for Working with Youth Whose Parents Are Ill

Youth with Ill Parents Need:

- Information regarding the illness, including:
  - treatment side effects
  - alternative therapies
  - prognosis
  - tips on how to best help their ill parent
- Information on normal feelings of other adolescents in similar situations
- Reciprocal relationships as opposed to strictly being a recipient of information
- Support in environments that allow them to explore their concerns and learn adaptive coping strategies
- "Safe people" with whom they can discuss their experiences

Professionals Should:

- Routinely question adolescents about aspects of their lives (for example, ask directly about their family, school, etc.)
- Not assume but inquire from each adolescent regarding his/her information needs
- Provide accurate and timely information in response to adolescents' inquiries
- Support positive parent-child relationships by teaching about appropriate communication skills and developmentally appropriate behaviors for youth
- Help youth and their parents differentiate between controllable stressors and uncontrollable stressors
- Facilitate adolescents' access to support groups
- Be sensitive to the complexity of the caretaking role assumed by many adolescents
- Support adolescents as they pursue normal development (e.g., autonomy, peer relations, and the need to have fun)

own personal and family characteristics, what they already knew about breast cancer, the stage of their mothers' illness and their ages" (p. 115) suggesting that professionals not assume but inquire from individuals what their information needs include. Adolescents also stressed the importance of reciprocal, rather than strictly recipient, relationships. Despite having such clear needs outlined by the adolescents, most of them reported that information and support needs were poorly met in the family and outside the family.

HIV/AIDS

For children whose parent(s) have HIV/AIDS, several recommendations are noteworthy. First, Lee, Lester, and Rotheram-Borus (2002) suggest that parents delay disclosure until the parents have processed the experience themselves in order to be in a better position to support their adolescents' adjustment. Furthermore, other researchers recommend that adolescents receive appropriate support in environments that allow them to explore their concerns and learn adaptive coping strategies (Reyland, Higgins-D'Alessandro, &McMahon, 2002), and that parents provide "safe people," such as a therapist or family member (Murphy, Roberts, & Hoffman, 2002, p. 201) to whom adolescents can turn to discuss their experiences. Disclosure might be complicated by the associated stigma of AIDS; sensitivity to this complication on the part of concerned practitioners is integral. Beyond the stigma, if adolescents are aware that their parents' illness was primarily contracted via sexual contact, this awareness might compromise adolescents' capacity for healthy, intimate relationships (Rotheram-Borus et al., 2005). Finally, given the possibility of parental death (e.g., 50% of parents had died at 6-year follow-up), the importance of appropriate custody plans cannot be overstated.

Other Illnesses and Overall General Recommendations

In addition to those recommendations specific to cancer and HIV/AIDS, we make the following suggestions for families coping with other chronic and/or terminal illnesses. Beyond parents' provisions of safe people with whom adolescents may process their experiences, professionals should support positive parent-child relationships by

teaching appropriate communication skills and educating parents about developmentally appropriate behaviors and expectations for their adolescents (Fagan, 2003; Kopp et al., 1995). Professionals can also facilitate adolescents' access to support groups that can provide both informational and emotional support. Professionals should help adolescents (and their parents) differentiate between controllable stressors (such as chores) and uncontrollable stressors (such as parents' prognoses) (Korneluk & Lee, 1998). Additional effort and problem-solving are adaptive with controllable stressors; whereas emotional support appears more adaptive with uncontrollable stressors. Professionals can provide accurate and timely information in response to adolescents' inquiries and with sensitivity to each adolescent's needs (Kristjanson et al., 2004). Professionals can support parents with compassion to parents' physical and emotional stress related to their illness status, and support parents in their sense of responsibility to their adolescents and how their parenting is compromised by their illnesses. Professionals should be sensitive to the complexity of the caretaking role assumed by many adolescents whose parents are ill. Although frequently helpful to the parents and others (including professionals themselves), providing care can also compromise normative developmental processes including autonomy, peer relations and simply having fun. To this extent, adolescents need to be supported (by parents and professionals) to continue to pursue these outlets.

Professionals can facilitate adolescents' access to support groups that can provide both informational and emotional support.

In conclusion, armed with a commitment to the well-being of adolescents, current competencies, skills, and information, concerned professionals can intervene with adolescents individually and direct adolescents to their naturally occurring support systems of parents, family, friends, teachers, and so forth. To this end, adolescents affected by parental illness are not alone.

Note

1. In order to protect the privacy and respect the confidentiality of this adolescent, his name has been changed.

References

Birenbaum, L.K., Yancey, D.Z., Phillips, D.S., Chand, N., & Huster, G. (1999). School age children's and adolescents' adjustment when a parent has cancer. *Oncology Nursing Forum, 26*, 1,639–1,645.

Centers for Disease Control and Prevention (2003). Advancing HIV prevention: New strategies for a changing epidemic – United States, 2003. *Morbidity and Mortality Weekly Report, 52*, 329–332.

Centers for Disease Control and Prevention (2005). Quick facts: Perinatal April 2003–March 2005. Retrieved May 14, 2005 from the World Wide Web: http://www.cdc.gov/hiv/partners/AHP/QF_Perinatal.htm

Centers for Disease Control and Prevention (2004). Summary Health Statistics for U.S. Adults: National Health Interview Survey, 2002. *Vital and Health Statistics, Series 10, Number 222.*

Compas, B. (2004). Processes of risk and resilience during adolescence: Linking contexts and individuals. In R.M. Lerner, & L. Steinberg (Eds.), *Handbook of Adolescent Psychology* (2nd ed.) (pp. 263–296).Hoboken, NJ: Wiley.

DeJudicibus, M.A., & McCabe, M.P. (2004). The impact of parental multiple sclerosis on the adjustment of children and adolescents. *Adolescence, 39*, 551–569.

Fagan, M.A. (2003). Exploring the relationship between maternal migraine and child functioning. *Headache, 43*, 1042–1048.

Faulkner, R.A., & Davey, M. (2002). Children and adolescents of cancer patients: The impact of cancer on the family. *The American Journal of Family Therapy, 30*, 63–72.

Harris, C.A., & Zakowski, S. (2003). Comparison of distress in adolescents of cancer patients and controls. *Psycho-Oncology, 12*, 173–182.

Kopp, M., Richter, R., Rainer, J., Kopp-Wilfing, P., Rumplod, G., & Walter, M. (1995). Differences in family functioning between patients with chronic headache and patients with chronic low back pain. *Pain, 63*, 219–224.

Korneluk, Y.G., & Lee, C.M. (1998). Children's adjustment to parental physical illness. *Clinical Child and Family Psychology Review, 1*, 179–193.

Kotchik, B.A., Forehand, R., Armistead, L., Klein, K., & Wierson, M. (1996). Coping with illness: Interrelationships across family members and predictors of psychological adjustment. *Journal of Family Psychology, 10*, 358–370.

Kristjanson, L.J., Chalmers, K.I., & Woodgate, R. (2004). Information and support needs of adolescent children of women with breast cancer. *Oncology Nursing Forum, 31*, 111–119.

Lee, M.B., Lester, P., & Rotheram-Borus, M.J. (2002). The relationship between adjustment of mothers with HIV and their adolescent daughters. *Clinical Child Psychology and Psychiatry, 7*, 71–84.

Lewis, F.M. (1996). The impact of breast cancer on the family: Lessons learned from the children and adolescents. In L. Baider, C.L. Cooper, & A.K. DeNour (Eds.), *Cancer and the Family.* Chichester, U.K.: John Wiley & Sons.

Lewis, F.M., & Darby, E.L. (2003). Adolescent adjustment and maternal breast cancer: A test of the "faucet hypothesis." *Journal of Psychosocial Oncology, 21*, 81–104.

Murphy, D.A., Roberts, K.J., & Hoffman, D. (2002). Stigma and ostracism associated with HIV/AIDS: Children carrying the secret of their mothers' HIV + Serostatus. *Journal of Child and Family Studies, 11*, 191–202.

Naiditch, L., Levine, C., & Hunt, G. (2005). *Young Caregivers in the U.S.: Findings from a National Survey.* Bethesda, MD: National Alliance for Caregiving, in collaboration with the United Hospital Fund. Available online at www.uhfnyc.org.

Reyland, S.A., Higgins-D'Alessandro, A., & McMahon, T.J. (2002). Tell them you love them because you never know when things could change: Voices of adolescents living with HIV-positive mothers. *AIDS Care, 14*, 285–294.

Romer, G., Barkmann, C., Schulte-Markwort, M., Thomalla, G., & Riedesser, P. (2002). Children of somatically ill parents: A methodological review. *Clinical Child Psychology and Psychiatry, 7*, 17–38.

Rotheram-Borus, M.J., Lee, M., Leonard, N., Lin, Y.Y., Franzke, L., Turner, E., Lightfoot, M., & Gwadz, M. (2003). Four-year behavioral outcomes of an intervention for parents living with HIV and their adolescent children. *AIDS, 17*, 1,217–1,225.

Rotheram-Borus, M.J.,Weiss, R., Alber, S., & Lester, P. (2005). Adolescent adjustment before and after HIV-related parental death. *Journal of Consulting and Clinical Psychology, 73*, 221–228.

Santrock, J. (2003). *Adolescence (9th edition).* Boston, MA: McGraw-Hill.

Steck, B., Amsler, F., Schwald-Dillier, A., Grether, A., Kappos, L., & Burgin, D. (2005). Indication for psychotherapy in offspring of a parent affected by a chronic somatic disease (e.g., multiple sclerosis). *Psychopathology, 38*, 38–48.

Welch, A.S.,Wadsworth, M.E., & Compas, B.E. (1996). Adjustment of children and adolescents to parental cancer. *American Cancer Society, 77*, 1,409–1,418.

Worsham, N., Compas, B., & Ey, S. (1997). Children's coping with parental illness. In S.Wolchik & I.N. Sandler (Eds.). *Handbook of Children's Coping: Linking Theory and Intervention* (pp. 195–213). New York: Plenum Press.

NANCY L. WORSHAM has a PhD in Clinical Psychology from the University of Vermont and is a licensed psychologist in Washington State. She is currently an associate professor of psychology at Gonzaga University, Spokane,Washington. **EMILY CRAWFORD** completed her bachelor's degree in psychology at Gonzaga University and is now a doctoral student in Clinical Psychology at Pacific University, Forest Grove, Oregon.

From *The Prevention Researcher*, November 2005, pp. 3–5. Copyright © 2005 by Integrated Research Services, Inc. Reprinted by permission. www.tpronline.org

A Nation of Wimps

Parents are going to ludicrous lengths to take the lumps and bumps out of life for their children. However well-intentioned, parental hyperconcern and microscrutiny have the net effect of making kids more fragile. That may be why the young are breaking down in record numbers.

Hara Estroff Marano

Maybe it's the cyclist in the park, trim under his sleek metallic blue helmet, cruising along the dirt path . . . at three miles an hour. On his tricycle.

Or perhaps it's today's playground, all-rubber-cushioned surface where kids used to skin their knees. And . . . wait a minute . . . those aren't little kids playing. Their mommies—and especially their daddies—are in there with them, coplaying or play-by-play coaching. Few take it half-easy on the perimeter benches, as parents used to do, letting the kids figure things out for themselves.

Then there are the sanitizing gels, with which over a third of parents now send their kids to school, according to a recent survey. Presumably, parents now worry that school bathrooms are not good enough for their children.

Consider the teacher new to an upscale suburban town. Shuffling through the sheaf of reports certifying the educational "accommodations" he was required to make for many of his history students, he was struck by the exhaustive, well-written—and obviously costly—one on behalf of a girl who was already proving among the most competent of his ninth-graders. "She's somewhat neurotic," he confides, "but she is bright, organized and conscientious—the type who'd get to school to turn in a paper on time, even if she were dying of stomach flu." He finally found the disability he was to make allowances for: difficulty with Gestalt thinking. The 13-year-old "couldn't see the big picture." That cleverly devised defect (what 13-year-old can construct the big picture?) would allow her to take all her tests untimed, especially the big one at the end of the rainbow, the collegeworthy SAT.

Behold the wholly sanitized childhood, without skinned knees or the occasional C in history. "Kids need to feel badly sometimes," says child psychologist David Elkind, professor at Tufts University. "We learn through experience and we learn through bad experiences. Through failure we learn how to cope."

Messing up, however, even in the playground, is wildly out of style. Although error and experimentation are the true mothers of success, parents are taking pains to remove failure from the equation.

"Life is planned out for us," says Elise Kramer, a Cornell University junior "But we don't know what to want." As Elkind puts it, "Parents and schools are no longer geared toward child development, they're geared to academic achievement."

No one doubts that there are significant economic forces pushing parents to invest so heavily in their children's outcome from an early age. But taking all the discomfort, disappointment and even the play out of development, especially while increasing pressure for success, turns out to be misguided by just about 180 degrees. With few challenges all their own, kids are unable to forge their creative adaptations to the normal vicissitudes of life. That not only makes them risk averse, it makes them psychologically fragile, riddled with anxiety. In the process they're robbed of identity, meaning and a sense of accomplishment, to say nothing of a shot at real happiness. Forget, too, about perseverance, not simply a moral virtue but a necessary life skill. These turn out to be the spreading psychic fault lines of 21st century youth. Whether we want to or not, we're on our way to creating a nation of wimps.

The Fragility Factor

College, it seems, is where the fragility factor is now making its greatest mark. It's where intellectual and developmental tracks converge as the emotional training wheels come off. By all accounts, psychological distress is rampant on college campuses. It takes a variety of forms, including anxiety and depression—which are increasingly regarded as two faces of the same coin—binge drinking and substance abuse, self-mutilation and other forms of disconnection. The mental state of students is now so precarious for so many that, says Steven Hyman, provost of Harvard University and former director of the National Institute of Mental Health, "it is interfering with the core mission of the university."

The severity of student mental health problems has been rising since 1988, according to an annual survey of counseling center directors. Through 1996, the most common problems raised by students were relationship issues. That is developmentally appropriate, reports Sherry Benton, assistant director of counseling at Kansas State University. But in 1996, anxiety overtook relationship concerns and has remained the major problem. The University of Michigan Depression Center, the nation's first, estimates that 15 percent of college students nationwide are suffering from that disorder alone.

Overparenting can create lifelong vulnerability to anxiety and depression.

Relationship problems haven't gone away; their nature has dramatically shifted and the severity escalated. Colleges report ever more cases of obsessive pursuit, otherwise known as stalking, leading to violence, even death. Anorexia or bulimia in florid or subclinical form now afflicts 40 percent of women at some time in their college career. Eleven weeks into a semester, reports psychologist Russ Federman, head of counseling at the University of Virginia, "all appointment slots are filled. But the students don't stop coming."

Drinking, too, has changed. Once a means of social lubrication, it has acquired a darker, more desperate nature. Campuses nationwide are reporting record increases in binge drinking over the past decade, with students often stuporous in class, if they get there at all. Psychologist Paul E. Joffe, chair of the suicide prevention team at the University of Illinois at Urbana-Champaign, contends that at bottom binge-drinking is a quest for authenticity and intensity of experience. It gives young people something all their own to talk about, and sharing stories about the path to passing out is a primary purpose. It's an inverted world in which drinking to oblivion is the way to feel connected and alive.

"There is a ritual every university administrator has come to fear," reports John Portmann, professor of religious studies at the University of Virginia. "Every fall, parents drop off their well-groomed freshmen and within two or three days many have consumed a dangerous amount of alcohol and placed themselves in harm's way. These kids have been controlled for so long, they just go crazy."

Heavy drinking has also become the quickest and easiest way to gain acceptance, says psychologist Bernardo J. Carducci, professor at Indiana University Southeast and founder of its Shyness Research Institute. "Much of collegiate social activity is centered on alcohol consumption because it's an anxiety reducer and demands no social skills," he says. "Plus it provides an instant identity; it lets people know that you are willing to belong."

Welcome to the Hothouse

Talk to a college president or administrator and you're almost certainly bound to hear tales of the parents who call at 2 a.m. to protest Branden's C in economics because it's going to damage his shot at grad school.

Shortly after psychologist Robert Epstein announced to his university students that he expected them to work hard and would hold them to high standards, he heard from a parent—on official judicial stationery—asking how he could dare mistreat the young. Epstein, former editor in chief of *Psychology Today,* eventually filed a complaint with the California commission on judicial misconduct, and the judge was censured for abusing his office—but not before he created havoc in the psychology department at the University of California San Diego.

Enter: grade inflation. When he took over as president of Harvard in July 2001, Lawrence Summers publicly ridiculed the value of honors after discovering that 94 percent of the college's seniors were graduating with them. Safer to lower the bar than raise the discomfort level. Grade inflation is the institutional response to parental anxiety about school demands on children, contends social historian Peter Stearns of George Mason University. As such, it is a pure index of emotional over-investment in a child's success. And it rests on a notion of juvenile frailty—"the assumption that children are easily bruised and need explicit uplift," Stearns argues in his book, *Anxious Parenting: A History of Modern Childrearing in America.*

Parental protectionism may reach its most comic excesses in college, but it doesn't begin there. Primary schools and high schools are arguably just as guilty of grade inflation. But if you're searching for someone to blame, consider Dr. Seuss. "Parents have told their kids from day one that there's no end to what they are capable of doing," says Virginia's Portmann. "They read them the Dr. Seuss book *Oh, the Places You'll Go!* and create bumper stickers telling the world their child is an honor student. American parents today expect their children to be perfect—the smartest, fastest, most charming people in the universe. And if they can't get the children to prove it on their own, they'll turn to doctors to make their kids into the people that parents want to believe their kids are."

What they're really doing, he stresses, is "showing kids how to work the system for their own benefit."

And subjecting them to intense scrutiny. "I wish my parents had some hobby other than me," one young patient told David Anderegg, a child psychologist in Lenox, Massachusetts, and professor of psychology at Bennington College. Anderegg finds that anxious parents are hyperattentive to their kids, reactive to every blip of their child's day, eager to solve every problem for their child—and believe that's good parenting. "If you have an infant and the baby has gas, burping the baby is being a good parent. But when you have a 10-year-old who has metaphoric gas, you don't have to burp him. You have to let him sit with it, try to figure out what to do about it. He then learns to tolerate moderate amounts of difficulty, and it's not the end of the world."

Arrivederci, Playtime

In the hothouse that child raising has become, play is all but dead. Over 40,000 U.S. schools no longer have recess. And what play there is has been corrupted. The organized sports many kids participate in are managed by adults; difficulties that arise are not worked out by kids but adjudicated by adult referees.

"So many toys now are designed by and for adults," says Tufts' Elkind. When kids do engage in their own kind of play

A Dangerous New Remedy for Anxiety

Of all the disorders now afflicting young people, perhaps most puzzling is self-injury—deliberate cutting, cigarette-burning or other repetitive mutilation of body tissue. No one knows whether it's a sudden epidemic or has been rising gradually, but there appears to be an absolute increase in occurrence: "It has now reached critical mass and is on all our radar screens," says Russ Federman, director of counseling at the University of Virginia.

It's highly disturbing for a student to walk into a dorm room and find her roommate meticulously slicing her thighs with a shard of glass or a razor. But it may be the emblematic activity of the psychically shielded and overly fragile. People "do it to feel better. It's an impulsive act done to regulate mood," observes Armando Favazza, author of *Bodies Under Siege: Self Mutilation in Psychiatry and Culture*.

It's basically a very effective "home remedy" for anxiety, states Chicago psychiatrist Arthur Neilsen, who teaches at Northwestern University. People who deliberately hurt themselves—twice as many women as men—report "it's like popping a balloon." There's an immediate release of tension. It also serves an important defense—distraction—stresses Federman. "In the midst of emotional turmoil, physical pain helps people disconnect from the turmoil." But the effect is very short-lived.

Self-harm reflects young people's inability to find something that makes them feel fully alive. Earlier generations sought meaning in movements of social change or intellectual engagement inside and outside the classroom. "But young people are not speaking up or asking questions in the classroom," reports John Portmann, professor of religious studies at the University of Virginia and author of *Bad for Us: The Lure of Self-Harm*. It may be that cutting is their form of protest. So constrained and stressed by expectations, so invaded by parental control, they have no room to turn—except against themselves.

—HEM

the beginning play helps children learn how to control themselves, how to interact with others. Contrary to the widely held belief that only intellectual activities build a sharp brain, it's in play that cognitive agility really develops. Studies of children and adults around the world demonstrate that social engagement actually improves intellectual skills. It fosters decision-making, memory and thinking, speed of mental processing. This shouldn't come as a surprise. After all, the human mind is believed to have evolved to deal with social problems.

The Eternal Umbilicus

It's bad enough that today's children are raised in a psychological hothouse where they are overmonitored and oversheltered. But that hothouse no longer has geographical or temporal boundaries. For that you can thank the cell phone. Even in college—or perhaps especially at college—students are typically in contact with their parents several times a day, reporting every flicker of experience. One long-distance call overheard on a recent cross-campus walk: "Hi, Mom. I just got an ice-cream cone; can you believe they put sprinkles on the bottom as well as on top?"

"Kids are constantly talking to parents," laments Cornell student Kramer, which makes them perpetually homesick. Of course, they're not telling the folks everything, notes Portmann. "They're not calling their parents to say, 'I really went wild last Friday at the frat house and now I might have chlamydia. Should I go to the student health center?'"

The perpetual access to parents infantilizes the young, keeping them in a permanent state of dependency. Whenever the slightest difficulty arises, "they're constantly referring to their parents for guidance," reports Kramer. They're not learning how to manage for themselves.

Think of the cell phone as the eternal umbilicus. One of the ways we grow up is by internalizing an image of Mom and Dad and the values and advice they imparted over the early years. Then, whenever we find ourselves faced with uncertainty or difficulty, we call on that internalized image. We become, in a way, all the wise adults we've had the privilege to know. "But cell phones keep kids from figuring out what to do," says Anderegg. "They've never internalized any images; all they've internalized is 'call Mom or Dad.'"

Some psychologists think we have yet to recognize the full impact of the cell phone on child development, because its use is so new. Although there are far too many variables to establish clear causes and effects, Indiana's Carducci believes that reliance on cell phones undermines the young by destroying the ability to plan ahead. "The first thing students do when they walk out the door of my classroom is flip open the cell phone. Ninety-five percent of the conversations go like this: 'I just got out of class; I'll see you in the library in five minutes.' Absent the phone, you'd have to make arrangements ahead of time; you'd have to think ahead."

Herein lies another possible pathway to depression. The ability to plan resides in the prefrontal cortex (PFC), the executive branch of the brain. The PFC is a critical part of the self-regulation system, and it's deeply implicated in depression, a disorder increasingly seen as caused or maintained by

parents become alarmed. Anderegg points to kids exercising time-honored curiosity by playing doctor. "It's normal for children to have curiosity about other children's genitals," he says. "But when they do, most parents I know are totally freaked out. They wonder what's wrong."

Kids are having a hard time even playing neighborhood pickup games because they've never done it, observes Barbara Carlson, president and cofounder of Putting Families First. "They've been told by their coaches where on the field to stand, told by their parents what color socks to wear, told by the referees who's won and what's fair. Kids are losing leadership skills."

A lot has been written about the commercialization of children's play but not the side effects, says Elkind. "Children aren't getting any benefits out of play as they once did." From unregulated thought patterns—lack of intellectual rigor, if you will. Cognitive therapy owes its very effectiveness to the systematic application of critical thinking to emotional reactions. Further, it's in the setting of goals and progress in working toward them, however mundane they are, that positive feelings are generated. From such everyday activity, resistance to depression is born.

What's more, cell phones—along with the instant availability of cash and almost any consumer good your heart desires—promote fragility by weakening self-regulation. "You get used to things happening right away," says Carducci. You not only want the pizza now, you generalize that expectation to other domains, like friendship and intimate relationships. You become frustrated and impatient easily. You become unwilling to work out problems. And so relationships fail—perhaps the single most powerful experience leading to depression.

From Scrutiny to Anxiety . . . and Beyond

The 1990s witnessed a landmark reversal in the traditional patterns of psychopathology. While rates of depression rise with advancing age among people over 40, they're now increasing fastest among children, striking more children at younger and younger ages.

Parents need to give kids—and themselves—a break by loosening their invasive control: sooner or later, most kids will be forced to confront their own mediocrity.

In his now-famous studies of how children's temperaments play out, Harvard psychologist Jerome Kagan has shown unequivocally that what creates anxious children is parents hovering and protecting them from stressful experiences. About 20 percent of babies are born with a high-strung temperament. They can be spotted even in the womb; they have fast heartbeats. Their nervous systems are innately programmed to be overexcitable in response to stimulation, constantly sending out false alarms about what is dangerous.

As infants and children this group experiences stress in situations most kids find unthreatening, and they may go through childhood and even adulthood fearful of unfamiliar people and events, withdrawn and shy. At school age they become cautious, quiet and introverted. Left to their own devices they grow up shrinking from social encounters. They lack confidence around others. They're easily influenced by others. They are sitting ducks for bullies. And they are on the path to depression.

While their innate reactivity seems to destine all these children for later anxiety disorders, things didn't turn out that way. Between a touchy temperament in infancy and persistence of anxiety stand two highly significant things: parents. Kagan found

to his surprise that the development of anxiety was scarcely inevitable despite apparent genetic programming. At age 2, none of the overexcitable infants wound up fearful if their parents backed off from hovering and allowed the children to find some comfortable level of accommodation to the world on their own. Those parents who overprotected their children—directly observed by conducting interviews in the home—brought out the worst in them.

A small percentage of children seem almost invulnerable to anxiety from the start. But the overwhelming majority of kids are somewhere in between. For them, overparenting can program the nervous system to create lifelong vulnerability to anxiety and depression.

Teens use irony and detachment to "hide in plain sight." They just don't want to be exposed to any more scrutiny.

There is in these studies a lesson for all parents. Those who allow their kids to find a way to deal with life's day-to-day stresses by themselves are helping them develop resilience and coping strategies. "Children need to be gently encouraged to take risks and learn that nothing terrible happens," says Michael Liehowitz, clinical professor of psychiatry at Columbia University and head of the Anxiety Disorders Clinic at New York State Psychiatric Institute. "They need gradual exposure to find that the world is not dangerous. Having overprotective parents is a risk factor for anxiety disorders because children do not have opportunities to master their innate shyness and become more comfortable in the world." They never learn to dampen the pathways from perception to alarm reaction.

Hothouse parenting undermines children in other ways, too, says Anderegg. Being examined all the time makes children extremely self-conscious. As a result they get less communicative; scrutiny teaches them to bury their real feelings deeply. And most of all, self-consciousness removes the safety to be experimental and playful. "If every drawing is going to end up on your parents' refrigerator, you're not free to fool around, to goof up or make mistakes," says Anderegg.

Parental hovering is why so many teenagers are so ironic, he notes. It's a kind of detachment, "a way of hiding in plain sight. They just don't want to be exposed to any more scrutiny."

Parents are always so concerned about children having high self-esteem, he adds. "But when you cheat on their behalf to get them ahead of other children"—by pursuing accommodations and recommendations—"you just completely corrode their sense of self. They feel 'I couldn't do this on my own.' It robs them of their own sense of efficacy." A child comes to think, "if I need every advantage I can get, then perhaps there is really something wrong with me." A slam dunk for depression.

Virginia's Portmann feels the effects are even more pernicious; they weaken the whole fabric of society. He sees young people becoming weaker right before his eyes, more responsive to the herd, too eager to fit in—less assertive in the classroom,

Un-Advice for Parents

CHILL OUT! If you're not having fun, you may be pushing your kids too hard.

- Never invest more in an outcome than your child does.
- Allow children of all ages time for free play. It's a natural way to learn regulation, social skills and cognitive skills.
- Be reasonable about what is dangerous and what is not. Some risk-taking is healthy.
- Don't overreact to every bad grade or negative encounter your child has. Sometimes discomfort is the appropriate response to a situation—and a stimulus to self-improvement.
- Don't be too willing to slap a disease label on your child at the first sign of a problem; instead, spend some time helping your child learn how to deal with the problem.
- Peers are important, but young people also need to spend time socializing with adults in order to know how to be adults.
- Modify your expectations about child-raising in light of your child's temperament; the same actions don't work with everyone.
- Recognize that there are many paths to success. Allow your children latitude—even to take a year off before starting college.
- Don't manipulate the academic system on behalf of your child; it makes kids guilty and doubtful of their own ability.
- Remember that the goal of child-rearing is to raise an independent adult. Encourage your children to think for themselves, to disagree (respectfully) with authority, even to incur the critical gaze of their peers.

unwilling to disagree with their peers, afraid to question authority, more willing to conform to the expectations of those on the next rung of power above them.

Endless Adolescence

The end result of cheating childhood is to extend it forever. Despite all the parental pressure, and probably because of it, kids are pushing back—in their own way. They're taking longer to grow up.

Adulthood no longer begins when adolescence ends, according to a recent report by University of Pennsylvania sociologist Frank E. Furstenberg and colleagues. There is, instead, a growing no-man's-land of postadolescence from 20 to 30, which they dub "early adulthood." Those in it look like adults but "haven't become fully adult yet—traditionally defined as finishing school, landing a job with benefits, marrying and parenting—because they are not ready or perhaps not permitted to do so." Using the classic benchmarks of adulthood, 65 percent of males had reached adulthood by the age of 30 in 1960. By contrast,

in 2000, only 31 percent had. Among women, 77 percent met the benchmarks of adulthood by age 30 in 1960. By 2000, the number had fallen to 46 percent.

Boom Boom Boomerang

Take away play from the front end of development and it finds a way onto the back end. A steady march of success through regimented childhood arranged and monitored by parents creates young adults who need time to explore themselves. "They often need a period in college or afterward to legitimately experiment—to be children," says historian Stearns. "There's decent historical evidence to suggest that societies that allow kids a few years of latitude and even moderate [rebellion] end up with healthier kids than societies that pretend such impulses don't exist."

Marriage is one benchmark of adulthood, but its antecedents extend well into childhood. "The precursor to marriage is dating, and the precursor to dating is playing," says Carducci. The less time children spend in free play, the less socially competent they'll be as adults. It's in play that we learn give and take, the fundamental rhythm of all relationships. We learn how to read the feelings of others and how to negotiate conflicts. Taking the play out of childhood, he says, is bound to create a developmental lag, and he sees it clearly in the social patterns of today's adolescents and young adults, who hang around in groups that are more typical of childhood. Not to be forgotten: The backdrop of continued high levels of divorce confuses kids already too fragile to take the huge risk of commitment.

Just Whose Shark Tank Is It Anyway?

The stressful world of cutthroat competition that parents see their kids facing may not even exist. Or it exists, but more in their mind than in reality—not quite a fiction, more like a distorting mirror. "Parents perceive the world as a terribly competitive place," observes Anderegg. "And many of them project that onto their children when they're the ones who live or work in a competitive environment. They then imagine that their children must be swimming in a big shark tank, too."

"It's hard to know what the world is going to look like 10 years from now," says Elkind. "How best do you prepare kids for that? Parents think that earlier is better. That's a natural intuition, but it happens to be wrong."

What if parents have micromanaged their kids' lives because they've hitched their measurement of success to a single event whose value to life and paycheck they have frantically overestimated? No one denies the Ivy League offers excellent learning experiences, but most educators know that some of the best programs exist at schools that don't top the *U.S. News and World Report* list, and that with the right attitude—a willingness to be engaged by new ideas—it's possible to get a meaningful education almost anywhere. Further, argues historian Stearns, there are ample openings for students at an array of colleges. "We have a competitive frenzy that frankly involves parents more than it involves kids themselves," he observes, both as a father of eight and teacher of many. "Kids are more ambivalent about the college race than are parents."

Yet the very process of application to select colleges undermines both the goal of education and the inherent strengths of young people. "It makes kids sneaky," says Anderegg. Bending rules and calling in favors to give one's kid a competitive edge is morally corrosive.

Like Stearns, he is alarmed that parents, pursuing disability diagnoses so that children can take untimed SATs, actually encourage kids to think of themselves as sickly and fragile. Colleges no longer know when SATs are untimed—but the kids know. "The kids know when you're cheating on their behalf," says Anderegg, "and it makes them feel terribly guilty. Sometimes they arrange to fail to right the scales. And when you cheat on their behalf, you completely undermine their sense of self-esteem. They feel they didn't earn it on their own."

In buying their children accommodations to assuage their own anxiety, parents are actually locking their kids into fragility. Says the suburban teacher: "Exams are a fact of life. They are anxiety-producing. The kids never learn how to cope with anxiety."

Putting Worry in Its Place

Children, however, are not the only ones who are harmed by hyperconcern. Vigilance is enormously taxing—and it's taken all the fun out of parenting. "Parenting has in some measurable ways become less enjoyable than it used to be," says Stearns. "I find parents less willing to indulge their children's sense of time. So they either force feed them or do things for them."

Parents need to abandon the idea of perfection and give up some of the invasive control they've maintained over their children. The goal of parenting, Portmann reminds, is to raise an independent human being. Sooner or later, he says, most kids will be forced to confront their own mediocrity. Parents may find it easier to give up some control if they recognize they have exaggerated many of the dangers of childhood—although they have steadfastly ignored others, namely the removal of recess from schools and the ubiquity of video games that encourage aggression.

The childhood we've introduced to our children is very different from that in past eras, Epstein stresses. Children no longer work at young ages. They stay in school for longer periods of time and spend more time exclusively in the company of peers. Children are far less integrated into adult society than they used to be at every step of the way. We've introduced laws that give children many rights and protections—although we have allowed media and marketers to have free access.

There are kids worth worrying about—kids in poverty.

In changing the nature of childhood, Stearns argues, we've introduced a tendency to assume that children can't handle difficult situations. "Middle-class parents especially assume that if kids start getting into difficulty they need to rush in and do it for them, rather than let them flounder a bit and learn from it. I don't mean we should abandon them," he says, "but give them more credit for figuring things out." And recognize that parents themselves have created many of the stresses and anxieties children are suffering from, without giving them tools to manage them.

While the adults are at it, they need to remember that one of the goals of higher education is to help young people develop the capacity to think for themselves.

Although we're well on our way to making kids more fragile, no one thinks that kids and young adults are fundamentally more flawed than in previous generations. Maybe many will "recover" from diagnoses too liberally slapped on to them. In his own studies of 14 skills he has identified as essential for adulthood in American culture, from love to leadership, Epstein has found that "although teens don't necessary behave in a competent way, they have the potential to be every bit as competent and as incompetent as adults."

Parental anxiety has its place. But the way things now stand, it's not being applied wisely. We're paying too much attention to too few kids—and in the end, the wrong kids. As with the girl whose parents bought her the Gestalt-defect diagnosis, resources are being expended for kids who don't need them.

There are kids who are worth worrying about—kids in poverty, stresses Anderegg. "We focus so much on our own children," says Elkind, "It's time to begin caring about all children."

Reprinted with permission from *Psychology Today* magazine, Vol. 37, No. 6, November/December 2004, pp. 58, 61–62, 64, 66, 68, 70, 103. Copyright © 2004 by Sussex Publishers, LLC.

Teenage Fatherhood and Involvement in Delinquent Behavior

TERENCE P. THORNBERRY, PhD, CAROLYN A. SMITH, PhD, AND SUSAN EHRHARD, MA

The human life course is composed of a set of behavioral trajectories in domains such as family, education, and work (Elder, 1997). In the domain of family formation, for example, a person's trajectory might be described as being in the following states: single, married, divorced, remarried, and widowed. Movement along these trajectories is characterized by elements of both continuity and change. Continuity refers to remaining in a certain state over time (such as being married) while change refers to transitions to a new state (such as getting divorced).

The life course is expected to unfold in a set of culturally normative, age-graded stages. In American society, for example, the culturally accepted sequence is for an individual to complete his or her high school education prior to beginning employment careers and getting married, and all the former, especially marriage, are expected to precede parenthood. Despite these expectations, there is, in fact, a great deal of "disorder" in the life course (Rindfuss, Swicegood, & Rosenfeld, 1987). That is, many life-course transitions are out of order (i.e., parenthood before marriage) and/or off-time (i.e., either too early or too late).

A basic premise of the life-course perspective is that off-time transitions, especially precocious transitions that occur before the person is developmentally prepared for them, are likely to be disruptive to the individual and to those around the individual. Precocious transitions are often associated with social and psychological deficits and with involvement in other problem behaviors. Precocious transitions may also lead to additional problems at later developmental stages. This paper focuses on one type of precocious transition—teenage fatherhood—and investigates whether it is related to various indicators of deviant behavior.

Teen Fatherhood

Until recently, the study of teen parenthood has focused almost exclusively on becoming a teen mother, and relatively little attention has been paid to teenage fatherhood (Parke & Neville, 1987; Smollar & Ooms, 1988). Nevertheless, teen fatherhood appears to be associated with negative consequences, both to

the father and child, that are similar to those observed for teen mothers (Lerman & Ooms, 1993). These consequences include reduced educational attainment, greater financial hardship, and less stable marriage patterns for the teen parent, along with poorer health, educationally, and behavioral outcomes among children born to teen parents (Furstenberg, Brooks-Gunn, & Morgan, 1987; Hayes, 1987; Irwin & Shafer, 1992; Lerman & Ooms, 1993). Given these negative consequences, both to the young father and his offspring, it is important to understand the processes that lead some young men to become teen fathers while others delay becoming fathers until more developmentally normative ages.

One possibility is that becoming a teen father is part of a more general deviant lifestyle. If so, we would expect teen fatherhood to be associated with involvement in other problem behaviors, such as delinquency and drug use. There is some evidence for this hypothesis; teen fathering has been found to be associated with such problem behaviors as delinquency, substance use, and disruptive school behavior (Elster, Lamb, & Tavare, 1987; Ketterlinus, Lamb, Nitz, & Elster, 1992; Resnick, Chambliss, & Blum, 1993; Thornberry, Smith, & Howard, 1997). Some researchers suggest a common problem behavior syndrome underlying all these behaviors (Jessor & Jessor, 1977), a view consistent with Anderson's ethnographic data (1993). In the remainder of this paper, we explore the link between teen fatherhood and other problem behaviors, addressing two core questions:

1. Are earlier delinquency, drug use, and related behaviors risk factors for becoming a teen father?
2. Does teen fatherhood increase the risk of involvement in deviant behavior during early adulthood?

Research Methods

We examine these questions using data from the Rochester Youth Development Study, a multi-wave panel study in which adolescents and their primary caretakers (mainly mothers) have been interviewed since 1988. A representative sample from the population of all seventh- and eighth-grade students enrolled in the Rochester public schools during the 1987–1988 academic year was selected for the study. Male adolescents and students living in census tracts with high adult arrest rates were oversampled based on the premise that they were more likely than other youth to be at risk for antisocial behavior, the main concern of the original study. Of the 1,000 students ultimately selected, 73% were male and 27% were female.

Because the chances of selection into the panel are known, the sample can be weighted to represent all Rochester public school students, and statistical weights are used here. The Study conducted 12 interviews with the sample members, initially at 6-month intervals and later at annual intervals. This analysis is based on the 615 men in the study who were interviewed in Wave 11, when their average age was 21. Twenty percent of these individuals are White, 63% are African American, and 17% are Hispanic. The interviews, which lasted between 60 and 90 minutes, were conducted in private, face-to-face settings with the exception of a small number of respondents who had moved away from the Northeast and were interviewed by telephone. Overall, 84% (615/729) of the total male sample was interviewed at Wave 11. Due to missing data generated by cumulating data across interview waves, the number of cases included in the models for the analysis varies from 551 to 611. There is no evidence of differential subject loss [see Thornberry, Bjerregaard, & Miles (1993), and Krohn & Thornberry (1999) for detailed discussions of sampling and data collection methods.]

Measurement of Teen Fatherhood

In Wave 11, respondents were asked to identify all of their biological children, including the name, birth date, and primary caregiver of each child. If the respondent fathered a child before his 20th birthday, he is designated a teen father. The validity of the respondent's self-reported paternity is suggested by the 95% agreement with the report provided by the respondent's parent in their interview at Wave 11.

Problem Behavior Variables

In predicting teen fatherhood, we examine the effects of delinquent beliefs, gang membership, and three forms of delinquent behavior. These measures are based on data from early waves of the study, generally between Waves 2–5, covering ages 13.5 to 15.5, on average. As such, these indicators of problem behaviors precede the age at which fatherhood began for this sample, and they can be considered true risk factors for teen fatherhood.

Delinquent beliefs asks the respondent how wrong it is to engage in each of eight delinquent acts, with responses ranging from "not wrong at all" to "very wrong." The measure used here is a dichotomous variable denoting whether the respondent was above or below the median value on the scale. Gang membership is a self-reported measure of whether or not the respondent reported being a member of a street gang (see Thornberry, Krohn, Lizotte, Smith, & Tobin, 2003).

Three variables are used to measure deviant behavior: drug use, which is an index of the respondent's use of 10 different substances; general offending, which is an index based on 32 items reflecting all types of delinquency; and violent offending,

which is based on 6 items measuring violent crimes. For the risk factor analysis, all three indices are based on self-reported data and are trichotomized to indicate no offending, low levels of offending (below the median frequency), and high levels of offending (above the median).

These three indicators of offending are also measured during early adulthood (ages 20–22) in order to determine the effects of teen fatherhood on deviant behavior later in life. At this stage, they are simple dichotomies indicating offending versus non-offending.

Results

We present the results in three sections. The first examines the prevalence of teen fatherhood, and the second examines whether delinquency and related behaviors are significant risk factors for becoming a teen father. The final section focuses on whether the young men who became teen fathers, as opposed to those who did not, are more likely to engage in criminal behavior during early adulthood.

Prevalence of Teen Fatherhood

In the Rochester sample, 28% of the male respondents reported fathering a child before age 20. The age distribution at which they became fathers is presented in Figure 1. Seven subjects (1%) became fathers at age 15, truly a precocious transition. The rate of fatherhood increased sharply from that point on. At 16, 3% of the sample became fathers; at 17, 6% did; and at both 18 and 19 years of age, 9% entered the ranks of the young fathers.

Risk Factors

The link between delinquent behavior and becoming a teen father is evident from the results presented in Figure 2. One-third (34%) of the high-level delinquents during early adolescence fathered a child before age 20, as compared to 21% of the low-level delinquents and only 13% of the non-delinquents.

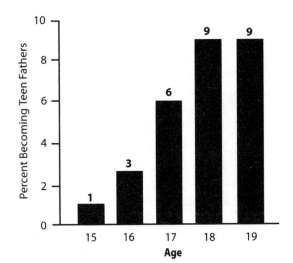

Figure 1 Relationship Between Age and Teenage Fatherhood

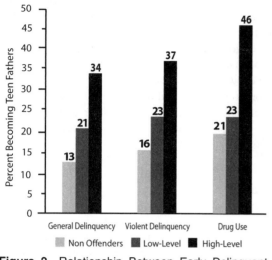

Figure 2 Relationship Between Early Delinquent Behavior and Teenage Fatherhood

The same dose-response relationship can be seen for violent behavior: the prevalence of teen fatherhood increases from 16%, to 23%, to 37% across the three groups. The pattern is a little different for drug use. The prevalence of teen fatherhood for the non-users and the low-level users is about the same, 21% and 23% respectively, but the rate for the high-level drug users is substantially higher, 46%. All three of these relationships are statistically significant.

In Figure 3 we present bivariate results for two variables closely related to delinquency, holding delinquent beliefs and being a member of a street gang. Both relationships are statistically significant. Younger adolescents who have higher levels of pro-delinquent beliefs are more likely (27%) to become teen fathers than those who do not (20%). Finally, gang members are more likely (38%) to become teen fathers than non-members (19%).

To this point, we have simply investigated bivariate associations, that is, the link between delinquency, say, and teen fatherhood, without holding the effect of other potential explanatory variables constant. In a fuller investigation of this

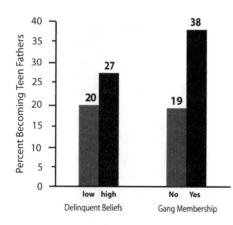

Figure 3 Relationship Between Delinquent Beliefs and Teenage Fatherhood and Between Gang Members and Teenage Fathers

issue, Thornberry et al., (1997) examined these relationships when the following variables were controlled: race/ethnicity, neighborhood poverty and disorganization, parent's education and age at first birth, family poverty level, recent life stress, family social support, parent's expectations for son to attend college, CAT reading achievement, early onset of sexual intercourse, and depression. When this was done, delinquent beliefs were no longer significantly related to teen fatherhood, but gang membership remained a significant and sizeable predictor of becoming a teen father. These two variables—delinquent beliefs and gang membership—were then added to the above list of controls when early adolescent delinquency, drug use, and violence were considered. General delinquency was no longer significantly related to the risk of teen fatherhood, but drug use and violent behavior were (figure not included).

Overall, it appears that early problem behaviors are a risk factor for teen fatherhood. This appears to be the case especially for the more serious forms of these behaviors—violence, high-level drug use, and gang membership.

Later Consequences

The final issue we investigate is whether becoming a teen father is associated with higher rates of criminal involvement during early adulthood, ages 20–22. The results are presented in Figure 4. Teen fathers, as compared to males who delayed the onset of parenthood until after age 20, are not significantly more likely to be involved in general offending or in violent offending during their early 20s. However, there is a significant bivariate relationship between teen fatherhood and later drug use. Of the teen fathers, 66% report some involvement with drug use as compared to 47% of those who delayed fatherhood. This relationship is not statistically significant once adolescent drug use is held constant (results not shown), however. The latter finding indicates that early adult drug use is more a reflection of continuing use than a later consequence of becoming a teen father.

Conclusion

This article investigated the relationship between teenage fatherhood and involvement in delinquency and related behaviors. Based on data from the Rochester Youth Development Study, it appears that an earlier pattern of problem behaviors significantly increases the risk of later becoming a teen father. This relationship is evident bivariately for the five indicators used in this analysis. Also, three of the relationships—violence, drug use, and gang membership—remain significant when the impact of a host of other important risk factors is held constant.

While earlier involvement in deviant behavior and a deviant lifestyle is related to the odds of becoming a teen father, teen fatherhood is not significantly related to later involvement in criminal conduct. At least during their early 20s, teen fathers are not more likely than those who delayed parenthood to be involved in general offending or in violent crime. They are more likely to use drugs, although that relationship is not maintained once prior drug use is controlled.

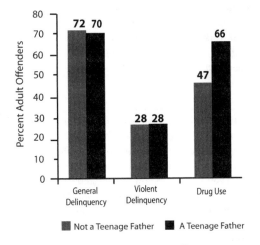

Figure 4 Relationship Between Teenage Fatherhood and Adult Offending

There is a clear link between teen fatherhood and earlier involvement in other deviant behaviors. Two kinds of explanations have been suggested for these effects. The first is that adolescent males immersed in a deviant lifestyle have many opportunities to develop a set of values and behaviors conducive to risky, adult-like adventures, some involving conquest and domination over others, including young women. This notion is supported by some ethnographic research (Anderson, 1993) and some gang studies (for example, Covey, Menard, & Franzese, 1992). Second, research has also documented that about one-fifth of teenage males feel that impregnating a young woman would make them feel "more like a man" (Marsiglio, 1993). There may be so few avenues for positive identity formation, particularly among poor adolescents and adolescents of color, that having a child is no deterrent to potential goals. Involvement in deviant behaviors, including early fatherhood, may at best be a means of achieving adult status and positive recognition or at least a means of making a mark in a world where even survival is in doubt (Burton, 1995).

Implications

It seems evident that becoming a teen father is not an isolated event in the lives of these young men. It is systematically related to involvement in a deviant lifestyle and, in a broader analysis of these data (Thornberry et al., 1997), to a variety of other deficits. These results have a number of implications for prevention programs designed to delay the transition to fatherhood and to improve the lot of these young men and their offspring. First, these programs need to be prepared to deal with this constellation of behavior problems and how teen fatherhood is intertwined with them. Focusing simply on reducing teenage fatherhood, absent a consideration of the broader context in which it occurs, may not be very effective. Second, prevention programs should include, or at least be prepared to provide access to, services to reduce involvement in antisocial behaviors for these adolescent males. Third, programs to

improve the parenting skills of these young fathers need to take into account their higher level of involvement in delinquency, drug use, and related behaviors. All of these behaviors have been shown to be related to less consistent, more erratic styles of parenting (Patterson, Reid, & Dishion, 1992) and efforts to improve effective parenting need to address these risk factors. Finally, programs and policies that try to maximize the teenage father's involvement in the rearing of his children need to be aware of the higher level of antisociality on the part of many of these young fathers. Insuring that risk to the young child is not elevated seems to be the first order of business.

Although there is a pronounced relationship between earlier antisocial behavior and the likelihood of becoming a teen father, we end on a somewhat more positive note. Not all antisocial adolescent males become teen fathers and not all teen fathers have a career of involvement in antisocial behavior. This relationship should not be painted with too broad a brush. Policies need to realistically assess the magnitude of the relationship and realistically take it into account when working with these men and their children.

References

Anderson, E. (1993). Sex codes and family life among poor inner-city youths. In R.I. Lerman & T.J. Ooms (Eds.), *Young Unwed Fathers: Changing Roles and Emerging Policies* (pp. 74–98). Philadelphia: Temple University Press.

Burton, L.M. (1995). Family structure and nonmarital fertility: Perspectives from ethnographic research. In K.A. Moore (Ed.), *Report to Congress on Out-of-Wedlock Childbearing* (pp. 147–166). Hyattsville, MD: U.S. Department of Health and Human Services.

Covey, H.C., Menard, S., & Franzese, R.J. (1992). *Juvenile Gangs.* Springfield, IL: Charles C. Thomas.

Elder, G.H., Jr. (1997). The life course and human development. In W. Damon (Ed.-in-Chief) & R.M. Lerner (Ed.), *Handbook of Child Psychology, Vol. 1: Theoretical Models of Human Development* (pp. 939–991). New York: Wiley.

Elster, A.B., Lamb, M.E., & Tavare, J. (1987). Association between behavioral and school problems and fatherhood in a national sample of adolescent fathers. *Journal of Pediatrics, 111,* 932–936.

Furstenberg, F.F., Brooks-Gunn, J., & Morgan, S.P. (1987). *Adolescent Mothers in Later Life.* New York: Cambridge University Press.

Hayes, C.D. (1987). *Risking the Future: Adolescent Sexuality, Pregnancy and Childbearing* (Vol. 1). Washington, DC: National Academy Press.

Irwin, C.E., Jr., & Shafer, M.A. (1992). Adolescent sexuality: Negative outcomes of a normative behavior. In D.E. Rodgers & E. Ginzberg (Eds.), *Adolescents at Risk: Medical and Social Perspectives* (pp. 35–79). Boulder, CO: Westview Press.

Jessor, R., & Jessor, S.L. (1977). *Problem Behavior and Psychosocial Development.* New York: Academic Press.

Ketterlinus, R.D., Lamb, M.E., Nitz, K., & Elster, A.B. (1992). Adolescent nonsexual and sex-related problem behaviors. *Journal of Adolescent Research, 7,* 431–456.

Krohn, M.D., & Thornberry, T.P. (1999). Retention of minority populations in panel studies of drug use. *Drugs & Society, 14,* 185–207.

Lerman, R.I., & Ooms, T.J. (1993). Introduction: Evolution of unwed fatherhood as a policy issue. In R.I. Lerman & T.J. Ooms (Eds.), *Young Unwed Fathers: Changing Roles and Emerging Policies* (pp. 1–26). Philadelphia: Temple University Press.

Marsiglio, W. (1993). Contemporary scholarship on fathers: Culture, identity, and conduct. *Journal of Family Issues, 14,* 484–509.

Parke, R.D., & Neville, B. (1987). Teenage fatherhood. In S.L. Hofferth & C.D. Hayes (Eds.), *Risking the Future: Adolescent Sexuality, Pregnancy, and Childbearing, Vol. 2* (pp. 145–173). Washington, DC: National Academy Press.

Patterson, G.R., Reid, J.B., & Dishion, T.J. (1992). *Antisocial Boys.* Eugene, OR: Castalia Publishing Company.

Resnick, M.D., Chambliss, S.A., & Blum, R.W. (1993). Health and risk behaviors of urban adolescent males involved in pregnancy. *Families in Society, 74,* 366–374.

Rindfuss, R.R., Swicegood, C.G., & Rosenfeld, R. (1987). Disorder in the life course: How common and does it matter? *American Sociological Review, 52,* 785–801.

Smollar, J., & Ooms, T. (1988). *Young Unwed Fathers: Research Review, Policy Dilemmas, and Options: Summary Report.* U.S. Department of Health and Human Services, Washington, DC: U.S. Government Printing Office.

Thornberry, T.P., Bjerregaard, B. & Miles, W. (1993). The consequences of respondent attrition in panel studies: A simulation based on the Rochester Youth Development Study. *Journal of Quantitative Criminology, 9,* 127–158.

Thornberry, T.P., Krohn, M.D., Lizotte, A.J., Smith, C.A., & Tobin, K. (2003). *Gangs and Delinquency in Developmental Perspective.* New York: Cambridge University Press.

Thornberry, T.P., Smith, C.A., & Howard, G.J. (1997). Risk factors for teenage fatherhood. *Journal of Marriage and the Family, 59,* 505–522.

TERENCE P. THORNBERRY, PhD, is Director of the Research Program on Problem Behavior at the Institute of Behavioral Science and Professor of Sociology, University of Colorado. He is the Principal Investigator of the Rochester Youth Development Study, an ongoing panel study begun in 1986 to examine the causes and consequences of delinquency, drug use, and other forms of antisocial behavior. Professor Thornberry is an author of *Gangs and Delinquency in Developmental Perspective* and an editor of *Taking Stock of Delinquency: An Overview of Findings from Contemporary Longitudinal Studies.* **CAROLYN A. SMITH,** PhD, is Professor in the School of Social Welfare, University at Albany. She holds an MSW from the University of Michigan, and a PhD from the School of Criminal Justice at the University at Albany. She has international social work practice experience in child and family mental health, and in delinquency intervention. Her primary research interest is in the family etiology of delinquency and other problem behaviors, and most recently the impact of child maltreatment on the life course. **SUSAN EHRHARD** holds an MA in Criminal Justice and is currently a doctoral student at the School of Criminal Justice, University at Albany, as well as a Research Assistant for the Rochester Youth Development Study. Her research interests include the sociology of crime, restorative justice, and capital punishment.

Impact of Family Recovery on Pre-Teens and Adolescents

VIRGINIA LEWIS, PHD, AND LOIS ALLEN-BYRD, PHD

When discussing parental alcoholism, it is often assumed that the parent's entry into recovery will resolve all problems. However, our research, which examined the impact of family recovery from alcoholism, shows that rather than being a unifying force for all family members, this process is traumatic, with pre-teens and adolescents frequently becoming the "forgotten" members of the family. The effects upon these forgotten members can be explained and understood in the context of recovery stages and family types. The purpose of this article is threefold: (1) to present a very complex process called family recovery, (2) to describe its traumatic impact on pre-teens and adolescents, and (3) to provide treatment suggestions for supporting young people.

The Family Recovery Project

In 1989, Drs. Stephanie Brown and Virginia Lewis were the first researchers to study the processes of family recovery from alcoholism. This research marked a dramatic shift from understanding how alcoholism affects all family members, to identifying the dynamics of family recovery and its influence on all aspects of family and individual functioning.

There were three questions of interest to this project: 1) What happens to the family when one or both parents stop drinking? 2) Is there a normal developmental process of recovery? and 3) What allows some alcoholic families to maintain recovery while others relapse (often repeatedly)?

Methodology

The research methodology was a cross-sectional design, studying 54 volunteer families who ranged in sobriety from a few months to 18 years. The study was multi-perspective (participants' data and researchers' observations) and multi-level (tests that measured individual, dyad, and family dynamics) in order to obtain a comprehensive picture of family recovery dynamics. In addition, two types of data analysis were used—qualitative (research team analyzing video tapes to determine individual and family functioning) and quantitative (a battery of paper/pencil measures administered to each family member). (Specific information on research methodology and results can be found in Brown & Lewis, 1995, 1999; Brown, Lewis, & Liotta, 2000;

Petroni, Allen-Byrd, & Lewis, 2003; Rouhbakhsh, Lewis, & Allen-Byrd, 2004.)

Due to the focus of this research, the drinking stage and its impact upon family members were studied retrospectively. Families were asked to describe the drinking years which, when combined with the data collected, provided a before and after sobriety perspective. Although painful for many, this journey into the past was necessary as family recovery cannot be fully understood without knowing what life was like, individually and systemically, during the drinking years.

Important Findings

Information from this research revealed that: a) there are normal developmental stages of recovery, b) there are different types of recovering families, and c) the early years of recovery are very traumatic. These latter two findings were surprising and clinically significant. For example, we found that the type of recovering family impacts stage development and requires different treatment approaches for both type of family and stage of recovery. The concept that the early years of recovery were traumatic came from the families' descriptions that this time was very disruptive, frightening, and dynamic. However, rather than being a negative, this "trauma" was normal, allowing for the disequilibrium and collapse of the addictive processes at the individual and system levels. In its place was a void without a map of how to navigate this necessary state. In time, the void was replaced with new knowledge, coping skills, and real-time functioning, providing the parents stayed in recovery through participation in 12-step programs, remained abstinent, and used various treatment modalities (individual, marital, familial) at different times during the recovery journey.

The early years of recovery are very traumatic.

These findings led to the emergence of two theoretical models: The Family Recovery Model and The Family Recovery Typology Model. Both models are briefly discussed below.

The Family Recovery Model

The Family Recovery Model captures the complex nature of family recovery. This complexity is critical for clinicians to understand because *rather than being the end point, abstinence is the beginning of a long and arduous journey that affects all functioning within a family.*

The Family Recovery Model has two dimensions: time and domain. Time is noted by four developmental stages: (1) drinking, (2) transition, (3) early recovery period, and (4) ongoing recovery period. Each domain is examined at three levels: the environment (family atmosphere); the system (family functioning—roles, rules, routines, communication patterns); and the individual (all family members, their emotions, cognitions, behaviors). The three domains are described in detail in *The Alcoholic Family in Recovery* (Brown & Lewis, 1999).

Developmental Recovery Stages

The following is a brief discussion of the three developmental recovery stages. See Box 1 for a summary of this information.

Transition Stage. This stage, which is characterized by the individual moving from drinking to abstinence, can last for several years during which there may be frequent shifts by the alcoholic between drinking and sobriety. The alcoholic feels completely out of control and the family system is in total chaos. The abstinence sub-stage is referred to as the "trauma of recovery"— there is the relief of sobriety and the utter terror of relapse. For example, although the adults in the family are feeling confused, frightened, and out of control, they are attempting to attend meetings and learning that recovery is possible. Their children, however, typically have no one available to them for support, information, or guidance, leaving them also feeling frightened and confused.

Early Recovery Stage. In this stage, the learning curve is steep for the parents as they are learning self-responsibility and self-care, and are slowly acquiring non-addictive lifestyles. It is a time of tremendous acquisition and application of knowledge. The alcoholic and co-alcoholic (spouse) are breaking addictive interactive patterns and learning to "separate" in order to develop their own individuality. Children and adolescents may cope by withdrawing, acting-out, "adopting" a friend's family, or attending 12-step meetings.

Ongoing Recovery Stage. In this stage, the process of recovery is becoming internalized. Recovery has become a central organizing principle (main force of focus) for the alcoholic and co-alcoholic. Life feels manageable and healthy. Problems, when they do occur, are addressed and resolved whenever possible. Parents can tolerate hearing about their children's pain and anger during the drinking and early recovery years. There is a process of healing between the parents and their now late adolescent or adult children.

Family Recovery Typology Model

The second theoretical model with significant implications for understanding recovery emerged from the finding that there were three types of families who differed dramatically from one another in terms of their recovery process. There were families who, regardless of time in recovery, seemed successful in their recovery processes while others appeared trapped in their dysfunctional patterns despite abstinence by the alcoholic.

The "successful" family style was the Type I family— both spouses were in recovery attending 12-step programs, accepting responsibility for change, and participating in therapy at different points in time. They practiced their sobriety, and recovery was a central organizing principle. The more rigid, stuck, and dysfunctional styles were found in the Type II and Type III families. In the Type II family, only one spouse was in recovery (typically the alcoholic who attended AA meetings), and the family environment and system retained the alcoholic dynamics, influences, and tensions. The alcoholic straddled two worlds: individual recovery and marital/family non-recovery. In the Type III family (of which there were only a few and the alcoholics were all males with short-term recovery), the alcoholics just quit drinking without participation in any 12-step program. Although they "looked" the best on the tests

---

Box 1
Family Recovery Model: Three Developmental Recovery Stages

	Drinking	Transition	Early Recovery	Ongoing Recovery
Alcoholic/Spouse:		Alcoholic moves from drinking to abstinence; may involve frequent shifts between drinking and sobriety, lasting several years.	Alcoholic and spouse are breaking addictive interactive patterns.	The family recovery process is becoming internalized.
Children:		Alcoholics' children typically have no supports, information, or guidance available at this time. They are left feeling frightened and confused.	Alcoholics' children may be left to cope by withdrawing, "acting out," "adopting" a friend's family, or attending 12-step meetings.	By this point, most children are now adult age. A possible healing process between the parents and children may begin.

(probably due to denial of any problems), they were the most rigid and stilted in the interviews.

Effects of Recovery on Pre-teens and Adolescents

Recovery is a life-long process for families that is very complex, traumatic, and utterly confusing in the early years. One major and disheartening discovery in our research was that pre-teens and adolescents were generally ignored in recovery (similar to their experiences during the drinking years). When one or both spouses became sober and began participating in 12-step programs, they became immersed in working at staying sober. For example, they attended meetings, spoke a new language (recovery terms), and developed new relationships. They were told that their number one focus was to stay abstinent. The result was that their children lacked much-needed effective and active parenting.

For pre-teens and adolescents, the early years of recovery were often worse than the drinking years. For example, they had learned how to "function" in the alcoholic system while the alcoholic was drinking; but with recovery, everything changed with no understanding of what was happening to their family. According to several adult children in the study, they "preferred" the drinking period to early recovery for a variety of reasons. For example, they had learned how to read some of the "signs" associated with drinking, (such as the alcoholic going on a binge, the first drink of the day), and, consequently, knew how to affect damage control. Initial recovery, on the other hand, was fraught with unpredictable, traumatic and out-of-control dynamics resulting in uncertainty on the part of the adolescent on how to deal with these new issues.

The following vignettes demonstrate the impact of alcoholism and recovery on adolescents.

Vignette 1

In one family, the oldest adolescent overdosed on over-the-counter medication (an attempt to break the denial that there was a problem). As she was going to the hospital, she handed her mother a note saying, "Please go to AA, you are an alcoholic." Initially her mother refused, but in time she became sober, both parents went into recovery, and they became a Type I family. For the first few months in the Transition Stage, the teens would come home, find no food on the table, and become angry. "Our parents got their own place (e.g., AA and AlAnon) and new 'parents' (sponsors), and we lost the parents we knew." Six months later, the youngest child left home as he found the changes and abandonment too painful. When this family was interviewed, they were in the Ongoing Recovery Stage and the parents had developed close relationships to their now adult children. This closeness and healing was hard-earned, requiring individual, couple, and family therapy at different times in the recovery years.

Vignette 2

A late adolescent child in the study became very anxious during the research interview. His parents had been in recovery for years and were a Type I family in the Ongoing Recovery Stage. While they were describing the drinking years, he became aware of how much he had denied that there was a problem in the family while growing up. His mother (who kept her alcohol stash in a closet in his room) would frequently drive him to school functions while drunk—behavior he would say was normal or not his problem. He began to frequently stay over at his friend's house thus "adopting" another set of parents in his early teens. Since no one commented, he thought it was normal. As the interview progressed, he said, "This is making me question my reality checks, my perceptions of life." What had been his constructed reality of himself and his family was being shattered. This is threatening for young people launching into adulthood as it questions their identity and their ability to understand reality and their place in the family system. His father said that there was one regret in recovery—that they had abandoned their son to meetings and new people (sponsors, AA members, etc.), and did not help him understand what was happening or how important he was to his parents. This was a common regret expressed by parents who had years of recovery and the ability to reflect on the past (Brown & Lewis, 1999).

Vignette 3

This last vignette is adapted from Lewis and Allen-Byrd (in press) as a brief portrayal of what an adolescent may experience in the transition/early periods of recovery.

Kayla, the oldest child, was the identified caregiver in the family and was gratefully supported by the non-alcoholic parent. She assisted in household decisions and duties, provided parental guidance to the younger children, and had special privileges because of her elevated role and status in the family system. When the parents/family went into recovery, Kayla was, in essence, demoted because as the recovering parent became more actively involved in the family, Kayla's role and functions were no longer needed. Her sense of worth and power, her identity and understanding of her family's reality were taken away when her parents went into recovery leaving Kayla feeling resentful, angry, and bewildered. Without appropriate intervention, adolescents in situations similar to Kayla's will typically act out and/or withdraw from the family.

Treatment Suggestions to Support Young People

With the awareness that family recovery is difficult for pre-teens and adolescents, positive and therapeutic action can be taken. Practitioners can play a vital role in helping children make the transition from drinking into early family sobriety. They can educate the parents, normalize the process of recovery, and provide a safe place for young people to express their fears and feelings. Box 2 provides a number of examples.

The family type will dictate how practitioners can approach parents and provide parenting guidelines. The Type I family will be open and receptive to new ideas and knowledge as both parents are in recovery and accept responsibility for change,

Box 2
Strategies for Facilitating Adolescents' Healthy Transition from Family Drinking to Early Family Sobriety

- Work with parents on basic parenting skills, inform them of the importance of these skills for abating turmoil within the pre-teen and/or adolescent.
- Explain alcoholism and recovery to the pre-teen and adolescent in age-appropriate terms.
- Educate parents on the needs of adolescents who are developmentally leaving the family and may not be interested in becoming involved in the new recovery family structure and dynamics.
- Provide safe parental substitutes for their children.
- Provide opportunities for children and adolescents to become involved in Alateen, Alakid, Alatot.
- Let children know they are not responsible for their parents' alcoholism, recovery, or relapse.
- Encourage parents to ask for help before parent-child problems become a crisis.
- Refer pre-teens and adolescents for individual therapy with a therapist who understands the recovery process and can help the young person navigate through the bewildering and newly emerging family system. The therapy focus should be on helping teens define their own individuality; work through new roles, rules, boundaries; and find their own voice.

(Adapted from Lewis & Allen-Byrd, in press)

growth, and the hope of a healthy family. In the early years, they will require a great deal of external support in the form of sponsors, 12-step members, and therapists.

The Type II and III families present additional issues. In the Type II family, one member is in recovery while the family system remains alcoholic. There is chronic marital and environmental tension that, while unnamed, is typically experienced by the children. For example, the recovering alcoholic becomes the scapegoat as a way to explain problems and tension in the family, or splitting may occur when the adolescent aligns with one parent against the other. Initially the therapist can effect change by working at the marital level and educating the adults on family recovery (e.g., the three domains of recovery, how every member in the family is impacted by alcoholism, and the danger for relapse when only one parent is in recovery).

Hopefully, with intervention, the Type II family will transition into a Type I family. If the "non-alcoholic" parent refuses marital treatment in order to change the alcoholic system into a recovery system, he/she could join a group that educates families about family recovery.

Pre-teens and adolescents may join another group to become educated about family recovery, to find alternative ways to cope with the tensions and changes, and to acquire healthy ways to begin the separation and individuation process. Frequently, without appropriate intervention, the adolescents in Type II and Type III families become involved in the rebellious, acting-out phase of life.

The Type III families (who were typically in therapy for parent-child issues because their children were identified as the "cause" of the family problems) presented unique challenges. Although the alcoholic stopped drinking, nothing else changed. The alcoholic may have cognitive rigidity (black and white thinking), emotional intolerance, and be on a collision course with the adolescent who is acting out and/or attempting to break away from a stifling, straight jacket, family dynamic. During our research Type III families remained the least clear because of their defensive stance in the interviews and paper-pencil measures. For them, the first step is to break individual and systemic denial. The least threatening approach is an educational format where the adults can attend a parent group to learn about the impact of alcoholism on family members, even though no one is currently drinking, and learn healthier parenting skills (e.g., learn what the developmental needs of the pre-teen and adolescent are). There could be a parallel education group for pre-teens and adolescents wherein they could learn the effect alcoholism had on their lives and the toll it took on their personality development, as well as help them become empowered to alter internalized alcoholic processes and develop healthy choices for their future.

Limitations

There were several limitations to the study, noted by the following: (1) the participants were all volunteers; (2) they were educated (high school graduates to all levels of college degrees); (3) they were predominantly Caucasians (multiple attempts were made to recruit a greater ethnic diversity) and, (4) small sample size. Further contribution to family recovery could be made by studying single-parent families, court-ordered families, and families from other cultures.

Summary

Family recovery from alcoholism is still an unfamiliar concept in the field of addictions and treatment (Lewis & Allen-Byrd, in press; Brown & Lewis, 1995, 1999). The more knowledgeable practitioners are in the dynamics of recovery, the more effective they will be in helping families and their children move through the normal developmental processes of recovery and launching young people into healthy adulthood.

Practitioners are on the front lines providing vital and appropriate treatment plans and referrals for recovering families with children. Their understanding of the normal processes in the stages of recovery and the knowledge of the different types of families can assist them in creating more successful interventions while minimizing family relapses and preventing adolescents from acting out or withdrawing. Pre-teens and adolescents need a voice and therapists can provide a safe and knowledgeable format for them to be heard and to help guide them through the bewildering times of adolescence in general, and in family systems of recovery, in particular.

References

Brown, S. (1985). *Treating the Alcoholic: A Developmental Model of Recovery.* New York: Wiley.

Brown, S., & Lewis, V. (1995). The alcoholic family: A developmental model of recovery. In S. Brown (Ed.), *Treating Alcoholism* (pp. 279–315). San Francisco: Jossey-Bass.

Brown, S., & Lewis, V. (1999). *The Alcoholic Family in Recovery: A Developmental Model.* New York: Guilford Press.

Brown, S., Lewis, V., & Liotta, A. (2000). *The Family Recovery Guide.* Oakland, CA: New Harbinger Publications.

Lewis, V., & Allen-Byrd, L. (2001). Family recovery typology: A new theoretical model. *Alcoholism Treatment Quarterly, 19*(3), 1–17.

Lewis, V., & Allen-Byrd, L. (in press). Coping strategies for the stages of family recovery. *Alcoholism Treatment Quarterly,* special edition.

Lewis, V., Allen-Byrd, L., & Rouhbakhsh, P. (2004). Understanding successful family recovery: Two models. *Journal of Systemic Therapies, 23*(4), 39–51.

Petroni, D., Allen-Byrd, L., & Lewis, V. M. (2003). Indicators of the alcohol recovery process: Critical items from Koss-Butcher and Lachan-Wrobel analysis of the MMPI-2. *Alcoholism Treatment Quarterly, 21*(2), 41–56.

Rouhbakhsh, P., Lewis, V., & Allen-Byrd, L. (2004). Recovering alcoholic families: When normal is not normal and when is not normal healthy. *Alcoholism Treatment Quarterly, 22*(2), 35–53.

VIRGINIA LEWIS, PhD, is co-founder and co-director of the Family Recovery Project and a Senior Research Fellow at the Mental Research Institute (MRI) in Palo Alto, California. **LOIS ALLEN-BYRD**, PhD, is a Research Associate at MRI. Dr. Lewis has co-authored two books on family recovery and both she and Dr. Allen-Byrd have published numerous articles on the subject.

After Incarceration
Adolescent-Parent Reunification

GRETCHEN NEWBY, MA

While children usually look forward to the day when the family is reunited after a parent has been incarcerated, reunification signals yet another stage in a long adjustment process that can be especially difficult for adolescents.

It is estimated that there are over 1.5 million children in the United States who currently have a parent in prison and 40% of them are between the ages of 10 and 17 years (Mumola, 2000). In spite of the large numbers of adolescents with an incarcerated parent, there have been few formal studies of their social and emotional experience during the incarceration and virtually none after reentry. This lack of information is demonstrated by the very uncertainty regarding the accuracy of the statistics: it is difficult to determine accurately how many children have an incarcerated parent because statistics are usually based on self-report, and neither families nor incarcerated parents are forthcoming about this information. Much of what we know about the effect of parental reentry has been learned from practitioners who work with families impacted by incarceration during this most difficult transition. Even more is learned from the recollections of adults who were themselves "children of incarcerated parents."

This article will explore some of the effects of parental reentry on adolescents who are already dealing with difficult issues associated with the emotional issues of parental incarceration, and some of the ways that practitioners, family members, and others can provide support for this often difficult transition.

Background

In order to understand the impact of parental reunification on adolescents, it is important to understand the overall impact of parental incarceration. Families often undergo dramatic changes when a parent is arrested and incarcerated. The first reaction is often disbelief, followed by feelings of helplessness, then anger that may border on rage. Poverty, if not already a concern, may become a daily issue and may result in the family moving to less expensive housing; the caregiver getting a second job; and as daycare becomes too expensive, older children may pick up responsibility for what was previously the responsibility of others. A change in residence may also mean a change in neighborhoods and schools and loss of social networks.

Visiting the incarcerated parent may also create numerous lifestyle changes. For some families, the cost of transportation may further drain their finances. Visits are likely to occur on weekends and holidays, which may limit the family's opportunities to participate in social and recreational activities, including gatherings of extended family and friends. Relationships with grandparents may be strained or lost due to relocation, grandparents' criticism of the incarcerated parent, or their anger directed toward the custodial parent. Religious observances and opportunities for weekend employment may also be forfeited in favor of maintaining contact with the incarcerated parent. Family members, including the children, may not only be deprived of opportunities to build and maintain social networks and support from family, but often they choose to be secretive about those visits to a prison.

The emotional and physical resources of caregivers can become strained as they attempt to cope with the stigma of incarceration, work longer hours and/or deal with extended responsibilities, and make do with less. Caregiver self-care may become neglected as children take priority and emotional resources are drained. Practitioners report that the needs of the most persistent children often tend to get met, while the oldest and the youngest tend to get less attention on the mistaken assumption that the older ones can take care of themselves and the youngest can "wait."

The result may be a family life characterized by chaos that begins with arrest (or perhaps earlier with criminal activity), and persists indefinitely. Families impacted by incarceration tend to become socially isolated (Braman 2002).This may happen in one or more ways, including 1) by circumstance, such as moving to another neighborhood or city, financial constraints, work schedules, or transportation problems; 2) social rejection by family members, friends, or colleagues who are blaming or judging; or 3) self-imposed isolation. Self-imposed isolation is often an attempt to protect family members from social blaming or judgment. It often arises from a pervasive sense of shame and guilt. On occasion, the caregiver is afraid of retaliation from the incarcerated parent's victims or criminal associates, harassment by creditors, or loss of employment due to disclosure.

Additionally, children and adolescents are often not told the truth about the incarcerated parent. They are told that the missing parent is in the army, recovering in a hospital, away at college, or away for "work." If they know the truth, they are admonished never to tell anyone. They move from social isolation to social silence (Braman, 2002).

Emotional Impact

The emotional impact of parental incarceration on children and adolescents can be devastating. For a majority of children of incarcerated parents, childhood is characterized by repetitive and enduring trauma (Johnston, 1995a). The extent to which the trauma of parental incarceration is likely to affect a young person is dependent on a variety of factors, including resilience, quality of the parent-child relationships, and other protective factors.

For some, the trauma begins by exposure to criminal activity, parents' victimization or victimization of others, or victimization of the child themselves. For others, trauma begins with parental arrest. Characteristics of enduring trauma include hypervigilence, aggression, attention and concentration problems, and withdrawal (Johnston, 1995a). The emotional impact of childhood trauma may affect the ability to respond to all future trauma, if it is not resolved. Children with inadequate coping skills whose families are overburdened by stress to the point that they cannot offer support may be less likely to overcome the emotional effects of trauma.

Practitioners, teachers, and others report that children of any age grieve deeply for the missing parent. They experience persistent sadness and they worry about the health and safety of their incarcerated parent (Johnston, 1995a). They also fear that the remaining parent or caregiver will be taken from them, creating a greater sense of uncertainty and instability. At some point, the grief may turn to anger over what they have lost. They mourn the loss of what was familiar, the loss of the missing parent, the loss of the caregiver's attention as the caregiver struggles to meet responsibilities, and the loss of a childhood relationship that they will never have again because they can never be that child again. They also mourn the loss of childhood, particularly if they have been encouraged to take on responsibilities that place them in the parental role. They might blame the incarcerated parent or the caregiver, and it is likely that they will also blame themselves.

Transition

The success of adolescent-parent reunification depends in large part on several preliminary factors, including the quality of relationships before the incarceration, support and contact while the parent is incarcerated, the parent's participation in rehabilitation programs, and realistic expectations for the reentry period.

Quality of the Relationship before Incarceration

Children who lived with the incarcerated parent and who previously had a positive relationship with their parent may be more likely to resume a positive relationship after reentry. Factors contributing to the quality of the relationship include the parent's

use of acceptable parenting skills and practices (Parke & Clarke-Stewart, 2003).

Frequency of Contact during Incarceration

Regular visits, phone calls, and written correspondence are likely to support the potential for a successful reunification (Johnston, 1995b). Regular contact allows the possibility of maintaining the relationship through parent-child interaction, albeit in the unnatural setting of a prison visiting room. Contact supported by phone calls and correspondence may encourage successful reunification through ongoing communication about daily events, activities, interests, and thoughts. Regular communication encourages discussion about expectations and allows parents to see developmental changes as they occur. Absence of communication between parent and child encourages fantasy thinking.

Family members can support and encourage visits and other forms of communication. Money to pay for phone calls and suggestions of topics to discuss, in person or by phone or mail, may encourage meaningful communication. Teachers and others can encourage letter-writing, and can provide school reports to be sent to the incarcerated parent to keep them engaged in school progress. Caregivers may need support in order to accomplish visits, like offers of transportation, someone who might "chaperone" if the caregiver is unable to visit, or helpful information about visiting.

Caregiver Support of the Parent-Child Relationship

Successful reunification can be sabotaged by the caregiver. Building the co-parenting relationship is the responsibility of both the caregiver and the incarcerated parent, and both are required so that a quality parent-child relationship can take precedence over any past differences. Encouragement and support of the caregiver may be helpful, with reassurance that one relationship getting stronger (child-incarcerated parent) does not in itself cause the other to get weaker (child-caregiver).

Incarcerated Parents' Participation in Rehabilitation Programs

Reunification is less likely to be successful if factors influencing the parent-child relationship are not addressed. Programs such as substance abuse treatment, anger management, domestic violence treatment, and English language proficiency may be available to the incarcerated parent. Adolescents and other family members may have the capacity to influence the incarcerated parent, and their encouragement of participation in rehabilitation programs may support the parent's personal growth. Practitioners who work with adolescents and other family members may have an impact in encouraging parent participation in these programs. In most cases, practitioners and other professionals are permitted to write to incarcerated parents about family reunification, providing the family members have given consent to share information. It is appropriate to include an inquiry about available programs or conduct that inquiry with prison staff by phone.

Incarcerated Parents' Participation in Parenting Programs

Parenting programs may be available to incarcerated parents within the prison or jail. These programs may provide additional parenting skills and knowledge, and may play an important part in influencing successful reintegration and family reunification. Improving the quality of interaction between parent and child may instigate other positive outcomes that will ultimately impact the success of reunification (Eddy & Reid, 2003). As with other programs, family members, adolescent children, and practitioners may all be able to influence participation.

Realistic Expectations

Practitioners agree that while the above preliminary factors are important to successful reunification of adolescents with their incarcerated parent, the most essential factor are reasonable expectations for that reunification. According to practitioners who work with them, incarcerated parents are not likely to forget how their criminality and incarceration has damaged their families in the past, but they tend to be optimistic about reunification. Practitioners report that planned activities are often a reflection of the dependency that is fostered by incarceration. During this adjustment time, the returning parent may be overwhelmed by sights, scents, and sounds that are unfamiliar. They may feel tired and miss the set routine of prison life. In prison, people rarely show their emotions and it is considered a weakness to talk about feelings. The returning parent may see family life as very emotional, disorganized, and chaotic. They may need time alone.

The returning parent may seem self-indulgent in their desire to eat favorite foods, watch television, sleep late, and spend time with family and friends. They may resent expectations of others, which are perceived as demands. They plan to provide advice for problems and make decisions, assuming what they imagine to be the role of the "good parent." They believe that their requests will be honored and that they will have autonomy to do as they wish within the family.

Adolescents have their own idealistic expectations of what life will be like when their absent parent returns. They also tend to be optimistic about reunification. Adolescents' own reports indicate that they imagine a loving parent who made them laugh, made them feel special, and made the world a better place. This parent will be patient, understanding, and generous with their affection and attention. In order for the reunification to be successful, these unrealistic expectations need to be addressed prior to reunification.

Caregivers, family members, and others such as teachers and social workers, can help the adolescent to understand the parent's expectations upon return to the community and family, and to realize that some of these expectations may be based on needs.

According to those who work with families who are reunifying after a period of parental incarceration, it is likely that others will want to spend time with the returning parent, creating demands on their time and energy. There may be other children who also want time and attention, and it may be difficult for adolescents to see their parent's attention given to others. For the first time, adolescents may see their parent in a loving relationship with a significant other, or in an adversarial relationship with their caregiver. If they visited in prison, they may have seen their parent in a role that has become familiar. Discussions with adolescents have revealed that seeing their parent in street clothes, with loud voice and laughter as they joke with old friends, is disturbing to them because they had come to know a parent who was subdued and quiet in a prison visiting room. Visits are usually centered on discussions between the parent, adolescent, and close family members. Sharing their parent with others often becomes problematic.

As reported by participants in parenting programs for incarcerated parents, they assume that they are going to resolve problematic adolescent behaviors like avoiding homework, disrespect for elders, and difficulty following rules when they return home. Attempts to assert control after a long absence may provoke an adolescent response that is startling to a parent who hasn't seen it before, creating even greater attempts by the parent to assert control. This struggle for control is magnified if the adolescent has taken on an adult role in the family in the parent's absence. According to adolescents who have experienced reunification with their incarcerated parent, this may be the most traumatic and challenging event for both parent and child.

It may be helpful for family members, teachers, or practitioners working with the family to discuss the young person's expectations, with suggestions for first discussions with the returning parent, reasonable amount of time shared in the first days and weeks, and questions they would like to ask. This discussion may be helpful in organizing reasonable expectations for the early days of reunification. Some adolescents find it helpful to know that they are not alone in this situation. It may help them to know that there is someone they can talk to about the realities of reunification and who listens without judging. A weekly check-in with a caring adult may be helpful. It is also important for them to have opportunities to spend time with other young people who have also experienced the incarceration of a parent. Schools, youth workers, recreation specialists, faith based organizations, and others may have the potential to form peer groups of young people with this shared experience, so they can engage in discussion about issues without fear of being misunderstood or judged.

Summary

Statistics indicate that there are hundreds of thousands of young people who are affected by parental incarceration and who will experience reunification with their parent while they are still in their teens. Factors associated with incarceration and social

Box 1
Promoting Successful Reunification

- Encourage communication between the adolescent and incarcerated parent.
- Send school reports to the incarcerated parent to keep them engaged in the youth's school progress.
- Provide support to children and their caregivers so they can visit the incarcerated parent.
- Provide youth with opportunities to interact with peers who have also experienced parental incarceration.
- Encourage and support the caregiver.
- Encourage the incarcerated parent to participate in prison programs, such as substance abuse treatment or parenting programs, as needed.
- Encourage realistic expectations about reunification.

References

Braman, D. (2002). *Families and Incarceration.* Unpublished dissertation. Yale University.

Eddy, M.J., & Reid, J.B. (2003). The adolescent children of incarcerated parents. In J. Travis & M. Waul (Eds.), *Prisoners Once Removed,* (pp. 233–258). Washington, D.C.: The Urban Institute Press.

Johnston, D. (1995a). Effects of parental incarceration. In K. Gabel & D. Johnston, (Eds.), *Children of Incarcerated Parents* (pp. 59–88). New York: Lexington Books.

Johnston, D. (1995b). Parent-child visitation in the jail or prison. In K. Gabel & D. Johnston, (Eds.), *Children of Incarcerated Parents,* (pp. 135–143). New York: Lexington Books.

Mumola, C.J. (2000). *Incarcerated Parents and Their Children.* Bureau of Justice Statistics Special Report, Washington, D.C.: U.S. Department of Justice.

Parke, R.D., & Clarke-Stewart, K.A. (2003). The effects of parental incarceration on children: Perspectives, promises, and policies. In J. Travis & M. Waul (Eds.), *Prisoners Once Removed,* (pp. 189–232).Washington, D.C.: The Urban Institute Press.

isolation limit their access to social networks and other sources of family and community support may be lost. People working with the family, such as teachers, therapists, social workers, clergy, and others, may not recognize that problematic behaviors are actually symptoms of the social and emotional impact of parental incarceration. This article has highlighted a number of practical ideas which can help support children with incarcerated and returning parents (see Box 1). It is hoped that knowledge of the adolescent's experience may help improve the quality and character of support and assistance in order to help them cope with the transition from parental incarceration to reunification.

GRETCHEN NEWBY, MA, is Executive Director for Friends Outside National Organization. She holds a Bachelor's degree in Criminal Justice with an emphasis in Delinquency Prevention, and a Master's degree in Counseling Psychology (Marriage and Family Therapy).

As Executive Director of Friends Outside, she provides support to 140 staff who work directly inside state prisons providing case management services and support to incarcerated people and their families. Ten Friends Outside affiliates provide support to jail inmates and their families in the community. Gretchen drafted the original "Children of Incarcerated Parents: A Bill of Rights," which is based on her experience working with incarcerated people and their families.

When a Parent Starts Dating Again

Josh Bailey

Q: How should I talk to a parent who's dating again?

There are some situations that are always awkward no matter how mature you are. Having your own father ask you for dating advice would, I suspect, top almost anyone's list. But that's precisely what I found myself doing last Christmas, when I was home for a visit. The worst part of it was, I couldn't even complain. This was a role I had volunteered for.

In the first couple of years after my parents' divorce, I resisted the idea of their being with anyone but each other. But seeing my father lonely was even worse, and after 12 years without my mother it was time for him to move on. He wanted to meet women, but didn't know where to start. So I offered to help him post an online profile.

I didn't know quite what I was getting myself into. Before long, my father was asking me for tips on where to meet women, how to present himself, and what to wear. I suddenly felt like I was the father and he was the son.

Adults in their 20s and 30s will often see a parent start dating just as they themselves are settling down.

This kind of situation is more common today than ever before. The divorce rate remains celestially high. We live longer and stay fitter until much later in life. "Viagra alone has completely changed the landscape of sex for older men," says April Masini, author of *Date Out of Your League*. The upshot is that adults in their 20s and 30s will often see a parent start dating just as they themselves are settling down.

So how should you talk to a parent who's starting to date again? How do you deal with the awkwardness and discomfort you'll inevitably feel?

The first thing to realize is that it's natural to feel squeamish when parents talk about dating. Don't feel shy about drawing a line between the subjects you're willing to hear about and those you are not.

Once your parent understands that you're not interested in locker room stories, though, it's time to get over your embarrassment and put his or her happiness first, says Yvonne Thomas, a psychologist based in Los Angeles who specializes in relationships. "You have to accept them as living, breathing human beings who need love in their lives." In fact, she says, it's a good idea to say just that to your parent: *I don't want you to be lonely. You deserve love and happiness, and I want you to have a well-balanced life and be fulfilled in every way.* "The point is to give permission to your parent to start dating again," Thomas says.

In my case, by helping my father write his ad, I'd stepped up to the plate. After all, dating again is an enormous, frightening step for many people, and lending support was the least I could do.

"Do you think I have to be funny?" he asked me the next day. "Women are looking for a funny guy, right?"

I took a deep breath. "Dad, you're a handsome, intelligent man, you're physically fit, you're basically world-famous in your field. Any woman would be lucky to be with you." As hard as this was for me to say, I knew it gave him the nudge he needed, reminding him what a great guy he truly was. "It's traumatic to get divorced no matter how old your kids are," says Thomas. "You may not feel great about yourself, you forget your best qualities, you feel like you've failed. You're also older, you don't look the way you used to, maybe you've gained some weight."

"Point out any positive attributes you can," recommends Craig Knippers, a clinical psychologist at the Betty Ford Center in Southern California. "Remind them of the successes they've had, and point out that there are lots of people with their same interests who would find them interesting."

Still, he was nervous. He'd pace back and forth on the carpet while I sat on the bed, his Mac on my lap, typing. He felt embarrassed about posting a personal ad online. I assured him that I had done it, most of my single friends had done it, and that it was nothing to be embarrassed about. As awkward as this exchange was for me, I knew it was tough for him, too.

"Bear in mind," says Carole Brody Fleet, author of *Widows Wear Stilettos,* "that the role reversal feels strange to your parent as well. But they still need your reinforcement, just as you needed theirs when you first began to date."

We posted the profile, and I briefed him on what to expect. "Women online are constantly bombarded with messages, so send detailed messages," I explained. I told him to respond specifically to elements in their profiles. At all costs, he should avoid "winking," a feature that allows you to send an indication of interest without even writing a message.

The next day, he nonetheless "winked" at five women, sending a message that said "So-and-so has expressed interest in you!" with no accompanying letter. He was still feeling too tentative to commit fully to the process. I told him not to expect much response. But as it turned out, all five responded. One of them, a political activist and writer, responded, "I read your profile with appreciation for your sense of humor, accomplishments, and interests."

I felt a momentary flush of pride, then quickly got to business, giving my father advice about how to respond, whether to talk on the phone, and when to set up a date. He listened, but the next day he told me he'd taken down his profile. He just wasn't ready, he said.

Someday soon, he will be ready. Meanwhile, writing the profile was a way to feel closer to him and express the things that I don't always feel comfortable telling him directly—how highly I think of him, what wonderful qualities he has, and how much I care about him. Helping my father with his profile turned out to be a reward in itself.

A: Put your Parent's happiness ahead of your own discomfort. Communicate to your parent that you want him or her to be fulfilled in every way, including romantically, and give them permission to go out and pursue that. But it's OK to draw reasonable boundaries. Nobody should have to hear details about a parent's sex life, so if the dialogue ventures into territory you're uncomfortable with, say so. Supporting this phase of your parent's life is a chance for you to demonstrate your love and support for your parent during a difficult time—as good a time as any to start interacting as peers.

Josh Bailey is a writer in New York City.

Learning to Chill

Overloaded at school and overscheduled at home, stressed-out kids—with their parents' blessing—are saying 'Enough!'

SUSAN SCHINDEHETTE ET AL.

L ast year, not long after entering Peterson Middle School as an accelerated sixth grader, Wendy Gregg hit the wall. "If you were late or your homework was incomplete, you got a gold note, and three gold notes was detention," says the formerly perfectionist 11-year-old from Sunnyvale, Calif. "I had seen detention in movies, but I didn't know what it was. I thought only weirdos got it, or people who smoked."

Wendy never actually did time herself, but despite three hours a night of homework, she soon saw her usual A's replaced by B minuses. "I felt pretty stupid," she says, recalling how mortified she was at being assigned to write about why she had fallen off the honor roll. She began to break out in cold sweats and often had stomachaches. In her class photo, says principal Bob Runyon, "Wendy was the only one not looking at the camera. She was staring off to the side."

In January, when Wendy's "scary feelings" were diagnosed as anxiety attacks, her parents—Jenny, 37, a homemaker, and Bill, 41, an aerospace engineer—did a major rethink. "My husband and I decided to pull her out of the pressure cooker," says Jenny. The Greggs took Wendy out of Peterson and homeschooled her for a semester. They reprioritized, making more time for her piano lessons, basketball and I Love Lucy videos. Says her mother: "We reclaimed a lot of her time."

Last month a buoyant Wendy returned to Peterson as a seventh grader in a standard curriculum. Whenever she starts to tense up, she pulls out the "stress kit" that she made in her local Girl Scout troop—a white paper bag painted with a lake and stocked with Silly Putty (for squeezing out tension), notes from friends, an origami bird and her favorite blue nail polish. "Last year I would have been scared," she says of returning to school. "This time I was so excited I couldn't stop smiling."

Wendy's story is hardly unique. From Portland to Peoria, experts say, plenty of kids are nearing meltdown from stress. The evidence is obvious: third graders hauling 25-lb. book bags to class; 12-year-olds juggling their soccer schedules on PalmPilots; a growing number of teens teaming up with $200-an-hour business consultants to teach them CEO-style time-management skills.

According to studies by such groups as the Centers for Disease Control and the American Institute of Stress, nearly half of kids report stress symptoms from headaches to short tempers; children as young as 9 are now experiencing anxiety attacks; and from 1980 to 1997 the number of 10-to-14-year-olds who committed suicide increased 109 percent. In an era when 40 percent of school districts have eliminated recess and 21 percent of teens rate a lack of time with their parents as a top concern, children risk becoming what a paper by the Harvard University admissions office recently termed "dazed survivors of some bewildering lifelong boot camp."

The source of the trouble is easy to track: anxiety-ridden moms and dads. Determined to get their children into increasingly competitive colleges and a tight job market down the

---

How to Help Your Kid Cope

If your child seems unduly worried or scared, is daydreaming too much or having trouble sleeping because of academic pressure and overscheduling, says Georgia Witkin, director of the Stress Program at Mount Sinai School of Medicine in New York City, try the following:

- Establish regular mealtimes and bedtimes. Predictability helps reduce kids' stress.
- Schedule unstructured play periods. If neither parent can be home, hire a responsible teen as an overseer.
- As a role model, make sure your kids see you relaxing with a book or listening to music—not just paying bills and cleaning house.
- Plan stress-reducing family time with your children, whether it's a picnic, outdoor games or just a round of Monopoly.
- If your kids are overwhelmed by homework, don't be afraid to let teachers and school administrators know.

road, today's parents are demanding more academic rigor (and thus more homework), even in grade school. To further beef up future resumes—and, often, to keep the kids occupied while both parents hold down jobs—they're also cramming after-school hours with extracurricular activities. The upshot, says Dr. Alvin Rosenfeld, a New York City psychiatrist and author, is that "parenting has become the most competitive sport in America. "Adds Georgia Witkin, assistant professor of clinical psychology at Mount Sinai School of Medicine: "It's as if an epidemic is spreading from us to them."

The good news is that some families—and organizations—have begun to fight back. Last September, for instance, the Girl Scouts introduced a Stress Less badge, awarded so far to more than 60,000 8-to-11-year-old girls (including Wendy Gregg). The entire town of Ridgewood, N.J., encouraged its citizens to clear their calendars for a "Ready, Set, Relax!" family night last spring. In Austin 6-to-12-year-olds can enroll in a program that teaches them painting, dancing and acting—without the pressure to achieve that often accompanies such extracurriculars. "Once in a while we get a call from a parent saying they want their child to be in a 'real' production, like Oliver! or Annie," says Jeanne Henry, the city's cultural arts education supervisor. "We explain that if the kids come here after school and feel like doing nothing, that's okay. They can do nothing."

Public schools are joining the stress-busting movement as well—and not only in affluent communities. When teachers in San Francisco noticed in 1997 that students were stressed out, they started teaching yoga. Today Cathy Klein, 30, offers it to her second graders at the inner-city Daniel Webster Elementary School. "Yoga calms me," says 6-year-old Filoi Sevatase, a regular at the twice-weekly, 20-minute sessions. "I like doing it when I'm mad or sad, like when my sister hits me or makes me cry." That relaxation technique is also on the curriculum in Atlanta preschools, where 4-year-olds learn to center themselves with the help of a Copee Bear hand puppet. Reports program director Gloria Elder: "Ninety-five percent of their teachers say it helps."

But the biggest push comes from parents like Bill Doherty, 57, a social sciences professor and father of two who lives in Roseville, Minn. In 1999, when he began noticing "6-year-olds with daily planners," Doherty helped launch Putting Family First, a local organization dedicated to reclaiming family time. One of the group's first seal-of-approval certificates went to the conference-winning Wayzata High School football team coached by Brad Anderson, 38. The team has long refused to bench players when they skip practice for family obligations.

Josh Rounds, 18, a senior middle linebacker, says that when he missed the first week of practice because of a family vacation, "it was no problem. I got right back into football when I came home."

Anderson says his own family has experienced scheduling overload firsthand. "As a parent you want to provide opportunities for your kids—gymnastics, swimming, church choir, Brownies, piano lessons. But my wife and I had to sit down with our PalmPilots to figure out how we were going to get them from one thing to another." Instead the couple decided to pare back, limiting their two girls to no more than two after-school activities each. Now, he says, "the kids' favorite thing is family night—playing a game of Battleship together or going to an outdoor concert."

In the nearby town of Plymouth, the Peterschmidt family came to a similar decision three years ago, when they almost lost themselves in a blur of frenetic activity. "I can't bear to look at the calendar from that year. It was crazy," says mother Margaret, 45, who goes by the nickname Bugs. "Every night we'd say, 'What's next?' before running to get Max to his church group or Betsy to soccer." Max, 14, who is just starting ninth grade at Wayzata High, also shudders at the memory: "Trumpet, Scouts, violin, advanced math, church youth group, recreational soccer. And I was depressed because I felt like I had no time to do anything at all." Adds Betsy, now 11, who was equally overscheduled: "I needed a break."

The kids weren't alone in feeling stressed out. In the fall of 1999 a chronically tired Bugs went to the doctor, who found that she had walking pneumonia. During a week of mandatory bed rest, she recalls, "my kids gave me all kinds of stress-relieving gifts—an aromatherapy candle, a little fountain for the kitchen counter. It was a clear message."

One that she and her husband, Eric, 47, a marketing director for Honeywell, finally heeded. Today, after curtailing their schedules, the Peterschmidts are enjoying a newfound tranquility. "Life is so much better now," says Bugs. "But it's like finding religion or quitting smoking: You don't realize how good you feel until you've done it." These days dinner's on the table at 6:15—no phone calls allowed. Family members talk to one another. The kids roast marshmallows and play flashlight tag—"like tag but with light," Betsy explains. "And it's in the dark, so it's much funner."

Each week, Max has a violin lesson, while Betsy takes piano from a teacher who comes to the house. "We don't have huge blowups like we used to," says Bugs. As for Peterschmidt pere: "When I come home from work," marvels Eric, "the first thing my son says is, 'Dad, how was your day?' Isn't that neat?"

UNIT 6

Peers and Contemporary Culture

Unit Selections

Key Points to Consider

- What behaviors are considered to be "risk-taking" behaviors? What can be done to help reduce these problems?

- Does the computers rob students of important social and physical experience?

- Should our youth be taught to kill?

- Is teenage drinking associated with common forms of mortality?

- How does the fear of terrorism interfere in adolescent normal functioning?

Student Web Site
www.mhcls.com/online

Internet References
Further information regarding this Web site may be found in this book's preface or online.

National Center on Addiction and Substance Abuse at Columbia University
   http://www.casacolumbia.org

Adolescents are without a doubt more peer-oriented than any other age group. But it is simplistic to assume that peer influence is always negative and that it outweighs parental influence. Research demonstrates that the nature of the parent-child relationship is consistently the best predictor of adolescent psychological health and well-being. Adolescents who have poor relationships with their parents are precisely the adolescents who are most susceptible to negative peer influences. Poor parent-adolescent relationships are not the norm during the pubertal years; but, rather, conflicted relationships more likely represent a continuation of poor family relationships from childhood.

Research also indicates that most adolescents feel close to and respect their parents. Most adolescents share their parents' values, especially when it comes to moral, religious, political, and educational values. The school the adolescent attends, the kind of neighborhood the parents live in, whether the parents attend religious services, and what parents do for a living all influence their children. Parental choices such as these have a definite impact on their children for the network of friends they select.

Several factors have contributed to the misconception that adolescents reject their parents in favor of peers. First, peers play a greater role in the adolescent's day-to-day activities, style of dress, and musical tastes than do parents. Second, parents often confuse the adolescent's struggle for autonomy with rebellion. G. Stanley Hall's views of adolescence as a biologically necessary time of "storm and stress" contributed to this confusion as well. Similarly, Anna Freud, arguing from her father's psychoanalytic tradition and her own experience with troubled adolescents, maintained that the adolescent-parent relationship is highly laden with conflicts causing adolescents to turn to their peers. According to Anna Freud, such conflicts ensure a successful resolution of the Oedipus/Electra complex. This model of intense parent-adolescent conflict has not been empirically supported and can be detrimental if parents fail to seek help because they believe intense conflict is "normal" during adolescence.

Another myth about peer influence during adolescence is that it is primarily negative. As Thomas Berndt discusses in his research, peer influence is mutual and has both positive and negative effects. Peer pressure is rarely coercive, as is popularly envisaged. It is a more subtle process where adolescents influence their friends and the friends influence them. Just as adults do, adolescents choose friends who already have similar interests, attitudes, and beliefs.

Until recently, researchers paid little attention to the positive effects of peers on adolescent development. Among other things, friends help adolescents develop role-taking and social skills, conquer the imaginary audience referred to in the last unit, and act as social supports in stressful situations. Although they decry peer pressure as an influence on their children, no thinking parents would want their son or daughter to be a social outcast without friends. Another misconception about peer relations is that teen culture is a unified culture with a single way of thinking and acting. A visit to any secondary school today will reveal the variety of teen cultures that exist. The formation of peer groups and adolescent crowds is partly a function of a school

Royalty-Free/CORBIS

structure and school activities. As in past decades, one can find jocks, populars, brains, delinquents, and nerds. One would also encounter members of today's grunge and body-piercing crowds. Media attention is often drawn toward bizarre or antisocial groups, further contributing to the myth that peer influence is primarily negative.

Music is very much a part of youth culture, although there is no universal type of music liked by all adolescents. One way adolescents have always tried to differentiate themselves from adults has been through music. On the other hand, today, adults are concerned that music, movies, and television have gone too far in the quest for evermore shocking and explicit sexual and violent content. Widespread and easy access to the Internet has also compounded concerns about the types of material today's adolescents are exposed to.

In addition to school and leisure activities like sports, adolescents today spend considerable time in the part-time work force. Work has usually been seen as a positive influence on adolescent development. Society points to the positive outcomes of developing responsibility and punctuality, knowledge of the working world, and appreciating the value of money. Research does corroborate the existence of the positive effects of work, but adolescents have been spending an increasing number of hours in the work force. Recent studies find that adolescents who work over 20 hours per week are more involved in drug use and delinquent activity, have more psychological and physical complaints, and perform more poorly in school. Although there may be a tendency for adolescents who are predisposed toward such behaviors to be disengaged from school in the first place and, therefore, work more. Longitudinal data suggest that working exacerbates these tendencies.

The first article in this unit discusses risk-taking behavior among adolescents, which sometimes results in risky business. The author provides the readers with teaching techniques to help the teacher work with these teens. The next two articles examine the over-dominance of computers, and then Tom Neven explains how some computer programs teach teens to kill. Alcohol drinking is next examined by Michael Windle; and finally the media exposure to terrorism is considered.

Risky Business: Exploring Adolescent Risk-Taking Behavior

TAMMY JORDAN WYATT AND FRED L. PETERSON

Ongoing behavioral research has documented the growing prevalence of adolescent health risk behaviors, such as tobacco use, sexual activity, alcohol and other substance use, nutritional behavior, physical inactivity, and intentional injury.[1] Newer youth risk behaviors, such as pathological gambling, are emerging as threats to public health.[2] Risk, risk taking, and risk behavior are important and relevant topics for exploring in health education classes. The goal of health educators, teachers, administrators, and parents alike should be to encourage youth to engage in constructive risk-taking behavior rather than alternative destructive behavior.

Risk has been defined as any action where the opportunity exists for success as well as some possibility for failure.[3] Risk taking can be defined as the participation in potentially health-compromising activities with little understanding of, or in spite of an understanding of, the potential negative consequences. The behavior is volitional, has an uncertain outcome (either positive or negative), and results from an interplay between the biopsychosocial processes of adolescence and the environment.[4] Risk taking is essential for positive growth and maturation. Risk taking may come in many forms such as physical, social, emotional, psychological, and financial. The challenge is to channel youth risk taking into positive, health-enhancing experiences and to provide realistic alternative options to destructive behavior. Constructive risk taking is an essential tool in the life of an adolescent. It allows for discovery and establishment of one's identity. Constructive risk taking is health enhancing in nature and may result in positive outcomes. Constructive risk-taking behavior includes activities that fulfill the need for thrill seeking that are healthy and legal. Examples of constructive risk taking include outdoor physical activities such as wilderness hiking and camping, swimming, bicycling, riding a motorcycle, or rock climbing; volunteer community service that is spiritually uplifting but also challenging such as working at an urban homeless shelter; and choosing to serve in a leadership role as an officer in an extracurricular organization. Risk taking only becomes destructive or negative when the risks are dangerous. Positive risks, often referred to as challenges, can turn negative risks in a more health-enhancing direction or prevent them from ever occurring. However, a key to enhancing involvement in constructive risk taking is the ability for young people to assess risks throughout one's lifetime. Youth need guidance, support, and opportunities to explore their values and attitudes regarding the risk-taking activities that they may face on a daily basis. Helping an adolescent understand and define his or her own risk taking is critical to risk assessment. Questions adolescents should ask themselves regarding various risk-taking activities include the following: What are the potential negative risks? What are the potential benefits? Do the benefits outweigh the dangers? Does this activity put others or me in danger? Is there a safe and enjoyable way to engage in this activity[5].

Lesson Objectives

Following completion of Risky Business, students will be able to

1. Understand the concepts of risk, risk behavior, and risk taking.
2. Review different risk behaviors and rank order them according to importance.
3. Identify positive alternative risk behaviors to the risk behaviors portrayed.
4. Engage in risk-assessment thinking skills.

National Health Education Standards

1. Students will demonstrate the ability to practice health-enhancing behaviors and reduce health risks.
2. Students will demonstrate the ability to use interpersonal communication skills to enhance health.
3. Students will demonstrate the ability to use goal-setting and decision-making skills to enhance health.[6]

After introducing and providing concrete examples of the concepts of risk, risk behavior, and risk taking, the instructor will begin the Risky Business learning activity.

Materials and Resources

Each student will need a plain sheet of 8.5 × 11-inch paper cut into 12 equal pieces of any shape and a pen/pencil.

Grade Level/Subject Area

This lesson may be used with middle school, high school, and/or college-aged students. The technique can be modified to fit the age and maturity level of different groups. For example, some characters and definitions may be omitted or modified for age appropriateness. Total time needed to facilitate the activity will vary with the age of the audience. The activity requires about 30–45 minutes to complete.

Activity and Strategies

Inform students that no talking, discussion, or remarks will be allowed during the initial stage of the activity. Provide each student a plain sheet of 8.5 × 11-inch paper. Instruct students to tear the paper into 12 equal pieces of any shape. Inform students that "I will state a character name and ask that you print that name on one piece of paper. I will then give you a definition, which is related to the character. Put the character name on the paper and the definition in your head. Don't worry; the definitions will be easy to remember. I will then state a second character name and its definition. Place that name only on the second piece of paper and keep its definition in your head. We will continue this process until all 12 characters have been identified and defined." Box 1 lists the character names used in this activity as well as the definitions of each character. While stating each character name, it may prove beneficial to write the name on a chalkboard or dry erase board so students see the name as they hear it. Once all 12 characters and definitions have been stated, repeat them to refresh each student's memory of the various definitions.

Part 1: Individual Rankings

Instruct students to rank each character from most important to least important. Once each character has been ranked, have the students list them on paper from 1 to 12. Again, with 1 being most important and 12 being least important. Students will ask what is meant by most and least important. State that they should decide what most and least important means to them.

Part 2: Small Group Rankings

Once students have their own ranking, divide the class into groups of 4–5. Using only discussion (not voting), have each group come up with a consensus or group ranking. This should take approximately 15 minutes. Tell each group that a spokesperson for their group will present to the class their rankings as well as their reasons for those rankings of most to least important. Each group should be given approximately 5–10 minutes to present group rankings and reasons for those rankings. Each group should be able to justify the rankings based

> ## Box 1
> ## List of Activity Characters and Definitions
>
> | | |
> |---|---|
> | Safer Sex | 14-year-old is sexually active and uses condoms correctly and consistently 100% of time. |
> | Hetero | College freshman engages in unprotected sex with multiple partners of opposite gender. |
> | Fight | High school basketball player injures teammate in physical fight after a game. |
> | Thin | Eighth-grade student uses starvation and exercise as a means of weight control. |
> | Blunt | 16-year-old smokes 1–2 marijuana joints on weekends. |
> | Drive | High school senior rides in car with classmate who has been drinking alcohol. |
> | Cut | Middle school student engages in self-mutilation (cutting) to ease pain and depression. |
> | Scream | Seventh-grade student regularly verbally abuses classmates. |
> | Homo | High school student engages in oral sex with same-sex partners but uses barrier methods 100% of the time. |
> | Binge | College student regularly binge drinks on weekends with friends. |
> | Goth | 15-year-old wears black clothing, is obsessed with death, and has multiple tattoos and body piercings. |
> | Feel | Middle school student is overweight and eats excessively large amounts of food when feeling sad or depressed. |

on discussions that occurred in the group process as well as the manner in which the rankings were made. Similarly, each group should state its definition of most and least important. While each group discusses the group rankings, place them in order on the chalk/dry erase board, allowing the class to compare the rankings of each small group.

Part 3: Large Group Discussion

After the groups have presented their rankings, return the class to their individual seats for a class discussion. Box 2 contains questions designed to summarize and bring closure to this activity. Comparisons of the small group rankings and definitions of most and least important should be discussed. Elaboration into

Box 2
Activity Discussion Questions

- How did you proceed to rank these characters?
- How did you define "most important" and "least important"?
- Did you have any problems coming to a consensus regarding the rankings?
- What gender are each of these characters?
- We each have perceptions, prejudices, and biases. How did these interfere with the communication within your group?
- Risk assessment questions for each character's behavior
    What are the potential negative risks?
    What are the potential benefits?
    Do the benefits outweigh the dangers?
    Does this activity put others or myself in danger?
    Is there a way to engage in this activity that is enjoyable and safe?
    What positive alternative behaviors might you suggest for replacing the risk behaviors exhibited by the characters?

Finally, use the following questions to conduct a risk assessment for each character: What are the potential negative risks to this behavior? What are the potential benefits? Do the benefits outweigh the dangers? Does this activity put others or myself at risk? Is there a safe and enjoyable way to engage in this activity? What are alternative constructive risk-taking activities for each of the 12 characters that would provide the same physiological, psychosocial, and emotional outcomes?

Although this activity can be completed in 1 class period, it may be useful to continue the discussion of risk, risk behavior, and risk taking in a follow-up period to reinforce concepts and facilitate understanding of the role of risk taking in one's life.

References

Centers for Disease Control and Prevention. Surveillance summaries, May 21, 2004. *MMWR.* 2004;53(SS-2):1–29.

Dickson L, Derevensky JL, Gupta R. The prevention of youth gambling problems: a conceptual model. *J Gambl Stud.* 2002;18(2):97–160.

Peterson F. The nuts and bolts of adolescent risk-taking behavior: a primer for Texas school health professionals. *Tex Sch Health Brief.* 2002; April:6–8.

Irwin CE, Jr., Millstein SG. Biopsychosocial correlates of risk-taking behaviors during adolescence. Can the physician intervene? *J Adolesc Health Care.* 1986;7(suppl 6):82S–96S.

Ponton L. *The Romance of Risk—Why Teenagers Do the Things They Do.* New York, NY: Basic Books; 1997.

The Joint Committee on National Health Education Standards. *National Health Education Standards: Achieving Health Literacy.* Atlanta, Ga: American Cancer Society; 1995.

the differences among group rankings and definitions should occur, noting that differences in definitions are analogous to differences in opinion, ideas, etc. Encourage students to discuss any problems that occurred during the group process regarding coming to a consensus. Elaboration on teamwork and group dynamics may be necessary.

Within the large group setting, ask students to visualize each character. Repeating the definitions of each may be necessary. Ask each student to state the gender of each character. Note that each definition is purposely written in a non–gender specific manner. It is here that prejudices or biases may emerge. Ask students to elaborate on any perceptions, prejudices, and biases that may have influenced the rankings.

TAMMY JORDAN WYATT, PhD, Assistant Professor, (tammy.wyatt@utsa.edu), Health Education, Department of Health and Kinesiology, University of Texas at San Antonio, 6900 North Loop 1604 West, San Antonio, TX 78249; and **FRED L. PETERSON**, PhD, Associate Professor, (fpeterson@mail.utexas.edu), Child, Adolescent, and School Health, Department of Kinesiology and Health Education, University of Texas at Austin, Bellmont Hall 222, 2100 San Jacinto Blvd, Austin, TX 78712.

The Overdominance of Computers

Our students need inner resources and real-life experiences to balance their high-tech lives.

Lowell W. Monke

The debate chums on over the effectiveness of computers as learning tools. Although there is a growing disillusionment with the promise of computers to revolutionize education, their position in schools is protected by the fear that without them students will not be prepared for the demands of a high-tech 21st century. This fallback argument ultimately trumps every criticism of educational computing, but it is rarely examined closely.

Lets start by accepting the premise of the argument: Schools need to prepare young people for a high-tech society. Does it automatically follow that children of all ages should use high-tech tools? Most people assume that it does, and that's the end of the argument. But we don't prepare children for an automobile-dependent society by finding ways for 10-year-olds to drive cars, or prepare people to use alcohol responsibly by teaching them how to drink when they are 6. My point is that preparation does not necessarily warrant early participation. Indeed, preparing young people quite often involves strengthening their inner resources—like self-discipline, moral judgment, and empathy—before giving them the opportunity to participate.

Great Power and Poor Preparation

The more powerful the tools—and computers are powerful—the more life experience and inner strength students must have to handle that power wisely. On the day my Advanced Computer Technology classroom got wired to the Internet, it struck me that I was about to give my high school students great power to harm a lot of people, and all at a safe distance. They could inflict emotional pain with a few keystrokes and never have to witness the tears shed. They could destroy hours of work accomplished by others who were not their enemies—just poorly protected network users whose files provided convenient bull's-eyes for youth flexing newfound technical muscles.

I also realized that it would take years to instill the ethical discipline needed to say *no* to flexing that technical power. Young people entering my course needed more firsthand experiences guided by adults. They needed more chances to directly connect their own actions with the consequences of those actions, and to reflect on the outcomes, before they started using tools that could trigger serious consequences on the other side of the world.

Students need more than just moral preparation. They also need authentic experiences. As more students grow up spending much of their time in environments dominated by computers, TV, and video games, their diminished experience with real, concrete things prevents them from developing a rich understanding of what they study on computers. The computer is a purely symbolic environment; users are always working with abstract representations of things, never with the things themselves. In a few months my students could learn to build complex relational databases and slick multimedia presentations. But unless they also had a deep knowledge of the physical world and community relationships, they would be unable to infuse depth and meaning into the information they were depicting and discussing.

Do Computers Help Achievement?

Educational technology researchers, who tend to suffer from a severe inability to see the forest for the trees, typically ignore the impact that saturating society with computers and other screen environments is having on children. University of Munich economists Thomas Fuchs and Ludger Woessmann recently examined data from a study of 174,000 15-year-olds in 31 nations who took the Programme for International Student Assessment tests. They found, after controlling for other possible influences, that the more access students had to computers in school and at home, the *lower* their overall test scores were (2004). The authors suggest that rather than inherently motivating young people or helping them learn, computers more likely distract them from their studies. But there may be other problems behind this phenomenon that point to inherent contradictions in the use of educational technology.

For example, although we know that computer programs can help small children learn to read, we also know that face-to-face interaction is one of the most important ingredients in reading readiness (Dodici, Draper, & Peterson, 2003). As a result of increased time spent with computers, video games, and TV the current generation of elementary students will experience an estimated 30 percent fewer face-to-face encounters than the previous generation (Hammel, 1999). Thus, teachers may be employing the very devices for remediating reading problems that helped cause the problems in the first place.

Nearly everything children do today involves technologies that distance them from direct contact with the living world.

The issue is not just balancing computer time with other activities in schools. Both inside and outside school, children's lives are dominated by technology. Nearly everything a child does today—from chatting with friends to listening to music to playing games—tends to involve the use of technologies that distance children from direct contact with the living world. If the task of schools is to produce men and women who live responsible, fulfilling lives—not just human cogs for the high-tech machinery of commerce—then we should not be intensifying children's high-tech existence but compensating for it. Indeed, as advanced technology increasingly draws us toward a mechanical way of thinking and acting, it becomes crucial that schools help students develop their distinctly human capacities. What we need from schools is not balance in using high technology, but an effort to balance children's machine-dominated lives.

To prepare children to challenge the cold logic of the spreadsheet-generated bottom line, we need to teach them to value what that spreadsheet cannot factor in: commitment, loyalty, and tradition. To prepare them to find meaning in the abstract text and images encountered through screens, we need to first engage them in physical realities that screen images can only symbolize. To fit students to live in an environment filled with human-made products, we need to first help them know and respect what cannot be manufactured: the natural, the living, the wild. To prepare students to live well-grounded lives in a world of constant technological change, we need to concentrate their early education on things that endure.

The Cost of Failing to Compensate

Anyone who has spent time in schools knows that what is keeping today's youth from succeeding academically has nothing to do with a lack of technical skills or access to computers. Rather, it is the lack of qualities like hope, compassion, trust, respect, a sense of belonging, moral judgment, stability, community support, parental care, and teacher competence and enthusiasm that keeps so many students imprisoned in ignorance.

Ironically, what students will most need to meet the serious demands of the 21st century is the wisdom that grows out of these inner human capacities and that is developed by community involvement. If the 20th century taught us anything at all, it should have been that technology can be a very mixed blessing. Children entering elementary schools today will eventually have to wrestle with the mess that their elders have left them because of our own lack of wisdom about technology's downside: global warming, increasingly lethal weapons, nuclear waste, overdependence on automobiles, overuse of pesticides and antibiotics, and the general despoiling of our planet. They will also have to take on ethical conundrums posed by advanced technology, such as what to do about cloning, which decisions are off-limits to artificial intelligence devices, and whether or not parents should be allowed to "enhance" the genetic makeup of their offspring (only the wealthy need apply).

Those decisions should not be left to technicians in labs, CEOs in boardrooms, or politicians in debt to those who stand to profit from the technology. Our children should be at the decision tables as adults, and we want them to be able to stand apart from high technology and soberly judge its benefits and detriments to the entire human race.

How can young people develop the wisdom to judge high technology if they are told from the moment they enter school, implicitly if not explicitly, that they need high-tech tools to learn, to communicate, to think? Having been indoctrinated early with the message that their capacity to deal with the world depends not on their own internal resources but on their use of powerful external machines, how can students even imagine a world in which human beings impose limits on technological development or use?

Where to Go from Here
Keep to Essentials in the Early Years

So how, specifically, should educators make decisions and policies about the appropriateness of digital technologies for students of different ages?

One approach to tackling this dilemma comes from the Alliance for Childhood. During the last eight years, the Alliance (whose board of directors I serve on) has engaged educators, children's health professionals, researchers, and technology experts in developing guidelines for structuring a healthy learning environment for children, and has developed a list of essential conditions. Educators should ask themselves to what extent heavy use of computers and the Internet provides children in the lower grades with these essential school experiences:

- Close, lining relationships with responsible adults.
- Outdoor activity, nature exploration, gardening, and other encounters with nature.
- Time for unstructured play as part of the core curriculum.
- Music, drama, puppetry, dance, painting, and the other arts, both as separate classes and as a catalyst to bring other academic subjects to life.

- Hands-on lessons, handicrafts, and other physically engaging activities that provide effective first lessons for young children in the sciences, mathematics, and technology.
- Conversation with important adults, as well as poetry, storytelling, and hearing books read aloud.

This vision places a high priority on a child's direct encounters with the world and with other living beings, but it does not reject technology. On the contrary, tools are an important part of the vision. But at the elementary level, the tools should be simple, putting less distance between the student and the world and calling forth the students own internal resources.

Schools must also be patient with children's development. It would strike anyone as silly to give the smallest student in a 2nd grade class a scooter so that the child could get around the track as fast as the other kids his or her age. But our society shows decreasing willingness to wait for the natural emergence of students' varying mental and emotional capacities. We label students quickly and display an almost pathological eagerness to apply external technical fixes (including medications) to students who often simply aren't ready for the abstract, academic, and sedentary environment of today's early elementary classrooms. Our tendency to turn to external tools to help children cope with demands that are out of line with their tactile and physically energetic nature reflects the impact that decades of placing faith in technical solutions has had on how we treat children.

Study Technology in Depth After Elementary School

After children have had years to engage in direct, firsthand experiences, and as their abstract thinking capacities emerge more fully, it makes sense to gradually introduce computers and other complex, symbolic environments. Computer hardware and software should also become the focus of classroom investigation. A student in a technological society surrounded by black boxes whose fundamental principles he or she does not understand is as functionally illiterate as a student in a world filled with books that he or she can't read. The only thing worse would be to make technology "invisible," preventing children from even being aware of their ignorance.

By high school, digital technologies should take a prominent place in students' studies, both as tools of learning and as tools to learn about. During the last two years of high school, teachers should spend considerable time outfitting students with the high-tech skills they will need when they graduate. This "just-in-time" approach to teaching technical skills is far more efficient—instructionally and financially—than continually retraining younger students in technical skills soon to be obsolete. In addition, students at all education levels should consciously examine technology's role in human affairs.

Techno-Byte

Percentage of U.S. students who used computers in school in 2003:

- 97 percent of high school students.
- 95 percent of middle school students.
- 91 percent of students in grades 1–5.
- 80 percent of kindergarten students.
- 67 percent of nursery school students.

—National Center for Education Statistics, 2005

I am not suggesting that we indiscriminately throw computers out of classrooms. But I do believe it's time to rethink the past decision to indiscriminately throw them in. The result of that rethinking would be, I hope, some much-needed technological modesty, both in school and eventually in society in general. By compensating for the dominance of technology in students' everyday lives, schools might help restore the balance we need to create a more humane society

The irony of postmodern education is that preparing children for a high-tech future requires us to focus our attention more than ever before on the task of understanding what it means to be human, to be alive, to be part of both social and biological communities—a quest for which technology is increasingly becoming not the solution but the problem.

References

Dodici, B. J., Draper, D. C., & Peterson, C. A. (2003). Early parent-child interactions and early literacy development. *Topics in Early Childhood Special Education, 23*(3), 124–136.

Fuchs, T., & Woessmann, L. (2004, November). *Computers and student learning: Bivariate and multivariate evidence on the availability and use of computers at home and at school.* CESifo Working Paper Series (#1321). Available: www.cesifo.de/~DocCIDL/1321.pdf

Hammel, S. (1999, Nov. 29). Generation of loners? Living their lives online. *US. News and World Report,* p. 79.

LOWELL W. MONKE is Assistant Professor at Wittenberg University in Springfield, Ohio; 937-342-8648; lmonke@wittenberg.edu.

Author's note—The Alliance for Childhood has produced two publications to help parents and educators guide children toward a healthier relationship with technology: *Fool's Gold: A Critical Look at Computers in Childhood,* and *Tech Tonic: Towards a New Literacy of Technology* (both available online at www.allianceforchildhood.org).

Teaching Kids to Kill

TOM NEVEN

What do a 15-year-old chronic video gem and a U.S. Marine have in common?

A lot more than you might think. Each has achieved a level of reflexive conditioning that makes him deadly with a weapon, and each has been desensitized to the act of pointing his weapon at another human being and pulling the trigger. There's a crucial difference, however. The Marine is part of an organization that instills discipline in the use of violence. He operates under strict rules of engagement. The teen doesn't.

A Study of Killing

How did we get to such a state of affairs? David Grossman, a retired Army psychologist, has written extensively about the process that takes immature, untrained teens and turns them into killers. His research, called "killology," is documented in his Pulitzer Prize-nominated book, *On Killing,* which tells how the military confronted a unique problem: Not enough of its soldiers were actually shooting their weapons in battle. Studies after the Civil War and World Wars I and II found that a relatively small number of soldiers—as few as 15 percent—actually fired at the enemy. "Obviously, you can't have that situation in war," he says.

> **"The kid had never fired an actual pistol in his life. But he'd been on the simulator for nearly a lifetime."**
>
> —Author, speaker and "killologist" David Gossman

The military realized that simply learning to shoot at a round bull's-eye did he not condition soldiers to the battlefield reality of sighting another human being and taking a life. There was a psychological barrier that had to be overcome. "Hardwired into the brains of most healthy members of most species in response against killing their own kind," Grossman explains. By using human-shaped pop-up targets and other means, the military was able to desensitize soldiers to the act of aiming at a human shape, which increased the firing rate to as high as 90 percent by the Vietnam War.

With the invention of video game technology, the military began to use this equipment to further train its soldiers. The Marine Corps, for example, adapted a version of the popular game *Doom* to hone Marines' reactions in a combat environment. In many ways, video games, particularly first-person shooters, exactly mimic the process used by the military. Teens (including the gunmen at Columbine High School) log countless hours with these same games—but without the discipline that comes from military training and, obviously, without any need to develop these skills in the first place.

The psychological process involved in this type of training is called "operant conditioning." Not only is the mind desensitized to a certain level of violence and to the process of sighting on an enemy, but the shooter also develops the muscle memory necessary to become an expert marksman. Grossman cites the example of one school shooter, Michael Carneal, who fired into a group of students at a high school in Paducah, Ky., in 1997.

"The kid had never fired an actual pistol in his life," says Grossman, who was an expert witness at Carneal's trial. The teen stole a .22-caliber pistol from a neighbor's house and practiced with two clips of ammo the previous night. That was the sale extent of his marksmanship training—at least with live ammo. "But he'd been on the simulator for nearly a lifetime," Grossman says. The boys family had converted their two-car garage into a playroom lined with point-and-shoot arcade games, a genre Grossman calls "murder simulators."

Carneal took the stolen gun to school and open fire on a group of students with an astounding degree of accuracy. "You have kneeling, scrambling, screaming targets," Grossman explains. "Carneal fires eight shots at eight different targets. Five of them are head shots, the other three upper torso. Now, I have trained Navy SEALs, Green Berets and Texas Rangers, and when I tell them about this case, they're simply stumped. Nowhere in the annals of law enforcement, military or criminal history can we fine equivalent achievement."

It was, Grossman says, a classic case of operant conditioning.

Feeding the Dog Brain

Until recently, manufacturers of hostile video games and other violent media have pooh-poohed the connection between their products and teen violence, claiming that any correlation has been, at best, anecdotal. But science is now proving the connection.

The Indiana University School of Medicine has conducted a series of tests using functional Magnetic Resonance Imaging (fMRI). This allows researchers to compare the brain activity of teens consuming a heavy diet of violent media to those

> "After the first ambush we were in Lt. Fick and I were discussing [Grossman's book *On Killing*] and how today's guys have no problem firing their weapons. For instance, Fick remarked after a firefight, 'Did you see what they did to that town? They [expletive] destroyed it.' Cpl. Trombley, the machine-gunner who was next to me in that ambush, he'd each been sort of ecstatic, comparing it to *Grand Theft Auto,* the video game."
>
> —Evan Wright, author of *Generation Kill,* about his experience of being embedded with a U.S. Marine reconnaissance unit in Iraq

Just What Is Media Violence?

According to David Grossman and Gloria DeGaetano in their book *Stop Teaching Our Kids to Kill,* media violence includes:

- Plots driven by quick-cut scenes of gratuitous violent acts delivered with rapid-fire frequency and graphic technical effects
- Graphic, sadistic revenge, torture techniques, inhumane treatment of others in a context of humor, trivialization, glibness and/or raucous "fun"
- Explicitly depicted violent acts shown through special effects, camera angles, background music or lighting with the intent of having them appear glamorous, heroic, "cool" or worthy of imitation
- Depictions of people holding personal and social power primarily because they are using weapons or using their bodies as weapons, and dominating other people through the threat of violence or through actual violence
- Extraneous, graphic, gory, detailed violent acts shown with the intent to shock
- Violent acts shown as an acceptable way to solve problems or presented as the primary problem-solving approach

not as heavily exposed. The scans (right) show decreased brain functioning in the prefrontal cortex, the part of the organ that regulates emotions, impulsivity and conscience.

Grossman explains it this way: "Our frontal lobes are what make us human. This is where the written word and the spoken word are processed and where, incidentally, abstract concepts like God and spirituality exist. Lying underneath the forebrain is the midbrain, the mammalian brain, the part of your brain which is identical to your dog's brain. Images, particularly violent images, bypass the forebrain and go straight to the dog brain."

The differences are also apparent between left and right brain, he adds. "The right brain is your artistic, creative, innovative brain. The left brain is your logical, rational, predictive brain. Your right brain really is kind of like the little devil who sits an one shoulder and thinks foolish things. The left brain is sort of like the little angel who sits on the other shoulder and says, 'Oh, that will get us in trouble; we can't do that.' The left brain really does have veto power."

While young people who suppress left-brain activity by feasting on violent media may not open fire in the school cafeteria, there are still consequences. "This kid just won't do his homework, because the ability to understand the logical ramification of not having his homework done tomorrow morning doesn't click," Grossman says. "Who knows what he'll do behind the wheel of a vehicle. This kid is cocked and primed to do drugs. He does not understand, because the left brain is catastrophically shut down."

The good news is that this change in brain functioning does not appear to be permanent. Studies have shown that children weaned from a heavy media diet do better on school aptitude tests, and school administrators report fewer incidents of playground violence and bullying.

A Cultural Problem Needs a Cultural Response

The American Medical Association, American Psychological Association, American Academy of Pediatrics, and American Academy of Child and Adolescent Psychiatry made a joint statement to Congress in 2000 regarding the link between media and societal violence. "They said that 30 years of research and a host of sound, scholarly studies have proven that media violence causes violence in our society," Grossman says.

The solution, it would appear, is obvious. But as much as parents may wish to ban violent media, it's not going to happen. We can, however, prevent impressionable children from consuming it. "There's a social cost to several things that we allow for adults but not kids," Grossman states. "Driving. Alcohol. Tobacco. . . . We can say there are some things adults can have that kids can't."

> "The evidence is overwhelming. To argue against it is like arguing against gravity."
>
> —American Psychological Association on the link between media violence and teen violence

Of course, we've all heard the entertainment industry argue, "If you don't like the violence, just turn it off." Grossman's rebuttal is simple. He shares a personal story from one of the first school shootings, which happened to take place in his hometown of Jonesboro, Ark. He stood helplessly, watching a forlorn, single mother as she waited for the final identification of her daughter's body at the morgue. "This mom had lost everything she had in the world because of two kids who decided to act out a violent video game," Grossman recalls. "You tell that single mom who lost her daughter to just hit the 'off' switch."

Alcohol Use among Adolescents

MICHAEL WINDLE, PhD

A dolescent alcohol use is statistically normative behavior in the United States. By their senior year of high school, the vast majority of adolescents have drunk alcohol at some point in their lifetime, with a substantial subset of adolescents drinking at high levels and experiencing a range of serious alcohol-related problems. On the basis of national survey data, the occurrence of a heavy drinking episode (i.e., having five or more drinks on a single occasion) was reported by about 25% of tenth graders and 30% of twelfth graders, and the average age of alcohol use initiation (or first drink) has decreased from 17.8 years in 1987 to 15.9 years in 1996. Alcohol use among teens has been associated with the three most common forms of adolescent mortality: accidental deaths (such as fatal automobile or boat crashes), homicides, and suicides. On average, eight adolescents a day in the U.S. die in alcohol-related automobile crashes, and nine out of ten teenage automobile accidents involve the use of alcohol. With a national school sample, suicide attempts were 3 to 4 times more likely among heavy drinking adolescents relative to abstainers.

In addition, alcohol use among adolescents is significantly associated with a range of other health-compromising behaviors. Higher levels of alcohol use are associated with more frequent, often unprotected, sexual activity among adolescents, which poses increased risk for teen pregnancy and sexually transmitted diseases, including potentially life-threatening diseases such as HIV. An earlier onset of alcohol use and higher levels of use among adolescents have also been associated with poorer academic functioning and higher rates of school dropout.

Adolescent Alcohol-Related Behaviors

The systematic, large-scale study of adolescent alcohol-related behaviors (for example alcohol use, alcohol problems, binge drinking episodes) is, historically and scientifically speaking, a relatively recent phenomenon. Among the most long-standing and well-known U.S. national studies of adolescent substance use (including alcohol use) is the Monitoring the Future Studies (MFS), which were initiated circa 1975 to provide national surveillance data on adolescent substance use practices. The MFS has provided annual national surveys of adolescent substance use practices and associated attitudes about various features of

substance use (such as perceived harmfulness, perceived availability). Over approximately the first 20 years of the MFS, the annual survey samples consisted solely of high school seniors. In recent years, the MFS has expanded to include eighth and tenth graders; this is important because of historical trends in substance use that indicate an earlier age of onset for substance use among children.

The following presentation of epidemiological findings about adolescent alcohol use are based largely on the MFS; findings from other regional or local studies are used to substantiate other significant considerations.

The data provided in Figure 1 indicates that the prevalence of using alcohol increases across grade levels for three racial/ethnic groups. However, it is important to note that by eighth grade over 50% of these children report having consumed an alcoholic beverage. Racial/ethnic group differences indicate a particularly high prevalence of lifetime alcohol use among

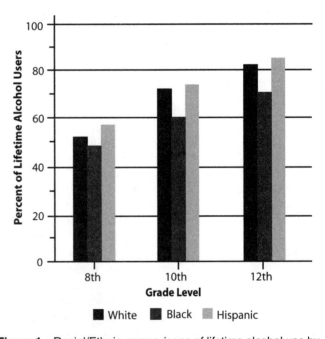

Figure 1 Racial/Ethnic comparisons of lifetime alcohol use by grade level

Source: Johnston, L.D., O'Malley, P.M., and Bachman, J.G. (2001). *Monitoring the Future National Survey Results on Drug Use, 1975–2000. Volume I: Secondary School Students* (NIH Publication 01–1924). Bethesda, MD: NIDA

Hispanic children. Similar to findings in previous studies, black adolescents have the lowest rate of lifetime alcohol use. Research findings from earlier MFS cohorts and from other epidemiological studies have also indicated very high (if not the highest) prevalence of lifetime alcohol use among Native American children and adolescents, as well as quite low rates among Asian-Americans. Parenthetically, it should be recognized that drinking practices among adolescents (and adults) may vary considerably for subgroups (for example, for different Native American tribes, for Mexican-Americans versus Puerto Ricans) within the broad racial/ethnic groups used to present these data.

In addition to lifetime use of alcohol, another useful index of trends in adolescent drinking references heavy or binge drinking episodes. Binge drinking refers to the consumption of five or more drinks in a single setting over the last two weeks. In contrast to lifetime alcohol use, the binge drinking index is designed to assess potentially problematic drinking that may contribute to current problems (for example poorer school performance) and may be prognostic of longer term difficulties. The data presented in Figure 2 indicates both high rates of binge drinking and increases across grade levels. Differences are also indicated for the three racial/ethnic groups. Hispanic adolescents had substantially higher rates of binge drinking than whites or blacks among eighth graders. Black adolescents had the lowest prevalence of binge drinking across all three grade levels, substantially lower than their white and Hispanic counterparts. White adolescents had the greatest increases in the prevalence of binge drinking across grade levels.

Alcohol use among teens has been associated with the three most common forms of adolescent mortality.

While there is variability across grade levels and racial/ethnic groups, the prevalence of binge drinking among adolescents, considered collectively, is quite high.

Gender provides yet another potential source of variation among adolescent drinking practices. It has been proposed that historical shifts toward more gender equality in work and family roles among adults may be contributing to a convergence in drinking practices among male and female adolescents. If lifetime use is evaluated, there are few gender differences in alcohol use (80.9% of males vs. 79.5% of females report lifetime use). However, for more serious indicators of alcohol use, such as binge drinking and daily alcohol use, boys have a significantly higher prevalence than girls (36.7% of males report binge drinking compared to 23.5% of females and 4.7% of males report daily drinking vs. 1.1% of females). These findings are consistent with other studies in supporting the inference that boys are more likely than girls to engage in more serious levels of alcohol use (i.e., more frequently and at higher quantities) and to have more alcohol-related problems.

These epidemiological findings provide a broad picture of the drinking practices of adolescents. It is evident that the vast

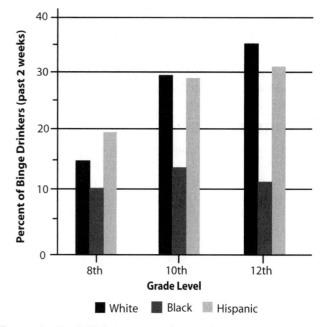

Figure 2 Racial/Ethnic comparisons of binge drinking by grade level

Source: Johnston, L.D., O'Malley, P.M., and Bachman, J.G. (2001). *Monitoring the Future National Survey Results on Drug Use, 1975–2000. Volume I: Secondary School Students* (NIH Publication 01–4924). Bethesda, MD: NIDA.

majority of adolescents consume alcohol at some time during adolescence, with a substantial number also engaging in binge drinking episodes. The study of more extensive alcohol problems among adolescents is a relatively recent phenomena, but the current data highlight high rates of such problems among adolescents. These alcohol problems are of concern because of their potential compromising influences on both current and future health functioning.

Adolescent Alcohol Disorders

As the preceding information demonstrates, data on adolescent alcohol use practices has increased substantially over the past 25 years or so. However, these national and regional survey studies have not included data on the number of adolescents meeting formal clinical diagnostic criteria for alcohol disorders. The available evidence, based on a few recent community studies, suggests that between 3% and 32% of adolescents meet lifetime criteria for an alcohol disorder.

In one study, 3–4% of adolescents between the ages of 14–16 years had an alcohol disorder. However, the prevalence of alcohol disorders of adolescents between the ages of 17–20 years was 8.9% for girls and 20.3% for boys. In another study, 32.4% of 386 older adolescents, mostly seniors in high school, had a lifetime alcohol disorder. Boys (37.6%) were more highly represented than girls (26.8%) with regard to the prevalence of an alcohol disorder. With a community sample of 3,021 adolescents and young adults in Munich, Germany, 25.1% of men and 7.0% of women had an alcohol disorder. Furthermore, the occurrence of alcohol disorders indicated low rates at age 13–14 years, with a rapid increase to a peak at 15–17 years, followed by a gradual decrease from

18–24 years. Cultural differences between the U.S. and Germany may contribute to this somewhat earlier onset of heavier alcohol involvement by German youth. Nevertheless, it is evident that the prevalence of alcohol disorders among adolescents is sufficiently high to merit increased concern and responsiveness from those concerned with the health and welfare of our youth.

Summary

Scientific studies of alcohol use among adolescents over the past 30 years or so have indicated high rates of usage as well as an earlier age of onset for alcohol use. More recent surveys have also indicated high rates of binge drinking and the manifestation of multiple alcohol problems. Although based on a limited number of local community studies, it has been estimated that between 3% and 32% of adolescents meet lifetime criteria for an alcohol disorder. These data clearly indicate the need for increased intervention efforts that target the initiation, escalation, and maintenance of alcohol use, as well as the treatment of alcohol disorders during adolescence.

MICHAEL WINDLE, PhD, is professor of Psychology and director of the Center for the Advancement of Youth Health at the University of Alabama at Birmingham. This research was supported by Grant No. K37-AA07861 awarded to Michael Windle from the National Institute on Alcohol Abuse and Alcoholism.

This article is adapted from M. Windle (1999). *Alcohol Use Among Adolescents.* Sage Publications. It appears here with permission from the publisher, all rights reserved.

Terrorism, the Media, and Distress in Youth

ROSE L. PFEFFERBAUM, PhD, MPH, ET AL.

The 1995 bombing of the Alfred P. Murrah Federal Building in Oklahoma City ushered in a new focus in childhood trauma that accompanies disaster. Prior research in the United States in this area had primarily addressed natural disasters and man-made incidents with relatively few casualties such as school shootings. Because children were widely believed a target in the Oklahoma City bombing—19 died in the day care center in the building—concern about the welfare of youth, in general, was heightened. Since a goal of terrorism is to create fear and intimidation in the broader society, monitoring the reactions and recovery of the extended community was also important. Furthermore, since media coverage may influence reactions to a traumatic event, studies following the Oklahoma City bombing examined the relationship between exposure to media coverage and emotional reactions of youth in the community. The results of these studies suggest prevention and intervention strategies with respect to the media and its impact on victims and the public.

Most studies of youth in Oklahoma City used post-traumatic stress reactions as the primary outcome measure. Post-traumatic stress disorder (PTSD) includes three clusters of symptoms that develop in response to an extreme traumatic stressor: persistent intrusive re-experiencing of the stressor, persistent avoidance of reminders of the event and numbing of general responsiveness, and persistent symptoms of arousal. According to the American Psychiatric Association (APA), the trauma can be experienced directly or indirectly. Physical presence at a disaster site, such as the scene of a terrorist attack, constitutes exposure. Witnessing and/or close relationship to victims are also recognized as exposure, but other potential mechanisms of indirect exposure are not specifically addressed. Exposure to intensive media coverage of a horrific event, for example, is not included as a form of exposure in APA diagnostic criteria for PTSD. Nonetheless, extended exposure to media coverage may result in heightened anxiety and worries about safety and security. Concerns about reoccurrence may also increase if exposure to the coverage becomes a focal point of daily activity. Although individuals are unlikely to meet criteria for a diagnostic disorder, the resulting distress can interfere with normal functioning and may be cause for concern.

Findings in Oklahoma City middle and high school students seven weeks after the bombing revealed a small but significant relationship between bombing-related television viewing and post-traumatic stress reactions. This sample did not include youth physically present at the bomb site, and most students in the study who knew direct victims were not closely related to them. One might expect different results in youth who were directly exposed. In any case, this work has important implications with respect to the response of youth to media coverage of terrorist events.

The relationship between media exposure and emotional reactions to the Oklahoma City bombing was explored in another sample of indirectly exposed middle school students residing 100 miles from Oklahoma City. This study was completed two years after the bombing, just as the federal trial of Timothy McVeigh was beginning. The study found a small but significant association between enduring post-traumatic stress reactions and both print and broadcast media exposure. Print exposure, in fact, was more strongly associated with post-traumatic stress than broadcast exposure, but this may reflect uneven distribution of broadcast exposure since most students in the study were highly exposed to broadcast coverage while there was a wider variation in the amount of print exposure across the sample. It is possible, however, that the findings reflect true differences in the effects of print and broadcast exposure. In some instances at least, print exposure may require intentional effort reflecting greater interest and perhaps greater distress. Those with more intense reactions to the incident may have actively sought print coverage. These findings suggest the importance of monitoring all forms of media coverage rather than limiting concern to television.

Although individuals are unlikely to meet criteria for a diagnostic disorder, the resulting distress can interfere with normal functioning and may be cause for concern.

The relationship between post-traumatic stress reactions and media exposure in the sample of middle school youth residing 100 miles from Oklahoma City was contingent upon their psychological reactions to media coverage. Thus, one is advised to monitor reactions to coverage as well as amount and content of exposure without necessarily assuming that media exposure is responsible for adverse reactions. Youth with increased arousal, for example, may seek media coverage to obtain information or to maintain the heightened state of arousal. Therefore, it is important to discuss with youth their reactions to traumatic events and to media coverage of those events, to listen to and reassure them about safety without misleading them, to assist them in processing emotions, and to redirect them to other activities as warranted. See Table 1 for a summary of interventions.

There may be developmental differences in children's responses to media exposure. Much younger children do not have the same cognitive abilities as older children and adolescents and may process images differently. Preschool children viewing repeated newscasts of the World Trade Center being attacked and then falling, for example, may have believed that each replay represented a different building being destroyed, Adolescents would understand the reality of thousands killed in the terrorist attacks while younger children would not have the cognitive schema to understand the importance of these numbers or the irreversibility of death. Furthermore, media coverage of disasters presents actual events that are novel and that carry information different from the usual fictional and non-fictional violence youth are routinely exposed to in their television viewing. In young children, the relationship between exposure to a traumatic event and reaction to it may be complicated by a child's difficulty distinguishing fictional and non-fictional events.

Recent studies suggest that the effects of media coverage may differ depending on various aspects of exposure. Jennifer Ahern and colleagues, for example, found an association between the frequency of viewing certain images and both PTSD and depression in adults directly involved in or affected by the September 11, 2001, attacks but not in study participants who lacked this tie to the attacks. For victims directly exposed through physical presence, media reminders of an event may rekindle arousal associated with the event. For those less directly exposed, media coverage itself may be the trigger for initial arousal and later, repeated media viewing may be retraumatizing.

Studies emerging since the September 11, 2001, attacks have examined the content of television coverage as well as the amount of viewing. Ahern and colleagues, for example, found a trend between increased frequency of viewing certain images, such as people falling or jumping from the building, and the prevalence of PTSD and depression using their measures. Frequency of viewing the image of the building collapsing was not associated with either PTSD or depression.

It is important to remember that the relationship between media exposure and both acute and later reactions does not establish cause and effect. While it is tempting to assume that media exposure leads to adverse outcomes, this conclusion ignores other plausible explanations. The relationship between acute reactions and media exposure may also suggest that youth who are aroused are drawn to the information provided by the media and/or that information seeking itself is a coping strategy for some. It is possible that other factors are responsible for the link between media exposure and these emotional states as well.

Table 1 Steps in Media-Related Trauma Intervention

- **Observe and assess media exposure even in those not directly exposed to traumatic event**
- **Take a media history**
  - Address all forms of media coverage (not just television)
  - Ascertain amount and type of media exposure especially relative to established patterns
  - Determine extent to which media exposure is deliberate as opposed to passive
  - Identify when media exposure occurs (e.g., in the morning, after school, at bedtime)
  - Ascertain whether media exposure occurs alone, with adults, or with peers
  - Evaluate content
  - Assess reactions to coverage including behavioral as well as emotional states
  - Determine impact on functioning at home, in school, and in other settings
- **Discuss traumatic events and media coverage**
  - Address reactions and concerns
  - Clarify misperceptions
- **Assist in processing emotions related to media coverage**
  - Explore feelings aroused by images and/or words
  - Validate feelings expressed
  - Observe and reflect, but do not reinforce hostile feelings
  - Encourage journaling and drawing as methods for expressing and processing feelings
- **Reassure about safety**
  - Listen to concerns
  - Identify activities and precautions to enhance safety
  - Avoid making false or misleading assurances
- **Suggest and practice coping strategies**
  - Redirect to other activities
  - Share relaxation exercises
  - Teach thought-stopping techniques
  - Explore cognitive restructuring
  - Designate focused time for media exposure
- **Limit media exposure to highly traumatic events and reminders**
- **Assist parents**
  - Teach about reactions to traumatic events
  - Allow adults to process their thoughts and feelings about the events and coverage
  - Discuss how adult conversations and distress related to media coverage can adversely impact youth
  - Provide permission for adults to limit media coverage
  - Provide guidelines for television viewing
  - Provide guidelines for discussing media coverage of events

The findings of these Oklahoma City and September 11 studies have implications for prevention and intervention. While these studies did not address a number of important issues such as if and how information was processed with others, it would seem prudent that exposure to media coverage of terrorist events be limited and monitored by parents. The pervasiveness of the media in Western society and the potential for passive exposure, especially in youth, suggest the importance of a proactive approach on the part of professionals who should routinely take a media history, especially following major events such as terrorist attacks, even in those not directly exposed. Such a history would include amount and type of exposure, changes in amount and type of exposure relative to established patterns, assessment of content, extent to which exposure is deliberate and focused as opposed to passive, when exposure occurs, whether others are present when exposure occurs and relationship to those others, as well as emotional and behavioral changes associated with exposure.

Youth may turn to the media when experiencing heightened arousal and/or as a method for managing distress, providing parents and professionals with excellent opportunities for prevention and intervention with them by eliciting and addressing concerns, clarifying misconceptions and misattributions, and suggesting and practicing coping strategies. Youth who do not want to discuss an event should not be forced to do so. Rather, they should understand that the topic is acceptable for discussion at the time or in the future.

In assisting adolescents as they process emotions related to media coverage, it is helpful to explore how images and words make them feel and to validate expressed feelings. Reflect but do not reinforce hostile reactions, such as extreme hatred and strong desire for revenge, since such feelings do not aid healing and may impair functioning. Intervention is warranted if one expects these negative feelings to result in angry or hurtful action against others.

Parents may benefit from educational materials in the form of age-appropriate guidelines for television viewing and for discussing media coverage with their children. They also may need to discuss their own thoughts and feelings about events and media coverage. Teaching parents about normal reactions to traumatic events may enable them to identify adverse reactions more quickly.

While the media are often criticized, they do have a vital role in information sharing in the aftermath of terrorist incidents. In fact, at times of crisis, most adults in our society quite naturally turn to the news media to obtain information. Moreover, a free press goes to the heart of who we are as a nation. Nonetheless, given that terrorists seek opportunities to transmit their messages and to instill fear and intimidation, and given that media coverage of terrorist events may lead to adverse consequences for youth, parents and professionals will want to be attentive to the exposure and reactions of youth to media coverage of horrific events. As professionals learn more about the relationship between media exposure to trauma and distress reactions in youth, we will be better able to develop and refine guidelines for parents and the media.

ROSE L. PFEFFERBAUM, PhD, MPH, is director of the Terrorism and Disaster Preparedness Center, Phoenix College, Phoenix, Arizona. ROBIN H. GURWITCH, PhD, is associate professor in the Department of Pediatrics, University of Oklahoma Health Sciences Center, Oklahoma City, Oklahoma. MADELINE J. ROBERTSON, JD, MD, is associate professor and EDWARD N. BRANDT, JR., MD, PhD, is Regents Professor, in Health Administration and Policy, College of Public Health, University of Oklahoma Health Sciences Center. BETTY PFEFFERBAUM, MD, JD, is professor and chairman of the Department of Psychiatry and Behavioral Sciences, University of Oklahoma Health Sciences Center.

Acknowledgment—Supported under Award Number MIPT106-113-2000-020 from the Oklahoma City National Memorial Institute for the Prevention of Terrorism and the Office of Justice Programs, National Institute of Justice, Department of Justice. Points of view in this document are those of the authors and do not necessarily represent the official position of the Oklahoma City National Memorial Institute for the Prevention of Terrorism or the Department of Justice. Also supported by grants from the Commonwealth Fund, the Presbyterian Health Foundation, and the Open Society Institute's Project on Death in America.

UNIT 7
Teenage Sexuality

Unit Selections

Key Points to Consider

- Why is sexual activity so high in seventh and eighth graders?

- What are the sexual activities of high school students?

- Should sex education teach abstinence or not?

- Is the abstinence movement a good idea?

- How can living together make mate selection more difficult?

Student Web Site
www.mhcls.com/online

Internet References
Further information regarding this Web site may be found in this book's preface or online.

Girls Inc.
  http://www.girlsinc.org

Like other aspects of psychological development, sexuality is not an entirely new issue that surfaces for the first time during adolescents. Children are known to be curious about their bodies at a very early age. And of course, sexual interest and development continues after adolescence. Most would argue that adolescence is a fundamentally important time for the development of sexuality.

During adolescence there is an increase in the sex drive as a result of hormonal changes. During puberty, individuals become capable of sexual reproduction. Individuals also develop the secondary sex characteristics that serve as a basis for sexual attraction, and as dramatic indicators that the young person is no longer physically a child.

The nature and extent of adolescent sexuality clearly have changed in recent years. Several different patterns of sexual behavior characterize contemporary adolescents. Many of the patterns include engagement in sexual behaviors that place the young person at risk of experiencing health, psychological, and social problems.

In much of American culture, the link between marriage and sexual activity has practically disappeared. This means that there is no particular age for sanctioning the initiation of sexual activity. Largely as a result of such changes, sexual activity is initiated at earlier ages than in the past, by increasing proportions of adolescents.

Attitudes toward sex became more tolerant from the late 1960s through the 1970s. The changed attitude, which was generally more liberal, has had a major impact on several major implications for youth's attitude today toward sex. First, there has been a greater openness in our society in sexual matters. Both the printed page and media openly discuss such topics as abortion, rape, and sexual abuse. Just a generation ago, such topics were not discussed as openly as today. The natural consequence is that youth today, who have been brought up in this atmosphere, are much more open and often feel more comfortable discussing sexual issues openly and honestly with both peers and adults. A second attitude change is that more adults and teens than a generation ago consider sexual intercourse outside of marriage as acceptable. No longer do many consider legal marriage as a required sanction for sex. Many believe that sex is acceptable within a "relationship," and some youth have adopted the liberal attitude that casual sex or sex for primarily personal pleasure, whether or not a relationship exists, is acceptable.

Many adolescents are initiating sexual intercourse at an earlier age than in the previous generation. Gender attitudes continue to demonstrate a difference in belief systems. Young women are much more likely than men to desire a strong relationship or even marriage before engaging in sexual intercourse.

Many of the problems associated with teenage sexual activity have increased with more teens' sexual involvement. American teenagers have one of the highest rates of premarital pregnancies in the world. Although more teenagers are now using contraceptives than in the past, there are still a large number who use no method of birth control or fail to use it properly. Legal abortion is an option that has become increasingly available even though it continues to be highly controversial. Because youth often delay making a decision to abort the baby, more complications persist. In addition, mental agony and guilt accompany making such a major decision.

Getty Images/SW Productions

Increased sexual activity also corresponds to a rise in sexually transmitted diseases. The most common among youth are gonorrhea, chlamydia, and herpes. Although some of the sexually transmitted diseases (STDs) may continue in the body for the rest of their life and affect reproduction, the AIDS disease often results in an early, painful death. In an attempt to prevent a nationwide epidemic, educational programs teaching about sex, diseases, and how to prevent the spread of these are taught around the country. Although not accepted by many, abstinence is the only true method to prevent sexually transmitted diseases.

Sexual abuse of and violence toward youth is all too common in America. Many adolescent girls experience unwanted sexual activities by dates and boyfriends. These experiences have a profound impact on behavior and development of young people. Sexual abuse is often linked to problems such as binge drinking and suicidal idealism. The true prevalence of rape is further complicated by the fact that most rapes are committed by someone known to the teenage victim, rather than a stranger who jumps out of "nowhere." These "date rapes," as they are sometimes labeled, are much less likely to be reported to authorities than those in which the woman is assaulted.

A major problem today is that a majority of youth continue to get most of their education and information about sex from the least reliable source—their peers. Informal sex education usually begins in the home when the child is young, but many homes give little instruction about sex to their preteen or teen, a time when they need good solid information.

Kim Painter explains in the first article that the sexual revolution has hit junior high school. The second selection continues the topic and explains new development in sexual activity. Controversy over sex education is explained in the subsequent article. In the fourth article, Nancy Wartik explores the topic of living together.

The Sexual Revolution Hits Junior High

The kids are doing more than baring bellies: They're shocking adults with their anything-goes behavior.

KIM PAINTER

Picture the mating rites of middle-schoolers. Perhaps you imagine hand-holding and first kisses, girls trying out eye shadow, boys sneaking a peek at vulgar men's magazines.

Now look again, through the eyes of increasingly concerned educators and experts:

- Researchers in Washington, D.C., recently started a program to prevent early sexual activity. They planned to offer it to seventh-graders, but after a pilot study decided to target fifth-graders—because too many seventh-graders already were having sex.
- Jo Mecham, a nurse at a Bettendorf, Iowa, middle school, says she overhears "pretty explicit sexual talk" from boys and girls in her "conservative" community. And despite a dress code, girls come to classes looking like bare-bellied rock stars: "They'll leave the house totally OK, and when they get to school, they start disrobing."
- Joey Zbylut-Birky, a middle-school teacher in Omaha, recently asked students to think about "where they feel most comfortable" as part of an assignment to write song titles about themselves. A group of giggling boys piped up with comments about receiving oral sex.

The list goes on. Middle schools that used to do without dress codes now must send home exhaustive inventories of forbidden garments, from tube tops to too-low hip-huggers. Schools that used to handle crude language on a case-by-case basis now must have "no-profanity" policies. And sexual-harassment training is a normal part of middle-school curriculum.

The world "is rougher, it is sexier and it has reached down to touch boys and girls at younger ages," says Margaret Sagarese, who, with Charlene C. Giannetti, has written several books on parenting, including the new *The Patience of a Saint: How Faith Can Sustain You During the Tough Times of Parenting.*

Baby-boomer parents who thought that nothing would ever shock them are shocked by the way their young teens talk, dress and perhaps even behave, Sagarese says.

"Things have changed," says Jude Swift, 52, a mother of five whose youngest is an eighth-grade boy. "I think a great deal of it is due to the media and what kids see on TV, in magazine ads, in videos. . . . It's all about being sexy."

The world 'is rougher, it is sexier' and it's harder for teens to avoid it

Swift, of Camillus, N.Y., says she picked up a *Teen People* magazine the other day and "I was amazed. It was page after page of young teens dressed in very provocative ways and in very provocative poses."

Young girls "do not see anything wrong in looking that way," says Zbylut-Birky, the Omaha teacher. And, she says, "they don't see the difference between how they should look for a party and how they should look in an educational setting."

Boys Want to Look Sexy, Too

Even boys face increasing pressure to look sexy, says Sagarese: "There are 12-year-old boys going to GNC and taking all kinds of supplements because they want abs the same way girls want breasts."

Of course, many girls who dress like Britney Spears and many boys who talk like Eminem don't go beyond nervous note-passing in their actual romantic lives.

Zbylut-Birky, who overheard the oral-sex banter, says, "A lot of times they use that kind of language to impress their peers, but there's really nothing going on there."

But for some substantial minority of middle schoolers, something very risky—including intercourse and oral sex—is going on, some experts say. In 1995, government researchers asked teens over age 15 whether they'd had sexual intercourse by age 14; 19% of girls and 21% of boys said yes. In 1988, the numbers were 11% for girls and the same 21% for boys, says the

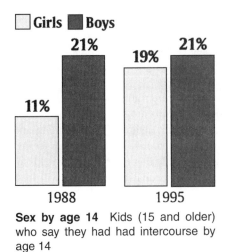

☐ Girls ■ Boys

Sex by age 14 Kids (15 and older) who say they had had intercourse by age 14

Washington, D.C.-based research group Child Trends. Data for 2002 are just being collected.

Another study, using different methods, followed 12- to 14-year-olds between 1997 and 1999 and found 16% of girls and 20% of boys reported sex at 14 or younger, says Child Trends researcher Jennifer Manlove.

As for oral sex, a 2000 study from the Alan Guttmacher Institute in New York caused a firestorm by suggesting that more young teens were engaging in that activity—possibly as a way of remaining technical virgins in the age of abstinence education. That study was based on scattered, anecdotal reports of increased oral herpes and gonorrhea of the throat.

No nationwide, scientific study has actually asked young teens, or older teens for that matter, whether they have oral sex.

"A lot of alarm parents feel on this issue is based on anecdotal information," says Bill Albert, spokesman for the Washington, D.C.-based National Campaign to Prevent Teen Pregnancy, a private, non-profit group working to reduce teen pregnancy.

But some of the anecdotes are hair-raising.

"The other day at school, a girl got caught in a bathroom with a boy performing oral sex on him," says Maurisha Stenson, a 14-year-old eighth-grader at a Syracuse, N.Y., middle school.

When the Lights Went On

Denyia Sullivan, 14, attends a different Syracuse middle school but says she's seen and heard about similar things. One time, a girl performed oral sex on a boy in the gym bleachers during a movie. "The teacher turned on the light and there they were," Sullivan says. "Everybody was looking and laughing."

The two girls also say there's more than oral sex going on. Sullivan can think of five pregnant girls at her school, which includes sixth-, seventh- and eighth-graders. Stenson guesses that "almost 50%" of kids at her school, for seventh- and eighth-graders, are engaging in some kind of sex.

"This is happening; they are telling the truth," says Courtney Ramirez, who directs the Syracuse Way to Go after-school program, designed to help kids succeed in school and avoid risks. Both girls are peer educators in the program.

"Youths are really getting involved in things a whole lot sooner than we thought," Ramirez says.

But other experts say that without good, current numbers on nationwide trends, they can't even say with any confidence that early sex is increasing. "It could be getting worse, it could be getting better, we just don't know," Albert says.

One problem is that the best government studies are done infrequently. Another is that researchers—and the public—are squeamish about asking detailed sex questions of young teens. And when they do ask, they aren't sure youngsters always understand the questions or answer truthfully. Albert's organization will try to fill in the gap later this year with a report based on data from around the country.

But many educators and parents have heard the alarms and are acting now. Krystal McKinney directs a program that offers sex education and life-skills training to middle-school girls in the Washington, D.C., area. Since the 2000 Guttmacher oral sex report, she and her staff have redoubled efforts to make sure that girls understand the risks.

"We have kids who think you can't get diseases from oral sex," she says. "Kids think they know everything, but we challenge that."

With the youngest teens, clear information is crucial, says Xenia Becher, a mental health educator at the Syracuse after-school program.

Recently, she says, she asked some 13- to 15-year-olds to define sex. "They had trouble coming up with an answer," she says. "Some said it had to be between a male and female and a penis and vagina had to be involved.

"So I asked, 'What about if two men were involved?' 'Well,' they said, 'I don't know what that is, but it's not sex.'"

Becher also trains parents to discuss sex with their kids. She tells them that their voices matter, even in a sex-soaked culture.

"When you get down to what's right or wrong, popular culture is going to have an influence, but the stronger internal voice comes from you," she says.

Becher admits that setting limits and encouraging independence can be a real balancing act. When her own 13-year-old daughter dressed for a dance in a pair of "those nasty hip-huggers" and a short top, Becher says, she asked her to think how she'd look when "she was waving her arms around on the dance floor." But she didn't make her daughter change.

"You've got to pick your battles," she says.

Parents Shouldn't Back Off

"Kids really do care what their parents think," says Kristin Moore, president of Child Trends. "They don't really want their parents to back away. But a lot of parents do back away at this age."

Some parents, she says, are so intimidated by a child's hostile behavior and demands for privacy that they give far too much ground. "Sometimes parents are home during a party but have no idea what is going on at the party."

Mark Gibbons, an Augusta, Ga., father of two girls ages 8 and 12, says that he and his wife are doing everything they can to stay involved. They try to talk to their daughters about everything. "We've told them that it may sometimes be embarrassing, but that we'd rather they get their information from us," he says.

"I talk to them all the time," says Lauryn, a seventh-grader who takes classes for gifted and talented kids. She does say that she prefers to discuss boyfriends with her mom.

Nevertheless, when Lauryn has friends over, Gibbons says he keeps his ears open. When she's instant messaging on the computer, he says, "Every once in a while, I'll just wander over there and ask who she's talking to. And I do look at her little directory and make sure all those user names are people that I know. We try not to show that we're being nosy, but we are."

Gibbons also chaperones middle-school dances. It's a window into his daughter's larger world—one that, even in a community of "pretty well-behaved kids," can be shocking, he says. "Some of the dancing they do is kind of risque, to say the least."

Lauryn says she appreciates her parents' involvement: "I believe it does makes a difference. . . . I have never gotten into trouble." And she says she does know kids who are getting into sexual trouble. "At some of the parties I go to, people playing 'Truth or Dare' will say that they've already 'done it,'" she says.

Meanwhile, Gibbons says he recently got a reminder that it is never too early to discuss sexual values. Third-grader Tayler "came home and said one little girl took a boy behind a tree and they were French kissing. . . . I said, 'Well, do you think that is wrong?' She said, 'Yes.'"

But while parents are right to watch and worry, some may be worrying too much and enjoying too little about their children's pubescent years, says Sagarese, the parenting author. "I can't tell you how many parents have come up to me at speeches and they are apoplectic that their daughter is kissing. They feel like the first kiss is a runaway train that will lead to AIDS or pregnancy."

Her co-author, Giannetti, says, "Parents need to take a deep breath and a step back and remember what it was like to be a young adolescent."

Sometimes, Sagarese says, a first kiss is just a first kiss—and the same lovely rite of passage it was in a more innocent time.

The Cuddle Puddle of Stuyvesant High School

Researchers find it shocking that 11 percent of American girls between 15 and 19 claim to have same-sex encounters. Clearly they've never observed the social rituals of the pansexual, bi-queer, metroflexible New York teen.

ALEX MORRIS

Alair is wearing a tight white tank top cut off above the hem to show her midriff. Her black cargo pants graze the top of her combat boots, and her black leather belt is studded with metal chains that drape down at intervals across her hips. She has long blonde curls that at various times have been dyed green, blue, red, purple, and orange. ("A mistake," she says. "Even if you mean to dye your hair orange, it's still a mistake.") Despite the fact that she's fully clothed, she seems somehow exposed, her baby fat lingering in all the right places. Walking down the sterile, white halls of Stuyvesant High School, she creates a wave of attention. She's not the most popular girl in school, but she is well known. "People like me," she wrote in an instant message. "Well, most of them."

Alair is headed for the section of the second-floor hallway where her friends gather every day during their free tenth period for the "cuddle puddle," as she calls it. There are girls petting girls and girls petting guys and guys petting guys. She dives into the undulating heap of backpacks and blue jeans and emerges between her two best friends, Jane and Elle, whose names have been changed at their request. They are all 16, juniors at Stuyvesant. Alair slips into Jane's lap, and Elle reclines next to them, watching, cat-eyed. All three have hooked up with each other. All three have hooked up with boys—sometimes the same boys. But it's not that they're gay or bisexual, not exactly. Not always.

Their friend Nathan, a senior with John Lennon hair and glasses, is there with his guitar, strumming softly under the conversation. "So many of the girls here are lesbian or have experimented or are confused," he says.

Ilia, another senior boy, frowns at Nathan's use of labels. "It's not lesbian or bisexual. It's just, whatever . . . "

Since the school day is winding down, things in the hallway are starting to get rowdy. Jane disappears for a while and comes back carrying a pint-size girl over her shoulder. "Now I take

her off and we have gay sex!" she says gleefully, as she parades back and forth in front of the cuddle puddle. "And it's awesome!" The hijacked girl hangs limply, a smile creeping to her lips. Ilia has stuffed papers up the front of his shirt and prances around on tiptoe, batting his eyes and sticking out his chest. Elle is watching, enthralled, as two boys lock lips across the hall. "Oh, my," she murmurs. "Homoerotica. There's nothing more exciting than watching two men make out." And everyone is talking to another girl in the puddle who just "came out," meaning she announced that she's now open to sexual overtures from both boys and girls, which makes her a minor celebrity, for a little while.

When asked how many of her female friends have had same-sex experiences, Alair answers, "All of them." Then she stops to think about it. "All right, maybe 80 percent. At least 80 percent of them have experimented. And they still are. It's either to please a man, or to try it out, or just to be fun, or 'cause you're bored, or just 'cause you like it . . . whatever."

With teenagers there is always a fair amount of posturing when it comes to sex, a tendency to exaggerate or trivialize, innocence mixed with swagger. It's also true that the "puddle" is just one clique at Stuyvesant, and that Stuyvesant can hardly be considered a typical high school. It attracts the brightest public-school students in New York, and that may be an environment conducive to fewer sexual inhibitions. "In our school," Elle says, "people are getting a better education, so they're more open-minded."

That said, the Stuyvesant cuddle puddle is emblematic of the changing landscape of high-school sexuality across the country. This past September, when the National Center for Health Statistics released its first survey in which teens were questioned about their sexual behavior, 11 percent of American girls polled in the 15-to-19 demographic claimed to have had same-sex encounters—the *same* percentage of all women ages 15 to 44 who reported same-sex experiences, even though the teenagers have much shorter sexual histories. It doesn't take a Stuyvesant education to see what this means: More girls are experimenting with each other, and they're starting younger. And this is a conservative estimate, according to Ritch Savin-Williams, a professor of human development at Cornell who has been conducting research on same-sex-attracted adolescents for over twenty years. Depending on how you phrase the questions and how you define sex between women, he believes that "it's possible to get up to 20 percent of teenage girls."

Of course, what can't be expressed in statistical terms is how teenagers think about their same-sex interactions. Go to the schools, talk to the kids, and you'll see that somewhere along the line this generation has started to conceive of sexuality differently. Ten years ago in the halls of Stuyvesant you might have found a few goth girls kissing goth girls, kids on the fringes defiantly bucking the system. Now you find a group of vaguely progressive but generally mainstream kids for whom same-sex intimacy is standard operating procedure. "It's not like, *Oh, I'm going to hit on her now.* It's just kind of like, you come up to a friend, you grab their ass," Alair explains. "It's just, like, our way of saying hello." These teenagers don't feel as though their sexuality has to define them, or that they have to define it, which has led some psychologists and child-development specialists to label them the "post-gay" generation. But kids like Alair and her friends are in the process of working up their own language to describe their behavior. Along with gay, straight, and bisexual, they'll drop in new words, some of which they've coined themselves: polysexual, ambisexual, pansexual, pansensual, polyfide, bi-curious, bi-queer, fluid, metroflexible, heteroflexible, heterosexual with lesbian tendencies—or, as Alair puts it, "just sexual." The terms are designed less to achieve specificity than to leave all options open.

To some it may sound like a sexual Utopia, where labels have been banned and traditional gender roles surpassed, but it's a complicated place to be. Anyone who has ever been a girl in high school knows the vicissitudes of female friendships. Add to that a sexual component and, well, things get interesting. Take Alair and her friend Jane, for example. "We've been dancing around each other for, like, three years now," says Alair. "I'd hop into bed with her in a second." Jane is tall and curvy with green eyes and faint dimples. She thinks Alair is "amazing," but she's already had a female friendship ruined when it turned into a romantic relationship, so she's reluctant to let it happen again. Still, they pet each other in the hall, flirt, kiss, but that's it, so far. "Alair," Jane explains, "is literally in love with everyone and in love with no one."

"Relationships are a bitch, dude."

Alair is having lunch with Jane, Elle, and their friend Nathan at a little Indian place near Jane's Upper West Side apartment. Jane has been telling the story of her first lesbian relationship: She fell for a girl who got arrested while protesting the Republican National Convention (very cool), but the girl stopped calling after they spent the night together (very uncool).

"We should all be single for the rest of our lives," Alair continues. "And we should all have sugar daddies." As the only child of divorced parents, Alair learned early that love doesn't always end in happily ever after and that sex doesn't always end in love.

Nathan looks across the table at her and nods knowingly. He recently broke up with a girl he still can't get off his mind, even though he wasn't entirely faithful when they were together. "I agree. I wholeheartedly agree," he says.

"I *disagree,*" says Elle, alarmed. She's the romantic of the group, a bit naïve, if you ask the others.

"Well," says Nathan. "You're, like, the only one in a happy relationship right now, so . . ."

Alair cracks up. "Happy? Her man is gayer than I am!" (Jane, the sarcastic one, has a joke about this boy: "He's got one finger left in the closet, and it's in Elle, depending on what time it is.")

"But at least she's happy," argues Nathan.

"When I'm single, I say I'm happy I'm single, and when I'm in a relationship I seem happy in the relationship. Really, I'm filled with angst!" says Elle.

Nathan rolls his eyes. "Anyone who says they're filled with angst is definitely *not* filled with angst."

He's got a point. In her brand-new sneakers and her sparkly barrettes, Elle is hardly a poster child for teenage anxiety. She makes A's at Stuyvesant, babysits her cousins, and is engaging in a way that will go over well in college interviews.

Then again, none of them are bad kids. Sure, they drink and smoke and party, but in a couple of years, they'll be drinking and smoking and partying at Princeton or MIT. They had to be pretty serious students to even get into Stuyvesant, which accepts only about 3 percent of its applicants. And when they're not studying, they're going to music lessons, SAT prep, debate practice, Japanese class, theater rehearsal, or some other résumé-building extracurricular activity.

Their sexual behavior is by no means the norm at their school; Stuyvesant has some 3,000 students, and Alair's group numbers a couple dozen. But they're also not the only kids at school who experiment with members of the same sex. "Other people do it, too," said a junior who's part of a more popular crowd. "They get drunk and want to be a sex object. But that's different. Those people aren't bisexual." Alair and her friends, on the other hand, are known as the "bi clique." In the social strata, they're closer to the cool kids than to the nerds. The boys have shaggy hair and T-shirts emblazoned with the names of sixties rockers. The girls are pretty and clever and extroverted. Some kids think they're too promiscuous. One student-union leader told me, "It's weird. It's just sort of incestuous." But others admire them. Alair in particular is seen as a kind of punk-rock queen bee. "She's good-looking, and she does what she wants," said a senior boy. "That's an attractive quality."

"The interesting kids kind of gravitate towards each other," Elle had explained earlier. "A lot of them are heteroflexible or bisexual or gay. And what happens is, like, we're all just really comfortable around each other."

Still, among her friends, Elle's ideas are the most traditional. Her first kiss with a girl was at Hebrew school. Since then, she's made out with girls frequently but dated only guys.

"I've always been the marrying type," she says to the table. "Not just 'cause it's been forced on me, but 'cause it's a good idea. I really want to have kids when I grow up."

"Have mine," offers Alair.

"I will," Elle coos in her best sultry voice. "Anything for you, Alair."

Jane blinks quickly, something she has a habit of doing when she's gathering her thoughts. "They will probably have the technology by the time we grow up that you two could have a baby together."

"But, like, if Alair doesn't want to birth her own child, I could."

"I'll birth it," Alair says, sighing. "I just want you to raise it and pay for it and take care of it and never tell it that I'm its parent. 'Cause, I mean, that would scar a child for life. Like, the child would start convulsing." Everyone laughs.

"You'd be an awesome mom, I think," says Elle. Her own mom puts a lot of pressure on her to date a nice Jewish boy. Once, Elle asked her, "'Mom, what if I have these feelings for girls?' and she said, 'Do you have feelings for boys too?' I'm like, 'Yeah.' And she's like, 'Then you have to ignore the ones you have for girls. If you can be straight, you have to be straight." Elle asked to go by a nickname because she hasn't told her mother that she's not ignoring those feelings.

Even as cultural acceptance of gay and bisexual teenagers grows, these kids are coming up against an uncomfortable generational divide. In many of their families, the 'It's fine, as long as it's not my kid' attitude prevails. Some of the parents take comfort in the belief that this is just a phase their daughters will grow out of. Others take more drastic measures. Earlier this year at Horace Mann, when one girl's parents found out that she was having a relationship with another girl, they searched her room, confiscated her love letters, and even had the phone company send them transcripts of all her text messages. Then they informed her girlfriend's parents. In the end, the girls were forbidden to see each other outside school.

Even Jane, whose parents know about her bisexuality and are particularly well suited to understanding it (her mother teaches a college course in human sexuality), has run up against the limits of their liberal attitudes. They requested that she go by her middle name in this story. "My mom thinks I'm going to grow up and be ashamed of my sexuality," she says. "But I *won't.*"

To these kids, homophobia is as socially shunned as racism was to the generation before them. They say it's practically the one thing that's not tolerated at their school. One boy who made disparaging remarks about gay people has been ridiculed and taunted, his belongings hidden around the school. "We're a creative bunch when we hate someone," says Nathan. Once the tormenters, now the tormented.

Alair is one of the lucky ones whose parents don't mind her bisexual tendencies. Her dad is the president of a company that manages performance artists and her mom is a professional organizer. "My parents are awesome," she says. "I think they've tried to raise me slightly quirky, like in a very hippie little way, and it totally backfired on them."

"'Cause you ended up like a hippie?" Nathan asks.

"No, 'cause I went further than I think they wanted me to go." Despite the bravado, there's a sweetness to Alair. She sings in the Trinity Children's Choir. She does the dishes without being asked. She's a daddy's girl and her mother's confidante, though she hasn't always managed to skirt trouble away from home. She got kicked out of her middle school, Columbia Prep, after getting into an altercation with a girl who had been making her life miserable. ("I threw a bagel at her head, all right? I attacked her with a bagel.")

"My mom's like, 'Alair, I don't understand you. I want to be a parent to you but I have no control at all . . . As a person you're awesome. You're hilarious, you entertain me, you're so cool. I would totally be your friend. But as your mother, I'm worried.'"

"I can't say I was pleased," her mother tells me about first learning of Alair's bisexual experimentation. "But I can't say I was upset either. I like that she's forthright about what she wants, that she values her freedom, that she takes care of herself. But I have all the trepidations a parent has when they learn their child is becoming sexually active."

Of course, none of these kids will have to deal with their parents quite this directly in another year or so—a fact of which they are all acutely aware. College is already becoming a pressing issue. Everyone thinks Elle is going to get into Harvard. "If I fail physics, my average drops like a stone," she frets. Alair and Nathan want to go to the same college, wherever that may be.

"You do realize," Alair tells him, "that, like, we're two of the most awesome people in the school."

"We would room," Nathan says. "We would totally room."

"Fuck yeah. But I'm gonna need a lock on my door for like, 'I'm bringing these five girls home, Nathan. What are you doing tonight?'" She mimics his voice, "'I'm reading my book.'"

"Ouch!" Nathan scowls at her.

"It's the Kama Sutra!"

"Oh, right, right."

"I've actually read the Kama Sutra," Alair informs the table. "Some of that shit just isn't gonna work."

"I know!" says Jane. "We have three editions at my house."

"Like, I've tried it. You need a man that's like 'Argh!'" Alair pumps her arms up above her head. "I've got one of those guys, actually." She's talking about Jason, the boy she was hanging out with last night, another frequenter of the cuddle puddle. "He's so built."

"He's in love with you," Jane says drily.

"No, he's not!"

"Yes he is!"

"How could he *not* be in love with Alair?" Nathan reasons.

Jane nods in Alair's direction. "He bought you gum."

"He bought you gum." This cinches it for Nathan. "Yeah, he loves you. He wants you so in his underwear."

Alair looks at him blankly. "But he already has that. We're friends." There's no need to bring love into it.

But later, back at Jane's apartment, as the afternoon is turning to night, Alair has the look of, if not love, at least infatuation, as she waits in the hallway for the elevator to take her back down. Only it's not Jason she's saying good-night to—it's

Jane. "You make my knees weak," she says. And then to cut the tension: "I showered for you and everything." She leans in and gives Jane a kiss.

It practically takes a diagram to plot all the various hookups and connections within the cuddle puddle. Elle's kissed Jane and Jane's kissed Alair and Alair's kissed Elle. And then from time to time Elle hooks up with Nathan, but really only at parties, and only when Bethany isn't around, because Nathan really likes Bethany, who doesn't have a thing for girls but doesn't have a problem with girls who do, either. Alair's hooking up with Jason (who "kind of" went out with Jane once), even though she sort of also has a thing for Hector, who Jane likes, too—though Jane thinks it's totally boring when people date people of the same gender. Ilia has a serious girlfriend, but girls were hooking up at his last party, which was awesome. Molly has kissed Alair, and Jane's ex-girlfriend first decided she was bi while staying at Molly's beach house on Fire Island. Sarah sometimes kisses Elle, although she has a boyfriend—he doesn't care if she hooks up with other girls, since she's straight anyway. And so on.

Some of the boys hook up with each other, too, although in far fewer numbers than the girls. One of Alair's male friends explained that this is because for guys, anything beyond same-sex kissing requires "more of a physical commitment." If a guy does hook up with other guys it certainly doesn't make the girls less likely to hook up with him; and the converse is obviously true.

Of course, the definition of "hooking up" is as nebulous as the definition of "heteroflexible." A catchall phrase for anything from "like, exchanging of saliva" to intercourse, it's often a euphemism for oral sex. But rules are hazy when you're talking about physical encounters between two girls. As Alair puts it, "How do you define female sex? It's difficult. I don't know what the bases are. Everyone keeps trying to explain the bases to me, but there's so many things that just don't fit into the base system. I usually leave it up to the other girl."

Elle elaborates by using herself as an example. At a recent party, she says, she "kissed five people and, like, hooked up with two going beyond kissing. One of them was a boy and one of them was a girl. The reason I started hooking up with the guy is because he was making out with this other guy and he came back and was like, 'I have to prove that I'm straight.' And I was standing right there. That's how it all began." The guy in question became her boyfriend that night; even though the relationship is all of a week old, she calls it her second "serious" relationship. "At least I'm intending for it to be serious." (It lasted eleven days.)

The cuddle puddle may be where a flirtation begins, but parties, not surprisingly, are where most of the real action takes place. In parentless apartments, the kids are free to "make the rounds," as they call it, and move their more-than-kissing hookups with both genders behind locked bathroom doors or onto coat-laden beds. Even for bisexual girls there is, admittedly, a *Girls Gone Wild* aspect to these evenings. Some girls do hook up with other girls solely to please the guys who watch, and it can be difficult to distinguish between the behavior of someone who is legitimately sexually interested and someone who wants to impress the boy across the room. Alair is quick to disparage

this behavior—"It kinda grosses me out. It can't be like, this could be fun . . . is anyone watching my chest heave?"—but Jane sees it as empowering. "I take advantage of it because manipulating boys is fun as hell. Boys make out with boys for our benefit as well. So it's not just one way. It's very fair."

She's not just making excuses. These girls have obliterated the "damned if you do, damned if you don't" stranglehold that has traditionally plagued high-school females. They set the sexual agenda for their group. And they expect reciprocation. "I've made it my own personal policy that if I'm going to give oral sex, I'm going to receive oral sex," says Jane. "Jane wears the pants in any relationship," Ilia says with a grin. "She wears the pants in *my* relationship, even though she's not part of it."

When the girls talk about other girls they sound like football players in a locker room ("The Boobie Goddesses of our grade are Natalie and Annette," or "Have you seen the Asian girl who wears that tiny red dress and those high red sneakers?," or "Carol is so hot! Why is she straight? I don't get it"), but there's little gossip about same-sex hookups—partly because the novelty has by now worn off, and partly because, as Alair puts it, "it's not assumed that a relationship will stem from it." It seems that even with all the same-sex activity going on, it's still hard for the girls to find other girls to actually date. Jane says this is because the girls who like girls generally like boys more, at least for dating. "A lot of girls are scared about trying to make a lesbian relationship work," she says. "There's this fear that there has to be the presence of a man or it won't work."

But dating gay girls isn't really an option either, because the cuddle-puddle kids are not considered part of the gay community. "One of the great things about bisexuality is that mainstream gay culture doesn't affect us as much," says Jane, "so it's not like bi boys feel that they have to talk with a lisp and walk around all fairylike, and it's not like girls feel like they have to dress like boys." The downside, she says, is that "gays feel that bis will cheat on them in a straight manner." In fact, there's a general impression of promiscuity that bisexual girls can't seem to shake. "The image of people who are bi is that they are sluts," says Jane. "One of the reasons straight boys have this bi-girls fantasy is that they are under the impression that bisexual girls will sleep with anything that moves and that's why they like both genders, because they are so sex-obsessed. Which isn't true."

If you ask the girls why they think there's more teenage bisexual experimentation happening today, Alair is quick with an explanation. "I blame television," she says. "I blame the media." She's partly joking, giving the stock answer. But there's obviously some truth to it. She's too young to remember a time when she couldn't turn on Showtime or even MTV and regularly see girls kissing girls. It's not simply that they're imitating what they've seen, it's that the stigma has been erased, maybe even transformed into cachet. "It's in the realm of possibilities now," as Ritch Savin-Williams puts it. "When you don't think of it as being a possibility, you don't do it. But now that it's out there, it's like, 'Oh, yeah, that could be fun.'" Of course, sexy TV shows would have no impact at all if they weren't tapping into something more innate. Perhaps, as research suggests, sexuality is more fluid for women than it is for men. Perhaps natural female intimacy opens the door to sexual experimentation at an age when male partners can be particularly unsatisfying. As one mother of a cuddle-puddle kid puts it, "Emotionally it's safer—it's difficult in this age group to hold onto your body. You're changing. There's a safety factor in a girl being with a girl." Then, laughing, she asked that her name be withheld. "*My mother might read this.*"

It's true that girls have always experimented, but it's typically been furtive, kept quiet. The difference now is how these girls are flaunting it. It's become a form of exhibitionism, a way to get noticed at an age when getting noticed is what it's all about. And as rebellions go, it's pretty safe. Hooking up with girls won't get them pregnant. It won't hurt their GPA. It won't keep them out of honor societies, social groups, the Ivy League.

In the end, the Stuyvesant cuddle puddle might just be a trickle-down version of the collegiate "gay until graduation." On the other hand, these girls are experimenting at an earlier age, when their identities and their ideas about what they want in a partner are still being formed. Will it affect the way they choose to live their adult lives? Elle is determined to marry a man, but Alair and Jane are not so sure. Maybe they won't get married at all, they say, keep their options open. "I have no idea," says Alair. "I'm just 16."

A few weeks later, the guys are hanging out in Nathan's room. Jason is stretched out on the bed and Ilia is leaning back in a chair by the desk, and it's pretty clear that nothing much is happening this afternoon. Just some guitar playing, some laying about. Then the girls show up and things get more interesting. Alair and Jane have brought a couple of friends, Molly and Nikki. Molly doesn't know for sure if she's bisexual, but "I have my suspicions," she says; she's hooked up with Alair before. Nikki is with her friend Jared, who she's sort of but not really dating. He makes out with boys but considers Nikki his "soul mate"; she's totally straight but kisses girls. "I kiss anything pretty, anything beautiful, anything worthwhile," she says.

Nikki runs her hands through Jane's hair. "You look awesome! I love this shirt. I love your hair." Jane crosses the room to sit in Alair's lap, and Alair wraps her arms around her. That reminds Nikki of something.

"Wait! Let me show you guys the next painting I'm doing," she says, pulling from her backpack a photograph of Alair asleep on the beach in a striped bikini. It's a sexy picture, and Nikki knows it.

Chinese food is ordered, guitars strummed, an ice cube is passed around and for no apparent reason everyone is required to put it down their pants. It's just another afternoon of casual flirtation. The boys showing off for the girls, the girls showing off for everyone. No strings attached. In theory, anyway. Most

of the kids say they hate relationships, that they don't want to be tied down, that they want to be open to different possibilities and different genders from minute to minute, but there is a natural tendency—as natural perhaps as the tendency to experiment—to try to find connection. Like it or not, emotions get involved. If you look closer, you can see the hint of longing, the momentary pouting, the tiny jealousies. Jared can't take his eyes off Nikki, but Nikki seems interested mainly in Alair. Jason, too, is angling for Alair's attention, but Alair is once again focused on Jane. And Jane, well, Jane might actually be in love.

She is in a particularly good mood today, quick to smile, and even more quick to drop into conversation the name of the boy she recently started dating, a tall, good-looking senior and one of the most popular kids at Stuyvesant. Later, while rummaging for silverware, she casually mentions that they may start dating exclusively.

"Ugh!" Alair exclaims, grabbing her by the hips and pulling her away from the drawer. "What about me?"

"Let's put it this way," Jane counters, grinning and snatching up a fork. "I'm not interested in any other *guys.*"

Still, it's clear that Jane really likes this guy. And Alair seems a little rattled. Her fortune cookie reads, "You are the master of every situation." Except perhaps this one.

Later, after the lamps have been switched on and the takeout eaten, both girls are on a love seat in the living room, leaning into each other, boys and dirty dishes strewn about. Jane starts showing off what she can do with her tongue, touching her nose with it, twisting it around, doing rolls. Everyone is impressed.

"My tongue gets a lot of practice," she says.

"Why don't you practice on me?" Alair demands. "I'll hook up with you." It's clear that she means more than kissing.

Jane blinks a few times. "I'm scared I'm going to be bad at it," she finally says. She's being coy, just putting her off, but there's a bit of sincerity to her nervousness.

"You won't be bad at it," Alair reassures her. She pulls Jane between her legs and starts giving her a massage, running her hands up and down her back, pushing her hair aside to rub her neck. When the massage is over, Jason comes over to Alair, grabs her hand, kisses it. For the rest of the evening, he stays close to her side, but she stays close to Jane.

The next day when I meet up with Alair on her way to choir practice, she tells me that nothing ever happened with Jane that night. She's decided to give up on her. Jane's with someone else, it's official, and there's no room in the relationship for her. "But you know what," she says, mustering a smile. "They're, like, monogamous together, and I'm really happy for them. And being their friend and seeing them so happy together totally beats a fling." She pauses. "It really does."

From *New York Magazine*, February 6, 2006. Copyright © 2006 by Reprint Management Services. Reprinted by permission.

Give Students the Knowledge to Make Wise Choices about Sex

Three out of four respondents to November's Your Turn believe schools should teach a comprehensive sex education curriculum. Abstinence-only education, they say, is unrealistic for media-savvy teens who may already be having sex.

As a Minnesota reader put it, "If public schools don't teach a comprehensive sex education curriculum, Madonna will."

This Your Turn marks the debut of the ASBJ Reader Panel, a group of readers who are joining an e-mail conversation with us to supplement the printed Your Turn question. (Interested? Sign on at www.asbj.com/readerpanel.)

At this early stage, the Reader Panel is a resounding success. We've received hundreds of responses and many thoughtful comments. We can't print them all, but we can offer a representative sample of your views.

In addition to the 75 percent who supported a comprehensive sex-ed curriculum, 16 percent favored abstinence-only education, 8 percent offered various other responses, and 1 percent said, "Don't teach sex education at all."

Like the reader who cautioned against ceding sex education to Madonna, many of you said it was unrealistic, dangerous, and even dishonest to teach abstinence only when many teens are having sex and will continue to do so regardless of what their teachers tell them.

"The program should stress the importance of abstinence but must be comprehensive," said Lee Doebler, a board member from Alabama. "We cannot ignore the fact that many teens are sexually active and that sexual activity is beginning earlier and earlier as children reach puberty at an earlier age."

"Teaching abstinence-only sex education is like teaching nutrition without covering sugars and fats," added another reader. "Abstinence should certainly be emphasized in the curriculum; however, students should be given all the information so they could make that determination for themselves."

William Higgins, a board member from Washington state, said he favors a strong abstinence message along with other information. "It is urgent that we get a handle on the number-one addictive drug of choice among our youth—sex," he said.

"I advocate a comprehensive program of graduated information, based on age and grade level, that has a strong emphasis on abstinence. The idea is to keep kids smart—and safe!"

While we want students to abstain, there are other things we need to teach them along with abstaining that will strengthen their resolve, said Kim S. Rogers, a board member from North Carolina. "We cannot force our children to abstain. And if we don't educate them on the emotional and physical stress of teen sex, that has the effect of diluting the importance of abstaining—which, in my opinion, is the ultimate goal of sex education. Not talking about it doesn't make it go away."

Many of those favoring the abstinence-only approach said sex education should be handled by parents, not schools.

"Parents have the right and duty to decide how to present this information to their children," said an Indiana board member.

Added Texas Superintendent Paul Vranish: "It seems that 'how-to' instruction should best be left to parents."

Such "how to" instruction can give teens a false sense of confidence, several readers said. As one Missouri board member put it, "There is too much false information being taught about the safety of the use of condoms as it relates to 'safe sex.'"

Ann Johnson, a registered nurse and Indiana board member, said she favors abstinence-only education as the best way to deter students from making choices that could harm them physically and psychologically.

"I believe students need to understand the anatomy and physiology of human reproduction," Johnson said. "It is also important to have some discussion on the emotional and hormonal changes that occur in developing from preteen to adolescent to young adult and on the financial, emotional, and physical demands that result from unplanned and too early pregnancies."

Among those favoring no sex education in school was Perry Shumway, a board member in Idaho. "If sex education weren't taught at all in public schools, private institutions, such as families, churches, and youth groups, would step up to the plate and fill in the void," Shumway said.

However, most respondents agreed with Linda Smith Kortemeyer, an Iowa board secretary/treasurer who said abstinence only isn't enough.

"If we adopt a curriculum limiting what children are allowed to learn because of our restrictive beliefs, we basically are telling children we don't believe in their ability to work through life's difficult problems," Kortemeyer said.

"When we encourage them to learn all they can, we tell them we have faith in their abilities to make the right choices. . . . Children may not make the same choices as we did, but they will have the opportunity to make decisions based on the knowledge we provided them. Hopefully, these choices are made with wisdom and courage."

The Perils of Playing House

Living together before marriage seems like a smart way to road test the relationship. But cohabitation may lead you to wed for all the wrong reasons—or turn into a one-way trip to splitsville.

NANCY WARTIK

Forget undying love or shared hopes and dreams—my boyfriend and I moved in together, a year after meeting, because of a potential subway strike. He lived in Manhattan, and I across the river in Brooklyn. Given New York City taxi rates, we'd have been separated for who knows how long. And so, the day before the threatened strike, he picked me up along with two yowling cats and drove us home. Six years, one wedding and one daughter later, we still haven't left.

Actually, if the strike threat hadn't spurred us to set up housekeeping, something else would have. By then, we were 99 percent sure we'd marry some day—just not without living together first. I couldn't imagine getting hitched to anyone I hadn't taken on a test-spin as a roommate. Conjoin with someone before sharing a bathroom? Not likely!

With our decision to cohabit, we joined the mushrooming ranks of Americans who choose at some point in their lives to inhabit a gray zone—more than dating, less than marriage, largely without legal protections. Thirty or 40 years ago, cohabitation was relatively rare, mainly the province of artists and other questionable types, and still thought of as "living in sin." In 1970 only about 500,000 couples lived together in unwedded bliss.

Now, nearly 5 million opposite-sex couples in the United States live together outside of marriage; millions more have done it at some point. Some couples do choose to live together as a permanent alternative to marriage, but their numbers are only a tiny fraction: More than 50 percent of couples who marry today have lived together beforehand. (At least 600,000 same-sex couples also cohabit, but their situation is different, since most don't have the choice to marry.)

"It's not this bad little thing only a few people are doing," says University of Michigan sociologist Pamela Smock. "It's not going away. It's going to become part of our normal, typical life course—it already is for younger people. They think it would be idiotic not to live with someone before marriage. They don't want to end up the way their parents or older relatives did, which is divorced."

In my and my husband's case, the pre-matrimonial experiment seems to have worked out well. But according to recent research, our year of shacking up could have doomed our relationship. Couples who move in together before marriage have up to two times the odds of divorce, as compared with couples who marry before living together. Moreover, married couples who have lived together before exchanging vows tend to have poorer-quality marriages than couples who moved in after the wedding. Those who cohabited first report less satisfaction, more arguing, poorer communication and lower levels of commitment.

Many researchers now argue that our penchant for combining households before taking vows is undermining our ability to commit. Meaning, the precautions we take to ensure marriage is right for us may wind up working against us.

From Toothbrush to Registry

Why would something that seems so sensible potentially be so damaging? Probably the reigning explanation is the inertia hypothesis, the idea that many of us slide into marriage without ever making an explicit decision to commit. We move in together, we get comfortable, and pretty soon marriage starts to seem like the path of least resistance. Even if the relationship is only tolerable, the next stage starts to seem inevitable.

Because we have different standards for living partners than for life partners, we may end up married to someone we never would have originally considered for the long haul. "People are much fussier about whom they marry than whom they cohabitate with," explains Paul Amato, a sociologist at Penn State University and one of the theory's originators. "A lot of people cohabit because it seems like a good idea to share expenses and have some security and companionship, without a lot of commitment."

Couples may wind up living together almost by accident. "People move in their toothbrush, their underwear, pretty soon a whole dresser," says Marshall Miller, coauthor with his partner,

Dorian Solot, of *Unmarried to Each Other: The Essential Guide to Living Together as an Unmarried Couple.* "Then someone's lease is up and since they're spending all their time together anyhow . . ."

Or, two people may move in together without a firm future plan because one partner isn't sure the other is good marriage material: He drinks too much; she gets really nasty during fights. Rather than commit, they take a trial run. Once they've shacked up, relatives start noodging: "So when are you going to get married already?" At friends' weddings, people ask, "When will it be your turn?"

"There's an inevitable pressure that creates momentum toward marriage," says Amato. "I've talked to so many cohabiting couples, and they'll say, 'My mother was so unhappy until I told her we were getting married—then she was so relieved.'" On top of the social pressure, Amato points out, couples naturally start making investments together: a couch, a pet—even a kid. Accidental pregnancies are more common among cohabiting couples than among couples who don't live together.

Once their lives are thoroughly entangled, some couples may decide to wed more out of guilt or fear than love. "I know a lot of men who've been living with women for a couple of years, and they're very ambivalent about marrying them," says John Jacobs, a New York City psychiatrist and author of *All You Need Is Love and Other Lies About Marriage.* "What sways them is a feeling they owe it to her. She'll be back on the market and she's older. He's taken up a lot of her time." Women in particular may be afraid to leave an unhappy cohabiting relationship and confront the dating game at an older age. "If you're 36, it's hard to take the risk of going back into the single world to look for another relationship," says Jacobs.

Younger people think it would be idiotic not to live with someone before marriage. They don't want to end up the way their parents did—divorced.

Charles, a 44-year-old New Yorker (who asked that his name be changed), admits that in his 30s, he almost married a live-in girlfriend of three years for reasons having little to do with love. The two moved in together six months after meeting when his sublet came to an end. "I thought it probably wasn't the best idea, but it was so much easier than looking for an apartment," Charles says. "I told myself: 'Keep trying, and maybe it will work.'"

Eventually his girlfriend insisted they either marry or break up, and he couldn't find the strength to leave. The two got engaged. Weeks before the date, Charles realized he couldn't go through with it and broke off the engagement. "Her father told me, 'I'm sorry horsewhips are a thing of the past,'" Charles recalls, still pained by the memory. Even now, he regrets moving in with her. "It was a terrible idea," he says. "You get entwined in each other's lives. If you're not sure you want to be entwined,

---

Would You Be My . . . Roommate?

EVERYONE WHO'S MARRIED remembers how, when and where the momentous question was popped. But when two people move in together, they're often much more cavalier about it. "It's a bigger decision than a lot of couples realize," says Galena Kline, a research assistant at the Center for Marital and Family Studies at the University of Denver. "It's really going to change their life and relationship more than they might think. But a lot of couples don't necessarily communicate about it."

• **TALK, TALK, TALK:** Sitting down to discuss the feelings and expectations about living together before making a move is the best way for couples to ensure a good experience. It's helpful for partners to talk about topics ranging from the sublime to the mundane: marriage, kids, life goals—and who will take out the garbage or feed the cat.

• **FINANCIAL FIRST STEP:** Decide how you'll deal with money matters. "We don't recommend immediately combining your accounts," cautions Marshall Miller, coauthor with Dorian Solot of *Unmarried to Each Other.* Keeping money and credit separate initially, he says, removes an area of potential conflict during a time of adjustment and lets partners see how compatible their financial styles really are.

• **THE SHAKEDOWN:** If you want to test the waters before hiring a moving van, do a "trial cohabitation." Solot and Miller suggest living with your potential partner for a week or two, but caution, "Don't be enticed by fantasies of spending long, lazy days in bed followed by heartfelt conversations while you prepare dinner elbow to elbow, looking adorable . . . Give yourselves a real feel for the pressure of the morning dash, the low energy I-just-want-to-crash-in-front-of-the-TV evening and the negotiation over who will do the dishes."

—NW

---

you shouldn't put yourself in a position where it's definitely going to happen."

Some evidence indicates that women have less control over the progress of the cohabiting relationship. She may assume they're on the road to marriage, but he may think they're just saving on rent and enjoying each other's company. Research by sociologist Susan Brown at Bowling Green State University in Ohio has shown there's a greater chance cohabiting couples will marry if the man wants to do so. The woman's feelings don't have as much influence, she found: "The guy has got to be on board. What the woman wants seems to be less pivotal."

Cohabiting men may carry their uncertainty forward into marriage, with destructive consequences. A 2004 study by psychologist Scott Stanley, based on a national phone survey of nearly 1,000 people, found that men who had lived with their spouse premaritally were on average less committed to their marriages than those who hadn't. By contrast, cohabitation didn't seem to change how women felt about their partners.

Based on this finding and others, Stanley, director of the Center for Marital and Family Studies at the University of Denver and another originator of the inertia theory, believes women should be especially wary of moving in before getting engaged. "There are plenty of young men who will say, 'I'm living with a woman but I'm still looking for my soul mate,'" he says. "But how many women know the guy is thinking that way? How many women are living with a guy thinking he's off the market, and he's not?" Men also get trapped in troubled relationships, admits Stanley, but women are more likely to bear the brunt of ill-considered cohabitation decisions for the simplest reason—they are the ones who have the babies.

Charles almost married a live-in girlfriend for reasons having little to do with love. "It was so much easier than looking for an apartment. I told myself: 'Keep trying, and it will work.'"

The Cohabiting Type

The inertia theory is not the only way to explain why couples who move in before marriage are less likely to stick it out for the long haul. There may also be something specific about the experience that actually changes people's minds about marriage, making it seem less sacrosanct. "A couple of studies show that when couples cohabit, they tend to adopt less conventional beliefs about marriage and divorce, and it tends to make them less religious," says Amato. That could translate, once married, to a greater willingness to consider options that are traditionally frowned upon—like saying "so long" to an ailing marriage.

Nonetheless, there's a heated debate among social scientists about whether the research to date has been interpreted properly or overplayed to some extent. Having a family income below $25,000, for example, is a stronger predictor of divorce in the first 15 years of marriage than having shared a premarital address. "Having money, a sense of an economically stable future, good communication skills, living in a safe community—all of those things are more important," says Smock.

Because it's impossible to directly compare the effects of marriage and cohabitation, there's just no way to prove cohabiters' higher divorce rates aren't a side effect of their other characteristics, says psychologist William Pinsof, president of the Family Institute at Northwestern University. They may just be less traditional people—less likely to stay in an unhappy marriage in observance of religious beliefs or for the sake of appearances. "Those who choose to live together before getting married have a different attitude about marriage to begin with. I think cohabiting is a reflection of that, not a cause of higher divorce rates," he says. One population of cohabiters also tends to have less money and lower levels of education, which in itself can strain a relationship.

In short, not everyone buys the idea that cohabitation itself is hazardous to your relationship. For some couples, it may serve a useful purpose—even when it lacks a happy ending. About half of all cohabiters split up rather than marry, and many of those splits save the parties involved from rocky marriages, miserable divorces or both.

That's the attitude Amy Muscoplat, 34, a children's librarian who lives in Santa Monica, California, now has about the man she lived with several years ago. She and Mr. X had dated for nine months when they got engaged; a few months later she gave up her rent-controlled apartment by the beach, sold most of her furniture, and the two moved in together. "We moved in in August, and by early September he flipped out," she says. "We were supposed to get married in early November. The invitations had gone out, and then he changed his mind. Living together was the reality check for him, the mirror that made him go, 'Gosh, this might not really work for me.'"

Though she and her family lost thousands of dollars when the wedding was called off, Muscoplat is grateful things fell apart when they did. If they hadn't moved in together, she says, "I think he might have been pushed to the same place at some later point, maybe some day down the road when I was pregnant. I have a religious take on it—God was really watching out for me and I dodged a bullet."

The debate over cohabitation is partly a rehash of the values and morals conflicts that tend to become political footballs in America today. But on one point, virtually all researchers agree: We need to understand the effects of cohabitation on children. Some 40 percent of all cohabiting households include kids—that's somewhere close to 3.5 million children living in homes with two unmarried opposite-sex grown-ups.

Cohabiting relationships, by their nature, appear to be less fulfilling than marital relationships. People who cohabit say they are less satisfied and more likely to feel depressed, Susan Brown has found. While the precarious finances of many cohabiters has something to do with it, Brown also points to the inherent lack of stability. Long-term cohabitation is rare: most couples either break up or marry within five years. "Cohabiters are uncertain about the future of their relationship and that's distressing to them," she says.

People who cohabit say they are less satisfied and more likely to feel depressed.

As a result, cohabitation is not an ideal living arrangement for children. Emotionally or academically, the children of cohabiters just don't do as well, on average, as those with two married parents, and money doesn't fully explain the difference. The stress of parenting in a shakier living situation may be part of the problem, says Brown. "Stability matters. It matters for the well-being of children and adults alike," she adds. "We're better off with commitment, a sense that we're in it for the long haul."

The Must-have Discussion

Cohabitation rates may be skyrocketing, but Americans are still entirely enchanted with marriage. That's a sharp contrast with some Western societies—Sweden, France or the

Canadian province of Quebec, for example—where cohabitation is beginning to replace marriage. In the United States, 90 percent of young people are still expected to tie the knot at some point.

Since most Americans are destined for marriage—and a majority will live together beforehand—how can we protect against the potentially undermining effects of cohabitation? Follow the lead of one subgroup of cohabiters: Those who make a permanent commitment to each other first. One study that tracked 136 couples through the initial months of marriage found that early intentions seem to make a big difference. About 60 of the couples in the study lived together before getting engaged, while the rest waited either until after they were engaged or after they were married to set up housekeeping. Ten months after the wedding, the group that had cohabited before being engaged had more negative interactions, less confidence about the relationship and weaker feelings of commitment than the other two groups. But the marriages of couples who had moved in together after getting engaged seemed just as strong as those who had moved in together after marrying.

Among other things, couples who get engaged before cohabiting probably have a clearer understanding of each other's expectations before they combine households. On that point, Mia Dunleavey, a 39-year-old online financial columnist living in Brooklyn, New York, can speak with the sadder-but-wiser voice of experience. In her late 20s, Dunleavey was involved with a man she hoped to marry. He reluctantly agreed to move in with her, spurred by the fact that his lease was running out, but he vacillated for so long about setting a wedding date that she finally ended the relationship. Soon after, she relocated across the country to move in with a new man she'd fallen in love with, only to find their living styles were utterly incompatible.

"When you leave the door open for quasi-commitment, quasi-commitment is what you get."

Back in New York again, she took stock. "I was terribly disappointed," Dunleavey says. "You have this faith that you're moving in with someone in order to deepen the commitment, and it doesn't necessarily happen at all. Those two things are not correlated.

"At that point, I said, 'Never ever, ever again,'" she continues. "Living together is a waste of time and energy. The piece of china you'd gotten from your mother gets broken in the move. My living-together experience was a catalog of lost and broken things, never mind my heart."

When she fell in love again, she did things differently. She moved in with her intended just two weeks before the wedding—because by that point, there was no question about their future together. "There was no take-it or leave-it," she says. "The commitment was the foundation of the marriage. Alas, my only experience of living with someone is that when you leave the door open for quasi-commitment, quasi-commitment is what you get."

Miller and Solot don't advise against cohabitation for couples without immediate plans to marry. But they do believe each partner needs to understand clearly what the other is thinking. "The most important thing is for people to treat moving in together as a serious decision, a major life choice," Miller says. "What does it mean to you both for the long and short term? If one person thinks living together means a quick path towards marriage and the other thinks it's just saving on rent and having a friend with benefits, there could be trouble. The important thing is to be on the same page."

As for my husband and me, we had this much going for us when we moved in together: We'd already discussed a lot of the important issues. We knew we wanted similar things: a family; a "for better or worse" kind of commitment; a partner who knew life had to stop on Sundays, when *Six Feet Under* or *The Sopranos* was on. Even before the ring, it was clear to me I'd found someone who'd be willing to work things through. And he has been.

Perhaps there's hope for us after all.

NANCY WARTIK is a freelance writer living in New York City.

What to Tell the Kids about Sex

KAY S. HYMOWITZ

S ex education has been the Middle East of the culture wars and one of the longest-running, most rancorous battlegrounds of American social policy. For nearly 40 years, conservatives—many of them, though by no means all, observant Catholics and fundamentalist Christians—have been battling the increasing presence in the public schools of a permissive strain of sex education that came to be known as "comprehensive sexuality education." Unlike sex-ed programs from the first half of the twentieth century that had frowned on teen sex, comprehensive sexuality education affected a morally neutral or even positive stance toward adolescent sexual activity, supporting what was usually described as teenagers' "autonomous decision making," and promoting their use of contraception.

The spread of comprehensive sexuality education in the schools coincided with a steep rise in teen sexual activity. The number of teen girls who had had sex went from 29 percent in 1970 to 55 percent in 1990. Fourteen percent of sexually active teens had had four or more partners in 1971; by 1988, that number had increased to 34 percent. But though sex educators had sought to encourage teens to practice what they called "responsible decision making," their efforts did not seem to be paying off. Throughout the 1970s and 1980s American teenagers were not just having more sex; they were getting pregnant—and at rates that far surpassed those in other industrialized countries. Between 1972 and 1990, there was a 23 percent increase in the rate of teen pregnancy, and there was a similar increase between 1975 and 1990 in births to teen mothers.

The Culture War

Thus it is hardly surprising that the new sex ed became a rallying point for the populist uprising that eventually gave rise to Reagan Democrats, the school-choice movement, and other grassroots groups chafing at the social upheavals of the sixties. Traditionalist parents opposed to sex education were often the working- and middle-class mothers of school-aged children. Sex educators, on the other hand, had influential friends in Washington and New York, including Planned Parenthood, the Sexuality Information and Education Council of the United States (SIECUS), and leading professional groups like the American Medical Association. While the federal government never directly funded comprehensive sexuality-education programs, over the years it did provide

numerous funding streams, such as that from the Centers for Disease Control's (CDC) Division of Adolescent and School Health (DASH), that were often used to support them.

True, in the early years of the Reagan administration, traditionalists had one notable success in Washington when Congress passed the Adolescent Family Life Act (AFLA), earmarking $11 million for programs to "promote chastity and self-discipline." But "the chastity bill," as it came to be called, became bogged down in the courts when opponents charged that it violated the separation of church and state, and it remained a marginal cause and the subject of much eye-rolling among health professionals. At any rate, by the time AFLA was passed, 94 percent of school districts saw "informed decision making" as the major goal of sex education according to a 1981 study by the Alan Guttmacher Institute, and for years after that, comprehensive sex education, though often sanitized for middle-class communities, was the national norm.

Today, the reign of comprehensive sex ed appears to be faltering. This is largely due to Title V, a junior provision of the Personal Responsibility and Work Opportunity Reconciliation Act (PRWORA), the landmark 1996 welfare-reform bill. Title V put substantial money behind what is now known as "abstinence education"—that is, teaching children to abstain from sexual intercourse. States could receive $50 million a year for five years in the form of a block grant as long as they matched three dollars for every four from the federal government. In 2000, Congress added another abstinence initiative called Special Projects of Regional and National Significance (SPRANS). Today, the federal government earmarks over $100 million annually for abstinence education. But despite close analysis by researchers and journalists on the legislation and its impact on welfare mothers and their children, in the seven years since Congress passed welfare reform, Title V's rationale and legacy remain somewhat clouded.

A Broad Coalition

Critics and supporters of Title V can agree on one thing: At the time it was passed, it was a profoundly radical initiative. The architects of Title V believed that they were challenging not just the sex-ed establishment but American society overall. In a paper written for the American Enterprise Institute, Ron Haskins and Carol Statuto Bevan, congressional aides closely involved in writing Title V, conceded that "both the practices and standards in many communities across the country clash with the standard required by the law." And this, they wrote, "is precisely the point . . . . [T]he explicit goal of abstinence education programs is to change both behavior and community standards for the good of the country." Determined to avoid the fate of AFLA, whose language had been broad enough to sneak through some programs that were all but indistinguishable from those run by sexuality educators, the authors of Title V introduced a strict eight-point definition of abstinence education. These were "education or motivational programs" that had as their "exclusive purpose teaching the social, psychological and health gains from abstaining from sexual activity." Abstinence from sexual activity outside marriage, the definition also required, is "the expected standard for all school-age children." The bill allowed some flexibility—funded projects could not be inconsistent with any part of the definition but they didn't have to emphasize each part equally—but Title V was unusually specific, as well as unusually radical.

Yet much as abstinence education was promoted by social and religious conservatives determined to overthrow the liberal, nonjudgmental approach to sex ed, it also benefited from the reluctant backing of moderates frustrated with the status quo and the policies supporting it. Many Title V supporters saw a direct connection between welfare reform and sex-education reform; both could contribute to the battle against out-of-wedlock births tied to government dependency. PRWORA allows states to use a number of strategies intended to discourage out-of-wedlock births, such as a family cap and an end of direct payments to teen mothers; abstinence education was partly intended to be another weapon in that arsenal. Title V's eight-point definition of abstinence education includes several points whose purpose is to plant the ideal of childrearing inside marriage in young minds and to promote the idea that "bearing children out of wedlock is likely to have harmful consequences for the child, the child's parents, and society."

Moderates who eventually got behind abstinence education were also troubled by continuing high rates of teen pregnancy. True, by the early nineties, a decline in teen sexual activity, pregnancy, and abortion began, trends that continue to this day. According to the CDC's Youth Risk Behavior Survey, in 1991, 54.1 percent of high school students reported having sex; by 2001 that number was 45 percent. Those reporting multiple (more than four) partners declined from 18.7 percent to 14.2 percent. Pregnancy rates declined too—the CDC just announced that teen-birth rates decreased by another 5 percent in 2002, for a cumulative 28 percent decline since 1990. However, according to a 2001 study by the Alan Guttmacher Institute, even after the declines of the last decade, teen-birth, pregnancy, and abortion rates in the United States remain considerably higher than those in France, Sweden, Canada, and Great Britain. Moreover, American girls are more likely to start having sex before age 15 and to have multiple partners than their counterparts in those countries. In the United States, a full 25 percent of high school seniors have already had four or more partners, a much rarer phenomenon in the contrasting countries.

What also made the 1990s decline in teen pregnancy and sexual activity look less impressive was the growing incidence of sexually transmitted diseases. When most parents of today's teenagers were their age, the only widely reported sexually transmitted diseases in the United States were syphilis and gonorrhea. By the last decade of the century, common STDs grew to encompass over 20 kinds of infections. They include not just the one everyone knows, HIV-AIDS, but other viral diseases that can be asymptomatic and that while not fatal, are difficult, and in some cases impossible, to cure. While condom use among teenagers increased—in 2001, 57.9 percent of teens who had had sex reported using a condom in the three months prior to the survey, up from 46.2 percent in 1991—teenagers were still contracting three million STDs every year, far exceeding rates in other industrialized countries.

Everyone for Abstinence?

Within a short time after Title V was passed into law, it began to seem that the idea of abstinence for teenagers wasn't so radical anymore. Just about everyone connected to the business of sex education had taken to embracing the word abstinence—to the point of meaninglessness and much terminological confusion. A mere decade ago, abstinence was something of a laughingstock at places like the CDC and state departments of health. These days it is hard to find a state authority, sex-ed program, or organization, including Planned Parenthood, that doesn't promote "teaching abstinence." In using the term, educators sometimes mean they tell teens that abstaining from sex is one option to consider, much as comprehensive sex educators do. By "teaching abstinence," others mean they strongly encourage teens not to have sex, but still offer them information about how to use contraception. Both of these approaches fall under the now commonplace rubric "abstinence plus."

"Abstinence only" educators, on the other hand, teach abstinence as the only acceptable choice and discuss contraception almost entirely in terms of its failure to protect kids from pregnancy and STDs. To make matters more complicated, some abstinence supporters reject the "abstinence only" label as an overly narrow description of their goals and prefer "authentic abstinence." Meanwhile, the National Campaign Against Teen Pregnancy, the most prominent, middle-of-the-road organization in the business, has begun to promote an "abstinence first" message, apparently in order to clarify the ambiguity of "abstinence plus." Significantly, "abstinence only" programs are the only ones eligible for Title V money.

These skirmishes over terminology highlight the fact that even as American opinion leaders have grown more comfortable with the abstinence message, the handshake agreement about "teaching abstinence" only papers over a bitter, ongoing culture war. Not surprisingly, money and jobs, as well as ideology, are at stake.

For all the recent success of the abstinence forces, comprehensive sexuality education remains deeply embedded in the public-health infrastructure. While the number of schools teaching "abstinence only" has clearly grown, they are still in the minority: According to a recent article in Family Planning Perspectives, in 1988, 2 percent of school districts reported teaching abstinence as the sole way to prevent pregnancy whereas by 1999, 23 percent reported doing so. The liberal SIECUS receives money from the CDC to train teachers of curricula on HIV and AIDS that are indistinguishable from comprehensive sex-ed programs. A host of organizations including SIECUS, Planned Parenthood, the National Abortion Rights Action League, various AIDS and gay-rights organizations, as well as the National Association of County and City Health Officials, have begun a campaign entitled NoNewMoney.org to stop the federal government from putting any more funds behind abstinence education.

Meanwhile, teacher unions often balk at abstinence curricula. The New Jersey Education Association has opposed a legislative proposal to "stress abstinence." The National Education Association (NEA) suggests that members in "abstinence only" districts "lobby for those funds to be used in after-school community programs so schools can be free to teach a more comprehensive program." In 2001, the NEA and 34 national organizations including Planned Parenthood, Advocates for Youth, and the ACLU, put out a joint statement declaring abstinence education "ineffective, unnecessary, and dangerous" as well as a form of "censorship" and an "affront [to the] principles of church state separation." A number of states, including California, Oregon, Missouri, and Alabama have introduced "medically accurate" laws on the books that abstinence supporters claim are backhanded attempts to sabotage their programs.

An Emotional Appeal

What is it these programs actually teach? The most common accusation against them is that they are crude, didactic efforts to get kids to "just say no." Whatever truth this generalization may have held years ago, it does not hold up to careful scrutiny today. For one thing, today's abstinence programs are extremely varied. Title V funds over 700 programs. The Abstinence Education Clearinghouse, a resource organization founded 8 years ago, has 1,300 paid affiliates and includes 74 curricula in their directory, up from 49 just 2 years ago. The early curricula funded by AFLA tended to be created with conservative middle-American communities in mind. Today, many programs—like Title V itself—are targeting lower-income kids. Some programs are aimed at preteens, some late teens, others even in their twenties. Some are community-based, others are school-based. Of those that are school-based, some are one or two sessions, others much longer. Some involve peer mentoring, some adult mentoring, some parental education. Community-based programs might use ad campaigns or cultural events or both. Some programs heavily emphasize delaying sex until marriage; others seem to be aiming to get kids to delay sex at least until they leave high school. Some programs get specific about what sexual behavior is permissible—one talks about avoiding the "underwear zone," another about going no further than holding hands and kissing—and some avoid these details altogether.

Still, today's abstinence programs share a few standard features. The first and most obvious is that they teach, as the Title V definition puts it, that "sexual activity outside the context of marriage is likely to have harmful psychological and physical effects." They aim to impress youngsters with the costs of ignoring the message, much the way drug or alcohol programs do, emphasizing the risk of pregnancy and sexually transmitted diseases. One widely used activity is a graphic slide show of the effects of STDs produced by the Medical Institute for Sexual Health in Austin, Texas. The gruesome slides of genital warts and herpes sores are reminiscent of pictures of diseased lungs shown in antismoking classes. Abstinence educators strongly emphasize—critics accuse them of actually lying about—the failure rate of condoms in protecting against pregnancy and STDs. Where comprehensive sex-ed programs promote safe sex and risk reduction—"Reducing the Risk" is the name of one well-known comprehensive program—abstinence programs are intent on risk elimination.

When critics charge abstinence education with being "fear based," they are overstating things; the newer abstinence curricula spend a relatively short amount of time on this sort of material. But there is no question that some of the warnings against sex tend toward the melodramatic. Abstinence educators are partial to stories of young people who have suffered heartbreak and misery after having sex with an unfaithful or diseased partner. In one of the more extreme examples of cautionary advice, "No Second Chance," a video sometimes shown in abstinence classes that has raised a lot of eyebrows in the media, a student asks a nurse, "What if I want to have sex before I get married?" "Well, I guess you have to be prepared to die. And you'll probably take with you your spouse and one or more of your children."

Most abstinence proponents believe premarital sex is genuinely destructive of young people's emotional and physical well-being, but some of them also cite several tactical reasons for their sensationalism. For one thing, they argue that kids should be scared. Early pregnancy does ruin lives; STDs can as well. It's not enough for kids to know how AIDS is transmitted, they argue; they need to dread the disease. For another, it makes sense to appeal to an age group partial to horror movies and gross-out reality shows—according to Health and Human Services, most programs are addressed to 9 to 14 year olds—through their emotions as well as their reason.

In fact, abstinence proponents believe that emphasizing the emotions surrounding sex sets them apart from the comprehensive sex-ed camp. They argue that comprehensive sex education gives the impression that sexual intercourse is a relatively straightforward physical transaction that simply requires the proper hygienic accessories. Abstinence proponents start with the assumption that sex elicits powerful crosscurrents of feeling that teenagers are unable to manage. Some cite new brain research showing that in adolescents the frontal lobes, the seat of judgment and self-control, are still undeveloped. They also believe that teens are not only incapable of mature, fully committed relationships but that teens have yet even to learn what such relationships are made of.

Character Counts

There is much more to these programs than an appeal to the emotions. In the later-model abstinence programs, delaying sex is treated as part of a broader effort to adopt a mindful, take-charge attitude toward life. Curricula usually incorporate goal-setting exercises; some of the more intensive also include character education. The tag line on the cover of the "Game Plan" workbook, part of a curriculum for middle schoolers sponsored by the basketball star A.C. Green from one of the oldest abstinence organizations, the Illinois-based Project Reality, says, "Everybody has one lifetime to develop your Game Plan." The booklet asks students to write down answers to questions like "What are some of your goals for the future?" "What will it take for you to reach these goals?" The workbook also tries to anticipate some of the temptations that lure kids away from their "game plan." "Describe some activities that could make it difficult for you to accomplish your goals," it asks. One section tells students to "think about how much time you spend each day on . . . TV, radio/CD's, the Internet," and asks them to analyze media messages and consider "whether those messages will help them achieve their goals."

Character education reinforces these sorts of activities. As Operation Keepsake, a Cleveland area program, puts it, the point is "to develop strong character qualities for healthy relationships to endure." Character education is also supposed to promote the autonomy that would help kids resist the unhealthy influence of a powerful peer group and glamorous media. "It's OK to stand against the crowd," Operation Keepsake urges its students. Some programs also add community-service requirements to their character component, such as reading to the elderly at nursing homes.

A Washington D.C.-based program called Best Friends, a highly regarded intervention project created by Elayne Bennett, also emphasizes character development. Bennett developed her program after working with at-risk girls and being struck by how depression and the sense of helplessness often led to sexual activity as well as drug and alcohol use. Bennett was determined to instill in drifting young women a sense of their own efficacy, or what is called in more therapeutic circles "empowerment." Best Friends' Washington D.C. program is used in schools with a large number of high-risk girls, the vast majority of them African-American. Looking at pregnancy rates of the 14 and 15 year olds in her targeted population, Bennett concluded that she had to begin her program at age 11 when "[girls'] attitudes are still forming."

What is unique about Bennett's approach is that instead of softening children's allegiance to the peer group, she tries to turn it into a force for individual improvement. "The best kind of friend is one who encourages you to be a better person," is one of the program's core messages. The girls in a selected class are designated "Best Friends" who meet at least once a month with a teacher, and once a week in a special fitness class, as well as at events like fashion shows, cultural activities, and recognition ceremonies. Once or twice a year there is a motivational speaker, a married woman with a successful career from the surrounding community who tells her life story, including how she met and married her husband, a narrative that Bennett says the girls particularly relish. The program also relies a good deal on mentoring. Each girl has a teacher-mentor from her school with whom she meets 30 to 40 minutes per week when she can complain about trouble with another teacher or talk about problems at home or with friends. Best Friends Foundation now licenses programs in 25 cities, reaching a total of 6,000 girls, and has recently started a Best Men program for boys.

Changing Hearts and Minds

The most common objection to abstinence education has always been that it turns its back on reality. Kids are going to have sex no matter what you tell them, and the best thing to do is to teach them how to be mature and responsible about it, the argument runs. What evidence do we have that it is possible to teach kids to abstain from sex?

One thing we can say with some certainty is that it is possible to change kids' attitudes on the subject. Mathematica Research, which was awarded a federal grant to examine the problem, is conducting the most rigorous study to date of abstinence education, examining 11 diverse programs each involving 400 to 700 subjects. Mathematica began following its subjects several years ago when the children's average age was 12 and one-half and will continue to do so until they are 16 or 17, so the organization will not have its final results until 2005. But its 2002 interim report confirms that teenagers are open to the abstinence message when teachers are clear about their message and appear committed to kids' well-being. "Youth tend to respond especially positively to programs where the staff are unambiguously committed to abstinence until marriage," the researchers write, "and when the program incorporates the broader goal of youth development." This change in attitude is not likely with less thorough curricula, which kids often view as "just another class."

Indeed, though it's not clear how much abstinence programs can claim credit for the decline in teen sexual activity since the early 1990s, this trend does appear to signal a growing conservatism among young people on sexual matters. In its annual survey of college freshman, the Higher Education Research Institute has shown a decline from 52 percent to 42 percent between 1987 to 2001 of the number of respondents who agree with the statement, "If two people really like each other, it's all right for them to have sex if they've known each other for a very short time." The National Campaign Against Teen Pregnancy conducted a survey in which it asked, "When it comes to teens having sex over the past several years would you say that you have become more opposed, less opposed, or remained unchanged?" Twenty-eight percent of teens said they were more opposed, as compared with 9 percent who said they were less opposed.

Surveys consistently show that somewhere around two-thirds of teenagers who have had sex say they wish they had not. In the most recent example, the National Campaign asked, "If you have had sexual intercourse, do you wish you had waited longer?" Eighty-one percent of 12 to 14 year olds and 55 percent of 15 to 17 year olds answered yes. Some of these responses are undoubtedly influenced by the bedeviling "social desirability" factor, but the very fact that kids believe they should give a positive answer suggests that the abstinence message is not out of line with social attitudes. Interestingly, there are indications that adults are more likely to be skeptical of abstinence than teens. The National Campaign asked in a 2002 survey, "Do you think it is embarrassing for teens to admit they are virgins?" Thirty-nine percent of adults said yes, while only 19 percent of teens agreed, though this finding may conflict with a Kaiser Family Foundation survey showing 59 percent of kids agreeing with the statement, "There is pressure to have sex by a certain age."

What the Data Show

Regardless, wishes are not horses, and we are still left with the question of whether abstinence education actually makes kids abstain. The answer to that question is less clear. Just about everyone agrees that the decline in teen pregnancy that began in 1991 is partly attributable to a growing number of teenagers delaying sex, though there is vigorous disagreement about just how much can be chalked up to abstinence and how much to improved condom use. At any rate, a national decline in teen sexual activity cannot prove the impact of abstinence education per se, something that has been difficult to measure.

The key problem is finding well-designed research. The few early abstinence programs that did seem to show an impact on attitudes or behavior didn't use the sort of randomized control groups that more exacting researchers tend to trust. There are many studies of kids before and after attending a program, but either there is no control group, the control group comes from a different school, the sample size is too small, there was a follow-up only three months after the invention, but nothing longer term, or some combination of all of these.

"Emerging Answers," a 2001 review of the research on sex education sponsored by the National Campaign Against Teen Pregnancy, included only those programs that had been subjected to research with a rigorous experimental or quasi-experimental design. Douglas Kirby, the report's author and a senior researcher at ETR, an education research organization that also produces comprehensive sex curricula, was able to find only three abstinence programs that satisfied the study's requirements. (By contrast, there were 19 comprehensive programs that did so, of which 5 were considered successful.) And while none of the three abstinence programs could be shown to affect either sexual initiation, pregnancy rates, or condom use, the results do not lead to generalizable conclusions about abstinence education. All three studies were of older-model programs, and as both Kirby's writings and Mathematica's research seem to confirm, straight didactic programs don't work with any message, abstinence or safe sex.

Another problem is that programs take time to test and refine. Up until two years ago there was little convincing evidence that comprehensive sex education was working. Four years before "Emerging Answers," Kirby wrote other less optimistic review of the research literature on sex education entitled "No Easy Answers," which concluded that "only a few programs have produced credible evidence that they reduced sexual risk-taking behavior," and even those results were limited to the short term.

Still, there are a few studies that provide what even the most scrupulous researchers might be willing to call "some evidence" that several abstinence programs are successful in getting kids to delay sexual initiation. One of the most intriguing, published in the Journal of Health Communication in 2001, looked at a community-based program called "Not Me, Not Now" in Monroe County, New York. In an effort to turn around high rates of teen pregnancy in and around the city of Rochester in the mid 1990s, the architects of "Not Me, Not Now" took a multifaceted approach to the problem: They spread the abstinence message through Internet sites, billboards, and community-sponsored events. Organizers also set up a youth-advisory panel, distributed 50,000 information packets for parents, and pushed abstinence curricula for middle schoolers. The results of the study show a decrease in the number of students who said they could "handle the consequences of intercourse" and a notable decline in sexual activity. Those who reported intercourse by the age of 15 dropped from 46.6 percent to 31.6 percent, and the rate of decline in teen pregnancy in Monroe surpassed that in comparison counties. But questions remain: Are students lying in their survey answers? Were there other interventions in the county that could explain the decline in teen pregnancy? These questions may yet yield firmer answers since "Not Me, Not Now" is one of the programs now being studied by Mathematica.

There are several reasons to anticipate that other abstinence programs will also have good results. The most suggestive finding in "Emerging Answers" is that service-learning programs that include time for contemplation and discussion are the most uniformly effective in getting adolescents to delay sexual initiation—even though they don't teach anything at all about sex. Kirby speculates that kids who are being supervised and mentored as they work in soup kitchens or hospitals develop close relationships with their teachers, increase their sense of competency, and gain a sense of self-respect from "the knowledge that they can make a difference in the lives of others." In general, Kirby finds that effective programs instill feelings of connectedness in kids. A number of earlier studies had shown that children who are more rooted in their peer group have earlier intercourse, while those more attached to their families and schools tend to begin having sex later. Connectedness, competency, and self-respect are precisely the goals of abstinence programs like Best Friends.

It's Not Just about Sex

But the truth is, even if evidence emerges that one particular abstinence-education program drastically reduces teen pregnancy and STDs—or conversely, of a comprehensive program that makes teenagers use condoms 100 percent of the time—sex education will remain a flashpoint in the culture wars. What a society teaches its young about sex will always be a decision founded in cultural beliefs rather than science. In the case of sex education, those beliefs are not about efficacy; they are not even only about sex. They are in part about clashing notions of adolescence. Sexuality educators emphasize teens' capacity for responsible and rational choices and their right to opportunities for self-exploration. They see their role as empowering the young to make their own decisions. Abstinence educators imagine a more impressionable and erratic adolescent. They see their role as guiding the young.

The two camps also presume different notions of identity. Comprehensive sex educators place a great deal of emphasis on gender identity and sexual orientation. Abstinence-only educators, who for the most part don't mention homosexuality, locate identity in character as reflected through qualities like respect, self-control, and perseverance. And finally, there are conflicting notions of freedom at stake. Sexuality educators see freedom as meaning individual self-expression while abstinence proponents tend to understand freedom in a more republican sense—the capacity for personal responsibility that allows individuals to become self-governing family members and citizens.

But it is likely that for most Americans outside the culture-war zone these are not absolute distinctions. One of the most striking flaws of the entire sex-ed dispute is that both sides talk about 13 year olds in the same breath as they do 18 or for that matter 23 year olds. It's unlikely that most Americans see age differences as insignificant. According to Mathematica's interim report, a good deal of Title V money is being directed toward middle schools because there is a general consensus that younger teens need a strong message that they are not ready for sex. Perhaps because they believe that as kids age they develop a firmer sense of identity and have even achieved some measure of character, Americans are not as likely to think the same about older teenagers and young adults in their twenties. Certainly, abstinence until marriage seems an improbable outcome in a society where people marry on average at the age of 26, and where acceptance of premarital cohabitation is widespread. Still, in their appeal to kids' higher aspirations and need for meaningful connections, abstinence proponents are on to something that has been missing in the lives of many children of baby boomers. "My father wasn't a very responsible man. I want to be a better father when the time is right," the 18 year old son of divorced parents told the Indianapolis Star about his decision to remain abstinent. Comprehensive sexual education promises pleasure, but abstinence education pushes honor—and a surprising number of kids seem interested in buying.

KAY S. HYMOWITZ is a contributing editor to *City Journal* and author of *Liberation's Children* (Ivan r. Dee, 2003).

Reprinted with permission From *The Public Interest,* Fall 2003, pp. 3–19.

UNIT 8

Problem Behaviors and Intervention

Unit Selections

Key Points to Consider

- What are the short-term and long-term effects on the victims of school bullying?

- What prevention methods for domestic violence work?

- What prevention strategies are helpful for at risk students who are self-injurious?

Student Web Site
www.mhcls.com/online

Internet References
Further information regarding these Web sites may be found in this book's preface or online.

National Youth Violence Prevention Resource Center
http://www.safeyouth.org

Choices in Sport
http://www.drugfreesport.com/choices

Focus Adolescent Services: Alcohol and Teen Drinking
http://www.focusas.com/Alcohol.html

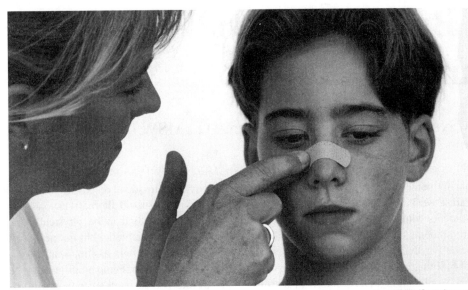

Russell Illig/Getty Images

That adolescents can and do engage in high-risk behaviors is not subject to much debate. The statistics on adolescent fatalities demonstrate their risk-taking behavior. The leading causes of death in adolescents are tragic: accidents, suicide, and homicide. Alcohol use is frequently involved, particularly in motor vehicle accidents. About half of the fatal motor vehicle accidents involving an adolescent also involve a drunken peer driver.

Why adolescents engage in high-risk behaviors is much debated. Some researchers believe that adolescent risk-taking is related to cognitive development. They propose that adolescents possess a sense of invulnerability. Adolescents believe they are special and unique; things that could happen to others could not possibly happen to them. Other researchers believe at best this may apply only to young adolescents. By their mid-teens, a majority of adolescents are too sophisticated to consider themselves invulnerable. Despite this, however, adolescents still take more risks than do adults.

If older adolescents do not perceive themselves as invulnerable, than why do they take risks? There are several possible explanations. One proposal is that adolescents may not perceive the risk. For example, adults may have a better sense of how fast they can safely drive given differing road conditions. Adolescents, simply because they are inexperienced drivers, may not recognize when road conditions are dangerous and so may not adjust their speed. Adolescents may engage in riskier behaviors than adults simply because they have the time and energy. Many adolescents have free time, money, and a car. Access to these may allow adolescents to put themselves in dangerous situations. Adults may work, do more household chores, and take care of their children. These adults may not have time to drink, take drugs, or joy ride.

Adolescents may also be less adept than adults at extricating themselves from high-risk behavior. For example, adults who attend a party where drugs are consumed may be more comfortable declining offered drugs than adolescents, or they may be able to leave the party without depending on transportation from others. Some researchers indicate that society may be somewhat to blame for adolescents' risk-taking. If impoverished adolescents have no chance of obtaining meaningful work, have limited access to recreational activities, and have little encouragement to go to school, then participation in drug-related or violent behavior may be the only options open to them. It may be up to society to provide these adolescents with an increased number of safe choices.

Adolescent risk-taking activities can take many forms. The U.S. Public Health Service identifies several categories of behavior related to health risks for adolescents. Included are behaviors that may cause injuries, such as suicide and violence, use of tobacco or illicit drugs (including alcohol), and risky behaviors related to sexuality or eating disorders. All these can clearly threaten adolescents. Moreover, alcohol use seems to exacerbate many of the other risks, as indicated by the statistics on alcohol use and violent death. And drug use can be related to accidents, health problems, and violence. Violent behaviors are an increasing concern to society. Murder is the second leading cause of death in adolescence; it is the leading cause of death for African American male teenagers. Suicide rates in young people have tripled since the 1950s. Eating disorders are another threat to adolescents. Millions of adolescents suffer from anorexia nervosa or bulimia in the United States.

In this unit, the first two articles focuses on school bullying and the long-term effects on the victims. The next selection examines domestic violence and emerging prevention efforts. The last article examines how schools provide intervention for teens who suffer from trauma and grief, and those who are involved in self-injury.

School Bullying: Who, Why, and What to Do

GORDON A. MACNEIL, PHD, AND JASON M. NEWELL, MSW

Bullying is typically perpetrated by stronger individuals or groups against weaker, isolated individuals; often while other students witness the interaction. It festers in environments where students do not raise the alarm about their plight, but is drastically reduced in schools where the ethos is for zero tolerance of bullying behaviors. No single intervention is effective, but a combination of prevention programs and swift, assertive responses to incidents of victimization can reduce incidents of bullying drastically.

Characteristics of Bullying, Bullies, and Victims

Bullying is commonly defined as an aggressive behavior (words, actions, or social exclusion) which intentionally hurts or harms another person; the behavior occurs repetitiously and creates a power imbalance such that it is difficult for the victim to defend him or herself. The necessary condition of the behavior(s) being repeated is particularly troublesome, as it reinforces the vulnerability of the victim. The passivity of bystanders often serves to enflame the bully's actions and increase the isolation and humiliation of the victim. Bullying may be perpetrated by one person or by a group. Bullying differs from normative peer-group altercations because it is based on an unfair match; the bully is either physically, verbally, and/or socially stronger than the victim. School bullying adds the dimension of the bullying behaviors either taking place on the school grounds or while the participants are enroute to or from school, or being initiated due to school-related relationships.

Characteristics of Bullies. Bullies tend to have poor self-concepts and feel relatively unloved or unnoticed by significant people in their lives. Verbal, physical, and emotional abuse is common in the families of aggressive youth. Bullies at school are frequently victims at home. Familial characteristics of bullying include inadequate parental supervision, family violence, hostile discipline techniques, and modeling of adversarial problem solving skills. Aggression is often passed from parent to child, through multiple generations. A common denominator among bullies appears to be their inclination to see hostile intent in the actions of others. Additionally, they tend to be less likely to recognize pro-social responses to problematic situations than others, so they see no alternatives to aggression.

Male bullies tend to be physically mature and dominant. They are usually athletic, but not necessarily involved in organized athletics. Others assume that the bully could be an athlete if he wanted to. Female bullies may be strong, but they are just as likely to be small since their bullying is commonly done verbally and focuses on social dominance rather than physical dominance. Although female bullying characteristics are less physical in nature, acts such as malicious gossiping and social exclusion are equally as harmful to victims' self-worth and self-concept.

Bullying creates a power imbalance such that it is difficult for the victim to defend him or herself.

Characteristics of Victims. Victims tend to be physically weak, either overweight or underweight. They tend to have difficulty relating to peers in general (not just bullies), and to have poor or ineffective social skills. They are frequently less popular than others, and therefore somewhat isolated from others. Victims tend to have rather poor coordination. They are typically younger, smaller, and weaker with lower energy levels and lower pain tolerances than other students. Finally, victims are often younger than their bullies (Besag, 1989; Jenson & Howard, 1999; Olweus, 1978).

Being victimized has painful social, emotional, and academic consequences. Victims of name-calling may experience embarrassment, rejection, and anxiety. Some victims retaliate with names of their own, and some withdraw. Some develop a tough facade, others may react with tears. As most victimization by bullies occurs at school, victims may develop anxiety about attending school all together, which may result in difficulty concentrating on schoolwork, the development of anxiety-related psychosomatic physical and emotional ailments, chronic absenteeism, and an overall decline in school performance (Lumsden, 2002).

Where Bullying Occurs. Bullying happens in all areas of a school. Bullying in classrooms is generally subtle due to the presence of the teacher, but it occurs there nevertheless. Most bullying takes place in areas of the school where supervision is limited such as in the lunchroom, on the playground, in hallways, and in restrooms. Additionally, bullying takes place off-campus while students are traveling to or from their homes.

Prevention Programs

Individuals who are sufficiently engaged and challenged in school have little need to victimize others. Of course this goal cannot be met by all students all of the time, but it does suggest that paying attention to the emotional needs of all students could lessen the likelihood of aggressive misbehavior (Rigby, 1996).

An additional prevention strategy suggests that in order for a transgression to occur several elements are necessary. There must be a law or school policy, a perpetrator, a targeted victim, and a suitable place for the act to occur. Without a location in which all of these intersect, bullying cannot occur. Therefore, reducing the number of viable places for bullying can serve as a prevention strategy. Specifically, schools can make accessing the target too difficult or time-consuming, and increase the likelihood of detection by reducing the amount of hiding places, reducing viable escape routes, and increasing supervision. Although it is difficult to alter the architecture of a school's physical layout, it is possible to minimize the potential for bullying by increasing the supervision of others and setting precedents for reacting to incidents in assertive and professional ways, including developing a school-based policy to address bullying behavior, creating classroom climates that enforce school policy, and developing support systems for victims.

Planning and developing anti-bullying policies with as many stakeholders as possible is a common element of successful anti-bullying models. Stakeholders should develop an anti-bullying philosophy, which may be translated into a policy to which all constituents agree. In turn, the policy should provide clear definitions of behavioral expectations that identify or define the culture of the school. Policy should also be implemented to address misbehavior or violation of the school bullying policy. This creates a system of accountability for those students who bully as well as those who do not react appropriately when they witness bullying.

Once a policy has been established, it must be clearly communicated to the students and parents. The old truism that actions speak louder than words holds in this situation; students (bullies, victims, and bystanders) will know how cohesive the school personnel are in enforcing anti-bullying policies by their actions (Hoover & Oliver, 1996).

A positive environment is created through the actions of the adults in creating a safe school. Assertiveness from adults in positions of authority to reports of victimization encourages future reports from students. If students feel unsupported or betrayed by these adults they will be unwilling to report further incidents of bullying. If adult responses do not solve the problem, they encourage further victimization by the bully(s).

In essence, the victim is violated twice; once by a bully and once by the system that is supposed to protect them (Elliott & Tolan, 1999; Rigby, 1996).

Additional prevention measures include the teaching of problem-solving or conflict-resolution skills, and the presentation of bullying-awareness programs and assertiveness-training programs. All of these can lessen the impact of incidents of bullying, but the most important aspect of prevention programs is that they be on-going rather than short-term (Hoover & Oliver, 1996). Only if the programs are infused into the curriculum can their effectiveness be sustained.

Interventions

Our culture often seeks to reduce social problems to simplistic levels and then apply simplistic interventions to them, but simplistic solutions typically prove unsuccessful or inadequate. There is no simple or single approach to maintaining a safe school. Efforts ranging from additional security officers, metal detectors and video cameras to threat-assessment consultants and software programs to track crime are available to address school violence problems. However, these approaches overlook the complexity of school violence problems and the multidimensional factors that create them. Those who desire successful prevention and intervention outcomes are likely to be disappointed by these tools if they are not augmented by efforts to build a positive atmosphere within the school. For instance, weapons are tools by which violence is inflicted, but their absence does not eliminate the threat of violence.

As bullying is by definition a repetitive behavior, the pattern should be addressed rather than a specific incident.

An important element of successful interventions is the elimination of "bystanding"—those who stand by and observe bullying behaviors without attempting to stop it. In schools where bullying is not tolerated, students who stand by as another is harmed are seen as facilitating the problem and are admonished for their inaction (Rigby, 1996). It is crucial that bystanding by teachers not be permitted. By ignoring name-calling, shoving, fighting, harassment, and psychological terrorism, teachers communicate that these behaviors are tolerated by society, thereby contributing to the victimization of bullied students.

Discipline and therapy are related to one another, but they are separate issues and should not be performed by the same people. Three basic tasks are necessary in an intervention program; recognition of the problem, enforcement of school or class policies, and counseling. Everyone in the school should perform the recognition task. Minor transgressions can be handled by teachers, but most problems are best resolved when the different tasks are performed by separate people. This procedure precludes the role confusion and distrust that can result when a single person is charged with multiple tasks. Fortunately, teachers, administrators, and counselors can be trained to perform specific tasks in this process.

Treating the Bully. Many people's first inclination when dealing with bullies is to give them a taste of their own medicine. This response is sure to lead to resentments and reprisals—exactly the opposite of the desired response. Thus, while punitive measures must be introduced to the extent necessary to maintain the safety of others, the greater need is to help the perpetrator understand why their behavior is unacceptable and help the individual develop alternative behaviors. As bullying is by definition a repetitive behavior, the *pattern* should be addressed rather than a specific incident. Responding to bullying in a non-punitive way is contingent on the spirit of the school and cooperation of parents of the participants. One should attempt to avoid humiliating the perpetrator, as this will likely lead to emotion-driven responses rather than thoughtful ones. It is often useful to minimize public scrutiny and defensiveness by addressing the problem one-on-one with an appropriate adult in a setting other than the classroom.

Bullies often come from homes where there is little nurturing and affection, and where they may be subjected to harsh physical discipline regardless of their age. Thus, although much of the bully's behavior may be related to their home life, tact and care must be taken when informing the bully's parents about their child's behavior. Attempts to address parent-child interactions should be based on the child's in-school behaviors, and should be offered under the auspices of the school social worker.

Goldstein suggests that many therapeutic failures result from a poor match between the model of intervention and the client (in this case, the bully). He contends that most youth from middle class backgrounds are taught to be introspective about their misbehaviors (Goldstein, 1999). For instance, the parent might respond to hair-pulling misbehavior by asking "Why did you do that? How do you think that makes Betty feel? You're old enough to not need to do that." Youth from low-income homes are more likely to be reared with a model that values authority more than self-control. Thus, in response to the hair-pulling behavior, the parent slaps child and tells him to stop the misbehavior. Children raised with the latter model of parenting are more likely to benefit from prescriptive models of intervention that focus on training youth to be competent in interpersonal interactions.

Treating the Victim. Following the basic tenets of crisis intervention to ensure the safety of the victim should be the first step of intervention with the victim (Roberts & Coursol, 1996). In addition to determining the physical injury of the victim, notification (perhaps mandatory) of authorities may be warranted. If this is the case, the limits of confidentiality should be explained to the victim.

Victims of bullying need two kinds of support: psychological support that allows the student to have his or her perceptions of the incident(s) and emotions related to the event heard, and a measure of psychological support that facilitates skill development so that the individual can better respond to bullying

behaviors he or she may encounter in the future (Rigby, 1996). In order to respond to bullying incidents, potential victims need to know how to make realistic appraisals of situations in which they may be hurt, they need to know how to respond in an assertive (but not aggressive) manner, they need to know how to enlist the help of others, and they need to know how to leave a dangerous situation.

Two interventions for victims of school bullying do not appear to be successful when used alone. Don't ask the victim to solve the problem by being assertive, ignoring the bully, or pretending to not be affected by the bully, because this approach places the responsibility for stopping the misbehavior on the victim. It teaches the victim that he or she needs to resolve problems without the assistance of authorities. Given that most victims are younger and weaker than the bully, this is not a reasonable demand. The second misguided intervention is whole-population education, where sensitivity training or alternatives to aggression are taught to build empathy. While the training may raise the empathy level of the general student body, the message is frequently missed by bullies who become bored or deny their own behavior due to the lack of self-awareness (Olweus, Limber, & Mihalic, 1999). Both of these interventions could produce positive outcomes for both bullies and victims, but only when they are components of more comprehensive intervention packages.

Conclusion

School bullying is a significant problem in American schools. It encompasses both physical and psychological intimidation and may have both short and long-term effects on the victim. Both the perpetrator and victim may be social outcasts, and both deserve help from adults in order to end the bullying behaviors. Schools that institute strong, sustained prevention programs coupled with interventions that are faithfully applied to those who transgress have had good success reducing bullying problems. Schools that have taken a less comprehensive approach (often focusing only on the punitive aspects of intervention) have had considerably less success. Creating a school ethos of safety and active participation by all school citizens in order to eliminate bullying appears to produce the greatest impact on all members of the school environment.

Selected References

Besag, V. (1989). *Bullies and Victims in Schools: A Guide to Understanding and Management.* London: Oxford University Press.

Elliott, D.S., & Tolan, P.H. (1999). Youth violence prevention, intervention, and social policy. In D.J. Flannery & C.R. Huff (Eds.) *Youth Violence: Prevention, Intervention, and Social Policy.* Washington, DC: American Psychiatric Press.

Goldstein, A.P. (1999). Teaching prosocial behavior to antisocial youth. In D.J. Flannery, & C.R. Huff (Eds.) *Youth Violence: Prevention, Intervention, and Social Policy* (pp. 253–274). Washington, DC: American Psychiatric Press.

Hoover, J., & Oliver, R. (1996). *The Bullying Prevention Handbook: A Guide for Principals, Teachers, and Counselors.* Bloomington, IN: National Education Service.

Jenson, J.M., & Howard, M. O. (1999). Prevalence and patterns of youth violence. In J.M. Jenson & M.O. Howard (Eds.) *Youth Violence: Current Research and Recent Practice Innovations* (pp. 3–18). Washington, DC: NASW Press.

Lumsden, L. (2002). *Preventing Bullying.* Office of Educational Research and Improvement (ED). Washington, DC.

Olweus, D. (1978). *Aggression in the Schools: Bullies and Whipping Boys.* New York: Wiley.

Olweus, D., Limber, S. & Mihalic, S.F. (1999). *Blueprints for Violence Prevention, Book Nine: Bullying Prevention Program.* Boulder, CO: Center for the Study and Prevention of Violence.

Rigby, K. (1996). *Bullying in Schools: and What to Do About It.* Melbourne, Victoria, Australia: ACER.

Roberts, W.B., & Coursol, D.H. (1996). Strategies for intervention with childhood and adolescent victims of bullying, teasing, and intimidation in school settings. *Elementary School Guidance & Counseling, 30,* 204–212.

Gordon MacNeil is an associate professor at The University of Alabama School of Social Work. His PhD is from Arizona State University, and his MSW is from the University of Iowa. **Jason Newell** is a doctoral student at The University of Alabama School of Social Work. He also holds a Master of Social Work degree from this institution.

This article is adapted from G. MacNeil (2002). School bullying: An overview. In L.A. Rapp-Paglicci, A.R Roberts, and J.S. Wodarski (Eds.), *Handbook of Violence* (pp. 247–262). New York: John Wiley & Sons, Inc. Copyright © 2002, John Wiley & Sons. This material is used by permission of John Wiley & Sons, Inc.

Bullying at School among Older Adolescents

SANDRA HARRIS, PhD

The Justice Department's Bureau of Justice Statistics and the Department of Education's National Center for Education Statistics (2001) reported that overall juvenile crime rates have dropped since 1992 from 48 crimes per 1,000 students ages 12 through 18 to 33 per 1,000 students. At the same time, data indicated that students who said they were victims of any crime of violence or theft at school decreased from 10% to 8%. However, before the 2003–04 school year had even completed the first quarter, there had been school shootings in and around Chicago and Minnesota, gang feuds in Arizona, stabbings in Texas and Florida, apparent murder-suicides in California and Kentucky; and armed students in standoffs in Washington and California (Toppo, 2003).

Many argue that school violence is a product of a sense of escalating alienation and rage that seems to exist in many of today's young people. The fuel for this violence is often considered to be school bullying. In fact, a 2002 report by the Families and Work Institute interviewed 2,000 students and found that small things, such as teasing, often trigger serious episodes of violence. On school campuses, studies have found anywhere from 20% to 30% of students are frequently involved in bullying incidents either as the victim or the bully (Juvonen, Graham, & Schuster, 2003). Consequently, high school students report that bullying has seriously affected their physical, social, and academic well-being.

Bullying is intentionally harmful, aggressive behavior of a more powerful person or group of people directed repeatedly toward a less powerful person, usually without provocation. The most common form of bullying among adolescents is verbal—name calling and hurtful teasing. Bullying also includes threatening gestures, hitting, stealing, spreading rumors, intentionally excluding others, and using weapons to threaten or harm. Sexual harassment is another harmful form of bullying that increases in adolescence. In fact, Stein (1995) has noted that even as early as kindergarten there appears to be bullying conduct with sexual overtones.

High school bullies tend to pick on students who don't fit in. Boys tend to select victims who are physically weak, who are short tempered, based on who their friends are, or by their clothing. Girls, on the other hand, choose victims based on looks, emotionalism, being overweight, or who get good grades.

Being a victim of school bullying causes students to feel less connected with the high school, which often leads to poor physical health, lowered participation in extra-curricular events, violence, substance use, and suicide (Resnick et al., 1997). The ability to form natural relationships is often impaired and this rejection by peers often leads to emotional disturbances in adulthood (Ross, 1996). In high school, victims of bullying are more anxious than their high school peers, are likely to be targeted for racism or actions that cross traditionally accepted gender behaviors (such as sexual orientation), and have poorer relationships with classmates and feel lonelier than bullies, especially boys (Nansel et al., 2001).

High school students are more likely to bully with ridicule, rejection, and other forms of emotional abuse, rather than using physical bullying.

While bullies demonstrate some of the same characteristics as their victims, they are more likely to be depressed than their victims; hold higher social status than victims; use alcohol and smoke; have poorer academic achievement and perceive a poorer school climate. They are more likely to manifest defiant behavior (Nansel et al., 2001) and are more likely to have racist attitudes (Ross, 1996). The students that seem to be the most seriously affected by bullying are the bully/victims. Bully/victims are more likely to smoke, drink and have poorer academic achievement than victims; and have poorer relationships with classmates and are lonelier than bullies (Nansel et al., 2001). They also need to retaliate following acts of aggression against them (Glover et al., 2000).

Table 1 What Kind of Bullying Do Students Observe at School?

	Never	Sometimes	Often
Being Called Names	485 (26%)	880 (47%)	503 (27%)
Being Left out of Activities	607 (33%)	792 (43%)	441 (24%)
Teasing	697 (37%)	846 (45%)	320 (17%)
Hit/Kicked	999 (53%)	665 (35%)	211 (11%)
Threatened	1,082 (58%)	619 (33%)	178 (9%)

Note. n = 1,893
Because stealing and sexual harassment were not included in earlier surveys, those categories are not reported here.

Study Design

It has only been within the last few years that bully studies have been done in the United States and many of these studies have concentrated on children and young adolescents. Since 2000, my colleagues and I have conducted several studies on bullying. For this article, I used data from students in grades 8–12 to gain an understanding of bullying among older adolescents.

Participants in the study included 1,893 students in grades 8–12. Ethnic breakdown of participating students was 11% African American, 22% Hispanic, and 77% Anglo. Fifty-one percent were boys and 49% girls. Twenty-two percent of the participants were in the 8th grade, 53% were in the 9th grade, 14% were in the 10th grade, 8% were in the 11th grade, and 3% were in the 12th grade.

A diverse group of schools were represented. They were located in rural and suburban areas in Texas, Georgia, and Nebraska, and sizes varied from a small school of 250 students to a large high school of 1,500 students. Schools were selected based on convenience to the researchers and willingness of administrators to permit the studies. None of the school leaders thought that they had a problem with bullying.

The survey sought to gather data regarding the types of bullying that occurred, where bullying took place, how safe students felt at school, how bullying made them feel, who they told when they were bullied, and how interested they felt their teachers and administrators were in stopping bullying. Surveys were administered in English classes or in physical education classes by the regular classroom teacher from 1999–2004. Since the survey was revised several times during this time frame, only selected questions on each survey were used. The survey has a reliability alpha of .69, which is appropriate.

Findings

What kind of bullying do students observe at school? As can be seen from Table 1, the most common form of bullying at school was being called names, followed by being left out of activities and teasing. Other studies have reported similar findings, noting

Table 2 Where Do Students Observe Bullying at School?

	Never	Sometimes	Often
Classroom	315 (17%)	1,162 (62%)	398 (21%)
Lunchroom	473 (25%)	1,051 (56%)	348 (19%)
At Break	556 (32%)	879 (50%)	319 (18%)
Extracurricular Events	676 (36%)	977 (52%)	215 (12%)
Initiations of Clubs/Athletics	924 (50%)	786 (42%)	147 (8%)
On the Way Home from School	1,137 (61%)	602 (32%)	123 (7%)
On the Way to School	1,279 (70%)	465 (25%)	83 (5%)

Note. n = 1,893
Because students frequently wrote in "restrooms" and "hallways" these locations were added to later surveys, but those categories are not reported here.

that high school students are more likely to bully with ridicule, rejection, and other forms of emotional abuse, rather than using physical bullying (Juvonen etal., 2003).

Where do students observe bullying at school? When students were asked how often they observed bullying in certain school locations, surprisingly, 83% identified the classroom as a place where bullying occurred at least sometimes. Seventy-four percent of the students reported that the lunchroom was a place where bullying occurred at least sometimes. (See Table 2).

Student Experiences Being Bullied. While 60% of students indicated that they were never bullied at school, an alarming 16% reported that they were bullied at least once a week, while 24% reported being bullied less than once a week. When students were asked how it made them feel when they were bullied at school, 15% admitted that it made them feel angry, and 16% said they felt sad and miserable. Thirty-four percent of students indicted that it did not bother them when they were bullied.

We asked students who they would tell if they were bullied or if they became aware of someone being bullied. Forty-six percent said they would tell a friend, 27% would tell their mother, and 14% would tell their father. However, only 13% of students would tell a teacher or an administrator.

Only half of the students responded to the next question which asked if students had told someone about being bullied and, if so, what happened. Nearly 37% reported that when they told, things got better. However, 17% said they never told anyone that they had been bullied, 37% reported that nothing changed even though they told, and 9% admitted that when they told the bullying only became worse.

A critical element in reducing bullying is the leadership of adults.

How safe do students feel at school? Despite the high reported occurrences of bullying, 39% of students reported that they always felt safe at school, and 45% indicated that they usually felt safe. However, 16% of students admitted that they did not feel very safe when they were at school. Consequently, 9% of students reported that they had even stayed home from school at least once because of bullying and 14% said they had considered staying home.

How interested is the faculty? When asked if administrators were interested in stopping bullying at school, 24% of students did not think that they were; while 34% admitted that they were not sure how administrators felt about this. Only 42% of students believed that administrators were interested in stopping bullying. Students felt nearly the same way about their teachers, with 22% admitting that they did not think teachers were interested in stopping bullying and 33% were not sure how their teachers felt. Only 45% felt that teachers were interested in stopping bullying.

The Dismal Conclusions

This study looked at 1,893 self-reports of older adolescents about bullying and findings suggested the following conclusions:

- Three out of four students are aware of name-calling, students being left out of activities, and teasing at least sometimes at school
- Bullying happens at many places on the campus, even locations where there is teacher supervision, such as the classroom

Bullying at School among Older Adolescents

- Nearly one-third of students admit that being bullied causes them to feel sad and miserable, or angry
- A small percentage of students tell school faculty about being bullied; and when they do tell, for more than one-third, nothing changes, and for a small but significant number of students, things get worse
- Over one-half of students are not convinced that administrators or teachers are interested in stopping bullying

What Can We Do about Bullying at School?

A critical element in reducing bullying is the leadership of adults. Lazarus (1996) identified the importance of adults in helping young people cope with stressful situations. Likewise in the early 1970s, Daniel Olweus led Sweden and Norway to implement an anti-bullying campaign characterized by adult involvement as a critical component. Two years later, incidents of bullying had been reduced by 50% (Olweus, 1993). Yet, too often, teachers cannot identify bullies or victims at school (Leff, Kupersmidt, Patterson & Power, 1999). Due in part to a lack of trust in adults, students very rarely break the "code of silence" to "rat" on bullies. Furthermore, studies indicate

that adults are not viewed by students as being committed to reducing bullying at school (Rigby, 1996). In fact, teachers are not even sure if other teachers are committed to reducing bullying, nor, they admit, do they know how to help when they do become aware of bullying (Harris & Willoughby, 2003).

Building on the importance of adult involvement, the following model for reducing bullying at school is recommended (Harris & Willoughby, 2003)

- **Be Aware.** Adults must first recognize bullying as harmful and a precursor to more severe forms of school violence.
  Strategies: Participate in training to recognize bullies and victims; survey students, teachers, and parents regularly to identify kinds of bullying and locations on campus that are high risk; increase supervision; and develop school policies that define bullying.
- **Build Trusting Relationships.** Adults must develop a culture of trust and respect on the campus.
  Strategies: Talk with students in class discussions about bullying; encourage students to share how bullying makes them feel; be responsive to bullies' needs, as well as victims' needs; and show students that adults care about student achievement and about personal achievements.
- **Accept the Challenge to Provide Support.** Adults must be willing to accept the challenge to provide support for all students.
  Strategies: Accept the responsibility to advocate for students in need; present a united front that establishes behavior guidelines that emphasize bullying is not acceptable behavior; encourage students to tell when bullying occurs; involve parents; and be encouraged to support one another in preventing and intervening in bully situations.
- **Know How to Help.** Adults must have the skills to be able to respond appropriately to bullying situations.
  Strategies: Work collaboratively with school and community personnel to adopt school policies with anti-bully guidelines; create policies that address appropriate consequences that include counseling for the bully, as well as the victim; participate in training that provides strategies for supporting students.

Conclusion

Bullying breeds violence. It teases, torments, and taunts. While many young people ignore bullying or overcome it, some succumb to the pain it inflicts. Most suffer in silence, but a few turn to horrible acts of school violence, such as 15 year old Charles "Andy" Williams. He brought a revolver to school, fired 30 bullets, and killed two schoolmates and wounded 13 others. His father later said, "[they] accused him of being gay . . . they made fun of him for being a country boy, for his big ears. It didn't matter what he did, they made fun of him" (Booth & Snyder, 2001, A1, A6). When adults are aware, when they build trusting relationships, when they accept the challenge to provide support, and when they have the skills to know how to help hurting students, schools will be safer for everyone.

References

Booth, W., & Snyder, D. (2001). No remorse, no motive from shooting suspect. *San Antonio Express-News,* March 7, A1, A6.

Bureau of Justice Statistics and DOE National Center for Education Statistics. (2001). *Indicators of School Crime and Safety.* Washington, D.C.: Author.

Glover, D., Gough, G., Johnson, M., & Cartwight, N. (2000). Bullying in 25 secondary schools: Incidence, impact and intervention. *Educational Research, 42,* 141–156.

Harris, S., & Petrie, G. (2002). *Bullying: The Bullies, the Victims, the Bystanders.* Lanham, MD.: The Scarecrow Press, Inc.

Harris, S., & Willoughby, W. (2003). Teacher perceptions of student bullying behaviors. *ERS Spectrum, 21*(3), 11–18.

Juvonen, J., Graham, S., & Schuster, M. (2003). Bullying among young adolescents: The strong, the weak, and the troubled. *Pediatrics, 112*(6), 1,231–1,237.

Lazarus, R. (1966). *Psychological Stress and the Coping Process.* New York: McGraw-Hill.

Leff, S., Kupersmidt, J., Patterson, C., & Power, T. (1991). Factors influencing teacher identification of peer bullies and victims. *The School Psychology Review, 28*(3), 505–517.

Nansel, T., Overpeck, M., Pilla, R., Ruan, W., Simons-Morton, B., & Scheidt, P. (2001). Bullying behaviors among U.S. youth: Prevalence and association with psychosocial adjustment. *Journal of American Medical Association, 285*(16), 2,094–2,100.

Olweus, D. (1993). *Bullying at School.* Cambridge, MA: Blackwell Publishers, Inc.

Resnick, M., Bearman, P., Blum, R., Bauman, K., Harris, K., Jones, J. et al. (1997). Protecting adolescents from harm: Findings from the National Longitudinal Study on Adolescent Health. *Journal of the American Medical Association, 278,* 823–832.

Rigby, K. (1996). *Bullying in Schools: And What To Do About It.* London: Jessica Kingsley Publishers.

Ross, D. (1996). *Childhood Bullying and Teasing: What School Personnel, Other Professionals, and Parents Can Do.* Alexandria, VA.: American Counseling Association.

Stein, N. (1995). Sexual harassment in school: The public performance of gender violence. *Harvard Educational Review, 65,* 145–162.

Toppo, G. (2003, October 21). Troubling days at U.S. schools. *USA Today,* 1A, 2A

SANDRA HARRIS received her PhD, in Educational Leadership from the University of Texas, Austin. She has more than 30 years of experience as a teacher and administrator and is currently an associate professor of educational leadership at Lamar University in Beaumont, Texas. She is the co-author of the book: *Bullying: The Bullies, the Victims, the Bystanders* (Scarecrow Press, 2003).

From *The Prevention Researcher,* Vol. 11, No. 3, September 2004, pp. 12–14. Copyright © 2004 by Integrated Research Services, Inc. Reprinted by permission. www.tpronline.org

Prevention of Domestic Violence during Adolescence

DAVID A. WOLFE, PHD, AND PETER G. JAFFE, PHD

Some days it seems that little progress has been made in addressing the fundamental causes and consequences of domestic violence and its effects on children. The problem seems as serious as ever, and the major underlying causes, such as abuse of power, inequality, and modeling of violence in the home, have remained largely unchanged over the past three decades. The government response has been to manage adult domestic violence, which involves providing services on an individual basis only when absolutely necessary. Crisis management is a necessary part of the response to adult domestic violence, but more proactive strategies of prevention are also strongly needed.

The news is not all bad; in fact, encouraging progress has been made in less than two decades. Scientific, professional, and activist groups have played a prominent role in recognizing the links between domestic violence and child adjustment problems, among other issues. A growing interest by researchers and clinicians in the field of domestic violence has made it possible to establish a scientific foundation for implementing prevention and treatment initiatives and public policy to end domestic violence. The field is in the process of finding alternatives to violence that can be activated in each community in a manner that stimulates interest, informs choices, and promotes action to decrease violence and abuse in the lives of children, youth, and families.

In this article, key issues in the prevention of domestic violence are reviewed. Included are discussions of the goals of prevention programs and theories of the causality of domestic violence and abuse. Next, prevention efforts designed to address the needs of children and adults are viewed through a developmental, or life-span, lens. Critical issues for prevention programs are described for adolescents. Finally, research and policy implications are explored for violence prevention endeavors in a number of settings, from homes, schools, and neighborhoods to courts and the culture at large.

Emerging Goals of Prevention Efforts

Emerging changes in public policy, legislation, and service delivery illustrate a commitment to finding ways to reduce the prevalence and harmful effects of adult domestic violence. Still, strategies that address the issue at a broader level need to be developed and evaluated. Such strategies must take into account the many factors that influence the likelihood of adult domestic violence and those that promote nonviolence. There are established precedents for such an approach, such as public health campaigns to eliminate health risks among adolescents and health promotion campaigns to encourage healthy (low-risk) behaviors among segments of the population (Hamilton & Bhatti, 1996; Sherman et al., 1998). These approaches, adopted primarily for known health issues, hold considerable promise for behavioral issues as well because they recognize that change occurs through finding positive ways to communicate messages about healthy families and relationships.

One way to envision the goal of prevention is to promote attitudes and behaviors that are incompatible with violence and abuse, and that encourage the formation of healthy, nonviolent relationships. The implications of this paradigm are significant and far reaching if attention and resources are primarily focused on the occurrence of undesirable behavior, such as identified acts of violence, prevention efforts are usually directed toward identification, control, and punishment. However, if the goal of prevention is the promotion of healthy, nonviolent relationships, attention and resources are more likely to be directed toward establishing and building trust, respecting others' thoughts and expressions, and encouraging and supporting growth in relationships. This perspective implies a different list of intervention and educational possibilities, such as school-based curricula, neighborhood-based health and social services, and family-based child and health care.

Theories of Causality

The prevention of domestic violence at first glance seems impeded by a lack of theoretical consensus as to its fundamental causes. However, the foundation of prevention programs might include several important principles:

- Domestic violence has been ignored as a major health, criminal, and social problem until recently and remains poorly understood among the general population.
- Domestic violence is a complex problem that cannot be understood by a single variable. Explanations require a multifaceted approach that recognizes individual behavior within a familial and cultural context (Dutton, 1995).
- The significance of childhood trauma, including witnessing adult domestic violence, is common to all theories even though there is disagreement as to the processes involved. In general, these processes include learning maladaptive behaviors through modeling and reinforcement by people in the child's family, neighborhood, and cultural environment (Emery & Laumann-Billings, 1998). In turn, prevention efforts may include efforts to prevent children from ever experiencing such trauma as well as community readiness to respond as soon as possible to children in violent homes.
- As long as domestic violence is seen as acceptable behavior or tolerated by silence through public attitudes, institutions, and the media, there is little chance of changing individual behavior. In other words, the prevention of domestic violence is everyone's business and is each human services provider's responsibility.

Although far from realized, domestic violence prevention efforts have begun to organize around the principle of building on strengths and developing protective factors in an effort to deter violence and abuse. Learning to relate to others, especially intimates, in a respectful, nonviolent manner is a crucial foundation for building effective prevention strategies for related forms of violence and abuse between partners.

Prevention Efforts

Because violence in intimate relationships is deeply rooted in early family experiences and in broader cultural and social influences, deciding where to focus prevention efforts for greatest impact is a critical starting point. In principle, prevention efforts should involve every aspect of social ecology. Societal, community, and neighborhood forces; schools and peer groups; family processes; and individual strengths and weaknesses have all been linked to adult domestic violence. Therefore, all of these influences play a role in the prevention of violence and care should be taken to ensure that the interventions are appropriate and beneficial. The following discussion will focus exclusively on interventions aimed at adolescents (for discussion of the other age groups, see Wolfe & Jaffe, 2001).

Adolescence is a time of important cognitive and social development, during which teenagers learn to think more rationally and become capable of thinking hypothetically. At the same time, they must develop and use effective decision-making skills involving complex interpersonal relationships, including an awareness of possible risks and considerations of future consequences and balancing their own interests with those of their peers, family members, and dating partners. Conformity to parental opinions gradually decreases, and the tendency to be swayed by peers increases until late adolescence. By mid-adolescence, romantic partners increase in their importance as social support providers (Furman & Buhrmester, 1992). Thus, early to mid-adolescence offers a unique opportunity for learning healthy ways to form intimate relationships, and teenagers are often keen to explore this unfamiliar territory.

Youth, especially those who grew up experiencing violence in their homes, profit from education and skills that promote healthy relationships and provide useful alternatives to violence and abuse. Clear messages about personal responsibility and boundaries, delivered in a blame-free manner, are generally acceptable to this age group, whereas lectures and warnings are less helpful. By offering youth the opportunities to explore the richness and rewards of relationships, they become eager to learn about choices and responsibilities. The initiation phase of social dating is a prime opportunity to become aware of the ways in which violent and abusive behavior toward intimate partners may occur, often without purpose or intention. This premise holds true not only for individuals from violent and abusive family backgrounds where negative experiences were prominent but also for other adolescents (Gray & Foshee, 1997).

A discussion of choice and responsibility for one's own behavior and how abusiveness has different consequences and meanings for young men and women is a critical step in enhancing youth awareness and recognition of dating violence (Gray & Foshee, 1997). Moreover, facilitating discussions about the meaning of violent dynamics, violent acts, and woman abuse simultaneously raises awareness of these issues and provides an opportunity to deal directly with issues of blame, responsibility, and victim-victimizer dynamics within the context of teenage dating relationships. Programs delivered universally through the high school often involve activities aimed at increasing awareness and dispelling myths about relationship violence. These activities can include: a) school auditorium presentations involving videotapes, plays, or a survivor's speech; b) classroom discussions facilitated by teachers and community professionals involved in domestic violence intervention, such as shelter staff or law enforcement personnel; c) detailed lesson plans, programs, and curricula that encourage students to examine those attitudes and behaviors that promote or tolerate violence (these exercises serve as an introduction to nonviolent alternatives in relationships); and d) peer counseling and peer support groups to assist students in developing empowerment initiatives.

The prevention of domestic violence is everyone's business and is each human services provider's responsibility.

Community-based programs for the prevention of relationship violence have goals similar to those of school-based programs, although they are intended for a more selective population, such as teenagers who are at greater risk of dating violence because of their early childhood experiences or similar risk factors. One example is the Youth Relationships Project (Wolfe et al., 2003), which was developed to help youth understand the critical importance of the abuse of power and control in relationship violence and relate these to their own social and dating relationships. The Youth Relationships Project involves adolescents referred from active caseloads of child protective service agencies who experienced violence and abuse in their families. They are informed of the program by their child protection caseworker, counselor, or other community agent. The program has an emphasis on building healthy, nonviolent relationships rather than attending treatment per se (which adolescents generally resist). Because the Youth Relationships Project is a secondary prevention program, participation does not require evidence of dating violence. Through group discussion and exercises, the youth learn how to select appropriate alternatives to abuse and violence with dating partners. This strategy builds on current strengths and identifies negative relationship factors at a time when teenagers are motivated to learn about intimate relationships.

Efforts to provide youth with such positive educational and cultural experiences in which power is understood, not abused, are very recent, and program evaluations are incomplete. Early findings, however, show that youth are responsive to such information, especially if they are involved in its design and delivery. Six dating violence prevention programs designed for high school teenagers have included evaluation components (Wekerle & Wolfe, 1999). Each program addressed specific skills and knowledge that oppose the use of violent and abusive behavior toward intimate partners. Positive changes were found across the studies in violence-related attitudes and knowledge as well as self-reported perpetration of dating violence. Although preliminary, such efforts indicate that adolescents are receptive to these learning opportunities.

Policy and Research Implications

Regardless of their attractiveness, prevention and health promotion efforts have not been popular strategies among professionals or the general public for addressing the problem of domestic violence. Prevention entails environmental and cultural explanations in addition to individual ones for causes of violence and necessitates a strong commitment to large-scale, proactive intervention using public resources rather than individually focused, private interests. Furthermore, prevention requires social and political action directed at achieving fundamental change. Nevertheless, we owe it to children, young people, and families to consider building other bridges that promote competency and adaptive behavior in an effort not only to prevent something unwanted but also to bolster potential and growth for individuals and society.

Although there is a paucity of evaluative data, there is general agreement that children and adolescents, especially those growing up in violent homes, are an important prevention focus. The following major prevention strategies and research issues stand out:

- Based on the collective wisdom of family court judges, child protection agencies, and domestic violence programs, there is a need to expand existing collaborative efforts by child protection and domestic violence agencies and staff to a more comprehensive primary prevention program (National Council of Juvenile and Family Court Judges, 1998).

- There is a growing recognition that crime prevention needs to focus on homes and communities to the extent that both are recognized as risk factors in violent behavior. Many children are exposed to violence not only in their homes but also in their neighborhoods and schools, which means there is a need for extensive collaboration among service systems. Thus, initial efforts may have to target high-risk neighborhoods and communities rather than assessing one client (potential victim) at a time (Earls, 1998).

- Primary prevention programs should be available in all schools and be developed as partnerships among students, teachers, parents, and community agents who have knowledge and expertise about domestic violence. For adolescents, the programs need to be relevant to their interests, such as dating violence, and actively involve counseling, such as peer support and peer models. A major challenge for the domestic violence field involves better collaboration with the more general crime prevention strategies that are being actively promoted in U.S. schools. There are overlapping strategies (e.g., clearly naming the problem), and domestic violence is often an underlying issue and concern for children. Although many parents and teachers are worried about violence in general, most children are more likely to witness and experience violence among people they know and trust. Therefore, the domestic violence issues are more relevant for them.

- Programs need to be planned according to both individual and institutional readiness for change. For example, boys and men may become defensive in discussions on violence against women and underlying issues of inequality until they have a better appreciation of the broader problems of violence in society. Therefore, programs have to acknowledge the stepping stones from awareness of a problem to a deeper understanding and ultimately an ongoing commitment for social change (for further discussion see Jaffe, Wolfe, Crooks, Hughes, & Baker, 2004).

In the prevention of adult domestic violence, a clear commitment is needed from all levels of government to address these issues comprehensively, with the goal of establishing a consistent, coordinated, and integrated approach for each community. Given the extensive nature of domestic violence and its accompanying human suffering, this commitment to prevention cannot be postponed.

References

Dutton, D.G. (1995). *The Domestic Assault of Women: Psychological and Criminal Justice Perspectives.* Vancouver, B.C., Canada: University of British Columbia Press.

Earls, F. (1998, September). *Linking Community Factors and Individual Development* [Research preview] (NIJ 170603). Washington DC: U.S. Department of Justice, National Institute of Justice.

Emery, R.E., & Laumann-Billings, L. (1998). An overview of the nature, causes, and consequences of abusive family relationships: Toward differentiating maltreatment and violence. *American Psychologist, 53,* 121–135.

Furman, W., & Buhrmester, D. (1992). Age and sex differences in perceptions of networks of personal relationships. *Child Development, 63,* 103–115.

Gray, H.M., & Foshee, V. (1997). Adolescent dating violence: Differences between one-sided and mutually violent profiles. *Journal of Interpersonal Violence, 12,* 126–141.

Hamilton, N., & Bhatti, T. (1996). *Population Health Promotion: An Integrated Model of Population Health and Health Promotion.* Ottawa, Ontario: Health Canada.

Jaffe, P., Wolfe, D.A., Crooks, C., Hughes, R., & Baker, L. (2004). The Fourth R: Developing healthy relationships through school-based interventions. In P. Jaffe, L. Baker, & A. Cunningham (Eds.), *Protecting Children From Domestic Violence: Strategies for Community Intervention* (pp. 200–218). New York: Guilford.

National Council of Juvenile and Family Court Judges. (1998). *Family Violence: Emerging Programs for Battered Mothers and Their Children.* Reno, NY: Author.

Sherman, L.W., Gottfredson, D.C, MacKenzie, D.L., Eck, J., Reuter, P., & Bushway, S.D. (1998, July). *Preventing Crime: What Works, What Doesn't, What's Promising* [Research in brief I (NIJ 171676)]. Washington DC: U.S. Department of Justice, National Institute of Justice.

Wekerle, C., & Wolfe, D.A. (1999). Dating violence in mid-adolescence: Theory, significance, and emerging prevention initiatives. *Clinical Psychology Review, 19,* 435–456.

Wolfe, D.A., & Jaffe, P.D. (2001). Prevention of domestic violence: Emerging initiatives. In S.A. Graham-Bermann & J.L. Edleson (Eds.), *Domestic Violence in the Lives of Children: The Future of Research, Intervention, and Social Policy* (pp. 283–298). Washington DC: American Psychological Association.

Wolfe, D.A., Wekerle, C, Scott, K., Straatman, A., Grasley, C, & Reitzel-Jaffe, D. (2003). Dating violence prevention with at-risk youth: A controlled outcome evaluation. *Journal of Consulting and Clinical Psychology, 71,* 279–291.

DAVID A. WOLFE, PhD, is with the Department of Psychiatry, Centre for Addiction and Mental Health, University of Toronto. **PETER G. JAFFE**, Ph.D, is with the Center for Children and Families in the Justice System, London Family Court Clinic, and is an Adjunct Professor in the Departments of Psychiatry and Psychology of the University of Western Ontario.

This article is adapted from David A. Wolfe and Peter G. Jaffe (2001). Prevention of domestic violence: Emerging initiatives. In S.A. Graham-Bermann & J.L. Edleson (Ed.,), *Domestic Violence in the Lives of Children: The Future of Research, Intervention, and Social Policy* (pp. 283–298). Washington DC: American Psychological Association. It appears here with permission from *The Future of Children,* a publication of the David and Lucile Packard Foundation.

Adolescents Who Self-Injure

Implications and Strategies for School Counselors

VICTORIA E. WHITE KRESS, PHD, DONNA M. GIBSON, AND CYNTHIA A. REYNOLDS, PHD

This article explores strategies for school counselors to use in intervening and managing adolescent students who engage in self-injurious behaviors. The school counselor's roles in intervention, referral, education, advocacy, and prevention are discussed. Implications and recommendations for school counselors are addressed.

In recent years, the media and popular literature have begun to address the issue of adolescent self-injurious behavior, and many counselors have had an increasing exposure to students who engage in these behaviors. Approximately 13% of adolescents sampled in one recent survey indicated that they engaged in self-injurious behaviors (Ross & Heath, 2002), and research has indicated that self-injury is becoming increasingly prevalent among adolescents (Hawton, Fagg, Simkin, Bale, & Bond, 1997). The incidence of self-injurious behaviors rises to 40% to 61% in adolescent inpatient settings and is ostensibly beginning earlier in the childhood and adolescent years (Conterio, Lader, & Bloom, 1998; Darche, 1990; DiClemente, Ponton, & Hartley, 1991).

Self-injurious behavior is discussed often with regard to the mentally retarded and developmentally disabled populations—people diagnosed with psychotic disorders, personality disorders, and dissociative identity disorder; however it is rarely addressed in discussions of the general adolescent population (Zila & Kiselica, 2001). This article focuses on self-injurious behaviors associated with adolescents in the non-severely mentally disabled population (e.g., mental retardation, schizophrenia, etc.). This article also is delimited to self-injurious behaviors involving self-cutting, interference with wound healing, scratching, and burning, but will not explore issues associated with hair pulling (e.g., trichotillomania), and extreme forms of self-injury (e.g., eye enucleation, amputation of body parts, breaking bones, etc.) as these are less commonly presented in school settings.

It is important to acknowledge that most cultures have forms of culturally acceptable and sanctioned self-injurious behaviors (Favazza, 1996). For example, among adolescents in Western culture, ear piercing, tattooing, and various forms of body piercing are becoming more commonplace. Deviant forms of self-injury are generally considered physically damaging and

occur in response to psychological crisis. These acts demonstrate a sense of disconnection and alienation from others; the line between socially sanctioned self-injury and deviant self-injury can be hazy (Dallam, 1997).

Self-cutting is one of the most common forms of self-injury found in the non-hospitalized population, followed by burning, pinching, scratching, biting, self-hitting, and interference with wound healing (Briere & Gil, 1998; Ross & Heath, 2002; Taiminen, Kallio-Soukainen, Nokso-Koivisto, Kaljonen, & Helenius, 1998). The areas that are most typically injured are the arms and wrists, legs, abdomen, head, chest, and genitals, respectively (Conterio et al., 1998; Zila & Kiselica, 2001). In the literature, many varied definitions abound as to what constitutes self-injury. In this article, self-injury will be defined as a volitional act to harm one's body without any intention to die as a result of the behavior (Simeon & Favazza, 2001; Yarura-Tobias, Neziroglu, & Kaplan, 1995).

In many ways, the current awareness of self-injurious behaviors parallels the appreciation of eating disorders that developed in the 1970s and 1980s. At that time, anorexia and bulimia were thought to be rare and interesting conditions, but as public and professional awareness increased, many people began to seek help (Conterio et al., 1998). Despite an increasing awareness of adolescent self-injurious behavior, little is known about what treatments work best with this population (Zila & Kiselica, 2001).

The age at which people first begin to engage in self-cutting behaviors varies; however, these behaviors usually begin in middle adolescence (Herpertz, 1995), with the freshman year of high school being the average age of the first self-injurious behaviors (Ross & Heath, 2002; Favazza & Conterio, 1989). One study found that mental health professionals identified 18 as the average age their clients last engaged in self-cutting behaviors (Suyemoto & MacDonald, 1995). Thus, with regard to self-injury, school counselors are in a unique position to intervene as these behaviors typically begin, and often end, during the adolescent years.

Gender issues may also be present with regard to rates of self-injury. It is commonly stated that females are more likely to engage in self-injury than males. In one study of self-injurious adolescents, 64% were female and 36% were males (Ross & Heath, 2002). Indeed, most studies have indicated the majority of hospitalized self-injuring patients are female (Herpertz, 1995). However, Briere and Gil (1998), using a community sample, found no gender differences with regard to self-injurious behaviors. The belief that females are more likely to engage in self-injury may be related to researchers' use of samples including help-seeking clinical populations, hospitalized patients, and sexual abuse and incest survivor populations; samples that are more likely to be comprised of females. Higher rates of male self-injury in community samples may be due to different definitions of self-injury with some researchers including deliberate recklessness and risk-taking behaviors in which males may be more likely to engage (Ross & Heath).

Many theories have been proposed concerning the etiology and function of self-injurious behaviors. Generally, theories of the etiology of self-injury tend to be based on biological, psychological, and sociological explanations. From a biological perspective, the seratonergic system has been implicated in the pathophysiology of self-injury (Dallam, 1997; Simeon et al., 1992) as well as the idea that the endorphin rush associated with self-injury can lead to an addiction to the behavior (Pies & Popli, 1995). Among mental health professionals, one of the more popular psychological theories (Suyemoto & MacDonald, 1995) involves the ability of self-injury to regulate emotions. The psychodynamic-oriented emotional dysregulation theory holds that self-injury is the result of anger turned inward on the self (Feldman, 1988) and that the self-injury results in emotional catharsis (Crowe & Bunclark, 2000). Similarly, Linehan's (1993) biosocial emotional dysregulation theory holds that self-injury in person's diagnosed with borderline personality disorder occurs secondary to a person being highly sensitive and reactive to emotional stimuli, yet having a deficit in emotion regulation skills. In other words, people who self-injure have an inability to distract themselves from their emotional experiences; thus the person self-injures as an attempt to modulate or cope with strong emotions.

Research investigations indicate that people who self-injure have identified the following as reasons for engaging in self-injurious behaviors: (a) feeling concrete pain when psychic pain is too overwhelming; (b) reducing numbness and promoting a sense of being real; (c) keeping traumatic memories from intruding into the consciousness; (d) affect modulation; (e) receiving support and caring from others; (f) discharge of anger, anxiety, despair, and expression of disappointment; (g) gaining a sense of control; (h) self-punishment for perceptions of being bad; and (i) an enhancement of self-esteem (Himber, 1994; Shearer, 1994).

Various life factors and clinical correlates are related to self-injurious behaviors in adolescents. Self-injury is often associated with childhood sexual abuse and subsequent posttraumatic stress disorder reactions (Darche, 1990; Favazza & Rosenthal, 1993; Ghaziuddin, Tsai, Naylor, & Ghaziuddin, 1992; Langbehn & Pfohl, 1993), as well as sexual assault/rape (Greenspan & Samuel, 1989), anxiety and depression (Ross & Heath, 2002) and eating disorders (Cross, 1993).

There are many correlates and predictors that are indicative of self-injurious behavior. Conterio et al. (1998) noted that other life conditions including loss of a parent, childhood illness, physical abuse, marital violence, and familial self-injury are related to self-injury. However, a history of sexual abuse and family violence are the best predictors of self-injury. Research also identifies adolescents' experiences that trigger self-mutilation, including the following: a recent loss, peer conflict and intimacy problems, body alienation or dissociation related to abuse, and impulse control problems (Conterio et al.; Welch, 2001). Indeed, all of these correlates can be useful in identifying at-risk adolescents for the purposes of intervention and prevention (Walsh & Rosen, 1988).

Many times, school counselors become aware of students' self-injurious behaviors prior to families and persons outside of the school setting. The school counselor's first awareness that a student is self-injuring can come from many sources: observations or physical indicators of self-injury, information reported to the counselor by the student, concerns of teachers and parents reported to counselor, or finally, other students reporting a peer's self-injury.

The dynamics of adolescent self-injurious behaviors and implications and strategies for school counselors in working with this population are important to understanding these behaviors. School counselors' functions as providers of interventions, referral agents, advocates, and as educators and prevention agents of student self-injurious behavior are essential in helping these adolescents.

School Counselors' Role in Intervening and Managing Self-injurious Behaviors

According to Dahir, Sheldon, and Valiga (1998), the heart of the National Standards for school counseling programs is a focus on student success being equated with academic development, career development, and personal/social development. Therefore, in terms of facilitating student success, school counselors have an important role to play in ensuring that students are safe and that they have the resources they need to develop in all of the aforementioned areas. School counselors can help facilitate student success by providing interventions, and referrals as well as acting as advocates, educators, and prevention agents with regard to student self-injurious behaviors.

Intervention

Most adolescents who self-injure are evasive about their role in the injury, attempt to avoid attention and embarrassment, and frequently wear clothes that hide their injuries (Alderman, 2000). Physical indicators of self-injury include numerous unexplained scars, burns or cuts. The scars are often more prevalent on the arm opposite the student's dominant hand and are more likely on the forearm at an angle. Some non-threatening questions that can be helpful in eliciting information about injuries are: "What is this from?"; "Could you say more about this?"; "Have you had accidents like this before?"; "What were you thinking or feeling prior to the accident?"; "Have you found a pattern to these accidents?"; and, "How did you feel after the accident?" (Barstow, 1995; Dallam, 1997).

The primary goal for school counselors intervening with self-injuring students is to help them create a safe environment. As many students who self-injure have been physically and sexually abused and thus have a history of adults abusing their power and disregarding their needs, it may be difficult for the student to trust the counselor. Therefore, care should be taken in fostering a strong alliance with the student. An emphasis on structure, consistency, and predictability can be stressed and modeled in the counseling relationship. Developing a plan with the student that emphasizes the students' taking responsibility for behaviors and making the safest decisions possible is one method for accomplishing this goal. A detailed safety plan should be developed including identifying self-injury triggers, physical cues, and reducers related to self-injury; exploring safe people and safe places to go when wanting to self-injure; and the deliberate avoidance of objects which could be used to self-injure (e.g., paper clips, staples, erasers, sharp objects). This plan should serve to help stabilize the student and to provide structure and support until community-based counseling can begin. Techniques that can be used in helping the student manage self-injurious impulses include increasing feeling awareness and recognition, increasing coping skills to be used in managing feelings, encouraging the use of self-soothing techniques such as relaxation exercises, and encouraging the use of a safe [place] (Kehrberg, 1997).

Research has indicated that two important factors contribute to a cessation of self-injury (Dallam, 1997). The first factor that contributes to a cessation of self-injury is developing an ability to identify and express feelings verbally. The second factor contributing to a decrease in self-injury is learning to use behavioral alternatives to self-injury. The short-term safety plan could be used as a means of fostering the students' development of impulse control and a sense of control in managing the self-injurious behaviors (Kehrberg, 1997). Encouraging the student to be around others when wanting to injure can be helpful, as self-harm is rarely done when others are nearby (Dallam).

Safety issues should also be explored with the student including the importance of not bringing dangerous objects such as razor blades or knifes to school. Students should be instructed on the dangers of using rusty blades or sharing blades with other people who self-injure so as to prevent disease transmission (Dallam, 1997; DiClemente et al., 1991). DiClemente et al. found that 61% of a hospitalized sample of adolescents self-injured, and of that sample, 27% reported that they had shared cutting implements with other adolescents. Clearly, school counselors can play an important role in educating students about the issues associated with sharing cutting implements.

One serious complication of self-injury is the possibility of accidental death as a result of damage inflicted on the body. Thus, in assessing a student's self-injury, it is important to consider the severity of the behaviors as well as possible medical complications. If there is any concern that the student has infections or is engaging in self-injury of a severe and chronic nature (e.g., infections secondary to recurrent cutting, etc.) that could cause severe medical complications, the student should be referred to a physician for an assessment.

To facilitate student safety, issues related to suicide should be assessed. Counselors should consider (a) an assessment of depression, helplessness, and hopelessness; (b) suicidal ideation, plan and intent, preparation and access to a means of suicide, and past attempts; (c) social support; (d) family history of suicide; and (e) recent stressors. It is important to note that suicide and self-injury are not necessarily related. Indeed, self-injury should only be thought of as suicidal if the student indicates intent to die. It should be noted however, that the link between suicide and self-injury is complicated; one can have suicidal ideation and self-injure and not be considered suicidal (Simeon & Favazza, 2001). An over-reactive stance could alienate students and fracture a developing student/counselor alliance.

The school counselor could provide support during aftercare and could be involved in helping to arrange home tutoring if needed. School counselors might also suggest modifications of the students schedule if needed through the use of a 504 plan. This type of plan allows students identified with a physical or mental impairment, yet not qualified for specialized education, to receive accommodations in their school schedule to receive help for the impairment. For example, the self-injuring student may need to leave class for counseling sessions, follow-up medical care, behavior modification scheduled checks, and time-out sessions to practice cognitive-behavioral intervention techniques. The 504 plan is an agreed upon arrangement between school, parent, and student.

Finally, an important part of a school counselor's intervention plan for self-injurious students is to follow their ethical duty in assessing and, if necessary, reporting the situation. School counselors are obligated to assess the student's behavior in doing harm to him or herself. Legally, school counselors are obligated to contact the student's parents or local authorities in helping the student. Although this task may appear clear, it is often difficult to decipher the severity of behavior and the intent of the self-injury. Part of the process should include assessing the family situation and determining if the student is safe in his or her home environment. If appropriate, parents should be called to the school and appropriate referral information should be given. However, parents should not be the first contacted if issues of abuse are part of the student's report. Following school protocol, the local social service agency or police should be contacted if abuse is suspected.

Referral Issues

In discussing the role of school counselors, Baker (2001) stated that their scope of practice primarily includes the intervention and prevention of mental and emotional disorders, but not the diagnosis and treatment of disorders. Thus, school counselors play an important role in the referral of students to qualified professionals. School counselors can make either a partial or a complete referral (Baker). A complete referral would involve dissociating from the student's case, and a partial referral would involve some continued involvement with the student while he or she works with outside mental health professionals. A referral for inpatient or out-patient treatment would be appropriate, and should be done in a sensitive manner so that the student does not feel abandoned or refuses to go. School counselors need to be knowledgeable of the practitioners and treatment centers that have specific training in the management of self-injury. If possible, the school counselor might use an in-service day to visit local treatment facilities and determine the steps a student would go through in receiving treatment. When counselors are aware of what the treatment process is like, they can better help students and their families in making decisions and developing intervention plans.

Once the student begins work with a community mental health professional, the counselor can collaborate with the community professional and can continue to play a role in the student's treatment process (e.g., being a safe person the student can talk to when wanting to injure). If the student goes for inpatient treatment, the school counselor could be involved in continuing the educational process through arranging in home tutoring or collaborating with the educational tutor at the residential center or hospital.

Advocacy and Education

Advocating for students, and educating school personnel are important roles of school counselors (Baker, 2001). Through advocacy and education, school counselors can help to dispel myths and break down stereotypes regarding self-injury.

School counselors can advocate for students through faculty in-services and parenting groups, and speaking in health classes to students regarding self-injury. It is important to inform staff, parents, and students that self-injury does not mean someone is crazy, but can be understood as a means of attempting to help one's self. In particular, educating school faculty regarding the etiology and function of self-injury can help in dispelling the myth that people who self-mutilate are attention seeking. Dispelling myths can help students gain access to support and needed services both within the school and in the outside community. For example, a teacher who is aware a student is self-injuring may not report self-injury as he or she may perceive it as trivial or as a way for the student to receive attention. With education, the teacher may be more likely to seek help for the student and to make the school counselor aware of the situation.

Education of staff and teachers is one manner in which school counselors can advocate for students who self-injure. By educating faculty about self-injury, they should feel more comfortable in managing the issue of self-injury. Also, educating faculty on ways to approach or manage student self-disclosure of self-injury can be helpful. In particular, the physical education teacher and the school nurse may be of critical importance in identifying and monitoring students who self-injure.

Advocating for students by educating faculty about the fact that self-injury is not equated with suicidality is also very important. Strong personal reactions to self-injury can lead to reactionary stances and extreme measures such as unnecessary

hospitalizations, pulling students out of school, or suspending students. Educating faculty and administrators on the differences between self-injury and suicide attempts can help in avoiding unnecessarily restrictive actions.

Prevention

Conterio et al. (1998) and Welch (2001) have noted that loss, childhood illness, physical and sexual abuse, marital violence, familial self-injury, peer conflict and intimacy problems, and impulse control problems are all related to self-injury. Thus, for the purposes of prevention, school counselors should consider these variables when targeting at-risk students. As with the issue of intervention, prevention efforts can include helping students to express and identify their feelings, while also developing healthy behavioral coping skills. Group counseling and counselor outreach activities that encourage at-risk students' development of these aforementioned skills may be helpful in preventing self-injury. Prevention efforts can also occur by providing pamphlets and handouts to students. Materials concerning self-injury can be distributed through health classes or directly through the school counseling office.

A sequence of events in which a person inflicts self-injurious behaviors and is imitated by others in the environment is referred to as contagion of self-injurious behaviors (Walsh & Rosen, 1985). The issue of contagion has received some attention in the research literature (Rosen & Walsh, 1989; Ross & McKay, 1979; Taiminen et al., 1998; Walsh & Rosen) Initial research indicated that in hospital and residential treatment settings, adolescents tend to imitate self-injurious behaviors. Self-injurious acts followed in 25 residents at a residential facility indicted that these acts are bunched or clustered in time across subjects, suggesting that adolescents in a residential setting trigger the self-injurious behaviors in each other (Walsh & Rosen). These findings suggest that a group process variable or social factors may contribute to the behavior in participants who already self-injure or are at risk for self-injuring. Walsh and Rosen noted that labeling self-injury as a behavior that is likely to be imitated actually decreases self-injury as many adolescents, for developmental reasons, do not want to be perceived as being imitative or be labeled as followers.

Similar to Walsh and Rosen (1985), Taiminen et al. (1998) have suggested adolescents' weak egos and diffuse identities make them susceptible to various forms of identification including self-injuring and refer to this phenomena as "rites of togetherness" (p. 215). Through intensive study (i.e., interviewing methods and empirical observation), Rosen and Walsh (1989) came to similar conclusions. They stated that adolescents in a residential setting engaged in contagious self-injury as a "concrete display of affinity between two people" (p. 657). Rosen and Walsh observed the following: (a) individuals involved in contagious self-injury are highly enmeshed; (b) they have difficulty with conventional forms of intimacy; (c) they find deviate acts (e.g., shared self-injury) to be compelling and exciting. Rosen and Walsh concluded that when contagious self-injury occurs, it is important to use interventions that target specific dyads. It is important to help the adolescents express emotions and negotiate intimacy in more normative ways. When this is not possible, it may be necessary to isolate the person being modeled from the rest of the group.

While the aforementioned studies all involved adolescents in residential treatment settings, Fennig, Carlson, and Fennig (1995) described their experiences consulting in a public school setting regarding a situation where an outbreak of self-mutilation occurred. They expressed concerns that this phenomenon may be more frequent in educational systems than reported. In describing their experiences they made the following observations: (a) the majority of students involved in the outbreak did not demonstrate any overt psychopathology and were not identified as emotionally disturbed; (b) the only overt sign of problems associated with self-injury was a drop in grades; (c) several initiators with more severe psychopathology seemingly induced the behavior in more passive students and all had anxiety and depressive related traits; (d) isolation of the more severely disturbed initiators was most effective in lowering the severity and frequency of the phenomenon.

While these suggestions are narrative and have not been empirically scrutinized, school counselors facing similar situations can use this information. Combined, the research related to contagion implies that social factors may contribute to the development and maintenance of self-injurious behavior. A related issue is to differentiate initiation self-mutilating behaviors of gangs or cliques from self-injuring behaviors related to psychopathology. Although both types of behaviors are significant, intervention and referral can take different directions. If an ostensible contagion situation occurs, consultation with other professionals may be necessary.

Personal Reactions

Counselors may have many strong feelings when faced with student self-injurious behaviors. Alderman (2000) stated that the typical clinician treating a client who self-mutilates is often left feeling a combination of helplessness, guilt, anger, betrayal, disgust, and sadness. Self-injury has been identified as the most distressing client behavior encountered in clinical practice and the behavior that many professionals find most traumatizing to encounter (Gamble, Pearlman, Lucca, & Allen as cited in Deiter & Peralman, 1998).

Writers on self-injury frequently address the issue of counselors' need to manage their personal reactions towards clients who self-injure. Issues such as the time and emotional investment required in working with this population, the strong reactions of counselors to self-injury, and the limits these reactions place on counselors' ability to work with clients have been noted (Levenkron, 1998; Zila & Kiselica, 2001). Self-injury is sometimes viewed as being manipulative or "attention seeking" (Simcon & Favazza, 2001). Counselors may sometimes feel frustrated with self-injury and may want to attempt to control the student by forcing him or her to stop engaging in the self-destructive behavior, or by lecturing or debating the problems associated with self-injury. A personal awareness and understanding of one's intentions when working with students who self-injure can be helpful in facilitating successful

interventions. Avoiding attempts to control the student or tell him or her to stop the behavior can facilitate student empowerment as well as prevent potential power struggles. A constant monitoring of personal reactions combined with ongoing consultation and supervision can help in ensuring that counselors maintain an objective perspective when working with this population (Deiter & Pearlman, 1998).

Conclusions

Self-injury is an increasing trend that has not been adequately addressed in the literature. Preliminary research indicates that the etiology, function, and interventions associated with self-injury are diverse and varied; counselors know little and must be careful, deliberate, and thoughtful in working with this population.

Counselors can serve as powerful advocates to students who self-injure through challenging a culture that may contribute to adolescents' challenges and by hearing adolescents' stories, validating their experiences, and providing a safe refuge. Counselors can also play a role in intervening and preventing self-injury; educating teachers, parents, and students; and making referrals to specialists who can help the self-injuring student. On a more macro-cultural level, counselors can serve to fight oppressive cultural systems that serve to disempower adolescents and hamper their voices by providing an environment that fosters self-expression and the use of positive coping skills (Conterio et al., 1998; Zila & Kiselica, 2001).

References

Alderman, T. (2000). Helping those who hurt themselves. *The Prevention Researcher*, 7(4), 43–46.

Baker, S. B. (2001). School counseling for the twenty-first century (3rd ed.). Upper Saddle River, NJ: Prentice Hall.

Barstow, D. G. (1995). Self-injury and self-mutilation: Nursing approaches. *Journal of Psychosocial Nursing and Mental Health Services*, 33(2), 19–22.

Briere, J., & Gil, E. (1998). Self-mutilation in clinical and general population samples: Prevalence, correlates, and functions. *American Journal of Orthopsychiatry*, 68, 609–620.

Conterio, K., Lader, W., & Bloom, J. K. (1998). Bodily harm: The breakthrough healing program for self-injurers. New York: Hyperion.

Cross, L.W. (1993). Body and self in feminine development: Implications for eating disorders and delicate self-mutilation. *Bulletin of the Menninger Clinic*, 57, 41–67.

Crowe, M., & Bunclark, J. (2000). Repeated self-injury and its management. *International Review of Psychiatry*, 12(1), 49–54.

Dahir, C. A., Sheldon, C. B., & Valiga, M. J. (1998). *Vision into action: Implementing the national standards for school counseling*. Alexandria, VA: American School Counselor Association.

Dallam, S. J. (1997). The identification and management of self-mutilating patients in primary care. *The Nurse Practitioner*, 22, 151–164.

Darche, M. A. (1990). Psychological factors differentiating self-mutilating and non-self-mutilating adolescent inpatient females. *Psychiatric Hospital* 21(1), 31–35.

Deiter, R J., & Pearlman, L. A. (1998). Responding to self-injurious behavior. In P. M. Kleespies (Ed.), *Emergencies in mental health practice: Evaluation and management* (pp. 235–257). New York: Guilford.

DiClemente, R. J., Ponton, L. E., & Hartley, D. (1991). Prevalence and correlates of cutting behavior: Risk for HIV transmission. *Journal of the American Academy of Child and Adolescent Psychiatry*, 30, 735–738.

Favazza, A. R. (1996). *Bodies under siege: Self-mutilation and body modification in culture and psychiatry* (2nd ed.). London: John Hopkins.

Favazza, A. R., & Conterio, K. (1989). Female habitual self-mutilation. *Acta Psychiatrica Scandinavica*, 79, 283–289.

Favazza, A. R., & Rosenthal, R. J. (1993). Diagnostic issues in self-mutilation. *Hospital and Community Psychiatry*, 44, 134–140.

Feldman, M. D. (1988). The challenge of self-mutilation, a review. *Comprehensive Psychiatry*, 29, 252–269.

Fennig, S., Carlson, G. A., & Fennig, S. (1995). Letter to the editor: Contagious self-mutilation. *Academy of Child and Adolescent Psychiatry*, 34, 402–403.

Ghaziuddin, M., Tsai, L., Naylor, M., & Ghaziuddin, N. (1992). Mood disorders in a group of self-cutting adolescents. *Acta Paedopsychiatrica*, 55, 103–105.

Greenspan, G. S., & Samuel, S. E. (1989). Self-cutting after rape. *American Journal of Psychiatry*, 146, 789–790.

Hawton, K., Fagg, J., Simkin, S., Bale, E., & Bond, A. (1997).Trends in deliberate self-harm in Oxford, 1985–1995. *British Journal of Psychiatry*, 171, 556–560.

Herpertz, S. (1995). Self-injurious behaviour: Psychopathological and nosological characteristics in subtypes of self-injurers. *Acta Psychiatrica Scandinavica*, 91, 57–68.

Himber, J. (1994). Blood rituals: Self-cutting in female psychiatric inpatients. *Psychotherapy*, 31, 620–631.

Kehrberg, C. (1997). Self-mutilating behavior. *Journal of Child and Adolescent Psychiatric Nursing*, 10(3), 35–40.

Langbehn, D. R., & Pfohl, B. (1993). Clinical correlates of self-mutilation among psychiatric inpatients. *Annals of Clinical Psychiatry*, 5, 45–51.

Levenkron, S. (1998). *Cutting: Understanding and overcoming self-mutilation*. New York: W. W. Norton.

Linehan, M. M. (1993). *Cognitive behavioral therapy of borderline personality disorder*. New York: Guilford.

Pies, R.W., & Popli, A. P. (1995). Self-injurious behavior: Pathophysiology and implications for treatment. *Journal of Clinical Psychiatry*, 56, 580–588.

Rosen, R. M., & Walsh, B.W. (1989). Patterns of contagion in self-mutilation epidemics. *American Journal of Psychiatry*, 146, 656–658.

Ross, S., & Heath, N. (2002). A study of the frequency of self-mutilation in a community sample of adolescents. *Journal of Youth and Adolescence*, 31(1), 67–77.

Ross, R. R., & McKay, H. B. (1979). *Self-mutilation*. Lexington, MA: DC Heath.

Shearer, S. L. (1994). Phenomenology of self-injury among inpatient women with borderline personality disorder. *Journal of Nervous and Mental Disease*, 182, 524–526.

Simeon, D., & Favazza, A. R. (2001). Self-injurious behaviors: Phenomenology and assessment. In D. Simeon & E. Hollander (Eds.), *Self-injurious behaviors: Assessment and treatment* (pp. 1–28). Washington D.C.: American Psychiatric Press.

Simeon, D., Stanley, B., Frances, A., Mann, J. J., Winchel, R., & Stanley, M. (1992). Self-mutilation in personality disorders: Psychological and biological correlates. *American Journal of Psychiatry*, 149, 221–226.

Suyemoto, K. L., & Macdonald, M. L. (1995). Self-cutting in female adolescents. *Psychotherapy*, 32, 162–171.

Taiminen, T. J., Kallio-Soukainen, K., Nokso-Koivisto, H., Kaljonen, S., & Helenius, H. (1998). Contagion of deliberate self-harm among adolescent inpatients. *Journal of the American Academy of Child and Adolescent Psychiatry*, 37, 211–217.

Walsh, B.W., & Rosen, R. (1985). Self-mutilation and contagion: An empirical test. *American Journal of Psychiatry*, 142, 119–120.

Walsh, B.W., & Rosen, R. (1988). *Self-mutilation: Theory, research, and treatment*. New York: Guilford.

Welch, S. S. (2001). A review of the literature on the epidemiology of parasuicide in the general population. *Psychiatric Services*, 52, 368–375.

Yarura-Tobias, J. A., Neziroglu, R. A., & Kaplan, S. (1995). Self-mutilation, anorexia, and dysmenorrhea in obsessive compulsive disorder. *International Journal of Eating Disorders*, 17, 33–38.

Zila, L. M., & Kiselica, M. S. (2001). Understanding and counseling Self-mutilation in female adolescents and young adults. *Journal of Counseling and Development*, 29, 46–52.

VICTORIA E. WHITE KRESS PhD, is an assistant professor, Department of Counseling, Youngstown State University, Youngstown, OH. E-mail: vewhite@ysu.edu. **DONNA M. GIBSON** PhD, is an assistant professor, School of Education, The Citadel, Charleston, SC. **CYNTHIA A. REYNOLDS** PhD, is an assistant professor, Counseling and Special Education, University of Akron, OH.

Test Your Knowledge Form

We encourage you to photocopy and use this page as a tool to assess how the articles in *Annual Editions* expand on the information in your textbook. By reflecting on the articles you will gain enhanced text information. You can also access this useful form on a product's book support Web site at *http://www.mhcls.com/online/*.

NAME: _____ DATE: _____

_____

TITLE AND NUMBER OF ARTICLE:

_____

BRIEFLY STATE THE MAIN IDEA OF THIS ARTICLE:

_____

LIST THREE IMPORTANT FACTS THAT THE AUTHOR USES TO SUPPORT THE MAIN IDEA:

_____

WHAT INFORMATION OR IDEAS DISCUSSED IN THIS ARTICLE ARE ALSO DISCUSSED IN YOUR TEXTBOOK OR OTHER READINGS THAT YOU HAVE DONE? LIST THE TEXTBOOK CHAPTERS AND PAGE NUMBERS:

_____

LIST ANY EXAMPLES OF BIAS OR FAULTY REASONING THAT YOU FOUND IN THE ARTICLE:

_____

LIST ANY NEW TERMS/CONCEPTS THAT WERE DISCUSSED IN THE ARTICLE, AND WRITE A SHORT DEFINITION:

We Want Your Advice

ANNUAL EDITIONS revisions depend on two major opinion sources: one is our Advisory Board, listed in the front of this volume, which works with us in scanning the thousands of articles published in the public press each year; the other is you—the person actually using the book. Please help us and the users of the next edition by completing the prepaid article rating form on this page and returning it to us. Thank you for your help!

ANNUAL EDITIONS: Adolescent Psychology 6/e

ARTICLE RATING FORM

Here is an opportunity for you to have direct input into the next revision of this volume.
We would like you to rate each of the articles listed below, using the following scale:

1. **Excellent: should definitely be retained**
2. **Above average: should probably be retained**
3. **Below average: should probably be deleted**
4. **Poor: should definitely be deleted**

Your ratings will play a vital part in the next revision.
Please mail this prepaid form to us as soon as possible.
Thanks for your help!

RATING	ARTICLE
	1. A Peaceful Adolescence
	2. Youth Participation
	3. The Future of Adolescence
	4. Youth Engaged for Action
	5. Why Do Kids Eat Healthful Food?
	6. Prescription for Disaster
	7. Youth Smoking Prevention: What Works
	8. Documenting Learning with Digital Portfolios
	9. Help Us Make the 9th Grade Transition
	10. Stories from Tween Classrooms
	11. My Year as a High School Student
	12. The Dropout Problem: Losing Ground
	13. Let Seniors Lead
	14. Studies Reveal Strengths, Weaknesses
	15. The New Cheating Epidemic
	16. Leading Adolescents to Mastery
	17. Healthier Students, Better Learners
	18. Fostering Social-Emotional Learning in the Classroom
	19. The Consequences of Insufficient Sleep for Adolescents
	20. Body Image: How Do You See Yourself?
	21. Adolescent Stress
	22. ADHD and the SUD in Adolescents
	23. Coping with Stress
	24. A Mother's Story
	25. Traumatic Stress in Adolescents Anticipating Parental Death

RATING	ARTICLE
	26. Parental Illness and Adolescent Development
	27. A Nation of Wimps
	28. Teenage Fatherhood and Involvement in Delinquent Behavior
	29. Impact of Family Recovery on Pre-Teens and Adolescents
	30. After Incarceration
	31. When a Parent Starts Dating Again
	32. Learning to Chill
	33. Risky Business: Exploring Adolescent Risk-Taking Behavior
	34. The Overdominance of Computers
	35. Teaching Kids to Kill
	36. Alcohol Use among Adolescents
	37. Terrorism, the Media, and Distress in Youth
	38. The Sexual Revolution Hits Junior High
	39. The Cuddle Puddle of Stuyvesant High School
	40. Give Students the Knowledge to Make Wise Choices about Sex
	41. The Perils of Playing House
	42. What to Tell the Kids about Sex
	43. School Bullying: Who, Why, and What to Do
	44. Bullying at School among Older Adolescents
	45. Prevention of Domestic Violence during Adolescence
	46. Adolescents Who Self-Injure

BUSINESS REPLY MAIL
FIRST CLASS MAIL PERMIT NO. 551 DUBUQUE IA

POSTAGE WILL BE PAID BY ADDRESSEE

McGraw-Hill Contemporary Learning Series
501 BELL STREET
DUBUQUE, IA 52001

ABOUT YOU

Name

Date

Are you a teacher? ☐ A student? ☐
Your school's name

Department

Address   City   State   Zip

School telephone #

YOUR COMMENTS ARE IMPORTANT TO US!

Please fill in the following information:
For which course did you use this book?

Did you use a text with this ANNUAL EDITION? ☐ yes ☐ no
What was the title of the text?

What are your general reactions to the Annual Editions concept?

Have you read any pertinent articles recently that you think should be included in the next edition? Explain.

Are there any articles that you feel should be replaced in the next edition? Why?

Are there any World Wide Web sites that you feel should be included in the next edition? Please annotate.

May we contact you for editorial input? ☐ yes ☐ no
May we quote your comments? ☐ yes ☐ no